STRANGERS
IN THE BIBLE

STRANGERS
IN THE BIBLE

Loved but Not
Embraced?

René M. Micallef

FOREWORD BY
David Hollenbach, SJ

Paulist Press
New York / Mahwah, NJ

Cover image : FESTIVAL OF LIGHTS. Copyright © 2000 - John August Swanson Trust
Cover and book design by Lynn Else

Nihil obstat: Mark A. Lewis, SJ, Academic Vice-Rector, Pontifical Gregorian University, 2022

Library of Congress Cataloging-in-Publication Data
Names: Micallef, René, author.
Title: Strangers in the Bible: loved but not embraced / René M. Micallef ; foreword by David Hollenbach, SJ.
Description: New York ; Mahwah, NJ : Paulist Press, [2024] | Includes index. | Summary: "The book links related concrete ethics issues of migration, hospitality, and integration of strangers with a methodological issue: the experience of the ethicist sojourning as a stranger in the landscape of the Bible"—Provided by publisher.
Identifiers: LCCN 2023020534 (print) | LCCN 2023020535 (ebook) | ISBN 9780809149964 (paperback) | ISBN 9781587686238 (ebook)
Subjects: LCSH: Emigration and immigration—Religious aspects—Christianity. | Christian ethics. | Group identity.
Classification: LCC BS680.E38 M53 2024 (print) | LCC BS680.E38 (ebook) | DDC 261.8/38—dc23/eng/20231026
LC record available at https://lccn.loc.gov/2023020534
LC ebook record available at https://lccn.loc.gov/2023020535

ISBN 978-0-8091-4996-4 (paperback)
ISBN 978-1-58768-623-8 (e-book)

Published by Paulist Press
997 Macarthur Boulevard
Mahwah, NJ 07430
www.paulistpress.com

Printed and bound in the
United States of America

To the staff of Jesuit Refugee Service in Malta, Italy, and Uganda, their collaborators, and the refugees and migrants whom they accompany and serve, and for whom they advocate

CONTENTS

LIST OF ILLUSTRATIONS

LIST OF TABLES

FOREWORD

The Bible and the Challenge of Refugees and Migrants

David Hollenbach, SJ
Georgetown University

The number of refugees and other migrants who have been forced to flee their homes has reached record levels today. Data assembled by the United Nations High Commissioner for Refugees indicate that in mid-2022, over one hundred million people had been driven from their homes as forced migrants. This extraordinary statistic means that one out of every seventy-eight people on earth had been compelled to migrate involuntarily. This is double the number of just a decade earlier. Most of these forced migrants were in flight from war, persecution, and serious human rights violations. Much of the very recent and dramatic increase in the number of forced migrants has been due to the war in Ukraine, from which eight million people had fled as of February 2022. But numerous people have also been fleeing conflict in other countries, including Syria, Venezuela, Afghanistan, and Myanmar. The danger is also rising that people will be driven from their homes by the harmful effects of climate change. The World Bank has conducted careful research on the involuntary displacements that are resulting from environmental causes. The Bank has concluded that without serious remedial action, by 2050 as many as 216 million people could be forced to move within their own countries due to the effects of climate change. These people will be compelled to migrate from areas with declining water availability and crop productivity or from regions affected by sea-level rise and storm surges. To offset these harmful effects, the Bank calls for intense efforts to reduce global emissions and to support green development.

The Catholic church, under the leadership of Pope Francis, has become a strong advocate for more effective response to the needs of refugees and other migrants. The leadership of Pope Francis has been particularly evident in two of his dramatic pastoral actions. On July 8, 2013, Francis made his first trip as pope outside Rome. He traveled to the island of Lampedusa in the Mediterranean Sea to call the world to a much stronger response to the needs of the many refugees arriving there, in flight from conflict in places such as Mali, Nigeria, Syria, and Libya. He challenged the nations of the world to replace what he called "the globalization of indifference" with action rooted in compassion and the capacity to "weep over the cruelty of our world."[1] His commitment to a compassionate response to the displaced was reinforced by his visit to the Greek island of Lesbos, a prime destination for numerous refugees seeking safety from conflict-ridden regions of Syria, Iraq, and elsewhere. At Lesbos he called the human community to build bridges for the displaced and to recoil from the idea of putting up walls to exclude them. He also suggested that though compassionate response by individuals is surely needed, so are multilateral political efforts that build peace, counter the arms trade, and strengthen international organizations and humanitarian agencies.[2] Pope Francis demonstrated his strong commitment to providing assistance to displaced people by taking three Muslim refugee families from Syria back to Rome with him on the papal plane.

Pope Francis's teachings and actions, of course, embody long-standing Catholic teachings on duties to refugees and migrants.[3] These teachings build upon the biblical call to respect strangers. For example, the story of the exodus—the migration of the people of Israel from slavery in Egypt to freedom in the land of God's promise—is central to the faith of both Jews and Christians. God saw the misery of Israel in Egypt, heard their cries, and through Moses led them to migrate across the desert into a land "flowing with milk and honey" (Exod 3:7–8). Thus both Jews and Christians have a special duty to respect strangers and migrants. Indeed, while the command to "love your neighbor as yourself" appears once in the Old Testament, the command to "love the stranger" appears no fewer there than thirty-six times (Exod 23:9; Lev 19:33–34, and many other places).[4]

The New Testament also highlights the importance of concern for those driven from their homes as forced migrants. In the Gospel of

Matthew, the narrative of the birth of Jesus includes an account of how Jesus, Mary, and Joseph were forced to flee to Egypt by King Herod in his effort to destroy the infant Jesus as a threat to his regime (Matt 2:13–15). Herod's action can be seen as a form of persecution and, since it resulted in Jesus's being driven across a border, we could say anachronistically that the newborn Jesus met the definition of a refugee in contemporary international law. Also in Matthew's Gospel, Jesus teaches that on the day of judgment, one's salvation or damnation will be determined by whether one has welcomed strangers (Matt 25:40). These biblical texts imply that Christians should understand that their relation with God is partly determined by the way they respond to strangers, migrants, and refugees.

The biblical texts on migration are the central foci of the reflections provided to us in René Micallef's careful study, *No Longer Strangers: Bridging the Divide between Scripture and Ethics.* The need for this scholarly exploration of the relation between the Bible and contemporary response to forced migrants is evident from the fact that the Bible and recent church teaching both call us not only to concern for strangers and the displaced but also to care for those who are members of our own communities. Thus the US bishops set forth three principles that should govern Christian response to migrants: first, people have the right to migrate to sustain their lives and the lives of their families; second, a country has the right to regulate its borders and to control immigration; and third, a country must regulate its borders with justice and mercy.[5]

René Micallef's study of the full range of the Scriptures shows that each of these principles has a genuinely biblical basis. Surely, the Bible calls us to respect the needs of the displaced. But it also calls us to have genuine concern for those who are members of our own communities, both for the people within our own nations and for those who are members of our own religious communities. Micallef shows that the Bible itself presents us with a complex mosaic of perspectives on these matters. It supports both duties to migrants and duties to our own people.

Micallef draws on careful study of a wide range of biblical materials to show us that obligations both to our own people and to migrants from elsewhere have solid biblical bases. He draws on recent efforts to clarify how we should interpret the complex teachings of the Bible on ethical matters. Thus part 1 of the book presents serious reflection on important recent approaches to biblical hermeneutics. Part 2 makes skillful use of these theories to interpret specific biblical passages that deal with migration and refugees. Thus *Strangers in the Bible* is a detailed scholarly reflection on how to read the Bible on duties to the migrants and refugees. In the face of the massive challenges of displacement today, Micallef's book makes a valuable intellectual contribution that is urgently needed.

PREFACE

As a case study, this book treats the plethora of ways Scripture presents the figure of the "stranger" to its reader, seeking to showcase how the Bible might be used honestly, respectfully, critically, and effectively to reflect on topical and divisive moral issues. Thus, my approach focuses on the ethical implications of biblical scholarship and its potential to transform the reader's action, rather than seeing that scholarship within its disciplinary autonomy. Ultimately this is a book about ethics, an ethics well-informed and wisely illuminated by Scripture, as all Christian ethics should be.

Familiarity and Strangeness

Who are the "strangers in the Bible" referred to in the title? The phrase is a play on words that hints at the originality of the approach, which links a concrete ethics issue with a methodological one. To inform ethical discourse about migration, hospitality, and integrating strangers, I explore how the ethicist can sojourn as a stranger in the landscape of biblical interpretation in ways that overcome (without abolishing or obfuscating) the barriers between exegesis and ethics.[1] This approach is unique in presenting the epistemological debates, the methodology, and the results of exploring an ethics issue in Scripture in one book, rather than separately.

I have written this book over many years, in Jesuit theological faculties in Boston, Rome, and Nairobi, cities built by migrants, and in Malta, the place from which I emigrated. In June of 2017, I was working in the vicinity of Kibera, the largest urban slum in Africa, full of migrant workers who provide cheap labor for the bustling city of Nairobi. Wherever you look in the informal settlement, you see Christian churches with biblical names and posters of pastors claiming to be familiar with Scripture. Yet back among my colleagues, mostly priests who hold doctorates in moral theology, the Bible is seen as a stranger, a book best left in the hands of expert exegetes and biblical theologians. The idea that a theological ethicist could write a book on biblical ethics is at times frowned upon, at times seen as a daring act of hubris. But is the Bible a relative or a stranger?

Having lived and studied in seven countries, I have learned in my life to underestimate neither the otherness of those persons and things that are most familiar to me, nor the closeness and banality of what I would instinctively consider "strange." In today's morally complex world, while it may be helpful and reassuring to classify objects, ideas, and persons into neat groups, it is always healthy to question those categories. Psychologists and philosophers like Julia Kristeva invite us to discover the stranger within ourselves.[2] In fact, since antiquity philosophers like Aristotle have taught us to take a step back from what we consider obvious and familiar, look at it from another perspective, stand in awe, and marvel at its otherness. At the same time, philosophers like Plato and the Stoics have challenged the idea that there is an unfathomable diversity in the world. They have taught us to dig under the surface of what appears to be strange and disparate to find the underlying pattern or structure ("logos") that upholds both the functioning of the universe and the intercultural consistency of what most humans deem good, just, or worthy of belief.

Acknowledging the usefulness of the tension between these two positions, I believe it is unwise either to exaggerate or to deny difference, and often a sign of manipulation and murky political games. People may exaggerate differences unfairly and irrationally to create divisions and exclude the other. Conversely, people may deny differences so as to assimilate the other and reduce her to a clone of the self.

The complementarity logic I propose does several things. It lets us see Scripture and ethics as disciplines sufficiently different as to require bridging to be able to talk to one another, yet sufficiently similar to allow such communication to be rich and fruitful when time and energy is invested wisely to build and maintain the bridge. Furthermore, it encourages us, on the one hand, to help Christians to marvel at the otherness of both Scripture and its implications for Christian ethics. On the other hand, it invites non-Christians and even nonbelievers to discover how close both the Bible and Christian ethics might be to their worldview and their deepest-held ideas of good and bad.

I am aware that this double-edged questioning of boundaries might sound dangerous and unsettling to many people today, but I believe nobody can live Christianly or ethically without facing internal struggles and questioning the ways of thinking and the cultural and social divisions that everybody else considers "obvious."

The Reader and the Author

I will assume that the reader has some background in contemporary ethics and Bible studies, and that they will have previously acquired a reasonably mature understanding of what professional theologians in mainstream Christian denominations mean when they say that Scripture texts are "true," "historical," and "inspired," but in ways different from what most modern agnostic readers or fundamentalist Christians think when using those words. Scripture texts are certainly not some kind of CCTV footage from antiquity converted into prose, nor are they texts dictated word-by-word by God to the human authors. I will also assume that my readers will have enough faith, psychological stability, or theological training not to be scandalized, but rather to be stimulated by a critical reading of Scripture that at times balances a "hermeneutics of appreciation" with a respectful "hermeneutics of suspicion." Much has been written about these topics that I do not have space to repeat in this book. Rather, my focus here is on understanding in what sense Scripture texts are "normative" or "ethically relevant."

The attentive reader will notice that in the notes, I cite sources in various languages. Important texts and authors in English are often translated into other languages like Spanish, French, and Italian. However, the reverse is less true, and English monolinguals risk missing out on a lot of rich scholarship published in other languages. Though I grew up speaking Maltese and English, I had the good fortune of being exposed to other languages in my adolescence, and this allowed me to profitably "read" philosophy and theology in universities in Italy, the United Kingdom, France, Spain, and the United States. This exposure is one of the factors that has made me a migrant, blessed with—and condemned to—crossing borders and dealing with otherness throughout my life. I am now a Jesuit priest, living in Rome and teaching in Italian. I moved into the realm of the humanities after studying biology and chemistry in my undergraduate years in Malta.

Though I am not a Scripture scholar, I have delved into biblical scholarship on the topic I teach and discussed many of the issues in this book with Scripture scholars. I currently coteach a course on the topic of this book with a colleague who is both a Scripture scholar and an archaeologist and historian of the ANE. Having doctoral degrees in both theological ethics and biblical sciences may be useful in writing a text like this, but I do not believe it necessary if we are willing to engage people in the other discipline honestly and seriously.

Why Does the Book Focus on a Single Social Ethics Issue?

In this book, I focus on a single social ethics issue and seek to use Scripture in a way that might shed light on current immigration and asylum debates. The issue of our relationship to the stranger is useful to my project for two major reasons. First, it is central to all other social ethics debates. Debates on property rights, unionization, strikes, fair wages, welfare, the role of governments in the economy, and the social responsibilities of businesses have shaped Catholic social ethics since *Rerum Novarum* was published in 1891. These debates arose when industrialization and rapid urbanization created "mass societies" and fomented social alienation. Millions of workers migrated from rural areas (and, later, from colonial territories and less industrialized countries) to burgeoning cities. These workers looked very "different" from premodern city artisans, and this strangerhood accentuated preexisting class differences. Eventually, after the Great Depression and the Second World War, and with the help of some great political and religious leaders (especially in Western democracies), social classes were encouraged to stop seeing each other as total strangers and to renegotiate their relationships in positive ways. The 1973 oil crisis and post–Cold War globalization reshaped the economies of most industrialized countries, and the resulting waves of international labor migration in this "post-Fordist" system have created new social tensions that have an impact on all the classical debates. We cannot honestly discuss unionization, wages, or welfare from an ethics viewpoint today without considering the rights of migrant workers, including unauthorized migrants.

Second, and on a more theoretical level, the notion of stranger-hood is central to many important debates on biblical hermeneutics in the second half of the twentieth century. There is a distance between the world of the text and that of the reader, which needs to be laboriously bridged in the interpretation exercise, without being abolished. Another distance that needs careful and respectful bridging is that between the world of modern ethics and the world of the Bible—a library of classical texts written for all sorts of reasons, and collected into a canon for theological purposes.

Many readers will note that by making such a choice, I avoid hotly debated (and possibly more stimulating) issues concerning the beginning and end of life, marriage, sexuality, and sexual orientation, and wonder whether I do so on purpose. The answer is yes, for several reasons. First, I avoid these topics since they are not within my area of expertise in theological ethics (I teach fundamental morals and social ethics). Second, I believe that trying to treat many ethical issues in a book of this length implies a serious risk of superficiality (as regards the ethical debates), and excessive selectivity or "random sampling" (as regards the use of Scripture). I have noticed that biblical scholars writing similar books tend to use a plethora of moral issues merely to illustrate exegetical and hermeneutical issues. I come to Scripture from the opposite direction, from my fields of expertise, so the issues I bring to my reading of scripture as an ethicist have real value to me. I discuss exegetical and hermeneutical tools to illustrate how they can help me use the Bible to reflect deeply on these issues, which I cannot afford to present fleetingly or superficially.

Third, though debates on immigration and relationships with strangers are topical and can be quite divisive in some political circles, sexual, family, and personal ethics issues have been fueling some of the most emotionally charged and polarizing debates in our societies and in our Christian churches in the last decades. The fact that they speak about our bodies and our most intimate relationships probably makes these debates more sensitive than immigration. From where I stand as a Catholic theologian working in Rome, I believe dealing with one charged issue is more than enough in an age of deep polarization. My main aim in this book is to use a current debate as an example to reflect on a series of important epistemological questions, hence, dealing with only one divisive issue should keep our discussion stimulating and topical, while hopefully still allowing us to reflect calmly on the foundational issues. The method presented here should allow the readers to go back to sexual, family, and personal ethics issues later, equipped with tools which might help overcome some of the polarization.

Finally, given the "privatization" of these moral issues during modernity, we often fail to appreciate how deeply the political, economic, demographic, and cultural realities of antiquity (which were very different from ours) shaped the way biblical authors understood sexuality, family ties, embodiment, and the generation of new life. In our current debates, the cultural distance, added to the current emotional and political weight of these issues, implies a high risk of manipulative, anachronistic, opportunistic, or apologetic readings, or simply missing the point of the passages in question. I can understand why these personal ethics issues are so delicate and important to most of us, and why our Christian traditions have often been tempted to guide us (in our search to act righteously) and assuage our anxieties (in an age of profound and rapid change) by seeking simple, universal, immutable, certain, and normative answers in Scripture.

It is not easy to accept the fact that such answers might not exist, and that we should rather trust the Spirit to inspire prophets and leaders to provide fresh answers that make sense in our "strange" postmodern societies, just as the Spirit did two thousand years ago among the first Christians hailing from non-Jewish communities. It may be hard to believe that the Spirit can slowly and prudently innovate, while challenging the veiled egoism, individualism, and narcissism that underpin certain forms of novelty in every age. The same Spirit can also guarantee an ongoing faithfulness to our tradition, one that is not irrational, slavish, or continually in denial of the vast societal changes we are experiencing. As a social ethicist and fundamental moral theologian who deeply believes in the guiding action of the Spirit within our churches and societies (while observing the boundaries of my discipline) I can only pray that my colleagues who specialize in these topics may be led by such a Spirit, and may use Scripture intelligently and responsibly in their research on particular personal, sexual, and family ethics issues.

xxii

How This Book Is Organized

The first chapter of this book serves as a musical overture introducing some of the major themes while exploring two well-known Scripture texts on the topic of dealing with strangers (Luke 10:25–37; Matt 25:31–46). Starting with chapter 2, the first part of the book is the more theoretical and conceptual part of our journey. It explores ways how the divide between Bible and ethics can be bridged, such that these two realities might no longer be strangers. Chapters 2–4 function as a unit, though chapter 3 delves into some arguments that are more easily appreciated by readers with some background in philosophy and linguistics. Should some readers find it too abstract, they may move on and revisit it at the end.

The book's second part applies the epistemological reflection in the first part to the particular theme of the stranger. It explores a selection of Bible texts in order to stimulate ethical reflection. At the same time, it showcases the use of some analytical approaches, such as rhetorical analysis and narratology. The point is to show the ethics student how to use exegetical tools responsibly, while challenging some of the aura surrounding exegesis as a series of operations so technically complex and daunting that only experts can dare attempt.

As we shall see in chapters 2 and 4, the approach adopted in this book differs from that found in other recent books in English on the use of Scripture in ethics. Many of these books adopt a taxonomic/typological approach. They classify authors into types, showing the pros and cons of how certain authors use the Bible in their publications on moral theology. They hope that this annotated taxonomy will help the student emulate the author they think is best, or figure out their way of doing things which avoids the shortcomings of many famous authors. However, this very "democratic" approach that avoids proposing a method often leaves the student perplexed as to how to proceed. Other books focus on Scripture uniquely as a source of private or communitarian moral character formation, hoping that the habituation loops established in this formation process will lead the person to act justly in public, in a stable and excellent manner. They tend to reduce everything to a discourse on virtue ethics paradigms, and avoid the questions surrounding explicit, public, scholarly, intellectually honest, and critical use of Scripture texts in sensitive political debates today. Yet others, including some of my former professors and friends, have coauthored insightful books on scripture and virtue ethics. Unfortunately, these books still feel quite disjointed to the reader, with the exegetical and ethical parts of each chapter often linked with a single concept or a thin thread.

I believe a higher level of cross-disciplinarity can allow us, exegetes and ethicists, to break out of our disciplinary silos, and to dance together gracefully, free of the fear of stepping on each other's toes. This book aims to cross that divide, halting the elegant but exasperating quadrille between "shy" or "brazen" dance partners. I believe we have all encountered "shy" exegetes who pretend they don't know anything about ethics (and write hundreds of pages of commentary on, say, a massacre text, pretending to avoid any discussion of the ethical issues at stake). Or "shy" ethicists who pretend they are incapable of doing exegesis or understanding rigorous commentaries. We may have also encountered "brazen" exegetes and ethicists who pretend to be experts in everything and capable of boldly resolving complex issues by simply collapsing them onto the concerns of their major discipline. It is time we move on to a more confident, candid, and respectful interaction.

ACKNOWLEDGMENTS

This book evolved from a chapter in my doctoral dissertation, which I submitted and defended at Boston College in 2013. I am grateful to Frs. David Hollenbach and James Keenan, and Dr. Christopher Frechette, who accompanied me in that process, as well as fellow Jesuits Lúcás Chan, Gonzalo Villagrán, Grégoire Catta, Bambang Irawan, and Nicholas Austin, who at the time were students like me, and who encouraged me and gave me useful feedback. I am also indebted to Frs. Enrique Sanz Giménez-Rico and Julio L. Martínez (at the Pontifical Comillas University in Madrid) and Fr. Alain Thomasset (at Centre Sévres–Facultés Jésuites de Paris) who shaped my understanding of how an adequate and fruitful dialogue might be established between Scripture and ethics and stimulated my interest in pursuing the subject further in a scholarly way. In my adolescence and early youth in Malta, well before I embarked on university studies in ethics and theology, I grew up debating matters of morality in the Bible with my parents, and then with Jesuit spiritual mentors such as Frs. Ray Pace, David Cefai, and Joseph Cassar. Their insightful, honest, and nuanced approaches, respectful of the complexity involved, was precious in my formative years.

Dr. Frechette eventually became my editor for this book, and I am especially grateful for his constant encouragement; the staff at Paulist Press (especially the publisher, Fr. Mark-David Janus, and editorial director, Paul McMahon) have also been particularly supportive during the moments when, due to other commitments, my writing came to a standstill. Among my current colleagues at the Pontifical Gregorian University, I am most indebted to Frs. Humberto Miguel Yáñez and Josef Mario Briffa, with whom I have taught several issues raised in this book to undergraduate and graduate theological ethics students, engaging in serious debates along the way. A final thank you goes to my students who have provided useful feedback over the last eight years of teaching on these issues.

ABBREVIATIONS

General Abbreviations

ANE   Ancient Near East
CST   Catholic Social Thought (or Teaching)
JB   Jewish Bible (or Jewish-Canon Bible, preferred to the more ambiguous term "Hebrew Bible")
NT   New Testament
OT   Old Testament (pre-Christian texts of the Catholic Canon; includes the JB and additional Greek texts)
PBC   Pontifical Biblical Commission

Catholic Church Documents[1]

AAS   *Acta Apostolicæ Sedis* (Official Gazette of the Holy See)
BM   *The Bible and Morality: Biblical Roots of Christian Conduct* (Pontifical Biblical Commission, 2008)
CCC   *Catechism of the Catholic Church* (1997)
CHM   *Church and Human Mobility* (Circular Letter by the Pontifical Council for the Pastoral Care of Migrants and Itinerant People, 1978)
CSDC   *Compendium of the Social Doctrine of the Church* (Pontifical Council for Justice and Peace, 2004)

---

1. The parts concerning migration in most of these documents have been published in Baggio and Pettenà (2009), including documents by the US Catholic Bishops and the Catholic Church in Asia. Most of the documents are also available at the Vatican website (www.vatican.va), and the originals are published in the Holy See's official gazette, the *Acta Apostolicae Sedis* (http://www.vatican.va/archive/aas/index_en.htm). In general, we will refer to these documents using the paragraph numbers in the Vatican editions of these documents published by the Libreria Editrice Vaticana.

DPMC	*De Pastorali Migratorum Cura / Nemo Est* (Instruction by the Sacred Congregation for Bishops, 1969)
EF	*Exsul Familia* (Apostolic Constitution by Pope Pius XII, 1952)
EM	*Erga Migrantes Caritas Christi* (Instruction by the Pontifical Council for the Pastoral Care of Migrants and Itinerant People, 2004)
FT	*Fratelli Tutti* (Encyclical by Pope Francis, 2019)
GS	*Gaudium et Spes* (Pastoral Constitution by Vatican Council II, 1965)
IBC	*L'interprétation de la Bible dans l'Église—The Interpretation of the Bible in the Church* (Pontifical Biblical Commission, 1993)
OTE	*Optatam Totius* (Decree by Vatican Council II, 1965)
SRS	*Sollicitudo Rei Socialis* (Encyclical by Pope John Paul II, 1987)
VG	*Veritatis Gaudium* (Apostolic Constitution by Pope Francis, 2018)

1

INTRODUCTION

The Bible: A Familiar Face or a Stranger?

In this introduction—intentionally written in a less scholarly and more conversational style—we invite readers to revisit two familiar Gospel texts: the parable of the good Samaritan (Luke 10:25–37), and the Last Judgment (Matt 25:31–46). The latter text is often cited in Catholic social ethics discourse and used in support of a classical list of the "Corporal Works of Mercy," or else to defend modern notions of social justice and human rights. Readers will discover that they have been reading these texts allegorically, one way or another. This chapter will challenge that reading by proposing other ways of allegorizing the texts, and changing the referents of the characters with whom readers may have identified in the past. Readers may thereby experience their visits to Bible texts also as sojourns in a strange land, even when passing through familiar territory.

In the process, readers will acquire some skills. They will learn how to perform "allegorical permutations." They will become acquainted with the "spiritual reading" of texts (Allegory 5), and learn to analyze and better understand how Scripture is used in many writings of the church fathers. Finally, readers will learn a technique that helps challenge stereotyped readings of Scripture by systematically looking for texts (on a given topic) that are less familiar, and that may not come to mind immediately.

1.1 Commonplaces and Clichés

Let us begin by diving straight into the middle of things, in media res, because that is how we usually experience things in life. It is only when, at some point, we take some distance from what we are doing that we become aware that we are actually doing *some* particular thing and may have been doing it for a long time. Then we start asking some interesting questions about our activity, and try to reach back to the origins, the wellsprings of our action.

I assume that my typical readers are already in the thick of things, having been exposed extensively to short quotes and narratives from the Bible, on the one hand, and having met and interacted with strangers on many occasions, on the other. Probably, they will have built links between these two elements in their heads. Readers, then, will have some ideas on what this book is about, or should be about. Hence, I would like to begin by asking the following: Which three Bible passages come to mind when you think about strangers and migrants? I suggest you take a moment now and write them down.

On this topic, I'm unaware of any surveys or rigorous studies spanning various countries and Christian denominations, but in most official Catholic discourses and documents, I usually come across the following three texts: the parable of the good Samaritan (Luke 10:25–37), the Last Judgment (Matt 25:31–46), and the injunction to love the stranger in Leviticus 19:33–34. These are wonderfully rich literary sources that people find familiar and think they know well, but that many of us tend to misuse and exploit inappropriately in our discourses, depending on our mood. When I'm in a critical mood I tend to dismiss texts like these as clichéd. When in a more apologetic mood, I see them as useful, but risky "commonplaces"[1] or "tropes." Think of the Scripture texts that moralizing parents throw at their misbehaving kids, or politicians use to flaunt their "Christian" credentials. Both suggest the same arrogant logic: "Even God agrees with me, so you don't dare disagree!"

1.2 The Good Samaritan

In philosophical and theological ethics, we often deal with "classics": rich, ubiquitous, and seemingly familiar stories and texts.[2] Moral classics include famous textbook cases, thought experiments, and narratives from religious traditions. Let us start by considering the parable of the good Samaritan (Luke 10:25–37), not only a favorite classic of popes and church leaders,[3] but also one that pops up in essays on migration by famous philosophers. Michael Walzer,[4] for instance, uses the parable to reflect on political membership and on what is owed to outsiders or strangers.

An Initial Approach: Allegorical Permutations

Classics have the ability to talk to us, even if we know little of the culture and historical context in which they were composed. I will argue, however, that serious moral reflection in Christian theology requires an acquaintance with the history and culture that underlie the Scripture passages we use for reflection. Before using them in our ethical arguments, we ought at least to be aware of what experts have discovered in those passages, using tools offered by modern historical and critical exegesis and other exegetical approaches. Yet before accessing that wealth of knowledge and before attempting "serious moral reflection," let us start our journey from where we are, in the midst of things. Let us try, with admitted naïveté, to delve deeper into the sense of a parable that is so very familiar.

In our "naïve" approach, we will consider the text as a single literary unit, assume that the translations in our Bibles are faithful to the ancient text, start with an allegorical reading, and try to figure out which of the characters "represent" the "stranger." In an allegorical reading, each character represents some social category, and the story points to some "moral." In our approach, which I call "allegorical permutations," we will try to match the stranger, allegorically, with various characters in the text, remapping the other characters accordingly, and assessing the results each time. Allegorical readings were popular in patristic exegesis. Allegory 5 below illustrates the common patristic practice that inspired the present exercise: comparing the allegorization proposals of various church fathers.

Before discussing allegorical readings, three points require attention. First, a parable does not necessarily point to a "moral," and most biblical texts do not fit nicely in a neat analogical construct linking them to our lives. They do not support a practical syllogism of this kind: "The hero did x in situation y; I am in an analogous situation y_1, so I should do x_1."

Already that kind of syllogism and analogical parallelism (hero:reader = $y:y_1$ = $x:x_1$) indicates that our action cannot mimic that of the hero of the narrative (x), since our situation is necessarily different (it is y_1, not y!). Hence, if anything, it has to be *similar*, but not *identical* (x_1, not x!). There is a measure of creativity and adaptiveness in moving from x to x_1 (from "What did Jesus/the Samaritan do?" to "What should I do?"). Yet even this structure is often inappropriate, since the point of a parable or Bible story is not simply that we imitate action x. Rather, we are to allow the parable to challenge and transform our way of thinking. We might come to see the particular issue being discussed in a new light, but this is secondary. The more enduring effect is that we absorb elements of the *type of logic*, the *worldview* and the *virtues* that the hero or protagonist exhibits when doing x.

Second, experts warn us that allegorical readings of parables can be too reductive and hence inappropriate,[5] even though the New Testament itself provides an allegorical interpretation of at least one important parable, that of the sower (Matt 13:1–9 / Matt 13:18–23). Though characters in parables may hint at social "types," the mirroring is not mechanical or unequivocal, as in Aesop's fables. Rather, Jesus's parables not only "throw us beside" their characters (to allow an analogical comparison) but also "throw us out of our regular orbit" (*paraballō*) into another world where things don't necessarily follow the logic prevalent in the "real" world. Yet, their logic is not completely unreasonable or incomprehensible, and it certainly does not leave the attentive listener indifferent. When we are back facing the real world, this emotional and rational "jolt" we experience in the "world of the parable" places a critical seed in our mind. This jolt can help us start to question deeply some behaviors, traditions, and social givens, since we now realize that things can be different, things that we have assumed can be only a certain way.

We might resist this idea initially, out of fear that it will turn our world upside down and make us question givens to which we jealously attach our identity or notion of order. We often assume that the only correct attitude in such and such a situation is the one our family, culture, ethnic group, profession, or personal history has presented to us as the normal one, if not the best or least harmful possible. At first, if we read carefully, some Bible characters may seem crazy. Slowly, however, we realize that it is we who are crazy for having thought until now that the *only* reasonable way of organizing reality is the one to which we are accustomed.

The third point builds on the second. This "strangerhood" of Scripture can be easily misunderstood. It is sacred and "totally other" (*ganz andere*, as Rudolf Otto would say), but not in the sense of a parallel

4

culture, standing in competition with other cultures, systems, or traditions. It is "other" to the "worldly" mentality that inhabits every sphere of human existence—including the most sacred institutions in Christianity, where humans are present with their cravenness, pettiness, and unbounded ambition. Yet, it appears "totally familiar" to most people (even the most atheistic), as soon as they flip a switch inside themselves and realize they can see things in a "spiritual" way. By "spiritual" I mean a "more authentically human" way; since we are created in the image of God, our authentic humanity is authentically spiritual.

The political and sociological ramifications of this third point are enormous. When we convert and degrade the "strangeness" of Scripture (or of Christianity) into something that can be identified socially and politically with some well-defined cultural group, movement, party, or ideology, using visible and measurable characteristics, that is exactly when the otherness disappears. Then we are back in a "worldly" mentality where faith becomes merely a social banner used by a group to negotiate privileges, spheres of power, and access to resources in a finite world, in competition with other social groups.

Allegory 1: The Stranger Is the Victim— An Issue among Individuals

Having stated these provisos, we may start our analysis. Many moral discussions use the parable of the good Samaritan (Luke 10:25–37) to reflect on how we should treat strangers, particularly those who are unthreatening and needy. These discussions usually remain at the level of single moral agents and avoid dealing with social structures (which we will discuss in Allegory 3). The most obvious analogical mapping entails linking the strangers (such as migrants and refugees) to the victim in the parable, and the "we" (the moral agents being addressed, who are usually Christians) to the good Samaritan. The final "go and do likewise" is transferred from the legal scholar in the passage to the readers, who are invited to use their "analogical imagination" to see themselves acting like the Samaritan in their various encounters with strangers in the twenty-first century. *Fratelli Tutti*, Pope Francis's 2020 encyclical letter on social kinship and friendship, dedicates the second chapter to the parable, in general following this analogical reading.[6]

There are two ethically relevant elements in this reading. The first is a matter of form (the "how"). Emulating the good Samaritan means not shunning opportunities (and possibly seeking) to assist people *through personal face-to-face encounters.* The second regards the "who" (object) and the "why" (motive). We should be the "good Samaritans" in our dealings with vulnerable migrants and refugees since they are needy persons, and *helping people in need is a decent thing to do.*

Let us start by discussing the *form* that neighborliness takes in this reading. The uniqueness of the event of the Samaritan's unscripted encounter with the victim is highlighted in a commentary of the parable entitled "The Socius and the Neighbor" penned in French by philosopher Paul Ricœur in 1954. The text is cited by Pope Francis in note 80 of *FT* as a source of inspiration for his own commentary.[7] Ricœur notes that "the event of the encounter is fleeting and fragile. As soon as it is consolidated into a lasting and stable relationship, it is already an institution. There are very few pure events, and they cannot be retained or forecast and organized without a minimum degree of institutionalization."[8] The point is that we should recognize the moment of the encounter at the beginning of the parable as a special moment that cannot be fully analyzed and explained sociologically. The way the Samaritan navigates the situation reveals his moral character, and it is not entirely conditioned by established notions of in-group/out-group duties or predetermined social dynamics regarding gifts and countergifts. There is a timelessness or eschatological element in such an event, and a grace-filled experience in his act of charity. Even so, we may correctly feel that acting this way is at the same time a matter of duty (and not an optional or supererogatory exercise of the virtue of charity), and furthermore that its "graciousness" and "gratuity" is something nonbelievers can fully appreciate.

As the story progresses, however, the relationship between the Samaritan and the victim becomes more stable. In the encounter the Samaritan is a "neighbor" (literally, the Greek word *plesion* indicates a nearby person, or person in proximity), which for Ricœur is not a sociological category, but rather a "happening" that has moral implications. He eventually becomes a "socius" of the victim, that is, an associate or fellow member within a sociologically recognizable human group. In verse 35, the Samaritan pays two denarii to the innkeeper and indicates that he intends to return to the inn (presumably in a relatively short period of time, if the promise of repayment is credible). At this point, the relationship with the victim starts to become more stable and to take on a historical and social dimension (allowing the victim or his family to discover the Samaritan's identity and eventually befriend or repay him).

The experience of the encounter is important, but Ricœur invites us theologians and believers not to focus all our attention on the individual encounter. We should also note the importance of social mediations: "When I reduce the theology of the neighbor to a theology of the encounter, I miss the fundamental meaning of the Lordship of God over history."[9] We will get back to the topic of institutions and social mediations when discussing Allegory 3, but it useful to note that institutionalization of assistance is not just a matter of large, anonymous welfare systems or public services, like those we activate when calling an emergency phone number (such as 911 in the United States). Even philanthropy and volunteering in a small-town community or in a parish is embedded in historical and social dynamics and rationalities and do not easily provide the experience of a singular, unscripted, unexpected event.

Let us now move on to the *motive and object*: the call to help people in need who are close-at-hand (proximate). There is nothing particularly Christian about being "good Samaritans," as *FT* itself notes (10–12; 271–75): the value of hospitality and our duties toward strangers in need are recognized in various ways in traditional cultures and mainstream philosophical ethics. As regards religious traditions, we could mention the notion of universal compassion of the Buddha (*karuṇā* and *anukampā* in Pali), Mencius's discussion of the case of the child about to fall into a well (*The Mencius* 2A:6), or the story of the first hijra (when Mohammad's companions were given asylum by the king of Ethiopia).[10] As regards philosophy, Peter Singer's "Shallow Pond" case (regarding our duty as passersby to wade into a shallow pond to save a drowning child) has stimulated an important ethics debate and I find the discussion of the case by Anglo-Ghanaian-American philosopher Kwame Anthony Appiah particularly enlightening.[11] The murder of Kitty Genovese in 1964 stimulated another debate in English-speaking countries that gave rise to the "Kew Gardens Principle." This posits that our duty to help a victim or person in danger increases with their need, our proximity and capability, and our aid being their last resort.[12] Of course, we may debate whether this ethics of hospitality and care of strangers in need is central or peripheral in these religious and philosophical traditions, and to what extent past contact or dialogue with Christian culture may have helped bring this ethics to the fore in other traditions.

It is interesting to see how this ethics undergirds public laws in different countries. Of course, law can justly impose or encourage particular ethical behavior only up to a certain point, or it risks becoming totalitarian (as the history of prohibition in the United States amply demonstrates). Yet some legal systems see the Samaritan's behavior as a moral standard that all citizens can appreciate and emulate. In Italy, for example, a capable bystander's "failure to assist or rescue" (*omissione di soccorso*) constitutes a criminal offense. Indeed, most civil law systems in continental Europe, Latin America, and Africa impose a far more extensive duty to rescue than do common-law systems prevalent in English-speaking countries. In common-law systems, duties are often limited to the perpetrator, such as in a hit-and-run traffic accident, or to people having a special relationship with the victim, such as relatives or chauffeurs.

Many countries whose law does not penalize "failure to rescue" have recently had to introduce "good Samaritan" laws to protect and motivate people who aid those in peril, given past incidents where innocent helpers were accused of being the perpetrators and were held liable for damages. For instance, in the Nanjing Peng Yu incident in China, in 2006, the court found that "experience from everyday life" sufficiently proves that no one would help someone in good conscience unless they felt guilty. This claim engendered a huge public outcry, but it did not keep other courts in China from reasoning in the same manner and punishing "Samaritans" until the Chinese Civil Code was updated in 2017.[13] In Italy, ship captain Carola Rakete (who worked for Sea-Watch, an NGO that rescues migrants at sea) was arrested for aiding and abetting illegal immigration after forcing her way into the port of Lampedusa on June 26, 2019. She had been trying to bring rescued migrants to safety for fourteen days, but the authorities were instructed by the minister, a populist far-right politician, to only allow a handful of the migrants to disembark, namely the most vulnerable and those needing urgent medical attention. Despite the minister's obvious and cynical political posturing and the Italian legal tradition regarding failure to assist, 61 percent of the Italian population believed the migrants should not have disembarked in Italy, presuming maybe that they should have been taken to the small island-nation of Malta or pushed back to Libya.[14]

These cases bring us to the thorny issue of what is "reasonable" and what isn't from the point of view of the individual rescuer. Most of the moral and legal debates at some point remind us that there is a limit to everything and that we can only help so many people. This means that in some cases, we may have to say no, hoping others will step in to aid and rescue people in need. Often, this means having to rely on the support of public and private institutions to aid the needy in our name, and then financially supporting these institutions. The Samaritan does not help every needy person he meets, and nothing tells us that his solution—that of using the services available at the nearest inn, since he probably doesn't live nearby—cannot be copied by the locals. From this perspective, going slightly out of our way to do the decent thing is not necessarily very demanding: we could simply leave undesirable and problematic strangers at an "inn." This could be some institution where professionals take care of needy people, and where we would leave some donation or contribute tax money to finance that institution. We wouldn't need to let them into our homes, bring them close to our kids, or spend too much time attending to their needs. Authors like Christine Pohl have written volumes on the costliness of true "Christian hospitality," but one might question in what sense (if any) the good Samaritan's hospitality was costly.

Let us stick to the action of the individual agent for now and note that overreliance on institutional support entails the risk of individuals becoming too removed from the experience of encounter. Such overreliance may be exploited by xenophobic demagogues such that public forms of assistance to vulnerable strangers, which have become "reasonable" and "not-so-costly" due to institutional support, are recast as burdensome and unreasonable from a more systemic viewpoint. Once we lose personal contact with "different" persons living in the peripheries of our lifeworld, we might quickly be convinced that these invisible persons do not really need help, but are taking advantage of generous welfare systems or private charities. Moreover, we may come to believe that helping them stand on their two feet entails removing the public safety net and forcing them to fend for themselves.

In many countries today, this operation is reinforced by circular arguments concerning the legality of actions of the person in need. If you cunningly craft a law that seems reasonable to most voters, whereby people are prohibited from lying on the ground along busy roads, you can then argue that the victim in the parable is not entitled to any help since he is probably acting illegally. Of course, in many countries, immigration law is more complex and less cynical than the law in the previous example, and some articles might even be written by persons who honestly seek to promote the common good in the best way possible at the time when the law was designed. Yet other articles are often built on shady political compromises made to the detriment of voiceless minorities or residents who are not allowed to vote, and even the most noble provisions in a law could become ethically blameworthy if not updated over time to account for changes on the ground, for instance, new migratory movements. Many citizens perfectly understand the moral ambiguity of law when discussing laws they dislike, but seem incapable of such critical distance when discussing migration law as it applies to strangers. The law may not be perfect, but "it's the law," according to a mindless tautology that many Christians strangely find convincing. Hence, many Christians insist that there is nothing racist, xenophobic, or anti-Christian in asking governments to keep out "*illegal* migrants," in upholding laws that make the entry of "*unwanted* migrants" *illegal*, or even in punishing Christian and other NGOs who aid and abet illegal entry and residence in one's country. All of this is deemed "reasonable," since "charity begins at home."

This rather linear attitude toward morality and legality is excessively trusting of human authority and concerned with keeping very complex matters as simple and reasonable as possible. It lacks curiosity and critical distance from the logic of the "world," and risks becoming a trap for readers of the Bible who seek guidance for moral life in the Sacred Scriptures. It is too attached to a neat and uncomplicated form of "orderliness," too wary of being surprised or shocked. This attitude may appear "pious," yet it is ultimately unwelcoming toward anything divine that dares to present itself in challenging ways, thus as a "stranger," to the moral agent.

My point here is not mainly about normative morality, the kind of blanket ethical rules we propose as general guidelines to every human person. Such morality, given the rigid duties it imposes on the conscience, normally needs to be "reasonable," "sensible," "practical," and not excessively "burdensome." Of course, to formulate moral norms (which can in turn inspire positive law in pluralistic democracies), we may need at some point to bracket some of the more utopian, idealistic, visionary, and subversive elements of Jesus's action and preaching, which echo the parrhesia of major Old Testament figures. Doing so may be necessary to come to terms with human reality: what is physically or morally impossible cannot obligate a person, and moral norms that seem to demand the impossible risk being discredited and ignored.

Nevertheless, there is much more to ethics than the formulation of general norms, and before we engage in that task, we should listen to Scripture in all its radicality, rather than confining it to what we deem "reasonable," thereby preempting any gratuitous exploration of what it is trying to tell us. Furthermore, Scripture has a lot to teach us that can shape our action as individuals and communities, but that cannot be formulated in normative language, nor imposed on others who do not have a particular relationship with Christ or Scripture.

Let us therefore go back to the text and allow it to surprise us. The first thing to ask is, "Are we sure that the stranger in the parable is the victim?"

Allegory 2: The Stranger Is the Samaritan

To be sure, nothing in the parable indicates that the victim (who "was going down from Jerusalem to Jericho") was not a Jew. The surprising element of story is precisely that *it is a stranger who helps the autochthonous victim*, and moreover, a stranger of the kind that first-century Jews tended to *look down on*. Some OT texts deem Samaritans detestable; one calls them "the foolish people that live in Shechem."[15] In *Jewish Antiquities* 18:29, Josephus describes a Passover incident (in the years 6–9 CE) in which Samaritans scattered human bones in the portico of the Jerusalem temple, defiling it, something akin to committing a heinous act during a solemn pontifical mass in St. Peter's. This reminds us of issue of defilement upon contact with the dead, an element of the parable we tend to overlook.

By focusing on the strangerhood of the rescuer we can propose a new analogy whereby the needy strangers of our day and age are linked to the character of the good Samaritan. This in turn allows us to associate autochthonous citizens and Christian readers today with the other characters, such as the priest and Levite, the innkeeper, and even the victim. In this latter case, the stinging irony whereby the villain (the detestable Samaritan) becomes the hero is hard to miss, and it is typical of Jesus and of Hebrew literature in general. Instead of employing the typical *captatio benevolentiae* in his inaugural speech in Nazareth (Luke 4:14–30), Jesus seems eager to provoke the anger and rejection of his audience. He hurts their nationalistic pride by implying that strangers were more worthy than Jews of God's benevolence:

11

"Doubtless you will quote to me this proverb, 'Doctor, cure yourself!' And you will say, 'Do here also in your hometown the things that we have heard you did at Capernaum.'" And he said, "Truly I tell you, no prophet is accepted in the prophet's hometown. But the truth is, there were many widows in Israel in the time of Elijah, when the heaven was shut up three years and six months, and there was a severe famine over all the land; yet Elijah was sent to none of them except to a widow at Zarephath in Sidon. There were also many lepers in Israel in the time of the prophet Elisha, and none of them was cleansed except Naaman the Syrian." (Luke 4:23–27)

We find such irony also in various Jewish Bible texts. In the Book of Jonah, the people of Nineveh, pagans reputed to be sinful and depraved, turn out to be so receptive and obedient to God's call to conversion that the Prophet Jonah is upset. His pride is offended since he was not prepared to see the powerful and wicked Assyrians showing such docility to the word of God (Jon 4). They implicitly make his fellow Jews (and Jonah himself, who is supposed to be a pious prophet) seem all the more resistant to God's word and reluctant to obey God, despite being God's chosen ones. Furthermore, the archetypical "blameless and upright man" in the Hebrew Bible is Job, who hailed from the (foreign) land of Uz (Job 1:1). To note such stinging irony against national and personal self-righteousness in Scripture is not anti-Semitic. It only becomes anti-Semitic and anti-Christian when we avoid being stung by it and deflect it toward someone else (for example, the Jewish nation). Deflection is, of course, a perfectly self-righteous and narcissistic reaction. In the context of the parable, deflection entails that we avoid transferring the ironic self-awareness to ourselves; we avoid questioning the idea that Christians are automatically or spontaneously kind toward strangers; and we avoid realizing that, even when we are welcoming the other, we are often being welcomed in turn by the other who might be holier and more generous than we are. Curiously, in many Romance languages, the same word is used for "host" and "guest." Indeed, both words in English are doublets, presumably derived from Proto-Indo-European *g^hóstis.

Are all strangers "needy" or "vulnerable"? Surely some are well capable of welcoming and helping us, and they actually do, even though we often fail to appreciate this. To be sure, the Samaritan in the parable is vulnerable. First, the robbers might still be around, and the whole "man on the ground" setup might be a trap. Second, if people in this part of the world do not dare or do not bother to stop and help their neighbors, members of the same ethnic and religious group, then who on earth would tend to him, an unwelcome stranger, were he to become the next victim? Third, what will keep the victim or the innkeeper from conveniently or xenophobically accusing the Samaritan of being himself the robber and assailant (now feeling guilty for having gone too far, but maybe intending to keep the rest of the victim's money)? Unusual acts of kindness by strangers are often suspected of masking an elaborate scam, as in the Peng Yu incident mentioned above. Xenophobia has a perverse way of convincing us that if the stranger is doing something right, it must surely be a smokescreen and yet another indication that he must be guilty of something.

Even so, despite being vulnerable, the good Samaritan has agency and refuses to let his fear of the other dictate his actions. We don't know what he is doing in Judea, what motives he might have to travel alone in an unwelcoming place, or if he might be involved in some shady business. Yet, he seems freer, stronger, and more morally mature than the priest and the Levite. They seem too concerned with avoiding the ritual impurity that would result from possible contact with a dead body to ponder their duty to attend to a person who is "half-dead" (*hemithané*; Luke 10:30). Such a choice runs contrary to first-century Jewish legal casuistry, in which life norms prevail over purity norms, as noted by Jesus in Luke 13:15. The Samaritan seems used to taking risks, to trusting in God and in human goodness. He sees the open road not only as a dangerous place, but also as a place where strangers meet, help one another, and become friends.

Many people find it hard to read the parable this way. They likely get stuck in the stereotype whereby "we" are the good guys, able and willing to help others, while "they," those we call "strangers," are either bad or needy individuals who cannot be of any help to us (except by making us feel good when we help them). It is humbling to admit that "strangers" can be courageous, hope driven, and resilient persons who put themselves at risk to come to our aid in many ways, and sometimes even when we are not even aware of it, while those we consider "friends" and "family" abandon us. Reading the parable in this way becomes easier and more obvious the more we get to know refugees and migrants personally, and the more we listen to their stories and come to appreciate their agency.

Xenophobia pushes back against this reading, asking us not to generalize from a rare case. For the skeptic, the exceptional "good" Samaritan does nothing to counter the reputation of Samaritans in general. They are still as evil as we were told they were. In 1960s London, due to the tabloids' simplistic representation of the city's underbelly, most people believed all Maltese immigrants to be gangsters or friends of mobsters. Those who had Maltese friends admitted they were decent people, but instead of doubting the stereotype, concluded that their friends must be exceptions.[16] Fear is a self-fulfilling prophecy: if you continue to treat strangers as a threat, even when they are consistently kind and generous, they risk becoming a threat. Hope, on the other hand, can bring out the best in people, even convicted criminals, as I learned in my years of prison ministry.

It is important to hope and believe that good Samaritans do not exist only in fairy tales or feel-good movies. Today, many practitioners involved in the accompaniment of vulnerable migrants recognize how the identity of these persons has been transformed by life on the road, an experience that allowed many of them to bracket their ethnic belonging and feel a sort of camaraderie with fellow travelers. More generally, they are among those people whose experience of vulnerability has made them keenly aware of, and empathic toward, the vulnerability of others. Of course, not all persons deal with vulnerability in this way; some clam up or become hostile or paranoid, but some become more solidary, and these are the people Jesus is inviting us (and the Torah expert or "lawyer") to imitate.

In answering the lawyer's question "Who is my neighbor?" Jesus's point is that neighborliness (proximity, "social kinship") is often not (and should not be) lived as a *matter of fact*, based on blood, ethnicity, or cultural communion. Such things can be studied using the tools of sociology. Rather, neighborliness is a *matter of choice*, though our freedom is anchored both by the "fact" of concrete vicinity and need, and by a common humanity present in us all. Hence, neighborliness is ultimately an object of parenetic and ethical discourse, not a sociological fact.[17] In this vein, in the text mentioned above, Ricœur writes, "There is no sociology of the neighbor [nearby person]. The science of the neighbor is thwarted by the praxis of the neighbor. One does not *have* a neighbor; I make myself someone's neighbor."[18] Of course, the readers of Luke's text needed to be constantly reminded of this. They were a disparate and marginalized band of Jews, Samaritans, and Gentiles brought together into a heterogenous "church" by their belief in Christ's resurrection, and deemed weird or heterodox by friends and family. Eventually, their church (assembly) will become an institutional "church," a visible association that can be studied sociologically, where charity is institutionally mediated. Institutions and established social groupings are an important channel for charity, but the inherent risk in this process is that some Jews, Samaritans, and pagans will now consider themselves part of yet another social group labeled "Christian," with a clear public identity, and will limit themselves to help other members of the "Christian" *society*, rather than choose to be neighbors to *whomever needs a neighbor*, no matter his or her sociological group of belonging.[19]

For now, as noted above, we have adopted a relatively loose method for analyzing the Luke 10:25–37 passage, or "pericope." Our reading is not totally "naïve" since it is aware of some well-known facts about Palestine in the first century CE regarding Samaritans, innkeepers, priests, and Levites. Nevertheless, it does not engage any of the contemporary exegetical literature on this passage (and the results of historical criticism, in particular). We are simply testing various ways of mapping the "neighbors" and "strangers" in the text onto the "neighbors" and "strangers" in our life contexts and commenting critically on the results. At the beginning of the passage, Jesus asks the Torah expert to engage in such an analogical mapping exercise. The point is to allow the expert to figure out who his neighbor is (or whom he should treat as "neighbor"), when Jesus invites him to "go and do likewise" at the end of the text, an exhortation the evangelist Luke also addresses to his readers.

Much has been said and written on the moral significance of the "analogical imagination"[20] promoted by Jesus in the text itself, which is central to the above discussion and to this whole book. Yet, methodologically, all we have done is taken a clichéd reading of a well-known biblical text and asked ourselves whether it really works or whether, by projecting so many stereotypes onto the text, it ends up skewing the text's meaning. Projecting *some* stereotypes or "precomprehensions" onto a text is normal and almost unavoidable. A problem arises when a powerful "classic" ends up so crushed and deformed by the meanings and concerns we load onto it that it loses its power to surprise us and to help us question some of those interpretative structures that we bring into our reading. At that point, the text simply mirrors us to ourselves, losing all its strangeness, its power to challenge us, to stand before us as a "vis-à-vis." It becomes just another "reasonable" text, a self-serving confirmation that "God agrees with me, so who will dare disagree?" We will discuss these hermeneutical issues later in the book. For now, let us continue our allegorical permutations exercise and see what new insights it may yield, despite allowing us to project stereotypes onto the text.

Allegory 3: The Stranger Is the Victim—a Structural Issue

In Allegory 1 we are the good Samaritans, and strangers or migrants are the needy victims. Allegory 2 allows us to swap the roles and see migrants as good Samaritans, whose experience of vulnerability drives them to help needy persons they meet on their journey (who might be us). Admittedly, in a culture that celebrates the myth of the individual pulling themselves up by their bootstraps from aversity to resounding success, Allegory 2 might lead to some callous and ethically problematic conclusions. The resilience of vulnerable strangers and their ability to help others may tempt us to conclude that we should let destitute and injured strangers alone to fend for themselves and their kind, and possibly fend for us as well, as mythical frontier heroes do. Allegory 2 may be used to conveniently let my readers and me off the hook (assuming we are not refugees and vulnerable migrants) when, in the Gospel, it is precisely we who are being asked to identify with the Samaritan and "go and do likewise."

Allegory 1 and Allegory 2 are similar in that they focus on the agency of individuals and can hence be read in a personal (and also in an overly individualistic) way. It is helpful at this stage to go back to the first allegory and discuss the victimhood of the stranger and our duty to assist and rescue victims at a deeper level—that of social structures. Might not the parable also point to a need to create institutions that help needy "outsiders" and to challenge the ingrained social behaviors, norms, and practices which hurt them?

I often drop a coin in the cups of Romani beggars sitting outside my university. I am fully aware that they might spend the money on alcohol or give most of it to a boss who preys on their earnings. Such acts of charity provide an important channel of noninstitutionalized contact with poor strangers, but they make little sense in the twenty-first century if not accompanied by institutionally mediated action. What does that mean for me? Eight minutes' walk from my office in Rome, there is

16

a soup kitchen for refugees and migrants run by fellow Jesuits, Centro Astalli, where some of the neediest are also provided with access to primary medical and psychological care, temporary housing, and job training. Should I go and volunteer there regularly? Certainly, a volunteer experience can be very formative, and I have done volunteer work with migrants in Malta, Italy, Spain, the United States, and Uganda. Should I go further out of my way and meet them on the road? Sure, a visit to the migration corridors and hotspots in Africa and Central America cannot hurt; I've done that as well. But can a twenty-first century obedience to Jesus's command—"go and do likewise"—limit itself to mimicking the actions of a Samaritan in first-century Judea, albeit with upgraded medical and catering technology?

One-on-one individual assistance or volunteering with small NGOs is not the only "true" form of charity and of being neighborly. We can and should also focus on the structural aspect of social problems— such as the plight of destitute or injured vulnerable foreign workers, refugees, and child migrants. This requires us to see beyond personal (what I do) and communal (what a local community does) charitable responses, and to recognize that an institutional response is often needed. At times, such a response may require forms of bureaucratization and professionalization which do not allow us to easily visit and volunteer. This is not just some "socialist" or "big government" idea. Ecclesial hospitality toward poor migrants was a hallmark of early Christianity.[21] The practice rapidly became institutionalized through city and state organs within medieval Christendom. In 1952, in an important doctrinal document on our duties toward vulnerable migrants, *Exsul Familia Nazarethana*, Pope Pius XII (a staunch antisocialist) wrote that while "charity may provide some remedy for many injustices that can be observed in social relationships, it does not suffice. First and foremost, justice needs to be enacted, observed, and truly put into practice."[22] Hence, "go and do likewise" in the twenty-first century may mean seeking social justice as a citizen, voter, and taxpayer, in addition to volunteering and making charitable donations to help poor strangers.

In his famous "I've Been to the Mountaintop" speech, delivered in Memphis on April 3, 1968—the night before his assassination—Martin Luther King Jr. adopted a more institutional reading of the parable of the good Samaritan. He focused on the winding road between Jerusalem and Jericho as the source of the problem. Following his line of thought, we may argue (perhaps anachronistically) that a really good Samaritan would not limit herself to helping one, five, or a hundred victims. She would start a road-improvement committee, or organize a nonviolent protest march from Jerusalem to Jericho to pressure the Roman administration to build a better, safer, road, while putting patrols in place to keep brigands at bay.

A modern, social reading of the parable and its final imperative shuttles us rapidly from the analogical "is" to the moral "ought." Helping vulnerable migrants today could entail advocating for migration law reforms that offer humane, legal, accessible, and sensibly regulated channels for entry and sojourn (and possibly access to citizenship) to vulnerable migrants and to poor workers. Scholars agree that the presence of migrants in the labor market does not noticeably harm the employment or enrichment of citizens, and is at times needed in many sectors of our countries' economies—notwithstanding the false economic claims to the contrary made by many demagogic, opportunist politicians.[23] Furthermore, following this reading, migration laws should punish human traffickers and criminals who prey on migrants, rather than punishing charities who help and welcome the destitute, whether they are documented or not. When making such observations, to some extent I am consciously projecting modern ideas and concerns onto the text, but I do so to nudge the text to address some of my questions as a reader today, while being careful not to overdo it.

Beyond helping particular victims of violence, poverty, and exploitation, recognizing the structural aspects of social problems moves us to change the evil structures that enable or coerce people to keep producing such victims. "Go and do likewise," according to this reading, implies that we should dare to challenge and try to resolve the causes of war, violence, and poverty that force people to flee. Today, many argue that traditional Christian political advocacy favoring peace and economic justice should take on the ecological dimension. If so, "go and do likewise" presumably includes convincing national and international political leaders to help poorer countries mitigate the effects and remove the causes of forced or undesired mass human displacement: natural disasters, environmental degradation, and human-induced climate change.

On one hand, we may need to push governments and international institutions to "walk the talk" and honor their commitments to help refugees and migrants "at home" by fostering safety, prosperity, and human rights in their countries of origin and neighboring transit countries. On the other hand, our world is mired in some very complex issues, such as the Israeli-Palestinian question, Sunni-Shia tensions in the Middle East, poor governance and rampant unemployment in many African and Latin American countries, the depletion of fish stocks off the Horn of Africa, and the perverse effects of globalization. We cannot expect such intractable situations to be resolved with the stroke of a pen, thereby relieving pressure on people to risk everything to seek a better life far from home. Hence there will be refugees and vulnerable migrants roaming our world for the foreseeable future. It is our choice (and especially that of Christian voters in wealthy countries) whether we allow our governments to hide these people from our sight and strong-arm poorer nations to welcome them, or whether we ask our representatives to take in as many as we can truly afford to welcome, and to allow us to encounter them face-to-face as "neighbors."

On a more local level, "go and do likewise" presumably means preparing our neighborhoods to welcome new migrants and refugees. It entails advocating for the improvement of the housing, public and private services available in the run-down peripheries of our major cities, which already house many migrants, and toward which poor newcomers tend to gravitate. Philanthropy and hashtag activism on a smartphone can help us be neighborly to people halfway across the globe, but meaningful structural change may be needed much closer to home, and does not bracket the need of physical and personal proximity, as in the parable.

Let us pause for a moment. The discussion in the above paragraphs pertains to social ethics, and some readers may feel it has taken us far from the text. Have we gone astray in our interpretation exercise? In most of this book, due to space limitations, I will avoid delving too deeply into social ethics debates. I will limit myself to showing how biblical hermeneutics can lead to certain debates that must then be explored further by the ethicist, by incorporating into her reflection several other sources (such as sociology, philosophy, jurisprudence, and the study of Christian moral traditions). The above discussion is included to make a point. If Scripture is to be relevant to current moral debates, it is important that we face the complexity of the issues raised in the course of our exegetical work, such as this allegorical reading.

Admittedly, discussions of poverty, meritocracy, and social justice in the United States (even within the Catholic Church) have become twisted in various ways: perennially by the myth of the frontier hero, in the 1950s by McCarthyism and its boogeymen, and in the 1980s by the myth of the "welfare queen." Today, many ethicists seeking guidance from

Scripture prefer to stay closer to the texts and avoid the polarization that surrounds such discussions, but I believe there is an urgent need of honest debate on these issues within our faith communities. Scholars note that the resurgence of social and spatial segregation (between the college educated and the high school dropouts) is striking when mapped.[24] Others describe how the wealthy "9.9 percent" unconsciously ignore the suffering of others and seem completely lost in the myth of pure meritocracy wherein the poor deserve their lot for being lazy.[25]

Of course, a social and structural reading does not invalidate or replace a more personal reading, like that of Allegory 1. Subsidiarity is important: as far as possible, family, friends, neighbors, and local churches and communities should be helped and encouraged to assist people in need directly, in order to avoid excessive professionalization, centralization, and bureaucratization of welfare. Otherwise, we risk making those receiving aid and those helping them into anonymous neighbors, linked only by a system of taxation and entitlements. Yet, subsidiarity should not lead to inequality when family, local charities, or small-town assistance networks cannot provide good quality assistance, or decentralization of welfare becomes too costly.[26]

There is value in an unmediated personal encounter with a person in need, but a more institutionalized encounter or form of assistance is not necessarily less "charitable." The Samaritan may "feel" he has done a charitable thing, but his act might be merely a form of exhibitionism and self-delusion. The innkeeper may not "feel" he has done anything other than his job when treating yet another victim and receiving some remuneration allowing him to do it again. However, his act may be a practice of virtue so woven into ordinary behavior that its goodness becomes hidden to the agent (see Matt 25:37–39) and to the onlookers: it is "unexhibited." As Ricœur notes, "Charity is not necessarily present wherever it is exhibited; it is also hidden in the humble, abstract services performed by post offices and social security officials."[27]

Allegory 4: The Stranger Is the Bandit

I can imagine politically conservative Christians having a radically different reading of the text than the one just discussed. Some might associate strangers and resident aliens with the story's robbers, perhaps thinking, "Those people prey on our fellow citizens night and day, while political and religious leaders do nothing. They don't recognize the problem, lest they be accused of 'political incorrectness' when dealing with the perpetrators." The good Samaritan in this reading might be the intellectual or politician whose words and behavior may make us feel uncomfortable, but who happens to be the only person willing to come down from some high horse in Washington, Brussels, or a fancy cathedral or university, call things by their name, and promise effective action. He or she will spell out the dangers lurking in "excessive and naïve" kindness and hospitality. They will suggest unpleasant but necessary remedies and will dirty their hands in efforts to save our country from foreign-looking criminals and terrorists. The Samaritan here is a "Jessica Delacourt" figure, like the one in Neill Blomkamp's 2013 movie *Elysium*, a modern parable that brilliantly uses futuristic science fiction to explore the big picture of human migration today.[28]

A radicalized version of this reading might ask, "The Samaritan is *good* because he tends to the victim, but wouldn't he be an even *better* person were he to pursue, imprison and even kill the perpetrators?" In the United States today, this implies that being a good Samaritan means hunting drug traffickers and terrorists hiding among vulnerable migrants, notwithstanding the collateral damage to human rights. I ministered for four years to migrants imprisoned in the correctional facilities of Massachusetts, people who have committed serious felonies. While I can appreciate such an interpretation, ultimately, I tend to dismiss it since it clearly projects an irrational and exaggerated fear of the stranger onto the text.

Nevertheless, let us explore the implications of this reading, since such underlying fear is present in many biblical texts (as we shall see later in the Conclusion). Many Christians today all over the world find it easier to relate to such an interpretation than to that of the "stranger as victim" that predominates in some of our homilies and official texts. Other faithful Christians (sometimes following the sensationalist mood swings of the media) demonstrate fundamental inconsistency when dealing with strangers. They jump continuously between Allegory 1 and Allegory 4. For instance, they might weep in front of the famous photo of Alan Kurdi, a Syrian child refugee who drowned near Bodrum, Turkey on September 2, 2015. At the same time, they might foam with rage at a photoshopped image of his father, Abdullah, attempting to cross an international border illegally, or a meme featuring the imaginary future Alan (had he survived), working in some foreign country without formal authorization, dressed up as a radicalized Islamist or wearing a suicide-bomb vest.

Some Christians who opt for this reading may feel that the many bishops and moral theologians who are keen to advocate for migrants' rights and to condemn racism and xenophobia are out of touch with what they are going through. They may see such figures as members of a liberal, cosmopolitan establishment, who, from their ivory towers, pontificate to poor people living in dysfunctional and crime-ridden neighborhoods, ordering them to "do their duty" and welcome strangers.[29] Ironically, often the Christians who actually live in such neighborhoods don't find such an interpretation of the parable most credible and attractive. Rather, it is those who live in "middle class" neighborhoods who do. They are worried about the economic future of their children, fearing they might end up facing poverty. Such Christians tend to sympathize and identify themselves with poorer autochthonous citizens living in burdened neighborhoods. Some politicians and social media influencers create a narrative depicting such poorer citizens as "invaded" and "assailed" by shady immigrants, who in turn are portrayed as potential criminals and terrorists, or at least people who "hate or misunderstand our culture and our values" or are unable to transmit them to their children.

The unresolved tension among the following four common inclinations is inherently destabilizing:

(1) our natural sense of empathy toward needy strangers,
(2) our natural sense of justice and solidarity toward our brethren suffering the impact of unregulated immigration,
(3) our anxiety over our ability to transmit our values to future generations (and hence our ability to reproduce socially), and
(4) our fear of "irrational" and unbridled violence breaking unexpectedly into our lives and those of our children (e.g., a terrorist attack or carjacking).

The situation can be even more destabilizing for people—such as some of our elderly and unemployed—who have the time to ponder and brood on it, but neither the inclination, patience, rigor, nor critical sense to attain a more adequate perspective on the reality of migrants and refugees today. They do not access either important and serious academic research or media outlets that respect such research, which might allow them to debunk popular myths and fake news on these subjects.

Let us move on, for now, but keep this interpretation in mind. Pope Francis and some other church leaders have been very careful to lead by example, not merely condemning xenophobia and promoting hospitality and social friendship. Not all pastors and theologians can or are willing to do so, and some will be seen as aloof and idealistic whatever they do. Yet it is very important for theological ethics, just like all theology, to be mindful of how the faithful "receive" the teaching of scholars and church leaders. In many of our parishes today there seems to be a lack of reception of readings of Allegory 1, 2 or 3, and of readings of the parable proposed by mainstream ecclesial authority and theology. Rather, we find there a greater willingness to adopt an Allegory 4 reading promoted by the right-wing media, keen to flaunt its Christian pedigree.

Allegory 5: The Stranger Is Christ, the Good Samaritan

Our final allegorical reading of the parable differs in a key respect from the previous four, and some would deem it even more "traditional" than our Allegory 1. Up till now we have engaged mostly in "moral allegorization" of the parable. We now turn to its "spiritual allegorization."

Moral allegorization existed in ancient and medieval Christianity and was important in the early church, but Christian documents from antiquity do not refer to the parable of the good Samaritan explicitly. They seem to assume that engaging communally in selfless acts of mercy and hospitality was an essential part of Christian identity. Historians such as Rodney Stark have shown how early Christians were committed to selfless acts of mercy and charity across the Roman empire, especially during epidemics.[30] He demonstrates that this was a powerful form of witness and source of conversion, even due to the simple epidemiological fact that plague victims tended to by Christians and included in a network of care had a higher chance of survival than those left untended, notwithstanding the contagion risk for the caregivers.[31] Since early Christianity, following Christ implied engaging in the seven Corporal Works of Mercy. These include feeding the hungry, giving drink to the thirsty, clothing the naked, visiting the incarcerated, sheltering the homeless, visiting the sick, and burying the dead (cf. Matt 25:35–36). A moral allegorization of the parable along these lines, as in Allegories 1 and 3 above, would see the victim representing the needy persons in our world, and the point of the story would be to invite us to act virtuously and live out mercy and justice in practice.

Nevertheless, in the major patristic texts available today, "moral allegorization" is not seen as the primary way of reading a biblical text allegorically (or "typologically," as some would call it). For some church fathers the moral allegorization of the parable might even have sounded overly self-righteous or Pelagian. Thus, at least in the texts we have, they considered the so-called spiritual allegorization more important. Saint Augustine, in his famous text on Bible interpretation, *On Christian Doctrine*, recognizes that some passages may sound shocking or morally problematic and for such passages, only a spiritual or symbolic interpretation is adequate.[32] Spiritual allegorization scans Scripture passages with a certain theological ingenuity, seeking to find in a given character a "typological" representation of a key figure (or "type") found in doctrines pertaining to dogmatic and fundamental theology. Such types include the persons of the Trinity, the church (historical and celestial), Adam and Eve (archetypical humans), Satan, and personified blocks of Scripture texts (the Law, the Prophets, and Wisdom).

Traditionally, some Christian authors have distinguished four possible levels of meaning in a given Scripture passage: the historical (or literal), the allegorical (or spiritual), the tropological (or moralizing), and the anagogical (or eschatological) meaning. This is summarized in a medieval Latin couplet: *Lettera gesta docet—quid credas allegoria; moralis quid agas—quo tendas anagogia* (The Letter teaches [historical] deeds; the Allegory teaches what you should believe; the Moral teaches you how to act; and the Anagogy what you should tend to [in the afterlife].)

Of course, the idea that God or the inspired author might have embedded all this in a simple text may sound a bit esoteric and forced to the modern reader, wary of the tendency of preachers and theologians of every age to project their meanings and theology onto Scripture. Yet there is a richness and a value in patristic exegesis, and these distinctions can help us even today to identify deeper motivations behind exegetical approaches using more modern methods.

> In a way, all readings, both the more "literal" (or "narratological-historical") and the more "allegorical"—in the triple sense of spiritual-allegorical, moralizing-allegorical, and eschatological-allegorical—have ethical implications. This is true in the sense that the exegete proposes them not solely to inform believers and the Church about dogmatic "facts," but also to have an impact on their action. Whatever concerns action or *praxis* is "ethical" in a broad sense.

Reimer Roukema examines how the parable is read by various commentators in ancient Christianity.[33] A typical "spiritual" reading presented by Roukema is that of Irenaeus, which roughly "decodes" the good Samaritan as Christ, the robbers as the devil, the victim as fallen humanity (or "Adam"), the innkeeper as the Holy Spirit, and the inn as the "we" (his readers), possibly implying "we redeemed/postpaschal humanity" or more specifically "we the church."

The other authors offer similar typologies, with minor modifications. In Clement's version, the innkeeper represents the angelic host. A presbyter quoted by Origen says he represents the (human) person keeping watch over the whole church (hence church leadership). In Origen's homily on the parable, the priest and Levite represent the Law and the Prophets and their inability to provide salvation. In Augustine the wine and oil poured on the wounds of the victim are the symbols of Christian initiation (and hence redemption from sin).[34] Most of the authors agree that Adam (the victim) loses his free will due to his fall, and that some freedom is restored in the healing process, which occurs either when the wounds are dressed, or slowly as he recovers in the inn.

Read in this way, the parable is transformed into a coded message that reminds us of some of the basic religious tenets we proclaim in the Creed. We are sinners, yet saved by Christ, the archetypical good Samaritan. We are kept safe in his church, in which we are both recovering victims (penitent sinners) and caregivers (disciples), helping other believers saved by Christ to overcome sin and stand up on their own two feet with us. We can do this not by our self-sufficiency, but under the guidance of our pastors and empowered by the grace of the Holy Spirit (the "innkeepers"), to live a life of virtue as children of God. To be sure, this reading does not place us on the road but rather places the reader in a more communitarian and institutionalized setting, the "inn." Its clear anthropological/soteriological focus does not *directly* invite us to engage in seven corporal works of mercy. Without becoming too self-righteous, might we nonetheless interpret our caregiver role in the inn as one concerning the seven Spiritual Works of Mercy? These include admonishing the sinner, instructing the ignorant, counseling the doubtful, comforting the sorrowful, bearing wrongs patiently, forgiving all offenses, and praying for the living and the dead.[35]

I believe that this spiritual reading has ethical import, at least in three ways. My first point invites some of my readers to widen their notion of ethics. Admittedly, the Spiritual Works of Mercy are not easily included in a *cross-cultural* system of ethical values or a system of moral *imperatives* that oblige all persons at all times, such as Thomistic natural law or Kantian ethics. These spiritual works are, nonetheless, an important part of Christian praxis and hence of Christian ethics. They strictly oblige *certain* people in *certain* situations (identified through discernment), but they invite *many more* people to "supererogatory" action in search of excellence in virtue, in response to the superabundance of God's love and grace, or moved by the desire to be as "thoroughgoing" (or "perfect") as the Father (see Matt 5—7).

Second, I believe that the spiritual reading should eventually lead us to a more classical moral reading. Overcoming our sinfulness and growing in virtue within the church would make little sense if all this leads to a disincarnate spirituality, that is, one that has no bearing on the material suffering of our fellow humans. To the extent that we are healed in the inn, and our free will is recovered, our action must extend to include the Corporal Works of Mercy, which may be supererogatory (as indicated above) at some levels, but strictly obligatory at other levels. Can a converted and "graced" Christian bracket the fructification of grace in her life history, and walk about Kew Gardens doing nothing while a Kitty Genovese or a refugee is being stabbed to death? The anthropology and soteriology that characterize this spiritual reading serve as a foundation of moral theology. On that foundation we can build a response pertaining to applied ethics (including biomedical ethics), even if we opt to avoid a "moralizing allegory" that leads us from the biblical text directly to concrete action.

Third, however, I believe we should ask ourselves in what sense can we say today that the church is a self-contained inn, a sinless place completely separated from the evils of the open road, devoid of self-interested priests, Levites, and robbers. A more critical reading of this spiritual tradition will point out that Jesus is truly a "Samaritan," and will remain one throughout human history, in the sense that he is often perceived as a stranger, even inside the Christian inn. He has been seen as such by the Judean political and religious establishment of his day, and any political and religious establishment in history could be tempted to do the same. To some extent, even those institutions that brand themselves as "Christian" and honestly seek to live up to the values of the gospel may at times struggle to recognize Jesus and let his deeds and words shape their way of proceeding. These words from John's Prologue capture an ongoing dynamic: "He came to what was his own, and his own people did not accept him" (John 1:11). This is because, no matter how much we *seek* the kingdom of God and strive to make its reality manifest in history, with the help of the Spirit, we will never *possess* it. Christ will continue to visit us as a Samaritan to shake up our "reasonable" approximations of the kingdom and unveil their flaws and fallacies.

Sometimes, human innkeepers will recognize, behind the Samaritan fabrics and accent, the presence of the very owner of the inn, and they will ask him for instructions and obey. Sometimes they will deem him a stranger and only tolerate him as long as he keeps out of trouble and pays his dues. Sometimes they will feel threatened by his presence or words and will show him the door. Is it truly possible for the church not to recognize Christ and treat him as a stranger? Catholics believe our leaders are assisted by the Holy Spirit to avoid betraying Christ in their teaching and in their efforts to govern and sanctify the church. In some cases, in history, they may receive extraordinary help to remain faithful to the mind of Christ and free from error in their teaching. Yet, this does not mean that popes and bishops haven't made some serious mistakes in history. St. John Paul II is famous for having asked pardon, on various occasions (including the Jubilee Year of 2000) for many past mistakes committed by his predecessors. Pope Honorius I was condemned for heresy after his death. The Catholic doctrine upholding papal infallibility in special circumstances does not warrant an "infallibilist" attitude whereby it is guaranteed that the church hierarchy will recognize Christ's voice automatically and effortlessly in history.[36]

This reappraised spiritual reading of the parable of the good Samaritan may be unsettling for an ecclesiologist, but it echoes the unsettling nature of the whole Judeo-Christian religious tradition. We follow a stranger God who likes to walk with God's people and hates being confined to a single image or shrine. This stranger God sends God's Son to the world to be born a Galilean, and to die a cursed death on a cross, abandoned by his friends and followers, after being condemned by the religious and political establishment as a blasphemer and apostate. Being "strange," being an "outcast," being "on the move," not fitting into a particular religious, political, or cultural stereotype, not having an "autochthonous" identity: these characteristics are quintessential not only to who our God is, but also to who we are called to be as followers of this Stranger-God. This has important implications for the use of Scripture in contemporary ethics, as we shall see in the following chapter.

1.3 God and God's Word as Strangers

Following the Divine "Outsider"

In our "allegorical permutations" exercise, and especially in Allegory 5, we were led to truly identify with and follow God, the divine Outsider. We were invited to become fellow good Samaritans with this God, but this is a costly analogy. When we picture ourselves as the assistants of the good Samaritan, we may do so because we like to identify with the "good" rather than with the "Samaritan" element in the traditional title of the parable. We readily tend to think of ourselves as good and charitable people, as the "good guys" in the story, but we do not naturally or consciously *choose* to identify with the *outcast* in the story, the shady foreigner whom the reader expects to search the body of the victim for any valuables the robbers might have missed, rather than dress the victim's wounds. Neither are we comfortable when asked to see Jesus, the Lord, in this character.

This second element of rescuer's identity cannot be bracketed. It is an essential part of Christian identity and would surely have reminded Luke's readers in the early church of how other people looked at them. Christian identity is paradoxical since it is built on the nonidentity of the outcast and the enduring strangeness of the stranger who doesn't belong anyplace. An early Christian document addressed *To Diognetus* tells us that "Christians are distinguished from other [persons] neither by country, nor language, nor the customs which they observe;…they dwell in their own countries, but simply as sojourners. As citizens, they share in all things with others, and yet endure all things as if foreigners."[37]

We may have a diminished sense of this in countries like Malta or Great Britain where Christianity was the dominant religion for many centuries, but recent secularization processes may have exposed the "outsider" element of our Christian identity once again. The issue is key to understanding what this book is about and what the Bible has to say about identity and strangers. Early Christians willingly saw themselves as born out of a humble band of misfits; this image of the church should help us remain humble. When we get too proud of our strangeness and uniqueness, thinking that it makes us automatically better than others, we betray the humility and critical self-awareness the gospel demands of Christ's disciples. Yet, when we desperately seek to fit into a particular political, cultural, or religious mold, and forget that we will always be strangers wherever we go, we are similarly led astray. This means that our Christian identity is not compatible with exclusivist and triumphalist ethno-nationalist ideologies, even though many Christians today seem to have a hard time figuring out why this is so, maybe because they see their faith and their "God" as either too "familiar" or too ostensibly "different."

The Last Judgment (Matthew 25:31–46)

At the beginning of this chapter, we mentioned three "commonplace" biblical texts used today to reflect ethically on our dealings with strangers and, in particular, with vulnerable migrants and refugees. We will, for now, bracket the injunction to love the stranger in Leviticus 19:33–34 but say a brief word about the Last Judgment (Matt 25:31–46), to which we referred above regarding the "Corporal Works of Mercy." This text, like the good Samaritan parable in Allegory 1, is often read in documents pertaining to the social teaching of the church as an invitation to Christians to advocate for social justice and human rights, and to commit themselves to works of mercy. Pope Francis often adopts this reading (for example, *FT* 84–86). In *FT* 74 he indicates that church fathers such as John Chrysostom support such a reading, citing one of his homilies: "Do you wish to honor the body of the Savior? Do not despise it when it is naked. Do not honor it in church with silk vestments while outside it is naked and numb with cold."[38]

Interestingly, many recent editions of the Bible (such as the NRSV) add the title "The Judgment of the Nations" at the beginning of this pericope. This reflects modern scholarship that, in part, tends to question

Francis's and Chrysostom's "activist" reading, which might sound too "Pelagian" to a *sola gratia* Protestant exegete. The Son of Man's questions are addressed to the "nations" gathered before him. This term, in biblical parlance, indicates the Gentiles (persons lacking the guidance of the Torah), hence non-Jews, and, by extension, non-Christians (since in Matthew's view, Jesus does not abolish the Torah but proposes a more complete and thorough interpretation that brings it to its fulfillment; cf. Matt 5:17).[39]

Thus, according to this reading, the text does not deal with the Last Judgment of Jews or Christians, but of unconverted Samaritans and pagans. It is *they*, the "strangers," who are judged according to the works of mercy they engage in toward *us*, the "members of [Christ's] family."[40] Despite their lack of explicit belief in matters known only through revelation, such just and caring strangers are deemed worthy of God's mercy, or, better, they are not automatically cut off from the community of the saved.[41] This idea reminds us of Allegory 2 above, in which the stranger is the Samaritan. It also echoes a Jewish tradition regarding Gentiles who obey the seven Noahide commandments: the prohibition of worshiping idols, cursing God, committing murder, sexual immorality, stealing, eating flesh torn from a living animal; and the command to establish courts of justice.[42] This tradition considers that such Gentiles abide by a parallel "covenant for gentiles" and deserve special treatment, including residency rights in a Jewish religious polity.[43]

By shining a light on the just and caring among the Gentiles—or the good and neighborly among the Samaritans, in Allegory 2 above—these readings help us recognize the agency and capacity for doing good that is present in the other. However, they might tempt us to conclude that strangers (such as non-Christian migrants and refugees) have a duty to help *us* and respect *our* rights (since this is their path to salvation), while we have no particular duty to help *them* and respect *their* rights (since our path to salvation is our faith and Christ's faithfulness). While insightful and possibly closer to the author's intention than the more traditional "Corporal Works of Mercy" interpretation, this contemporary reading of Matthew 25 risks being merely informative to the Christian reader. It implies that we should not fix our gaze upon the sheep in the story and "go and do likewise" since the soteriological implications of their actions are valid only for non-Christians and do not concern us. However, if we stop trying to figure out what Matthew "truly" intended (which is always hard to reconstruct objectively), we will note that such a clear-cut distinction between Christians ("my family") and non-Christians (sheep/goats) raises some serious questions regarding the theological presuppositions and implications of such a reading. Is it true that Christians are Christ's only family? Is it true that we can reduce our faith (or choice to be members of the community of those saved through Christ's faithfulness) to a purely cognitive action, completely devoid of any act of love toward others, such as that expressed in the Corporal Works of Mercy? If not, can we be so sure the text has no moral lesson to teach us Christians?

Arguably, Matthew's take on the duties of his Christian readers—and by extension, our duties—can be found in the logic of mature and wholehearted obedience to the spirit of the Torah. Such obedience is showcased in the so-called Matthean Antitheses (Matt 5:17–48), and more broadly in the Sermon on the Mount (Matt 5—7), which points to such lofty standards of mercy and justice that they might seem impossible to reach. In Matthew, such high standards are not intended to frustrate us and make us feel unworthy and impotent (e.g., so we may realize our need of salvation). Rather they remind us that with humble confidence, we can strive to achieve what is possible for us, recognizing that our successes are also due to the grace we have received, and that there is still a good way to go to reach the divine standard of completeness and wholehearted goodness (which should serve as goal and inspiration). If we use this logic to interpret Matthew 25:31–46, we realize that the text calls Christians to action, and not only "the pagan nations." It concerns us through an a fortiori logic: if even pagan strangers are expected to be hospitable toward the Christian, how much more can Christians, who are called to imitate a God so wholehearted and boundless in love (cf. *FT* 60), be expected to be welcoming of the stranger?

1.4 Delving into the Otherness of Scripture: An Exploration Exercise

Up to this point, we have explored Scripture texts that seem *familiar*, ones that readily come to mind when we think of a moral issue such as, "How should we treat the stranger?" Familiar as they may seem, do we know them well in all their *depth of meaning*? Familiarity often breeds arrogance and stereotyping; sometimes it needs to be strongly challenged even when it seems benign.

In his many popular books on "lateral thinking," Edward de Bono describes what he calls "the intelligence trap" and proposes a series of tools that encourage seeking unfamiliar or "strange" pathways to solve problems.[44] Highly intelligent people are often trapped in a game of finding the best shortcut. They see a problem, immediately link it to a tried-and-true, readily available solution, apply the solution and move on to the next problem: simplest and quickest is best.

By contrast, some people who are less intelligent (but more patient, inquisitive, and methodical) may end up being more creative. Before homing in on one solution, they may pause to consider other options, to consult a book or an expert, to brainstorm a list that might include complex, impractical, costly, unreliable, time-consuming, exotic, unpopular, and untested solutions. De Bono suggests that we all train ourselves to occasionally take this second and roundabout way to reach solutions to problems. It may not get us a quick promotion but can actually lead to a breakthrough.

Though we do not usually associate Scripture and ethics with "breakthroughs" and "innovation," many thinkers like Paul Ricœur have suggested taking the "scenic route" instead of the "shortcut" in our ethics thinking. Hermeneutical detours that force professional ethicists to wade through Scripture and literary classics before offering a solution to a moral problem can be particularly helpful. "Put out into the deep water and let down your nets for a catch" says Jesus to Peter (Luke 5:4): it may have sounded stupid, counterintuitive, and irrationally laborious to an exhausted experienced fisherman to fish during daytime and in places where shoals of fish were not known to gather, but fortunately, Peter was a patient and humble man.

At the beginning of this chapter, I asked readers to write down the three Bible passages that come to their minds when they think about strangers and migrants. At this point, let us put those texts aside, and think of another five texts related in some way to strangers and migrants, but that don't come immediately to mind. Should this exercise prove challenging, I recommend the following techniques:

- Leaf through a copy of the Bible, reading the section headers. Ask yourself, Does this passage touch on the topic I'm exploring?

- Make a list of related words (*stranger, foreigner, outsider, sojourner, resident alien, guest, intruder, migrant, outlander, wanderer...*) with the help of a thesaurus, and look up the word stems or the various forms of each word (such as *foreign, foreign*er, foreign*ers, foreign*ness...*) in a digital copy of the Bible.
- Alternatively, if you have some knowledge of Hebrew or Greek, you may look up and list the Biblical Hebrew and Biblical Greek words that express all these similar notions, and using their roots or word stems for a search in critical editions of the JB/OT and the NT. You may also use Strong's Numbers or Louw-Nida semantic domains to identify the headwords (lemmas) and relevant roots/stems, or the linguistics tools offered in modern Bible software programs.
- Use a more recent Catholic or ecumenical Bible concordance and exegetical biblical dictionary to look up the word stems in the original languages and build a list of relevant texts. This technique can be fruitful for beginners and for advanced Scripture scholars. The preliminary list can be expanded by going through some theological dictionaries and encyclopedias that might point to biblical texts that deal with a certain topic, while not actually using the words we associate with that topic. For instance, although the Prologue of the Gospel of John speaks about the strangerhood and familiarity of God and God's preexisting and incarnate Word, and the humanity's fundamental struggle with hospitality, it does so using a series of metaphors; hence, it is not readily identified using headwords.

Of course, we cannot possibly analyze thoroughly and include in our ethical discussion every single text in Scripture that touches upon the morally relevant issue we are exploring. Hence, after constructing such a list, we need to go through the texts and shortlist those on which we will focus while bracketing interesting alternatives that we will keep in reserve, hoping to analyze them later. In the tables below, I have included fifteen texts that I will not discuss in this book.

TABLE 1.1 UNFAMILIAR TEXTS ON STRANGERHOOD AND HOSPITALITY		
FIVE UNFAMILIAR TEXTS ON STRANGERHOOD AND HOSPITALITY THAT SUSPEND JUDGMENT ON THE STRANGER'S GOODNESS		
Passages	Title	Possible Relevance
1 Gen 10	Genesis Genealogies	Mapping of relationships among groups of strangers
2 Num 12	Moses's Cushite Wife	Miriam and Aaron punished for their xenophobia
3 2 Chr 36	Evil Kings and Foreign Invasions	Before blaming strangers, we should take a critical look at our leaders
4 Gal 2:11–20	Paul Confronts Peter	Challenging assimilation and excessive demands on strangers
5 Gal 5:13—6:10	Intergroup Conflict among Christians in Galatia	Hostility, provocation, and envy toward culturally different brothers is not Christian freedom
FIVE UNFAMILIAR TEXTS ON STRANGERHOOD AND HOSPITALITY THAT PRESENT GOOD STRANGERS		
Passages	Title	Possible Relevance
1 Gen 39—50	Joseph in Egypt	The powerful stranger can be welcoming
2 2 Kgs 4	The Role of the Servants in the Healing of Naaman	The importance of mediation by humble common people in overcoming nationalist pride
3 Jonah 3—4	Jonah and the Ninevites	The powerful stranger can be surprisingly open to God's word and to conversion
4 John 4:1–42	Jesus and the Samaritan Woman	Assertive and honest strangers can be great disciples
5 Acts 10	Cornelius the Gentile Receives the Holy Spirit	Overcoming the taboos that keep us segregated

	FIVE UNFAMILIAR TEXTS ON STRANGERHOOD AND HOSPITALITY THAT PRESENT EVIL STRANGERS		
	Passages	Title	Possible Relevance
1	Ps 137	Humiliation and Oppression by Foreigners	Recounting our painful past and admitting anger and resentment toward strangers can be an important first step toward justice and peace
2	1 Kgs 11:1–13; 16:31—19:18	Solomon's Foreign Wives; Jezebel and Elijah	Can the stranger turn away our heart from God and provoke cycles of violence?
3	Prov 5:7–23	Sharing Wells and Wives with Strangers	Concerns about interethnic marriages
4	Esth 3; 7	Haman Undertakes to Destroy the Jews but Esther Thwarts His Plans	Wise and courageous persons are needed to keep interethnic hatred from fueling mass violence
5	1 Macc 1—2	The Maccabee Rebellion	Assimilation, religious freedom, and violence

How did I come to choose the texts I dwell upon in this book? First, I sought a mix of texts that I deem familiar and ones that are less familiar. Texts that are less familiar can be more challenging and stimulating; however, these features do not imply that they are always the best texts to reflect on certain moral issues.. There is often good warrant for choosing and promoting certain texts in preaching, liturgy, literature and art, and catechism classes, implicitly creating a "canon within a canon."

Second, in my selection process, I have sought to reach a "reflective equilibrium."[45] Two elements need to be held in balance in this selection process, and tweaked and tested *through the lens of our judgments, beliefs, or intuitions* as readers, moral agents, and theological ethicists, as though we were weighing rice on a trip balance. The first element or scale arm consists of *our judgments* (including our beliefs and intuitions) concerning the **ethical principles** that govern the matter being investigated (such as duties toward strangers, duties of strangers), derived from several ethical systems used in our Christian ethics traditions (Platonic and Neoplatonic, Stoic, Aristotelian, Kantian, etc.). The second element consists in *our judgments* concerning the **biblical texts** we believe should inform our appraisal of the issue, both as individual texts and as a canonical synthesis ("What do the different voices in the Bible dealing with strangerhood boil down to, in my mind?").

Such a selection exercise is not necessarily a reductionist act of violence, disrespectful of the cultural and ideological differences and the rich historical layers present in the library of texts we call the "Bible." It might be frowned upon by some Bible scholars, but even professional exegetes are called to write synthetic articles in biblical dictionaries and encyclopedias. Some form of synthesis is all the more necessary for the theologian who believes Scripture *as a whole* to be something morally normative for Christian agents today, and not just a collection of random opinions that sometimes happen to touch on moral issues. I believe that some of the differences and tensions can be maintained in this synthetic process, and this book will showcase how. What we are looking for is not a unilateral thesis of the sort: "Scripture says X on topic Y." Rather the synthesis might look like this: "A, B and C are the three major positions on topic Y in Scripture; A being the most common and mainstream, while its contraries B and C are prevalent in situations/cases of type M and N, respectively." This may bring to mind US Supreme Court decisions, which often append dissenting opinions.

In the process, we might discover that a biblical text that we thought offered great moral insights on hospitality is actually much more pertinent to a modern reflection on social housing or the respect for autochthonous minorities. Hence, we might want to remove such a text from our synthesis, while possibly including another text we never would have thought pertinent to our topic had we not cast our net wide and taken the scenic route through the whole of Scripture. Similarly, we might be taken aback to find that many Scripture texts adopt a purely pragmatic, utilitarian, or even opportunist approach to the issue at hand.

Via reflective rebalancing, this realization might then temper our enthusiasm for modern normative proposals rooted in Thomist or Kantian ethical principles. Alternatively, it might make us admit that the biblical approach to the issue is not sufficiently developed or "morally grounded" to inform a debate in the twenty-first century (Scripture, of course, is not primarily a moral handbook, not even for a premodern society). Moreover, it might make us explore why what we consider obviously fair and ethical today might have completely eluded even the inspired authors. Of course, divine inspiration does not mean that culturally embedded human authors were given a glimpse of the world two thousand years later, and hence could envisage a world without licit torture, chattel slavery, unquestioned male dominance, subsistence agricultural economics, and so forth.

PART 1

NO LONGER STRANGERS

BRIDGING THE DIVIDE BETWEEN SCRIPTURE AND ETHICS

2

BRIDGING SCRIPTURE AND ETHICS IMPLICITLY

No longer strangers. The heading of the first part of this book (chapters 2–4) implicitly cites Ephesians 2:19 figuratively and out of context. Unlike that verse, part 1 concerns not the access of Gentiles to the Father, but that of ethicists to Scripture. It will guide readers through a series of debates on the use of Scripture in ethics and present some of the major models used to build a bridge between the biblical text and contemporary moral debates.

In this chapter, readers will first learn to distinguish between two major ways of bridging Scripture and ethics: the implicit channel and the explicit channel. The implicit channel is an intimate and individual way used in personal and communitarian discernment. The explicit channel is a more rigorous and critical way used in scholarship and serious debate when forming the consciences of the faithful and of people of good will, in a more public setting.

We will then focus on the implicit channel for the rest of the chapter, starting with a discussion on the transmission of Scripture-inspired concepts that are ethically relevant to secular culture (2.1–2.2). In section 2.3 the reader will learn how moral paradigms can be built using OT figures, following a bridging model proposed by Waldemar Janzen. Paradigms can then be held up as models of virtue that readers can emulate or propose to others. In section 2.4, we will explore a different paradigmatic approach described by William Spohn. The approach focuses on Jesus, as a character in NT narratives, and on some of the major characters that populate the strange world that this Jesus narrates to us through parables embedded in these narratives. Jesus and the parable characters can hone the moral sense of readers and help form their moral character. Readers will learn how this is achieved through traditional spiritual practices and, in particular, through imaginative contemplative prayer as understood in the Ignatian spirituality tradition.

Finally, the discussion in this chapter will help readers appreciate some of the strengths, but also the weaknesses, of a virtue ethics approach to implicit bridging between Scripture and ethics. We will raise several questions without yet providing complete answers. Can Scripture be honestly molded into a binary logic and used to construct simple paradigms of virtue and vice, as some ethicists would like? Is there value in critically engaging the complexity and ambiguity of Scripture characters, and distinguishing good and bad traits in each character, so to hone our moral sense precisely while making such distinctions? Can a paradigmatic approach be useful to reflect on issues such as hospitality and integration of strangers, which defy stereotyped distinctions between "the good guys" and "the bad guys"? Our critique of virtue ethics approaches will be reinforced by introducing a series of notions at various points in the chapter, such as preunderstandings, stereotypes, and dialectics.

2.1 Two Major Channels of Biblical Influence on Moral Reflection and Action

Our previous chapter illustrated how we can obtain a list of texts that might have something to tell us about our topic of ethical investigation. The next question is, What do we do with such texts?

Implicit and Explicit Bridging to Ethics

We can distinguish two major channels through which Scripture might influence the *actions* of a *moral agent*, whom we shall call the *Implicit-Channel Actor*, and the more theoretical general *reflections* of an *ethicist*, the *Implicit-Channel Theorist*, who spends her time reflecting on the goodness and badness of the kinds of acts the Implicit-Channel Actor is engaged in. Of course, the reflection of the Implicit-Channel Theorist is also a kind of action and can itself be appraised according to ethical standards (the first of which is its honesty and dedication to the truth). That is why we are standing at a distance and observing both the Implicit-Channel Theorist and the Implicit-Channel Actor (keeping in mind that even our observation is yet another action subject to ethical appraisal).

Agatha and Ethel are two friends who are interested in Scripture. Agatha is a physician, medical researcher, mother, and political activist; she is a good example of our Implicit-Channel Actor. Ethel is an ethicist and sits on various bioethics committees; she exemplifies our Implicit-Channel Theorist. We are told that Agatha's action and Ethel's reflection are influenced by Scripture, but after observing them for a certain period, we note that they never mention or quote Scripture to their colleagues, friends, or family and never analyze or comment on a biblical text in public. In private, every morning, they spend an hour mediating on Scripture texts. We are not sure why they do this; we suspect it is because they are devout Christians, but they might just as well be agnostics who were given this book to meditate on by an open-minded psychologist whose perspective on mindfulness goes beyond Buddhist-style meditation. Let us assume that this mediation has become part of their morning routine, and that they have been doing it every day for twenty-five years. It is difficult to imagine that something wouldn't "rub off on them" as a result of this practice. There must be some sort of biblical influence on the moral *action* of Agatha, and the moral *reflection* of Ethel, resulting from their increasing familiarity with the texts.

If so, Agatha and Ethel's case illustrates what I call the "implicit" channel. Our lives might well be transformed by Scripture, but there is no direct evidence linking our action and reflection to any biblical text, or to biblical culture as a whole. This channel is not necessarily individualistic. The Implicit-Channel Actor (Agatha) and the Implicit-Channel Theorist (Ethel) might discreetly participate in Bible camps during the summer, or listen to podcasts where famous preachers or exegetes offer their interpretations of the texts on which they are meditating, or receive guidance from a spiritual mentor every month. Yet this part of their life remains hidden when Agatha tries to explain to friends, family, and colleagues why she is choosing to do the things she is doing and when Ethel tries to justify her ethical views about Agatha's actions to her colleagues and readers. This behavior is not necessarily a sign that they are intentionally hiding their spiritual lives from other people. Doing so could nonetheless make sense if they lived in a country where Christianity was a minority religion, or if they were judges trying to seem impartial in a secular or multifaith judiciary setting. It could simply be the case that they themselves do not see the connection and do not have the tools to establish more direct links between the texts they are meditating on and the decisions they are taking in life.

In this first channel, *meditation* leads to *interpretation* of the texts (hermeneutics)—private or communitarian—and then to action and reflection, which is implicitly inspired by the text's interpretation and which we will call *appropriation*. Note that such appropriation might not necessarily be exegetically warranted or ethically acceptable, especially since there is limited opportunity here for a critical exchange with others on the interpretation of the texts adopted by the Implicit-Channel Actor and Theorist. For now, let us simply focus on the fact that some "contamination" of their actions and thoughts by Scripture—be it good or bad—simply happens. The appropriation is implicit, since Scripture implicitly informs Agatha's actions and Ethel's ethical reflections. Yet, if Agatha were to start suggesting to others to "do likewise" and Ethel to start encouraging other ethicists to "think likewise," they would not use any references to Scripture when doing so; they would resort to arguments based on other sources, such as common sense, shared values, logical argumentation, and social science data. Their public discourse is never explicitly linked to their appropriation of Scripture. The scheme is as follows:

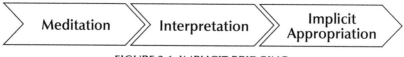

FIGURE 2.1: IMPLICIT BRIDGING

Now let us compare this with the explicit channel. Here, the actor and the theorist see the links between the Scripture texts they are spending time with and their actions and thoughts, and then go on to speak about this to others "publicly," be it in a religious or a lay setting, using explicit biblical references to explain some of their actions and thoughts. The public and explicit nature of this channel usually means that, at some point, the text must be revisited and analyzed in some manner, since in this case their interpretation might be challenged by others. They cannot simply stop the conversation by invoking a response based on intimate experiences and feelings: "Well, that's what I felt when I meditated on the text."

Spirituality, Affects, and Moral Discernment

According to certain spiritual traditions, such as the Ignatian Spiritual Tradition, people who meditate on or contemplate Scripture might receive a spiritual consolation at some point during their meditation and "feel something." The consolation might be hard to link rationally and argumentatively to the text, since it could have a cause outside the text itself. For instance, a minor detail of the text might bring back a fond memory, which then triggers a consolation, such as an increase in faith in God's providence, with a deep accompanying sense of relief and inner peace.

In some cases, the consolation might even have no identifiable immediately preceding cause and seem to appear "out of nowhere" as an experience of pure grace. Such consolations are very important for a person's spiritual life and moral decision-making, and should be shared and discussed with one's spiritual director. The appropriation of Scripture when accompanied by such consolations is usually private, and hence a case of the implicit channel, not the explicit channel.

In the explicit channel, we expect to be asked to provide a cogent argument linking the scriptural text, our interpretation of the text, and our action or moral reasoning to people who might question these links. We therefore need to approach the text with a more analytical and intellectual mindset, rather than simply stand in awe in front of it and let it inspire our imagination and conjure up images, memories, and spiritual emotions. We move here from analysis to interpretation to appropriation, but in this case our appropriation is explicit. The Explicit-Channel Actor and Theorist are linking Scripture—not just in their hearts and minds, but in front of a possibly critical audience—to a particular concrete moral action or a particular theory or a generalized claim regarding a value, norm, principle, virtue, and so on:

FIGURE 2.2: EXPLICIT BRIDGING

There might be other channels connecting our time spent with Scripture (as individuals or communities) and our actions and moral reflection, but in this book, we will focus on these two channels, implicit and explicit. I will dedicate most of this chapter to the implicit channel of transmission, though the rest of the book will tend to focus on the explicit channel, since the appropriate use of this channel is the one that requires the most attention from a standpoint of theological ethics as a scholarly and ecclesial discipline.

Public and Private (Devotional) Use

In his book *Using Our Outside Voice: Public Biblical Interpretation*, Greg Carey makes a distinction between a responsible public use of Scripture (our "outside voice") and a devotional one. The first "implies the ability to enter a conversation about the Bible, to understand the various arguments in play, to weigh the ethical and theological implications of our views, and to offer informed opinions that others can understand."[1] It requires certain skills and dispositions. Devotional approaches, on the other hand, are personal and individual, and expect Scripture to "speak" to the reader directly, who in turn is not required to consult experts or explain his interpretation to others.[2]

In our discussion above, the implicit channel that links Scripture to ethics is usually assumed to be "devotional" in Carey's sense, and the explicit channel is presented as predominantly "public." However, the thrust of my distinction is slightly different from that of Carey, and the two may be decoupled, since *public* is an ambiguous term that could mean "nondevotional" and "explicit." This is illustrated by the examples in table 2.1 below.

TABLE 2.1 IMPLICIT AND EXPLICIT BRIDGING TO ETHICS		
	Implicit Bridging to Ethics	Explicit (Public) Bridging to Ethics
"Devotional" use	A politician uses *private or mystical experiences* of Scripture-based prayer to ethically underpin her political decisions. However, she *does not say this explicitly* to the voters, or uses secular arguments to mask the biblical origin of her ideas and practices so to make her message more inclusive and appealing to non-Christians.	A politician *explicitly* justifies in front of the electorate the ethics underpinning her political decisions by referring to *private or mystical experiences* of Scripture-based prayer, not available for critical appraisal by others. There is no way to know whether the prayer or mystical experiences ever occurred in fact, and if the religious language is just a ploy to seduce Christian voters.
"Nondevotional" (public) use	The CEO of a family business uses *reasoned, expert-informed understandings of Scripture* to underpin the ethics of his business decisions. He discusses this regularly in a secret ethics committee that includes exegetes and ethicists, where his interpretation is exposed to scholarly critique. Yet he *never says this explicitly* to his business stakeholders, preferring to use lay arguments to explain his actions.	The CEO *explicitly* justifies the ethics underpinning his business decisions to the stakeholders, in part, by using reasoned understandings of Scripture. These are open to scholarly critique, based on widely accepted interpretation criteria, and on dialogue with experts' claims on the meaning of the texts. The CEO also uses nonscriptural arguments to build his case.

This book is primarily concerned with supporting the agent in the bottom right corner of the table, who is more typically a church leader, a faith-based organization activist, or a Christian politician. My core concern here is to note that even if one does not cite Scripture explicitly in justifying one's actions or one's more theoretical ethical reflections, those actions may still be deeply inspired by Scripture. Many moral theologians do not use Bible texts explicitly in their books and articles, not even the classic texts (such as the parable of the good Samaritan) that can speak eloquently and convincingly, even to nonbelievers, without being paraphrased in secular language. I, for example, often write theological texts about human rights, migration, peace and conflict, and other matters that do not explicitly quote Scripture. Sometimes I omit quotations intentionally, since using Scripture appropriately is no easy task and complicates academic writing considerably. Sometimes it simply doesn't cross my mind when I am writing that there might be a link to the Bible that I could mention. A few days later, after I have submitted my article for peer review, I might encounter a familiar Bible text once again and realize that some of the major ideas in the article had been brewing in my head ever since I had meditated on that text, say during a retreat two years prior.

Conversely, I often read articles full of biblical citations, but am not impressed and become suspicious of what seems to me a frivolous and ostentatious use of Scripture. A Christian ethicist serenely rooted in his faith and identity does not need to prove his Christian pedigree continuously to himself and to others in this manner. Proof-texting is common in theological ethics, and it can easily be used to decorate and disguise thinking that is very foreign to the Christian tradition and to the biblical worldview.

2.2 Implicit Transmission of Concepts

A Discrete Source of Moral Inspiration

The implicit channel is a very important route connecting Scripture to ethics, even though it may be hidden or indirect. It may be hidden to moral agents and theorists like Agatha and Ethel who might not be aware that their action or reflection is rooted in Scripture. In Christopher Nolan's 2010 sci-fi movie *Inception*, Leonardo DiCaprio plays a thief

48

who is convinced to implant in the subconscious of an heir to a business empire an idea coming from someone else. The plan is that the idea will eventually nudge the heir to act in ways that will benefit the people behind this operation. Scripture can act like the thief in this movie.

However, it is more often the case that the implicit link is hidden not from the person who makes it, but from their observers or interlocutors, who might see the link or not. If they do, they will find it hard to pinpoint precisely which text or element of biblical culture is being linked to a particular action committed by the Implicit-Channel Actor or theory being upheld by the Implicit-Channel Theorist. Agatha or Ethel, the *persons making the link*, may be aware of it but might feel it unnecessary, inconvenient, or counterproductive to point it out to their interlocutors.

On the one hand, it is true that many intelligent lay and non-Christian interlocutors today do understand and appreciate a reflection on a classic Christian text that everyone can relate to, such as the parable of the good Samaritan. Hence, we do not need to always hide from them the biblical roots of our action and thought. However, they might find references to other biblical texts too particularistic and peculiar for certain multicultural debates and an implicit bridging might be the best option in a dialogue with such interlocutors. On the other hand, Christian interlocutors on certain occasions may need to be exposed to cross-cultural arguments in ethics, and citing Scripture too often may sound artificial. Excessive explicit use of the Bible in Christian ethics may promote self-righteous, "holier-than-thou" attitudes when speaking of principles, norms, values, and virtues that we believe all human beings should be able to understand, accept, and put into practice.

Thousands of Jewish and Christian intellectuals, artists, politicians, judges, administrators, and educators have shaped their character and mindset during time spent every day with the Jewish and Christian Scriptures. In modern times, many have allowed that dynamic to seep into everything they did in their lives, without explicitly mentioning it to the people who observed them or asked them to reveal their source of inspiration or the wellsprings of their moral imagination and action. In many cases implicit bridging between Scripture and ethics happens when notions and concepts derived from the Bible or inspired by it are translated into the culture of the readers and are gradually transmitted to nonreligious disciplines and practices, such as secular philosophy or jurisprudence. We shall dedicate the rest of this section to a discussion of such a mode of transmission.

In the mid-1960s, German legal scholar Ernst-Wolfgang Böcken-förde ventured to ask the question, "Does the free, secularized State exist on the basis of normative presuppositions that it itself cannot guarantee?"[3] In other words, are some of the ethical and juridical norms underpinning German or American institutions prepolitical, thus making these states somewhat dependent on religious traditions and sacred texts? This complex problem was the central issue of a famous public debate held in Munich on January 19, 2004, between the secular German philosopher Jürgen Habermas and then cardinal Joseph Ratzinger. Habermas's answer is roughly that there is no explicit dependence, and modern states have ways to justify their norms without referring to their religious roots, but Western thought has genuinely assimilated Christian ideas.

> This work of assimilation has left its mark in normative conceptual clusters with a heavy weight of meaning, such as responsibility, autonomy, and justification; or history and remembering, new beginning, innovation, and return; or emancipation and fulfillment; or expropriation, internalization, and embodiment, individuality and fellowship. Philosophy has indeed transformed the original religious meaning of these terms, but without emptying them through a process of deflation and exhaustion. One such translation that salvages the substance of a term is the translation of the concept of "[a human] in the image of God" into that of identical dignity of all humans that deserves unconditional respect. This goes beyond the borders of one particular religious fellowship and makes the substance of biblical concepts accessible to a general public that also includes those who have other faiths and those who have none.[4]

Scripture and the Public Use of Reason

American philosopher John Rawls develops a similar, but not identical, position in a series of texts, revised and republished together in the expanded edition of *Political Liberalism*, in which he distinguishes between public and nonpublic uses of reason and uses the "neutral" arguments and language of US Supreme Court as "exemplar" of public reason.[5] Rawls compares the nonpublic use of reason by the US abolitionists in the 1800s, "who argued against the antebellum South that its institution of slavery was contrary to God's law," with many of the speeches of Martin Luther King Jr. against segregation, which appeal "to the political values expressed in the Constitution correctly understood," and to general arguments on the nature of just and unjust laws taken from Aquinas (which are not explicitly religious).[6]

The example used is an interesting one, since one cannot find a text in Scripture that explicitly condemns chattel slavery, discrimination, or segregation. It is much easier to find texts, even in the New Testament, that consider these acts and institutions a normal feature of a premodern social order approved of, or at least tolerated, by God.

Scripture, Slavery and the Valladolid Debate (1550–1551)

The Valladolid Debate was a landmark moral, theological, and legal debate regarding the treatment of indigenous people by European colonizers. Juan Ginés de Sepúlveda represented the European landowners (*encomenderos*). He argued that war against the natives can be morally justified if it served to prevent cannibalism and human sacrifices, to ensure better government of the territories, and to spread the gospel. Prisoners taken during the war could legitimately be enslaved (thus "saving" them from execution).

Spanish Dominican friar and bishop Bartolomé de Las Casas vigorously disputed Sepúlveda's claims and defended the rights of American Indians, but struggled to find biblical arguments against slavery, or simply avoided using them. Instead, de Las Casas made ample use of philosophical and legal arguments (in ways akin to Rawls's notion of public reason) to assert that American Indians could not be enslaved since they did not fit into the Aristotelian category of "slaves by nature." He won the legal dispute and convinced the Spanish monarchy, and thereby shielded the First Nations of the Americas from enslavement. However, until very late in his life, he did not frown upon the lucrative slave trade being developed by the neighboring Portuguese, which was based on the assumption that the enslavement of unconverted Africans could be morally legitimate.[7]

In the 1800s, Catholic and Anglican theologians, though often sympathetic to the abolitionist cause, struggled to find biblical and theological warrant for the claim that "slavery was contrary to God's law."[8] Today we might consider such a claim obvious, but this is the result of a long and complex hermeneutical process. In this process, a notion of human dignity and human rights was slowly built based on biblical anthropology and Roman law, already present in the works of medieval canonists.[9] These notions were then used to condemn chattel slavery, even pushing back against the biblical passages that present it as something normal.

This example illustrates how the implicit channel can transmit a series of biblically grounded but universally comprehensible concepts or notions to philosophical and theological ethics that enrich debates in fora that require a *public use of reason*. The transmission is not one-sided, however. Those debates, in turn, may shape the way we read other Scripture texts (such as Paul's Letter to Philemon), and bridge them explicitly to contemporary ethics debates. Biblical notions of good and evil and notions derived from our experience as citizens in multicultural and multireligious settings intertwine hermeneutically to temper and refine one another.

In his treatise on biblical interpretation, *On Christian Doctrine*, Augustine formulates a rule that is based on this interplay, which we mentioned in passing in chapter 1 (Allegory 5). "If the [biblical] sentence is one of command [or admonitive teaching], either forbidding a crime or vice, or enjoining an act of utility or benevolence, it is not figurative. Conversely, if it seems to enjoin a crime or vice, or to forbid an act of utility or benevolence, it is figurative."[10] By appealing to our notions of crime, vice, utility, and benevolence, Augustine indicates that we may often need to use criteria external to the passage to judge its moral relevance. To avoid bias, we may seek to corroborate and generalize those notions, together with others in our ecclesial and political communities. Traditionally, within Catholic moral thought, this is done with the help of "right natural reason," that is, human reason informed by the experience of shared practices of seeking the common good, by philosophical ethics and comparative jurisprudence, and possibly by references to other biblical passages that are not deemed morally problematic. Yet even when generalized and corroborated in this manner, these criteria remain extrinsic to the passage at hand.

Using concepts from contemporary hermeneutics, we may say that Augustine is asking us to depend on our moral "preunderstandings" when reading Scripture, which in the process reshapes and challenges our older preunderstandings or engenders new ones. We will further discuss the notion of preunderstandings in chapter 3; for now, a brief note on this topic should suffice. As readers, we are encumbered with experiential and intellectual baggage that helps us understand literary classics, such as the Bible, but may also condition our reading in negative ways. This baggage is what we call "preunderstandings." They cannot be shed a priori: they enable us to approach the text and attempt a first round of interpretation. Hopefully, as we progressively encounter the otherness of the text and its "world," we will also come to question the validity of those preunderstandings.

Taking Stock of Our Moral Baggage as Readers

In his book *The Use of the Bible in Christian Ethics,* Thomas Ogletree discusses three major models that shape our understanding of the moral life: consequentialism, deontology, and perfectionism. He presents them as important preunderstandings when approaching Scripture.[11]

- *Modern Consequentialist Thinking* focuses on the aftermath of the action and the maximization of morally and physically desirable effects intended or envisaged as its results or consequences. One form, utilitarianism, which is predominant in contemporary institutional rationality, is particularly concerned with the progressive improvement of general living conditions in the world. Ogletree seems to conflate this with *Premodern Teleological Thinking,* which has different ontological underpinnings and focuses on the intentionality and finality of the action and the quest for the common good.

- *Deontological Thinking* focuses on discovering a system of clear, public duties that all persons can understand and obey, deeming them fair and universal. In authors such as Kant, such duties shape right action, and they obligate the agent independently of any desirable or undesirable effects or any ends sought by the agent which are extrinsic to the action itself.

- *Perfectionist Thinking* focuses on the personal and moral perfection (flourishing) of the agent. In the Aristotelian tradition, this is achieved via her habituation and growth in virtue (i.e., stable and morally excellent action). Ogletree considers Nietzsche's notion of human self-transcendence a form of perfectionism, albeit peculiar.

Ogletree believes that when taken separately, none of these ethical frameworks are adequate, but that we should approach Scripture encumbered with "a synthesis of all three determined by the temporal horizon of experience."[12] A similar approach has been proposed by many Catholic theologians after Vatican II, such as Joseph Fuchs, Klaus Demmer, and Richard Gula. Though Catholic ethics is often associated with perfectionism and premodern teleology, traditional Catholic case analysis incorporates elements of consequentialist thinking (for example, in the estimation of the proportionality of the effects of an action) and of deontological thinking (for example, in the more Stoic, Neoplatonic, and Roman law notions of obligation underpinning the medieval and modern natural law tradition). Furthermore, increasing historical consciousness (the "temporal horizon of experience") was a central feature of Vatican II reform and is explored in works of authors such as Bernard Lonergan.

Ultimately, in the rule cited above, Augustine is implying that the Bible contains moral laws that should be obeyed, but only in the passages we deem morally sound. There is a circularity in this reasoning, which should not be problematic as long as it is understood within the hermeneutical framework sketched above. The problem arises when we become obsessed with finding in Scripture a codified, concrete, apodictic *lex divina* (divine law) that requires no effort of interpretation by the individual reader or her ecclesial community. We will discuss this further when discussing legalistic misuse of Scripture in chapter 4. For now, let us simply note the hermeneutical circularity between the notions and concepts by which Scripture teaches us moral values, and those that we bring with us when reading Scripture to determine what passages have moral value for us.

2.3 Transmission of Paradigms

Another kind of transmission of ethically relevant biblical content allowed by the implicit channel (as well as by the explicit channel) is that of paradigms of idealized social figures. Waldemar Janzen, a Mennonite biblical scholar who grew up in Stalinist Ukraine and lived part of his life as a refugee, develops this approach in *Old Testament Ethics: A Paradigmatic Approach* (1994).

Janzen's Concept of Paradigm

Janzen notes that in the Hebrew Bible, narrative literary genres are dominant and serve as an interpretive framework for texts written in legal literary genres. Therefore, he chooses to present Old Testament ethics by focusing on narratives and their ability to elicit a practical reaction from the reader, even one who is not a theologian or professional exegete. Janzen is not very interested in an analytical or intellectual speculation performed on the particular narratives to derive ethical principles. Rather, he envisages readers as moral agents who learn from the narratives the virtuous action of the characters and then emulate it in their lives.

Thus, the hermeneutical bridge between the Scripture text read and contemplated by the moral agent and her action in the twenty-first century is constituted by what Janzen calls "paradigms," a notion derived from Christopher J. H. Wright and from grammar. The conjugations of regular verbs in Romance languages are paradigms; they are partly idealized forms achieved by reflective equilibrium between the unruly and multiple verb forms found in spoken languages and the simplified, standardized verb forms envisaged by enthusiasts of perfectly regular languages. According to Janzen, the paradigmatic or ideal "king" (or institutional leader) in Scripture does not coincide perfectly with any particular biblical character; he is a composite, part David, part Solomon, part Hezekiah, part Josiah, part Cyrus the Persian. We can represent Janzen's proposal as shown in figure 2.3:

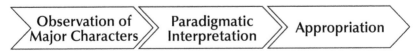

FIGURE 2.3: JANZEN'S PROPOSAL FOR THE USE OF THE OT IN ETHICS

Seen in this way, a paradigm is not easily reducible to a list of characteristics of the ideal "king," "father," "prophet," and so on. It is not usually transmitted to us via definitions or principles, any more than a native Italian speaker initially learns to conjugate verbs whose infinitive ends in -*are* by studying the list of verb endings in a grammar book, or a young automobile driver learns how to be a good driver by reading a highway code or state-issued driver's manual.[13] A "good driver" is a mental construct we build by fusing some of the best driving behavior we have experienced when riding with people whom we consider decent or competent drivers. We build these mental constructs using memories of those drivers' actions, both when they were alert and in a good mood and doing everything in a way that felt "right," and when they were tired and upset, but still focused on the road rather than on their feelings, doing their best to guarantee the safety of their passengers. This mental image imprints itself on us in an unmediated manner, and not through the medium of notions, concepts, and definitions.

Janzen distinguishes his approach from more legalistic or speculative ones. Here are some alternatives he does not find convincing (which I develop and comment on further in my descriptions below):[14]

- building an OT ethics on a compendium of texts or sentences written in legal literary genres arbitrarily chosen by the ethicist or exegete (therefore an ethics of norms or laws);
- speculating on narrative texts to extract from them a "biblical ethics" made of abstract principles, rather than inviting readers to emulate the main characters. Some authors do this because the best-known and best-developed characters of the OT sometimes act in morally ambiguous ways and make choices that we deem clearly immoral;
- focusing on the characters of the prophets (considered more advanced morally than other OT characters) and bracketing the characters of the Pentateuch and of the historical books for the above reasons;
- integrating the characters into a complex and progressive "history of salvation" that, however, risks reducing the individual characters to raw materials or half-baked samples in an ongoing historical process: the "moralization of humanity."

In contrast, biblical paradigms of ethical import, as understood by Janzen, encapsulate mental images of exemplary people in social roles and are transmitted through biblical narratives, which in turn are inserted into a single great narrative of God's relationship with God's people. On this basis, Janzen offers to read the OT in a canonical way and finds in this variegated set of books five major paradigmatic "social roles" or "types" that he considers useful for ethical discourse and formation (also found in the NT in the figure of Jesus), namely: priest, wise man, prophet, king, and human creature made in the image of God and embedded in a family structure. The last paradigm, which for brevity we shall call the "Family Member Paradigm," is the central one and allows Janzen to draw the contours of a biblical global ethics. Extended families in the Pentateuch include strangers who approach the main heroes (such as Abraham), stay on in "their" land, or host them in "theirs," since they are part of the hero's greater "family" in a real, if limited, sense. Thus, the OT proposes a global ethics, not through the universalization of maxims, but by extending the circle of kinship and the natural obligations that it implies.[15] This is why Janzen identifies three key components of the family paradigm (life, land, and hospitality) and presents two other examples (Ruth and Judges 19), claiming that "all laws stand in some relationship with the central paradigm, the 'familial paradigm.'"[16] There is a richness in Janzen's approach. I believe that by taking the scenic route (suggested at the end of the previous chapter) and bracketing some of the more clichéd texts, different readers of the Bible may find other interesting paradigms to emulate. The five paradigms he examines seem uniquely focused on leadership. They could be useful in a course on business ethics or ethics for politicians and community organizers, using the explicit channel to link Scripture texts to leadership models. Such use might be limited, however, by the fact that his theory seems to point more to a personal meditation on the texts and an implicit appropriation of the paradigms than to a rigorous analysis of texts and an explicit transmission of biblical "content" to a wide audience.

Janzen's approach offers a useful model to bridge Scripture and ethics and serves to enrich the hermeneutical and methodological debates in this book. From a social ethics viewpoint, however, our topic brings out some of the more serious limitations of Janzen's approach. It is not easy to build a paradigm of the "good friend of strangers" or the "good resident alien" and then show how this paradigm preannounces Jesus, who does not seem particularly friendly toward strangers, and is not presented as a stranger himself (ethnically speaking) in the Gospel narratives. We could try to use the Abraham narrative cycle in Genesis, the Book of Ruth, and some other lesser-known characters to try to build such paradigms, but this might seem like cherry picking. Even so, the more challenging question is this: Can we truly construct a biblical paradigm of the "good friend of strangers" or a "good resident alien?" The answer depends on the way the adjective *good* functions in these expressions.

Paradigms and Stereotypes

In Aristotelian ethics, when we add the adjective *good* to a noun like *mother* or *general* or *carpenter*, we qualify that noun so to build a model of virtue: a caring mother, a brave general, a skilled carpenter. However, as we have seen in chapter 1, when we add *good* to nouns like *Samaritan*, instead of simply qualifying that noun, we could end up challenging the stereotyped meaning of that noun. The idea that true "goodness" and "camaraderie" might be found in a Samaritan would have seemed like a contradiction to Jesus's audiences. Possibly, the expression "the good Samaritan" (which is not found in the text) would have sounded to them more like a provocative oxymoron or the start of a xenophobic joke than a reference to Aristotelian virtue ethics.

Attributing Goodness to Strangers in Film

In the title of the Steven Soderbergh's 2006 movie *The Good German* (based on Joseph Kanon's novel of the same name), the adjective may be ironic, with reference to the expression popular among Allied soldiers, "The only good German is a dead German." Alternatively, it may be skeptical, with reference to the expression "good Germans," used in the late 1940s to describe persons who did not support the Nazi regime but did nothing meaningful to resist it.

By contrast, at the end of Florian Henckel von Donnersmarck's movie of the same year, *The Lives of Others*, the main character dedicates a book entitled *Sonata for a Good Man* to a compassionate and anonymous Stasi (East German secret police) officer who had hidden incriminating evidence of the character's illegal journalism, instead of reporting him. The main character wrote articles that criticized the communist regime and leaked them to the West German press. We

don't expect a Stasi officer to be truly "good" by protecting the dissident with whom we tend to identify as spectators. He becomes "good" in our eyes by being a "bad Stasi,"
violating his professional duty as an intelligence officer to
hunt down traitors and dissidents. But the movie challenges
the stereotype and implies that the greatest saints might well
arise in social contexts that make holiness next to impossible, rather than in contexts where virtue is the norm.

By ironing out the kinks and character flaws, paradigms simplify
the moral ambiguity and vulnerability of Bible heroes and villains. Janzen doesn't dwell on villains, but his method can be inverted, of course,
to construct a paradigm of the "evil king" or "false prophet" with no
redeeming feature or hope of conversion. Clearly distinguishing between
good and evil is pedagogically useful, especially in cultures where moral
complexity often serves as an excuse for relativism. However, if we use
paradigms systematically to strip biblical heroes and villains of their
moral ambiguity and vulnerability, and to conceal their openness to corruption and conversion, we could end up severely impoverishing these
characters and keeping powerful narratives from functioning as effective windows into human reality.

Indeed, Janzen's paradigms seem to work like accurate, positive
stereotypes. When we use the word *stereotype* we are usually referring to
inaccurate and negative stereotypes, but stereotypes can be accurate and
positive. These stereotypes have an important cognitive function: they
help us make sense of complex social realities.

Types of Stereotypes

Let us imagine that we are members of a hiring team that
does not include Asians, and we are discussing the strengths
and weaknesses of various candidates for a job that requires
a good grasp of arithmetic, algebra, and geometry. Someone
recommends a candidate who is an engineer, noting that "all
engineers are good at math." This is a stereotype that is usually *positive* (in this context it is not being used to imply they
are "nerds") and *accurate* (their profession logically requires
mathematical proficiency).

Another team member comments that "Asians are good at math" to hint that we should hire a promising Korean candidate. This is another stereotype, which in this context is usually *positive* (though in some contexts, an Asian might construe it as a microaggression). It is usually an *inaccurate* stereotype since mathematical proficiency is not logically or biologically dependent on ethnicity. In some cases, it is not entirely *false* since some Asian parents are aware that this stereotype may help their kids get certain jobs (in countries like the United States). They may push their children to earn good grades in math for this very reason, lending some credibility to the stereotype a posteriori. When that pressure works, and these kids grow up and become parents, they may in turn be better equipped to help their own children improve their math proficiency, reinforcing the stereotype. Even so, the claim remains a priori inaccurate and might prove detrimental to Asian youths who desire an artistic career and are held back by another inaccurate stereotype: "good mathematicians make bad artists."

We use stereotypes all the time to simplify reality taxonomically. Since the 1950s, various studies on stereotyping by Gordon Allport and others show how this mechanism is part of our ordinary cognitive functioning. Prejudice, on various levels, implies a cognitive dysfunction and is treated by these authors as special case, though most people today conflate stereotypes and prejudices.[17]

Does the Bible have anything to say about such attempts to simplify and understand social and moral realities via generalization? I believe the answer is twofold when we consider the figure of Jesus in the NT. On the one hand, the Gospel narratives show us a Jesus seemingly taking several stereotypes for granted, like "Pharisee," "Torah expert," "tax collector," "prostitute/public sinner," "Canaanite," and "Greek/Gentile." On the other hand, traditional authors have often compared Jesus to the "Socrates" character in Plato's earliest dialogues, a gadfly who seemed to enjoy challenging popular stereotypes. Like the Socrates character, Jesus often used his parables to show his audiences that the people we usually expect to be wise, just, pious, or courageous (according to the prevalent stereotypes) often don't know or don't live up to what those virtues really entail. He took contradictions and incoherencies in human behavior seriously. He did not dismiss them as imperfections within an overarching process of unveiling either flawless Platonic forms by extrapolation and idealization or Aristotelian paradigms of practical excellence by finding the "golden mean" between two flawed extremes. This should make us wary of using paradigmatic approaches such as Janzen's as the only or the primary approach to bridging Scripture and ethics.

2.4 The "Jesus" Paradigm and Analogical Imagination

In his 1999 book *Go and Do Likewise: Jesus and Ethics*, William Spohn used a paradigmatic approach. According to Spohn, a paradigm is "a normative pattern or exemplar that can be creatively applied in different circumstances."[18] This does not completely coincide with Janzen's notion of paradigm, but is close enough to allow us to compare the two authors. Spohn's approach is unique in that it claims to focus on Jesus as the sole paradigm, even though it includes his parables and their characters, which function as narratives within narratives, fitting new paradigms within the Jesus paradigms. Spohn's book combines three "avenues of reflection":

(a) the New Testament story of Jesus
(b) the ethics of virtue and character
(c) certain Christian spirituality practices (mainly in the tradition of Ignatius of Loyola)

The book's exclusive focus on Jesus and the NT obviously limits access to the richness of the whole of Scripture but fits into a long Christian tradition of christocentric typological exegesis. Jesus "the Christ" has a special place in a Christian's approach to Scripture. He is both the timeless Logos that is theologically unveiled transversally through all Scripture (but especially through New Testament texts) and the main character of the Gospel stories. Focusing on Jesus's character as an archetypical moral paradigm has allowed ethicists and catechists to avoid dealing with most of the moral ambiguity present in many other biblical figures.

Nevertheless, the excommunication of Marcion of Sinope in 144 CE, along with the centuries-long debate over supersessionism and its repudiation by Pope John Paul II, should make us wary of facilely bracketing OT texts. Jesus was neither a political leader nor a Roman citizen; he lived far from Rome in a marginal province of an empire ruled by strangers where he and his people had no say on topics like borders or immigration. The Gospels show him constantly shunning the attitudes promoted by various political groups at the time. Thus, forcing ourselves to use the Gospels to try to reflect on social and political topics today implies a serious risk of anachronistic and ideological manipulation of the Bible. This is why the approach in this book focuses primarily on debates reflected in the OT that actually deal with political leadership and borders, while exploring their complexity and morally unattractive elements.

Still, Spohn's book can enrich our notion of implicit bridging, which is the main concern of this chapter. His title echoes the conclusion of the parable of the good Samaritan. He notes that doing "likewise" is neither doing "the exact same thing" nor doing "whatever you want."[19] Rather, it is an invitation to think using analogies. Spohn's approach reminds us of the work of authors such as Ricœur who tie together narratives, imaginative mimesis, and ethics. However, I believe that Spohn's book is overly concerned with promoting virtue ethics, while Ricœur's understanding of ethics is more complex and complete. It comprises "aiming at a good life, with and for others, in just institutions," combining elements from the perfectionist, consequentialist, and deontological preunderstandings of moral life discussed in section 2.2.[20] It also seeks to balance the "aristocratic" communitarian virtue ethics of Aristotle with the "universalist" cosmopolitan, deontological, normative ethics of Kant, wary of the one-sidedness of the enthusiastic but polemical movement of the rediscovery of virtue ethics in the 1980s by authors such as Alasdair MacIntrye.[21]

Spohn's Approach and Its Attractiveness

Spohn chooses to focus on virtue ethics, since, in his opinion, it "attends to the full range of moral experience, from vision to character, [and hence] it offers the most fruitful approach to [the NT Jesus narratives]."[22] Virtue ethics (also known as aretaics) gained traction in Catholic theological circles after Vatican II since it allowed theological ethicists to revisit the Aristotelian-Thomist moral tradition while avoiding the legalistic readings of Aquinas typical of neo-Thomism.[23] MacIntyrean virtue ethics received a considerable boost after the publication of Pope John Paul II's encyclical *Veritatis Splendor* in 1993, a hotly debated text that seemed to frown on the works of theologians who engaged in dialogue with other moral traditions. More recently, debates on virtue formation have also become popular in lay intellectual circles. Important psychological, neurological, and sociological research has been conducted on habituation cycles in recent years, popularized in self-help books by authors such as James Clear, Charles Duhigg, and BJ Fogg.[24]

Given this background, Spohn's approach was attractive in 2003 when his book was published and remains attractive now, which is why we will dedicate the rest of this chapter to his proposal. In Spohn's view, it is easy for Christians to read the gospel and learn important virtues from Christ; the problem lies in the transformation of their attitudes, desires, and behaviors. Pastors and committed lay leaders often complain that many practicing Christians remain stuck in vicious cycles of moral misperception and action, such as racism and xenophobia. Others resist habituating themselves virtuously to conform with a gospel worldview, despite many years of faithfulness to liturgical and devotional practices and Bible study groups. While commenting on Paul's experience in Philippians 3:4–21, Spohn proposes a spirituality focused on imaginative contemplative prayer (spiritual practices that help us interpret the text). This serves as a hermeneutical bridge between gospel-derived aretaics (observation/meditation of Jesus in the text) and habituative personal transformation (as a form of appropriation of the text):

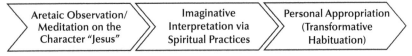

FIGURE 2.4: SPOHN'S MODEL FOR HONING MORAL PERCEPTION
USING PARTICULAR SCRIPTURE PASSAGES

The "devotional" bridging element uses both the "analogical imagination," which allows Christians who practice imaginative contemplation regularly to observe Jesus in the gospel and "go and do likewise," and "moral perception," which helps them to see reality as Jesus saw it: a place where God's reign manifests itself constantly and transformationally. This is quite different from the way social media influencers, TV anchorpersons, and television and streaming programmers present reality. Faith and justice give us eyes to see the world anew, but we need to be willing and receptive to gain this new kind of vision.

This honing of moral *perception* using classics is the first stage of the bridging process envisaged by Spohn. It leads in turn to the second stage: the formation of stable *dispositions* to act in certain ways that are good and excellent—otherwise called "virtues"—motivated by deep-seated spiritual emotions that help us desire a virtuous life. The final stage is *identity formation*, allowing action that is truly Christian and rooted in Scripture to flow from our character and deepest selves, and hence become second nature to us.

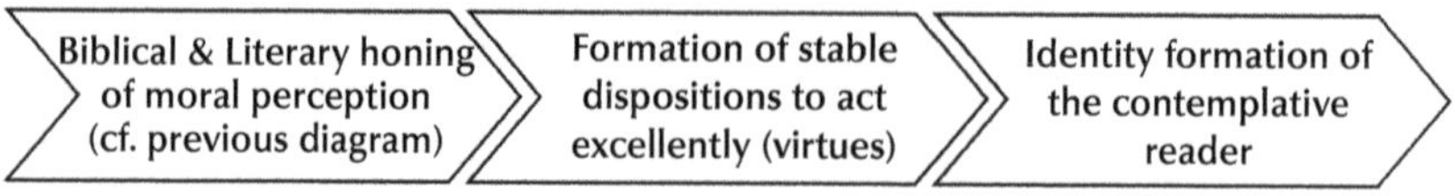

| Biblical & Literary honing of moral perception (cf. previous diagram) | Formation of stable dispositions to act excellently (virtues) | Identity formation of the contemplative reader |

FIGURE 2.5: SPOHN'S MODEL FOR IMPLICIT
BRIDGING OF SCRIPTURE AND ETHICS

The Importance of Spirituality

Spohn's bridge between Scripture and ethics depends on spiritual practices. Contemporary notions of spirituality may include a hodge-podge of religious practices, chosen and combined at will, within a dein-stitutionalized system of credence disconnected from doctrinal claims associated with particular traditions. Considering doctrinal claims either "intolerant" or "violent," contemporary postmodern culture sometimes finds even atheism and critical agnosticism too "dogmatic" and "structured" and opts for ad hoc mixtures of elements from different spiritual traditions that "feel good" or "feel true," provide health or social benefits, and are hassle-free.[25] Spohn understands spirituality in almost an opposite manner. For him, truth claims, institutions, and traditions are important. Spirituality, in the traditional sense, "signifies practical ways of praying, serving, and living that connect the faith convictions of a tradition to a particular time and place."[26]

Spohn notes that Judaism and Roman Catholicism have engendered new spiritualities during times of great historical changes and upheavals, and these spiritualities were lived within new religious orders or lay movements that found their niches within an institutionalized but generally tolerant and inclusive religious organization (a "church" in the sociological sense). Conversely, "new movements of intense religion with well-defined identities (often called 'sects') often left the Protestant churches in which they originated, seeking to form new denominations."[27]

Spohn indicates that he is primarily acquainted with the spirituality of the followers of Ignatius of Loyola and the first Jesuits. Ignatius developed a more complex and institutional "Jesuit Spirituality" for the vowed members of the Jesuit religious order, while also offering spiritual accompaniment to laypersons and other religious, shaped by what is now called "Ignatian Spirituality." Originally founded as a band of itinerant priests to promote spiritual encounters with God, the Jesuits quickly found themselves managing hundreds of schools and universities. To remain faithful to their origins, they incorporated elements of Ignatian Spirituality in their educational practices.[28] Over the centuries, several women's religious congregations were founded, shaped by the mystical and ascetical aspects of Ignatian Spirituality and also by some of the more institutional aspects of Jesuit Spirituality. These congregations promoted Ignatian Spirituality in the institutions they founded. Ignatian Spirituality is demanding but has a relatively wide following today, given these historical events and the fact that it has proven helpful to many laypersons, diocesan priests, and active religious navigating the complexities of life in the modern world.

Let us take a moment to detail three aspects of this spirituality that are important for our discussion in this chapter, but that Spohn seems to take for granted.[29] Ignatian spirituality entails a certain way of praying with Scripture, of being and of acting in the world. It includes meditative, social action, and governance practices, performed at a personal and communal level.[30] First, contemplative imaginative prayer is seen as a means to cultivate "a deep personal love for Jesus Christ," which is a central aspect of Ignatian Spirituality. Second, this relationship with Christ is active and practical, not monastic, hence a second important aspect is that of "being contemplative, even in the midst of action." Contemplation is not sought merely for the beauty of consciously placing oneself in God's presence; it is also a means to hone one's moral perception and receive guidance for decision-making and action.

A third important feature of Jesuit spirituality is the so-called *presupponendum* (from the *Spiritual Exercises*, 22). This is the attitude of seeking to interpret other people's words, thoughts, and actions in a positive way, even when they appear to be in error, thus opting to see the goodness in the other and to empower it, rather than being keen to spot and reveal their ignorance or moral blameworthiness. I have detailed these three aspects since they explain how Jesuits and persons trained in Ignatian Spirituality relate to Scripture and how they practice the more intimate and less "active" aspects of spirituality that we usually associate with the word *prayer*. Though Spohn dedicates some space in his book to liturgical and petitionary prayer, especially in chapter 5, he reserves chapters 6 and 7 to Scripture-based imaginative-contemplative-elective prayer. This is a kind of prayer that uses the various affects that well up in a contemplative imagination exercise by channeling it through a constant discernment process geared to decision-making. Habitually grounding our decision-making in such a discernment process results in moral character formation.

Ignatian Imaginative-Contemplative Prayer, Discernment, and Action

To understand better what Spohn is talking about, it is best to start with Ignatius's story, reconstructed as best we can from various documents. These include some reminiscences about Ignatius's past life that he once communicated during a brief conversation with another Jesuit, Luís Gonçalves da Câmara, who later wrote them down from memory. (They are sometimes referred to, misleadingly, as Ignatius's "Autobiography.")

In 1521, while slowly convalescing after painful surgery, Ignatius was given devotional books to fill the time, containing medieval narratives of the lives of the great saints and a digest of "The Life of Christ" based on the four canonical Gospels. He alternated romantic and chivalrous daydreaming with more "religious" daydreaming. There he imagined himself either as one of the saints in his book, but facing new, challenging, missionary scenarios, or as a disciple in one of the episodes of "The Life of Christ," creating a sort of "screenplay" in his head, shoring up the lack of a detailed scenic design by using his imagination. He started noticing the difference in the emotional tone and the kind of joy or pleasure afforded by each kind of daydreaming. During his imaginative games based on religious texts, he connected the stories to his life using an implicit analogy ("in *their day*—Jesus or St. Francis did x :: *today*—I might do x₁"). Ignatius found the emotional effects of these imaginative experiences to be of a wholesome and long-lasting nature, and he attributed them to a "good (honest) spirit." The other daydreaming exercises—fantasies focused on worldly pleasures, fame, glory, and wealth—provided intense, but hollow emotional experiences, which he attributed to a "deceitful" spirit (*malo espíritu*).

With help from monks and eventually from professional theologians, the "religious" daydreaming (or rather, use of the "analogical imagination," as Spohn would say) was eventually recognized as a form of prayer, and came to be seen as a peculiar form of the monastic *lectio divina* tradition,[31] especially when Ignatius learned enough Latin to be able to read a church-approved copy of the Bible and acquaint himself with the "original" Jesus stories. He did, however, continue to believe that imaginative contemplative prayer works best when we simplify complex narratives, reducing them to three major story "points" (*puntos*, in Spanish), and thereby creating ample space for our imagination to roam.

For Ignatius, this was not a disincarnate kind of prayer, done simply in the name of the doubtless beauty and worthiness of prayer in itself. Rather, he saw his practice of "discernment of spirits" flowing from his "kind" of prayer as something strongly oriented toward decision-making and action: it concerns "morality" in the wider sense of the term. Hence, this imaginative-contemplative prayer is also "elective." That is why a sympathetic but critical "spiritual guide" is essential. A wise "Ignatian prayer guide" is trained to avoid advocating for any options being considered by the agent, so long as they are ethically acceptable.[32] Rather, the guide is to ask probing questions to help the person they are accompanying situate their spiritual practice within an ecclesial framework, limit their tendencies toward self-deception, narcissism, and individualism, bring in other perspectives, and bear in mind that discernment should lead to a coherent and authentic *set* of life choices.

Within the framework of discernment, the "honest spirit" and the "deceitful spirit" are in many ways spiritual, moral, or psychological constructs, rather than direct manifestations of the Holy Spirit or Satan, and the "deceitful spirit" is generally the fruit of internal resistance to change or to ideas that challenge one's ingrained self-image and coveted social role.[33] Yet, Ignatius, together with his early followers, was convinced that the emotions provoked in him by the "good spirit" were not just moralizing projections of the superego, as Sigmund Freud might say. They had something to do with the Holy Spirit and with God indirectly or even directly nudging him to take certain life-transforming decisions and to act in certain ways.[34] However, when questioned by suspicious inquisitors, he denied having mystical experiences through which God told him what to do.[35]

In chapter 6 of his book, Spohn presents "imaginative-contemplative Scripture-based prayer" as a "school of the affects" (*schola affectus*) hinting at an expression Ignatius used to describe the final phase of Jesuit training.[36] Such prayer coaches us and tones our emotive muscles, creating dispositions. A key role is played by affects or, to use a better-known term, emotions (both terms are used to indicate something less self-centered and unstable than "sentiments" or "feelings"; Ignatius uses a peculiar

Spanish term, *mociones*). They are not completely under rational control, but neither are they necessarily "irrational" or "disordered," as Martha Nussbaum argues in some of her best-known books.[37] Affects can lead to (a) perceptive moral knowledge and (b) virtuous action (via dispositions), and hence have both a cognitive and a pragmatic dimension. Both are explained in the following scheme, which adds some order and details to what Spohn suggests in his book:

a.   Perceptive moral knowledge:
   • "Emotions resist systematic treatment, since some are primitive and others more structured."[38] Recognizing and naming the affects is an important first step (emotional intelligence). Modern "emotion wheels" such as that developed by Robert Plutchik can be helpful here. It is useful to note the salience of the emotion, that is, the level of our subjective engagement.
   • Recognition leads to the question "What is this emotion referring to?" and launches within us a process that seeks to determine its object.
   • We can eventually interpret the emotion using memorized past experiences, cultural references, beliefs, and paradigms.
b.   Virtuous action:
   • Even in people who struggle to identify and name them, emotions can "dispose the subject to a particular type of action."[39]
   • They can be channeled through habituation processes to provide energy to the will to act stably in a given way, that is, according to ends, values, principles, and rules recognized rationally as good. For example, anger can be let loose to hurt people, or when properly coached, used to fuel rational, strategic action in favor of justice.[40] Serenity can be either wasted in nonchalant, carefree behavior or trained to trigger within us a sense that this time is a precious opportunity we could use to deal with past trauma and to help others who are suffering.

Bible stories and images, as well as popular literary and even movie heroes, are important in this training. When unjustly insulted by a colleague, a moral agent might bring to mind the words and actions of Jesus and keep their tongue from automatically slapping back with a similar insult. They might turn their metaphorical "other cheek" meekly while thinking, "Father, forgive them, for they do not know what they are doing," or protest politely while thinking, "If I have spoken rightly, why do you strike me?" (cf. Matt 5:39; Luke 23:34; John 18:23). In any case, if properly trained, they will process the anger in ways that build God's reign effectively and lovingly, rather than simply lash out mindlessly until they feel vindicated, and then deal with the consequences. They will calmly evaluate whether their colleague is simply under stress and whether the situation can be diffused through compassion, or whether they are being systematically harassed and need to take strategic action to protect themselves and others.

2.5. The Utility of Dialectic and Dynamic Approaches

Should We Avoid Struggling with the Text? The Limitations of Static Approaches

Our discussion of Ignatian imaginative-contemplative prayer offers a good example of what Spohn means by using the "analogical imagination," nourished by Scripture, to shape our decision-making, character, and action. There is, however, a major tension in Spohn's approach that may confuse his readers. On one hand, his keenness on spirituality and on imaginative contemplation of biblical texts points toward an ethics that is comfortable with ambiguity, complexity, and personal freedom to follow the guidance of the Spirit. This would imply recognizing and being comfortable with the fact that when approaching a text, the contemporary reader will bring with her various moral preunderstandings of the moral life. She will introduce elements of perfectionism, classical teleology, deontology, and consequentialism into the contemplative exercise (as noted above when discussing Ogletree's proposal), and seek an interpretation that may include the individual, communal, and institutional levels of moral life (as underlined in Ricœur's definition, cited above). The variety of possible analogies we explore in chapter 1 illustrates such interpretive freedom.

On the other hand, we note Spohn's tendency to reduce the many literary elements of moral relevance in the NT to the sole figure of

Jesus Christ, and this figure to the aspects that make Jesus appear as a paradigm of virtue to the reader. This points to a desire to control the experience of the reader or imaginative contemplator, limiting it to a perfectionist ethics. Spohn's claim that Jesus is morally paradigmatic is true but can be misunderstood. Jesus's actions do not always fit neatly into classical virtue ethics categories, and when they seem to jar with such moral preunderstandings, this is not something we can afford to bracket. Consequently, Spohn tends to avoid serious discussion of the tension between the world of the text and the world of the reader, potentially creating conflict when these worlds find themselves disagreeing or challenging one another. In his book, Spohn brackets "hermeneutics of suspicion" in favor of "hermeneutics of appreciation." He politely mentions and brackets dialectics, strongly favoring analogy. Dialectics seeks to establish truth by contrasting two or more alternative claims or realities, rather than comparing them. It uses agonistic reasoned argumentation to refute alternatives, introduce distinctions (such as alternatives that are only true at a certain level or in a certain sense), or move toward a synthesis that supersedes the opposition between claims or realities that is posited at the start of the exercise. Spohn downplays the dialectical operations in traditional analysis of moral cases that emphasize the differences between the case and the "prime analogate," focusing rather on the analogical operations that seek to establish conformity.[41]

This eschewal of the conflictive dimension of all interpretation and moral formation—of Ignatius's combat between two "spirits"—is surprising, given Spohn's insistence on "transformation." Scripture portrays God as seducing and overpowering believers (Jer 20:7; Gen 32:23–32; Hos 2). Naturally, at first, we resist. Then it is hoped that we give in, not because we are gullible or cowardly, but because at some point in the struggle we fall in love.[42] We are transformed, we decide to stop resisting, and we reach a willing "naïveté" at a deeper, meta level.

The analysis of the parable of the workers in the vineyard (Matt 20:1–16) offers a useful example: we can combine analogy and dialectics in our analysis, or limit ourselves to analogy. Spohn seems to favor the latter. At the start of his analysis of this text, Spohn correctly underlines reversal and the "element of surprise" in Jesus's parables, comparing them with jokes, puns, and "shaggy dog" stories, noting that if the landowner's cheeky response "doesn't offend our sensibilities, it is hard to imagine what would." Two paragraphs later, however, in his interpretation of the parable, he takes the landowner at his word and concludes that he "has acted fairly because he honored their agreement."[43]

The point Spohn is trying to make is that the parable offends the people in the pews during Sunday Mass because it challenges the American mindset, imbued with a legalistic and meritocratic notion of fairness. This notion needs to be put into tension with other notions of fairness and desert to overcome our skewed sense of fairness. Yet in his rush to use analogical thinking and hence to defend the landowner of the parable and elevate him as a paragon of virtue for us to imitate, Spohn simply accepts his justification: "Did you not agree with me for the usual daily wage?" and "Can't I do whatever I want with my property?" Most people, outside the United States at least, would find his words preposterous. Naïvely accepting the landowner's justification simply pushes Spohn's US reader from disliking the landowner for scoffing at typical American meritocratic thinking to liking him for championing typical American notions of property rights and legal positivism, without ever challenging the reader's notions of fairness and desert. Now the people in the pews get it: Jesus is a capitalist defending absolute property rights and telling us that, so long as the letter of the contract is respected, nothing is amiss. Is that really what Jesus it trying to teach us?

Spohn doesn't seem to notice that this landowner has just made the exhausted, hard-working folk wait in line until the very end on purpose and has intentionally paraded in front of them the workers who came to work at the end of day, as well as paying the latecomers what he had promised to those who worked the whole day under the sun. When we introduce a dialectic voice in our analysis, we can clearly see that the landowner is no paradigm of goodness, generosity, or charity. His actions appear patently imprudent, capricious, and possibly spiteful and callous. We don't need to read treatises on virtue ethics to realize that true generosity and charity are neither random nor indiscrete; a virtuous person doesn't pay all the latecomers ten times the normal rate because they came late for work, and doesn't *make a show* of it. Rather, if she suspects some of them had valid reasons for coming late and actually need additional financial help, she investigates and then discretely offers them the help they need.

Jesus is not proposing the landowner as a paradigm of virtue. The hero of the story, if we may call him that, is a typical arrogant landowner of his day, possibly more histrionic than callous. The point of the story, just as in a joke, is to question the notion of fairness and rewards held by the listener (who automatically identifies with the workers who complain) without immediately proposing the behavior of the landowner as a corrective.

Upon reflection, after struggling with the narrative and trying to make some sense out of what initially seems absurd, some readers will realize that the latecomers have families to feed and may have reasons for seeking work so late; the behavior of the landowner may not be as vicious as it seems, despite his theatrics. Some may realize that the apparent virtue of the early birds is in part a product of moral good luck, and the apparent vice of the latecomers is in part a product of moral bad luck; many factors that facilitate or hinder our virtuous behavior are not under our control. Different readers will find different ways of dealing with the strangeness of the parable and convert it into a story to which they can relate. In any case, I believe a dialectical approach wherein we try to figure out what is really wrong and what might be somehow right in the behavior of the three main character types (landowner, latecomers, and early birds) can be much more fruitful here than trying to figure out which of the protagonists Jesus is supposedly holding as a paradigm of virtue. Then we can use our analogical imagination to "go and do likewise."

Jesus's parables and behavior are eminently transmissible as narratives, since they challenge reality as we know it, just like all good narratives. They do not function as propaganda or brainwashing where an impeccable model is simply held up for us to emulate, merely asking us to tweak as needed in our situation. Rather, his parables often present a horribly inadequate model to confound us at first, and then to challenge our way of thinking. Whether and to what extent we should try to emulate the model is secondary. Jesus does suggest analogical behavior at the end of the good Samaritan parable, but this isn't necessarily the approach we should take with all the protagonists of the parables. Furthermore, as Spohn himself notes, asking a first century CE Jewish audience to emulate a Samaritan would have been as palatable as asking churchgoers today to emulate "the good terrorist."[44] There is no escaping the dialectic side of the equation.

Should We Only Look for Virtuous Moral Agents to Emulate? The Limitations of a Paradigmatic Approach

This debate leads us to conclude that a virtue ethics or paradigmatic approach, even when focused solely on the Gospels, is valuable, but implicit bridging between Scripture and ethics should envisage other approaches as well. If many of the characters in Jesus's parables cannot be used to instantly fuel the analogical imagination and point it immediately to ethical behavior, we might at least learn something from them using a dialectical exercise where we struggle with their strangeness. In many ways, parables, like folktales, are short wisdom stories, intended to make a point rather than to set an example. Often, the protagonists are the very opposite of Aristotelian models of virtue. Consider the parable of the sower, for instance (Matt 13:1–23; Mark 4:1–20; Luke 8:4–15). At face value, and by Aristotelian standards, the farmer seems wasteful and cannot possibly provide a paradigm of a "good" sower. Though fields in antiquity were often small and irregularly shaped and included many unproductive areas, the sower makes no attempt to avoid or improve those areas, for instance by removing the thorns. Similarly, the prodigal father (Luke 15:11–32) shows us a "bad" father, who lets his sons disrespect him and enables their vices and arrogance rather than disciplining them.

The parable of the talents (Matt 25:14–30) shows us a greedy landowner in a subsistence agriculture economy who expects his less business-savvy servants to resort to usury to satisfy his towering greed. In Luke's version (Luke 19:11–27), the protagonist's tyrannical nature is revealed at the end. "As for these enemies of mine who did not want me to be king over them—bring them here and slaughter them in my presence." The story might have reminded the original audience of Herod the Great.

The parable of the dishonest manager (Luke 16:1–17) shows us a finance officer too eager to write off debts, while possibly swindling his employer. After getting caught he tempts clients to forge revised copies of their contracts, probably with the intent of currying favor with them or blackmailing them as soon as he gets fired. We then hear that the employer commends the administrator on his shrewdness. As we struggle to make sense of this bizarre commendation, in our imagination, we might hear the boss laughing sardonically at the administrator's picaresque behavior while he fires him.

Of course, not all of Jesus' parables, metaphors, and teachings are iconoclastic in this manner; some take for granted, and build on, common stereotypes. For instance, the distinction between the Good Shepherd and the hired hand in John 10:11–18 seems a straightforward "good" versus "bad" image (though shepherds were often seen as uncouth scofflaws who went around stealing and damaging harvests).

Yet, assuming that what we are after is to bridge Scripture and ethics via Gospel paradigms of virtue, if the narrative literary genres of the parables in the Gospels won't provide what we need, all we are left with are the pericopes describing the actions of Jesus. That leaves us with very little to work with.

Furthermore, focusing on Jesus's actions does not necessarily provide the perfect virtue paradigm that Christian ethics has taught us to expect. For instance, let us just focus on our topic: dealing ethically with strangers. A quick scan of the way Jesus treats the Canaanite woman (Matt 15:21–28), the Syrophoenician woman (Mark 7:24–30), the Samaritan woman (John 4:1–42), and the Greeks (Gentiles) who ask to see him (John 12:20–23) indicates that his initial attitude toward non-Jews (outside of the parables) was usually one of indifference, if not haughtiness and hostility, with some notable exceptions (such as that of the Judeophile centurion in Luke 7:1–10; Matt 8:5–13). Certainly, compassion toward strangers is not what first comes to mind when we read these texts. And yet, inspired by Diana Fritz Cates, Spohn makes "compassion" the prototypical "emotion" in his conception of "moral perception."[45]

In this chapter, we have presented a few models of explicit bridging between Scripture and ethics. The transmission of Scripture-inspired values through concepts that can be expressed adequately in debates featuring a public use of reason is an important piece of the puzzle. Another significant piece is the transmission of paradigms and virtues, and the models provided by Janzen and Spohn are insightful. The questions we have just raised indicate that we are still missing some pieces of the implicit channel puzzle, but we will not attempt to fill in the void with yet another model: the focus of this book is on the explicit channel. The following chapter may provide some clues by revisiting the discussion above concerning the imaginative contemplation of literary texts, using hermeneutics debates from twentieth century philosophy and linguistics. This may help us to envisage other ways in which a literary work may have an impact on the moral thinking and action of its readers.

3

ENGAGING THE "WORLD OF THE TEXT"

The common feature in our diagrams depicting implicit bridging between exegesis and ethics (fig. 2.1) and explicit bridging (fig. 2.2) is what we call the "interpretation" phase. The study of interpretation is called hermeneutics. In this chapter, the reader will learn about some of the major hermeneutics debates of the second half of the twentieth century, before moving on to explore models of explicit bridging in the following chapter.

The first part of the chapter focuses on Paul Ricœur's notion of the hermeneutics of distanciation and his critique of Romanticist and structuralist approaches to hermeneutics. Readers will learn to distinguish between the world of the original authors, editors, and hearers/readers of a text—such as that which gave birth to several literary works of poetry or narrative fiction included in our biblical canon—and the world that the text itself unveils to its readers by its own weight as a literary work.

The second part of the chapter focuses on Umberto Eco's notion of presupposition. This notion will help readers temper Ricœur's tendency to reduce the meaning of "interpretation" almost exclusively to "understanding oneself in front of a literary work of fiction." Eco claims that there are chains of meaning linking the world of the reader to the world of the author and the original readers, allowing us to have knowledge of the words and concepts used in a text independently of the text, and hence to read it effectively. Readers will discover that texts are lazy machines that *presuppose* that we activate those meaning chains if we want them to project their worlds to us.

This chapter functions as both a bridge and a watershed between chapters 2 and 4. As a watershed, it uses Ricœur's hermeneutics to conclude our previous discussion of intrinsic bridging and of the character formation of readers through imaginative encounters with literary works. It does so by linking the reflections of authors like Janzen and Spohn to wider existential debates in contemporary Continental philosophy, which should inspire readers to conceive new models of intrinsic bridging. As a bridge, the balance between Ricœur's hermeneutics of the self and Eco's notion of presupposition should help the reader to better appreciate the theoretical underpinnings of many of the choices made throughout this book.

3.1 Hermeneutical Considerations

Hermeneutics: Preliminaries

In both implicit and explicit bridging processes (see figs. 2.1 and 2.2), the central link concerns the task of interpretation. This task occurs between meditation and implicit appropriation in the implicit channel, and between analysis and explicit appropriation in the public/argumentative explicit channel.

Scripture itself notes the importance and necessity of interpretation. For instance, in Acts 8:30–35, the Lord sends Philip to help an Ethiopian eunuch interpret a passage from Isaiah and in 2 Peter 3:16–17, Christians are warned that some passages in Paul's letters can be easily misunderstood by "the ignorant," implying that formation and community support are necessary to interpret Scripture correctly (*IBC* introduction-A). Interpretation is a complex process, and its success cannot be taken for granted: given the cultural, linguistic, and temporal distance between modern readers and the text, we as interpreters of Bible texts face a significant difficulty. Today, the reader may feel confused by the availability of so many scientific exegetical methods and approaches to assist us in responsible interpretation, on the one hand, and the many voices within Christianity promoting spontaneity and claiming that methods are "unsettling" or "overrated," on the other.

The problem with "spontaneity" is that it can be a chimera. We might end up projecting our problems, our mindset, our psychology onto the text, and force it into our system of prejudices and precomprehensions, rather than liberating its meaning and allowing it to build us and to challenge us. The problem becomes more acute with Scripture, rather than, say, with Shakespeare, since reducing a Shakespearian play to a mouthpiece for our concerns may not be an issue for theological ethics. By contrast, converting God's word into the interpreter's idiosyncratic mouthpiece and making it say what it doesn't really say can seem disrespectful to a believer, if not blasphemous.

Some may object to this critique by noting that traditional Christian interpreters, such as the church fathers, did not use modern exegetical methods. They tended to use Scripture creatively to support their philosophical and theological claims, and from a modern exegetical perspective, their fanciful spiritual readings—and even what they called "literal" readings—often took too many liberties with the text. Theologians have traditionally justified such use of Scripture by the church fathers, claiming that the same Spirit that "inspired" the divine authors also "assisted" their reading, given that the fathers were authoritative voices within their local churches, embedded with others in processes of ecclesial discernment (*IBC* iii-B3-4). That Spirit is still present among us as a church, assisting us, our communities, and our leaders. But spiritual assistance is not a concept to be used carelessly to excuse ignorance, laziness, ethnocentrism, authoritarianism, anachronism, or manipulation of Scripture texts, especially in our context today, which is marked by narcissism, individualism, secularism, and relativism.

Furthermore, it is unfair to assume that premodern readers let their interpretive imaginations run wild based on some patristic commentaries that seem fanciful to the critical modern reader. The church fathers were aware of some of the risks inherent in their search for the "spiritual" sense of Scripture and sought to limit those risks. For instance, Augustine wrote three commentaries on Genesis, moving from the very allegorical *On Genesis: A Refutation of the Manichees* to the more sober *The Literal Meaning of Genesis* later in his life.[1] Augustine dedicated a whole treatise to the topic of responsible interpretation of Scripture, *On Christian Doctrine*, seeking to establish certain ground rules; we have already discussed one of his rules in section 2.2 above. In this text, he claims that "anyone who understands in the Scriptures something other than intended by them is deceived"; these interpreters cannot be accused of lying if they do so innocently, but they need to be corrected.[2]

Augustine's Fundamental Rules for the Responsible Interpretation of Scripture

Augustine was determined to provide guidelines for the responsible interpretation of Scripture. Though he had little regard for Donatist schismatics, in his treatise *On Christian Doctrine* (3.30–37) he recognized the usefulness of a series of hermeneutical rules formulated by a Donatist called Ticonius.

There is a twofold logic undergirding Augustine's treatise as a whole, and his adoption and justification of Ticonius's rules. First, there is an attention to dogmatic coherence, sometimes referred to as the *rule of faith*. Augustine equates "the expositor and teacher of the Divine Scripture" and "the defender of the right faith and the enemy of error" (4.4). "When investigation reveals an uncertainty as to how a locution should be pointed or construed, the rule of faith should be consulted as it is found in the more open place of the Scriptures and in the authority of the Church" (3.2). He uses the example of John 1:1–2 to illustrate how, by shifting punctuation (which is lacking in some of the oldest copies of the original), an Arian heretic might avoid admitting that Jesus is God. Such an interpreter would translate the text: "...(In the beginning was the Word, and the Word was with God, and) God was. The Word, he was in the beginning with God," instead of "...(In the beginning was the Word, and the Word was with God, and) God, was the Word. He was in the beginning with God" (NRSV, amended by author). The addition of punctuation and translation already implies a first level of interpretation.

Second, there is an attention to moral probity, sometimes referred to as the *rule of love*. "Whoever thinks that he understands the divine Scriptures or any part of them so that it does not build the double love of God and of our neighbor does not understand [them] at all" (1.36). Augustine is quite tolerant with the reader who "is deceived in an interpretation which builds up charity, which is the end of the commandments" (1.36). He may have taken a wrong turn but managed to get to the destination all the same. He still needs to be corrected, lest this wandering become habitual, and he is led astray (1.36; see also 1.40). On the other hand, Augustine critiques the interpreter who speaks wisely and eloquently but lives wickedly: though he may benefit many students with his wisdom, "the life of the speaker has greater weight in determining whether he is obediently heard than any grandness of eloquence" (4.27).

Cultural and philosophical movements, especially since the mid-twentieth century, have focused our attention on the individual self, and hence on the reader. Despite the dangers of individualism, these movements have brought about a positive transformation in hermeneutics; they have helped us to look for the effects that literary works have on the reader (pragmatics) and to ask the question, "How does this text speak to me and to my community today?" This question directs us to a more concrete and fruitful appropriation. Past hermeneutics debates focused excessively on (a) trying to get to the original author and their intentions, (b) reconstructing the historical *context* (*Sitz im Leben*) of the communication, or (c) analyzing the code underlying the message. Scholars often avoided focusing on (d) the *recipient* of the message because that same person includes the "me," the exegetical scientist, and they did not want to introduce themselves in the object being analyzed, thus vitiating the neutrality of their observation. In the seventeenth and eighteenth centuries, the dogma of observational neutrality set the standards of scientific practice in the natural sciences, which other sciences attempted to emulate.

Continental philosophers like Dilthey, Husserl, Heidegger, Gadamer, and Ricœur helped us realize that in the "sciences of the spirit" (humanities), there is always some of "me" under the lens of my microscope. Yet, such "contamination" can become a help rather than a hindrance if we can deal with it wisely and aptly, using the specific tools of these sciences. When engaging and analyzing literature, we will always approach texts with our stereotypes and presuppositions. Gadamerian philosophical jargon calls them "preunderstandings" (or "precomprehensions," in some translations), as noted in section 2.2 above. This neutral-sounding neologism is used to avoid the term *prejudices* and its negative connotations, and to indicate that such baggage can be a good thing, if it helps us "comprehend" rather than "judge." Preunderstandings can also act like prejudices, restricting or warping the text and blocking the encounter between our world and that of the text. Gadamer speaks of a "fusion of horizons" to help us picture this encounter. If our preunderstandings are too ingrained and inaccurate, as in the case of racial prejudices or strong and inaccurate stereotypes (see section 2.3), our world and horizon of meaning might crush and absorb those of the text. But if the fusion occurs in a more balanced way and we allow the text to stand on its feet and speak to us with its own voice, our preunderstandings can help us to read and appreciate the text better. In this case, we allow the text and its horizon of meaning to push back against our conscious or unconscious attempts to manipulate it into telling us what we want to hear.

Like a screw or helical coil, upon every turn, good hermeneutics takes us from our world, at the base of the helix, and brings us back to our world at the same point in the circle. But it is actually not the same point since we are now slightly higher up the screw. As we ascend to a different plane, our preunderstandings start to be gently challenged. Thus, in a healthy encounter with the text, the vicious circularity is broken, and our world and our self-understanding shift up, notch by notch. How can we ensure that such a healthy encounter takes place? This book will not only show how exegetical methods can help us do this, but also illustrate different types of distanciation whereby we bring our world closer to that of the text, while recognizing and maintaining a certain distance. The rest of this chapter will deal with the notion of distanciation in hermeneutics.

We who are Christians may be tempted to pretend that we bring no preunderstandings to our reading of Scripture. Yet, *IBC* iii (introduction) notes that "Catholic exegetes approach the biblical text with a pre-understanding which holds closely together modern scientific culture and the religious tradition emanating from Israel and from the early Christian community." Hence, we come to the text with double baggage, tradition and exegetical science, which can both help and hinder the encounter with the text. If we think we don't carry any baggage, we are deluding ourselves. If we try to drop one of these two preunderstandings, we unbalance our hermeneutics. Any attempts at faking "premodern" nonscientific hermeneutics while being embedded in a modern reality will be just that, a bogus exercise.

Furthermore, *IBC* iii-D notes that,

> on the one hand, systematic theology has an influence upon the [preunderstandings] with which exegetes approach biblical texts. On the other hand, exegesis provides the other theological disciplines with data fundamental for their operation. There is, accordingly, a relationship of dialogue

between exegesis and the other branches of theology, granted always a mutual respect for that which is specific to each.

Most of our bridging diagrams in chapter 2 contained arrows pointing right, leading from the analysis or meditation of a text to its appropriation, but keeping this dialectic in mind will help us appreciate that there is also a reverse flow. The *IBC*'s text patently refers to the influence of speculative systematic theology (for instance, the christological and trinitarian dogmas) on exegesis. This book is about practical systematic theology (better known as "fundamental morals" or "fundamental theological ethics"), which, according to most experts, lacks dogmatic definitions as such. This should make our baggage a bit lighter than that of speculative systematic theology. Yet theological science as a whole cannot bracket what faith and tradition teach us about the Trinity, Christ, human nature, and other essential elements of Christian dogma that have some impact on our action and ethical reasoning.

The "World of the Text" and Its Ethically Relevant Dynamics

How can we best understand distanciation in our task of interpreting Scripture and bridging between the Bible and ethics? In his 1996 book *The Moral Vision of the New Testament*, Richard B. Hays lists four major modes of appeal to Scripture for the purpose of doing ethics: theologians often look for (a) rules, (b) principles, (c) paradigms, or (d) elements allowing us to perceive and reconstruct a biblical "symbolic world," which then becomes for us a lens through which we interpret reality. Hays distinguishes, for the sake of analysis, "two different, but correlated, aspects of the New Testament's symbolic world: its representations of the human condition and its depictions of the character of God," in other words, a biblical anthropology and theology.[3] I believe that in all these modes, what scholars seem to be looking for is not simply an effective bridge between Scripture and ethics, but a device for producing standard, precast building blocks for ethical discourse and action.

The World of the Text and the World of the Reader

When Hays speaks of symbolic "world," he seems to refer to a reconstruction of a panbiblical symbolic world using individual Scripture texts. However, the word *world* brings to mind an important concept in contemporary hermeneutics. In Ricœur's jargon, each major text, qua literary work, has its "world" (discussed below). The notion of world in Gadamer and Ricœur is built on the philosophy of Martin Heidegger and other phenomenological thinkers.[4]

Sandra Schneiders aptly summarizes the concept: "World is not a spatial container, or even an environment. It is an ever-changing, moving equilibrium of relationships of which we are the locus and in which, consequently, we participate. No two people inhabit the same world, although our worlds overlap. The interaction between the world of the text and the world of the reader is a dialectic between two complex and never totally objectifiable networks of meaning, and the dialectic affects both."[5]

Given the multinational and multiethnic context in which I teach, I am very sensitive to the inculturation of "Mediterranean" and "Eurocentric" moral notions in other settings (cf. *IBC* iv-B), but I do not conceive the inculturation process as one of crystallization and dissolution of a cultureless moral stuff (like pure sugar derived from sugar cane juice) extracted from Scripture and tradition. Rather, what I propose is simply boiling the biblical sugar cane once to produce dark, viscous, strongly flavored, and combustible "first molasses" (cane syrup) with some precipitated sugar crystals, and asking my students to go ahead and taste that mix and react to the taste. Some processing is required, but only to produce something we can interact with fruitfully. I do not believe that we should be looking for a pure ingredient to make moral "desserts" using Scripture texts, but rather for experiences to train our taste buds and stimulate our creativity as moral *pâtissiers*. If anything, inculturation happens through osmosis once the methods described in this book are put into practice.

In chapter 2, we presented different paradigmatic approaches for bridging Scripture and ethics, namely, those of Janzen and Spohn. I believe that the *processes* they ask their reader to engage in, leading to paradigm construction and to moral character formation, are more important than obtaining the paradigm itself or the accomplishment of a fully developed virtuous moral character (possibly at the end of one's life). Many skirt these processes seeking shortcuts and easy mediations.

For instance, an ethicist may rapidly look up a moral issue in a Bible dictionary or in a book on the moral message of the NT or the OT, or read a brief commentary on a single text, and then derive some useful notions or principles from the work of the "Bible experts" and use those for her ethical reflection, without closely and methodically engaging Scripture in the ways we discuss in this book.

There is great value, however, in undertaking the more time-consuming processes if we want to bridge Scripture and ethics responsibly and fruitfully. These processes yield what I call "ethically relevant dynamic encounter experiences," which we gain by facing and grappling with the "world of the text," not only in a spiritual, personal, or communitarian setting but also in scholarly, critical, and public encounters with Scripture. By the term *dynamic experiences* I refer to encounters with Scripture (and other classics) that feature an interplay between two poles. On the one hand, we have the various institutional and traditional claims of ethical import held in a balanced tension in the text, matching similar claims embedded in the reader's moral preunderstandings. On the other, we find the irruptive forces that risk unbalancing that tension or radically questioning its foundations, both within the text or the biblical corpus, and within the reader. The former pole appeals to the analogical imagination, and the latter beckons to the dialectical imagination. Narratives, for instance, are usually constructed with a background equilibrium of forces and an inciting incident (or catalyst), which unbalances the situation and leads to a climax, after which the plot heads toward an event of resolution or revelation. Other literary genres in Scripture have dynamics of their own. In many cases, the dynamics involve a surprise, which leads the reader to an experience of wonder, shock, or awe. Similarly, on the side of the reader who is standing in front of the narrative, an affective stimulus welling up in the imaginative contemplator, or the argumentative gadfly buzzing inside the critical reader, can be powerful elements that enable an enriching and transformative encounter between the world of the reader and the world of the text.

What ultimately results from that fleeting, but transformative, encounter depends on the reader and the context and modality in which the text is read. Moral agents and theorists might let it shape their moral action and reflection implicitly, as Agatha and Ethel in chapter 2. Alternatively, they might wield scholarly methodological tools to navigate the text and then use elements of the text to construct an explicitly

Scripture-based argument to guide others in spiritual direction, or write a homily, or craft a theological ethics paper for a peer-reviewed journal. The argument might include norms, principles, or virtue paradigms, based on the elements gleaned from the text combined with extrabiblical sources and reasoning that allow Scripture to talk to our world. At the center of it all, however, is the encounter between our world as readers and the world of the text, an encounter that might be facilitated or hindered using an exegetical method. This dynamic encounter makes things happen within us.

It is by lingering in the world of the text, letting its tensions and dynamics push us and pull us in various directions, inspiring imitation (analogy) at times, and rejection (dialectics) at others, that we manage to build the most fruitful bridge between Scripture and ethics. Such an approach may unsettle us at first since it may seem random or piecemeal. It doesn't lead to a grand theory or overarching pattern allowing the whole canon of Scripture to speak on some moral issue with one single or dominant voice. It is at the level of moral theology that grand generalizations can be made, after factoring in reflections from many nonscriptural sources, and not on the level of the analysis of single Scripture texts and corpuses. We should be wary today of books that seek to present the "moral message of the New Testament" (or some OT/NT corpus), though they have proven useful in the twentieth century to jump start a dialogue between modern exegesis and ethics. Rather, many stimuli for moral thinking can be provided by the literary worlds of the NT and OT to those who spend time with the texts, and these stimuli can be used to explore a particular topic and build a Scripture-nourished moral message for Christianity and humankind in the twenty-first century on that topic.

The Interplay between Ideology and Utopia

In this book, we are looking for elements that enable ethically relevant dynamic encounters between the reader and the text. There are currents, tensions, and moving parts in the text that confirm, on one hand, and challenge, on the other, the beliefs of the implied reader, that is, the ideal reader whom the text or corpus is seeking to address. In a fruitful dynamic encounter, the text's elements should similarly confirm and challenge the real reader's sense of reality and how things ought to be. In this book we have chosen a sociopolitical issue—our relationship with the stranger—to illustrate this interplay between the confirming and the challenging pole of such encounters; hence a brief reference to Ricœur's notions of ideology and utopia should prove helpful.[6]

Any debate on sociopolitical issues involves an interplay between positions that seek to confirm the current state of affairs, and others that seek to challenge it. As listeners in such debates, assuming that we are not completely polarized and that both sides provide rhetorically effective arguments, our sympathies and convictions move us between the confirming and the challenging position, between ideology and utopia. Ideology can be understood as a system of discourses and images that seek to defend and legitimize reality as we know it (that is, the status quo, tradition, established authority), shielding it from subversion, irrational and unnecessary transformation, volatility, and chimeric novelty.[7] It may concede that some improvements could be necessary over time, but claims the current system already caters to gradual amelioration. Utopia is a similar but opposite system of discourses and images seeking to question, delegitimize or upend the status quo, deeming it obsolete, inadequate, corrupt, or simply evil, and seeking to rebuild social reality from scratch and in one go, not via incremental changes.[8]

Both ideology and utopia can become pathological and violent in their extremism, seeing one another as an existential threat. However, when kept within certain limits, the tension between the two can be healthy, and these two poles of sociopolitical discourse have complementary roles. Healthy ideology allows valuable events and realities to be integrated ritually and institutionally into the collective memory, while healthy utopia keeps the horizon of our hopes and possibilities from collapsing, cynically, onto the horizon of our present givenness. Likewise, successive, fruitful encounters with Scripture can serve at times to legitimize and at times to delegitimize aspects of our view of reality. Such encounters, which can also be scholarly, may be much more interesting for the moral agent and the theological ethicist than ones that simply allow us to construct abstract and static paradigms, norms, symbolic worlds, or principles on the basis of Scripture.

3.2 Paul Ricœur's Notion of the "World of the Text"

Unmediated Truth or Method-Induced Distortion? The Literary Classic as a Third Option to Encounter Reality Authentically

In her book *The Revelatory Text*, biblical scholar Sandra Schnieders claims that Ricœur is the most important figure in a crucial contemporary discussion on the mediated quality of human understanding and on the importance of language and texts in such mediation.[9]

To better appreciate this, in the following paragraphs we engage with an important article in English published by Ricœur in 1973. The article describes a process by which a discourse—pronounced by a speaker or conceived by an author—distances itself from the "world of the author" or "world behind the text," to become a literary work with its own world, the "world of the text," that is available to be encountered by the reader and her world.[10] In this article, Ricœur talks mainly about narrative fiction and poetry, and we should exercise care when applying his claims to Scripture.

The article opens by presenting to the reader an unpalatable alternative found in Gadamer's *Truth and Method*. We can seek truth using a limited and risky *unmediated grasp of reality*, that is, without using a method that objectifies reality and alienates the observer from what is observed. Or we can opt for a *mediated* grasp of reality and use a method. But in this second case, we may end up without the truth, holding a chimera or a biased, partial rendering of reality that has been warped and distorted in the process of being captured by our methodological tools. If you give Warren a ruler, Carmen a thermometer, and Rani a watch, teach them how to use them and send them out to observe a giraffe, each will come back with different and partial understandings of the giraffe, convinced that their understanding is the correct one, since they observed the method rigorously.

This debate raises a key question: Is access to biblical moral truth only something that happens spontaneously, in an ineffable encounter, without the use of methodological tools, and then somehow shapes our thoughts and actions in implicit ways, just as in the case of the Implicit-Channel Actor and Theorist in chapter 2? Or can we also use a method to explicitly bridge Scripture and ethics, one that does not objectify Scripture to the extent of rendering its deeper truth inaccessible?

To be sure, we cannot fully comprehend the reality of the author of the "world behind the text," neither by grasping its truth intimately through "participation by belonging," nor through the use of a method that implies objectification and "alienating distanciation" and ultimately warps our access. However, Ricœur rejects Gadamer's dilemma by claiming that through the medium of a literary work we can more fully come to know reality, a reality that is beyond that of the original author and his world. A text is not a giraffe; it is the human experience of other Warrens, Carmens, and Ranis packaged in a way that our three friends can open and experience, using a wide range of instruments already present within themselves.

I like to compare the literary classic, as understood by Ricœur, to a tinted, semitransparent mirror in dim lighting, like the French window in front of me, reflecting my face and allowing me to enjoy the Valletta night skyline while I write this page.[11] The mirror/window is an object that I could observe by itself using various types of microscopes, to analyze the vitreous solid and aluminum film and understand how it was made; this is analogous to using a literary text to reconstruct the world of the author and her intention (the "world behind [embedded in] the text"). However, such a mirror is much more useful and powerful as a medium that serves both as a window into reality as a whole (the Valletta skyline) and as a mirror onto which I may project my reality, set against the wider reality beyond the mirror. A literary work can do the same, reflecting my world and transforming it by setting it against a larger world seen through the text. What I see is already a fusion of two things: the "I" and the "world out there" as I understand them (that is, my world as a reader, the "world in front of the text") and the "me" and "world out there" as the text wants me to see them (the "world of the text").

I cannot disentangle myself and my way of seeing reality from the text, since, in Ricœur's view, attempts to know reality in an unmediated way or using a totally objective and neutral scientific method result in the Gadamerian dilemma. Yet I have my own consistency and can know reality (mine and that outside me) through other texts and possibly through nonliterary means. Like the mirror, the "world of the text" has its own consistency; sitting where I am sitting, anyone can see the same section of the Valletta night skyline, framed and tinted by the window just like I am seeing it. The text can show its world to many other people, and what I see does not entirely depend on me. Furthermore, I would need to see through many similar French windows to get a 360-degree view of the Valletta skyline, just like I would need to read many Scripture books, together with other literary classics, to get a better picture of myself and the reality beyond me.

What is not fully captured in this analogy is the fact that literary works can be analyzed to better allow us to see their world and ours, but such analysis (typical of explicit bridging to ethics) should not be overly concerned with "the world behind (embedded in) the text," the glass and aluminum particles in our analogy. Texts allow such analysis precisely by taking four steps away from the original author or oral communicator. This distanciation is what gives readers a structure they can analyze using literary tools and a world they can encounter existentially, but that also makes objectification or unmediated access harder or more distorted. Let us follow these four steps as presented by Ricœur in his article: language to discourse, discourse to structured work (opus), opus to "world of the work," and "world of the work" to self-understanding.[12] The texts Ricœur is referring to in this article are mainly literary works, so by "world of the text" he means "world of the [literary] work," though this latter expression may sound less intuitive and more cumbersome and is not used consistently by the French philosopher.

Step 1: Language → Discourse[13]

Ricœur starts by distinguishing between language and discourse. Language is a *code* (made of phonological and lexical signs), while discourse "happens" as an *event* that is understood by some of its participants as a *meaningful message* (made of sentences). As an event, discourse has (a) a footing in time, (b) a communicator, (c) a recipient, and (d) a reference in the world it claims to describe—features that language, as code, does not possess. As a meaningful message, discourse is a locution, but the *locutionary* act (saying "x," for example, "Open that door!") may imply an *illocutionary* force (what we do *by* saying "x," that is, we order John to open the door behind him) and sometimes even a *perlocutionary* one (what we do *by the fact* of saying "x," that is, we annoy John because he feels we are being bossy).

Step 2: Discourse ⟶ Opus (Structured Work)[14]

Many of the above features of discourse may be lost when it is converted into a text that becomes part of a structured work; hence an important dimension of distancing is that between discourse and work. When a text grows to become longer than a single sentence, and takes the shape of a structured work, it takes on a certain autonomy in relation to its author. Its meaning is determined by three further features: (a) its *composition* (a work is composed of a finite group of sentences that constitute a *composite whole*, which shapes the meaning of its parts: the meaning of the work is not just the meaning of the sentences), (b) the *literary genre* (a mechanism that codifies discourse as opus), and (c) the individual *style* that colors that particular work.

The style of written works maintains a link to their authors and their subjectivity even when they are long dead or otherwise unknown. It does not, however, allow us to penetrate the psychology of historical authors and unearth their deepest intentionality or commune with their creative "genius," as Romanticist or Diltheyian hermeneutics sought to do and believed possible. Yet, it allows us to see a literary work as something more personal than what European structuralism[15] reduced it to: an arrangement of precast literary building blocks fitted together according to the rules of a given genre.

Step 3: Opus ⟶ World of the Work[16]

A further level of distancing is that between the work itself, which can be one of pure fiction, and the world that it presents to its reader, which can be real in a powerful sense. A written work is peculiar; it is not just an oral work transcribed symbolically and fixed on a material medium. Writing involves a kind of objectification, or distanciation, whereby a message is detached from the psychological and sociological conditions of the original writer and from intended first readers and is given the freedom to be decontextualized and recontextualized in new situations. This peculiarity of texts, especially works of narrative fiction and poetry, allows us to overcome the Diltheyan understanding/ explaining dilemma, the Gadamerian truth/method dilemma, or the need to choose between Romanticist hermeneutics and structuralism.

To be sure, the physical, temporal, and sociological or psychological distance between the original communicator and the new recipients affects the message's *reference*, which is no longer ostensive, since it cannot be simply pointed to or discovered using the common historical situation of the interlocutors. Yet, according to Ricœur, the external *reference* is not simply reduced to an idealized object, purely immanent to the text, what Gottlob Frege would call the *sense*.[17] Despite its inherent distanciation from the original context, a written work points to something outside itself. Even in fantasy or science fiction, where the authors themselves seek to disguise any first-order reference that might have inspired them, the text finds a way to connect with external reality through a second-order reference. Just think of how the eternal human questions we are concerned with in this book—identity, hospitality, strangerhood, inclusion, exclusion, and so forth—feature in many folk tales and science fiction stories.

Fiction hence introduces a new level of distanciation where reality is distanced from itself via a counterfactual literary work, which then could reveal the most profound essence or sense of that reality by mimicking it and re-imagining it. This new reality can metamorphose everyday reality by shaping the actions of the reader.

Step 4: World of the Work → Self-Understanding[18]

Ricœur rejects the Romanticist notion of interpretation (a quest for the intention of the author or for access to his "genius" and his psychology), as well as the structuralist one (an operation whereby a text's constitutive structures are dismantled and classified). Inspired by Martin Heidegger's *Being and Time*, Ricœur claims that "to interpret is to explicate the type of being-in-the-world unfolded *in front of* the text,"[19] rather than simply digging *within it* to identify and dismantle structures, or *behind it* to get to the psyche of the author. He proposes that we use classic literary works, especially narrative and poetic ones, to understand neither "what the author really meant," nor "how the building blocks fit together," but rather "how our ownmost possibilities—those which are our very own as humans, in the most authentic manner—are projected onto the text."

In this process, we understand and touch the truth, not of something outside us (such as the original reference of the text) but of our very selves. Given the clearly Heideggerian spirit of this section of the article, and Ricœur's appreciation of the social and institutional dimensions of the moral life (see chapter 1, Allegory 1), there is no hint of individualism or solipsism here. For Heidegger, we are beings who exist constitutively *with* others (*Mitsein*), embedded in a given reality (*In-der-Welt-sein, Dasein*), and the basis of such an embedded existence is care or concern (*Sorge*) for what is beyond our givenness. Understanding ourselves, understanding the world, and understanding the text are all enmeshed, given the conception of knowledge assumed by these authors (known as phenomenological intentionality). The analogy of the semi-transparent mirror, which allows us to see ourselves, the world, and the glass all at once, can help us visualize all this.

In conclusion, according to Ricœur, "we understand ourselves only by the long detour of the signs of humanity deposited in cultural works. What would we know of love and hate, of moral feelings, and, in general, of what we call the self if these had not been brought to language and articulated by literature?"[20] This way of understanding the impact of the text on the reader and his transformation by the "world of the text" allows the French philosopher to rethink the classical notions of appropriation (*Aneignung*) and application (*Anwendung*) of literary works in traditional hermeneutics. What we appropriate is not, according to Ricœur, the hidden intention of the author, but a proposed world, the "world of the work," which allows us to interpret and understand our reality imaginatively and transform it.

3.3 Reaching beyond Ricœur's Notion of Distanciation

Ricœur's conception of texts and structured works—as media that allow a distanciation from reality without falling into an alienating objectification—is useful. His discussion of the peculiar nature of texts and literary works helps us understand why both implicit and explicit links are possible when bridging Scripture and ethics, and why both meditation and analysis are possible when approaching a biblical text.

However, Ricœur's hermeneutics have raised many debates when applied to Scripture, which is not a simple work of fictional narrative or fanciful poetry. Using our semitransparent mirror metaphor above, we recognize the Bible's great value as a literary work that mirrors our reality and opens a window onto one beyond ours. But is the biblical text really as transparent and reflective as my French window? Can we truly manage or afford to stop seeing in Scripture the referents it presents as historically real, and the meanings which it proposes as nonmetaphorical? Two major issues come to the fore in this debate. First, is the distance that Ricœur's theory places between literary works and the history and culture that generated them excessive for biblical hermeneutics? Second, does his theory link the work's meaning and value too closely to the existential experiences of its readers in front of the text?

The Bible's Unbreakable Bond to Its Sources

Some authors, when appraising Ricœurian hermeneutics, believe that if we bracket historical referents and author's intentions, all interpretations become valid, as long as they reveal something to us of ourselves. The French philosopher would probably deny this, since the words and genre of the work are what they are, and the style bears the mark of the author. These elements, which are relatively fixed for the reader, place certain limits on what the imagination can honestly and reasonably do with such a text. A more fundamental objection, however, concerns the possibility of truly bracketing historical referents. In the case of high-fantasy literary works such J.R.R. Tolkien's *The Lord of the Rings*, it is quite clear how the various steps of distanciation described by Ricœur can create an impressively consistent and original "world of the text." But even here, readers who have no concept of British identity, medieval Europe, nineteenth-century Western industrialization and militarization, wizardry, Christianity, and Germanic and Norse legend would be hindered in making sense of the trilogy by an inability to understand many of the words of the English text. They would need, at least, to consult other sources outside the book that enable them to link the words in the book to the historical referents in the "real" world at which they hint. The text of the Bible, which contains fictional elements but is not a work of high fantasy, is even harder to extricate from its cultural and historical setting, despite the distanciation process described above. Single words in a language can contain a universe of meaning, part of which is culturally and historically rooted; for instance, the first European missionaries in Latin America and Asia struggled to translate biblical words like *God*, despite their rigorous theological training. Weary of disconnecting the term from Western European theological history, they often ended up using phonetic simulations for the Latin *Deus*.[21]

Therefore, the main limitation in applying Ricœur's approach to Scripture as the sole or primary hermeneutical framework is that he seems to lack, at least in the article we have analyzed, a robust notion of *presupposition* (*presupposizione*). In his important 1979 book *Lector in Fabula*, Umberto Eco uses this word as an umbrella term that includes various phenomena in logic, semiotics, semantics, and pragmatics, such as entailments and implicature.[22] While Gadamerian *preunderstanding* is the baggage we bring with us when approaching a text, often unconsciously, *presupposition* here indicates what the author is asking us to bring with us, or to fetch if we haven't brought it along.

Eco starts with Charles S. Peirce's discussion on the act of *defining* |lithium|, which can become a very "pragmatic" affair and include a series of instructions and operations by which one can produce lithium from a mineral and do things with the metal. He concludes that each *sememe* (linguistic element of meaning, such as |lithium|) encapsulates a virtual text linking it to a potentially infinite web of meanings, which we limit to a finite encyclopedia of meanings by *defining* that sememe. Hence, definitions and the encyclopedic dictionary systems that contain them are not closed and complete systems as they may seem at first glance; they are not *simple* dictionary systems.[23] To better understand Eco's point let us consider a pocket dictionary: Here simple words in modern English are defined using other simple words from the same system, giving the impression that languages and texts are closed systems pointing only to themselves, and not to a "real" world beyond them (that of the author or that of the reader). But in the twenty-volume *Oxford English Dictionary*, entries are connected to words in other languages, the transformation of their form and meaning over time is explained, and references to material artifacts outside the dictionary are used in the process of defining. An online encyclopedia goes even further, linking words to huge bodies of knowledge, eventually including the whole of the World Wide Web and much more.

Without a vast network of cultural, pictorial, artefactual, and linguistic mediations (not merely a single "Rosetta Stone") linking our world with that of the Fertile Crescent, we would never be able to make sense of hieroglyphic inscriptions and cuneiform tablets. In the case of the Bible, that network is immense. We do not stand in front of biblical texts as though they were isolated literary works disconnected from us and from the Mediterranean world that generated them; rather, we bathe in the same sea in which they have always bathed, even though our shores may seem far apart.

Given the encyclopedia of meanings attached to each sememe, the reader needs to cooperate with the text to make it express something.

He needs to select and activate what is "presupposed" in the text—the things left unsaid, or entailed, or implied, or hinted at, or previously mentioned in some other part of the work. Texts are lazy presuppositional devices that need to be kickstarted and pedaled along by the reader. Eco explains how a good writer strategically plans the cooperation of the reader, assuming that her model reader will possess the knowledge necessary to understand her text and providing hints to an unintended or ignorant reader who does not possess that knowledge that this text was not written for him and that he should do some extra work to inform himself better or assume a certain mindset if he desires to better understand the text.[24] The author thus burdens the reader with "philological duties."[25]

It is interesting to note the implications of this reflection today in the age of Big Data and neural networks. We can understand whether the adjective *wicked* in an English sentence means "very evil" (Standard English usage) or "very good" (slang) because we can roughly place that sentence in a historical, social, and geographical context. Probably, an artificial intelligence like Google Translate will eventually figure out the intended meaning if you add enough text beyond a single sentence. Using massive archives of real historical texts, and not just a dictionary system, such an artificial intelligence will estimate if the text is more similar to an Oxonian ethics manual from the 1950s or to an informal exchange among Londoners in 1985, and interpret it accordingly. Similarly, at the level of the literary opus, a work of irony or sarcasm will be taken to mean the contrary of what it was written to communicate by a reader without any historical background to help her detect that she must subvert the immediate meanings of the words to understand it "properly."

A hard-core Ricœurian might frown at this word, *properly*, but we care about reading things "properly," striving to fit into the shoes of the implied reader. While harboring few illusions that we might be able to reconstruct the psyche, genius, or full-blown intention of the author when reading Scripture or any important literature, as readers we care about more than just having an enriching existential experience in front of the text. If we didn't, we might just as well spend our time reading books composed by an artificial intelligence like GPT-3. We hope that our reading experience has some anchoring, at least minimal, to the reality behind the text.

We care about great books that can teach us all about "love and hate [and] moral feelings [and] the self,"[26] not just because they have an air of antiquity or fame that creates hype around them and entices us to read them to appear "learned" to our peers, but also because we believe they have something to teach about these matters that is not just a projection of our world. Of course, what we learn comes from an encounter with the "world of the work," made possible by the style, genre, and composition. Moreover, these elements are right there, in the text itself, not in the decomposing brain of some deceased writer. Yet, some part of our ability to appreciate these elements comes from a thread of presupposition linking us to the "world behind the work" belonging to the original writer and intended recipients. This thread passes through a community of interpreters bound through history, and further empowered in modernity with sophisticated archeological, historical, and linguistic tools.

Distancing the Bible from the Self

A second question that Ricœur's approach raises concerns his Heideggerian claim that interpreting a text (such as Scripture) is mainly a question of encountering its world for the purpose of projecting our possible selves onto it, to ultimately understand ourselves. This claim takes the previous discussion a step further: not only does the meaning of the text appear when we stand in front of it, independently of its history and origin, but, furthermore, the meaning we should be primarily concerned with is the self-understanding we gain when exposed to the text. As noted above, Ricœur is talking mainly about fiction and poetry and his claim does not promote individualism or narcissism, but rather reacts against the impersonal and reifying approaches to hermeneutics typical of the generations which preceded his. However, the contemporary reader might exaggerate the "hermeneutics of the self" element in Ricœur and reduce the "hermeneutics of the text" to something purely instrumental in the quest for self-understanding. He might end up considering all Scripture as fantasy literature.

All this indicates that Ricœurian hermeneutics should be used critically in our dealings with Scripture and needs some rebalancing in our cultural context. Critics such as Tom Deidun have a point when he writes, "It is one thing to say that there is no interpretation without some involvement of the interpreter, and quite another to make the interpreter's involvement a methodological imperative."[27] We appreciate the richness that the hermeneutics of the self in Ricœur's fourth step of distanciation brings to implicit bridging between Scripture and ethics. However, our claim in this book is that an argumentative and rigorous encounter with the world of the work and its dynamics is possible and can set us thinking critically and systematically, as *communities* of readers and thinkers, about current moral issues. To be sure, the reader in the fourth step might well be a collective reader, but the rhetorical device used in Ricœur's article—starting with Gadamer's apparently insoluble truth/method dilemma and then regaling us with a single, brilliant solution after a laborious thought process—seems to discourage us from searching for rigorous, falsifiable, and public methods of enquiry that can give us some authentic access to the truth.

The explicit bridging between Scripture and ethics that I propose in the following chapters is mediated by a variety of methods, in the hope that they can reinforce one another and the existential experiences of the moral actor and theorist as readers and offer us an authentic access to moral truth. Special attention is given to the literary modes of interpretation that were developed in response to hermeneutical issues raised by Gadamer, Ricœur, and Anglo-American New Criticism, while recognizing the great value of historical and critical exegetical methods. Bridging that is mediated by such a variety of methods—and is aware of their tendency to distort their object of inquiry to make it fit the method—is not necessarily an alienating objectification of the original work, and a corruption of its truth, as we hope to demonstrate in the second part of this book. Rather, it helps us fend off the opposite risk, that of creating an *incestual fusional bond* (to use imagery from the psychology of Jacques Lacan[28]) with a text written in antiquity, projecting our world onto it in such a way that all otherness is voided and its possible chastising and subverting influence on our world is neutered.

4

BRIDGING SCRIPTURE
AND ETHICS EXPLICITLY

This chapter introduces readers to the forms that explicit, scholarly, argumentative, and public uses of Scripture in ethics debates can take, as we continue to probe the distinction between implicit and explicit bridging introduced in chapter 2. We begin with a discourse on reasonable hope, to help readers appreciate why explicit uses of Scripture are necessary within the realm of scholarly theology, and why they should also feature in important documents on moral issues produced by church leaders. Even in pluralistic democracies, our hope as Christians pushes us to find ways of engaging in an intellectually honest public use of Scripture that is respectful of nonbelievers who do not see the Christian Bible as normative. The reflection on hope leads to a short history of modern exegesis that will allow readers to situate some of the major debates on the use of Scripture in ethics chronologically.

The systematic part of the chapter presents three approaches that authors have adopted in recent years to reflect on explicit bridging between Scripture and ethics. Readers will first learn how, by building taxonomies, we can distinguish different ways ethicists use the Bible and Scripture scholarship to engage moral issues. While comparing different bridging styles, readers may come to adopt or adapt one for themselves, building on the best practices found in the works of renowned schools or scholars.

In addition, readers will learn to detect misuse of Scripture in ethics by exploring how instrumentalization, legalism, fundamentalism, and secularism can warp our access to the Bible. They will also be introduced to the constructive approach that we use in this book by learning a series of rules informing this approach. This chapter concludes the series of epistemological debates launched in chapter 2, and hence the first part of this book.

4.1 Ethics, Hope, and the "Heart"

The Second Vatican Council's Dogmatic Constitution on Divine Revelation, *Dei Verbum*, claims that "the study of the sacred page is, as it were, the soul of sacred theology" (24). This claim is all too often truncated and misquoted, omitting the incidental "as it were" (*veluti*), which expresses an uneasiness with the soul metaphor, and the original subject, "study." Asserting that "the Bible is the soul of theology" gives the false impression of an unmediated bridging, as though the council fathers thought theology might be animated or ensouled by a simple exposure to the texts and paradigms of virtue within Scripture, rather than a rigorous, methodological study of these texts and paradigms. *Optatam Totius*, the Council's text on priestly formation, repeats the phrase almost word for word, substituting "study of the Sacred Page" with "study of Sacred Scripture," and then insists that moral theology ought to be "nourished more on the teaching [doctrine[1]] of the Bible" (16).

The emphasis on explicit, scholarly mediations is perfectly clear, and this indicates that our bridging work cannot limit itself to personal, intimate, communitarian, and implicit appropriation of Scripture. The soul metaphor evokes, on one hand, pervasiveness, and, on the other hand, intimacy and invisibility. The council fathers' uneasiness probably has to do with the latter. The study of Scripture should be pervasive in our theology but not invisible or confined to the private sphere of personal appropriation and small group devotion; rather, a scholarly approach is often warranted. Let us briefly turn to a Scripture text that can help us better understand the point being made by Vatican Council II.

"Accounting for the Hope That Is in You"

"Always be ready to make your defense to anyone who demands from you an accounting for the hope that is in you; yet do it with gentleness and reverence" (1 Pet 3:15–16).

TABLE 4.1: 1 PETER 3:15–16: TEXTUAL CRITICISM TESTS	
Test 1 (Use the Apparatus of a Critical Edition or the Notes of a Good Study Bible)[2]	
Is the original text clear and grammatically consistent?	✓
Are there textual differences among the major sources that could raise serious doubts on the meaning?	✗
Test 2 (Compare Various Translations, Possibly in Different Languages)	
Do most other translations provide a text similar in meaning to the one we are working with?	✓

At one end of this exhortation, the issue is our hope and what we do with it. Hope is an important concept in fundamental theology as well as a key theological virtue that shines brightly in some of the great Christian martyrs, but it may also be present as a dimmer light in the actions of people who consistently act justly, even if they consider themselves agnostics or nonbelievers. For people who have had to face moral bad luck for a long time,[3] it can be nearly impossible to get out of bed in the morning without latching onto some underlying hope. Hope is the "fuel" of ethical action; even Immanuel Kant famously invites us to reflect on "what we *may permit* ourselves to hope."[4]

At the other end of Peter's text is the question of "making our defense." Having, deep down in our hearts, good reasons to hope and to let that hope fuel our just actions is a great thing, but it is not enough. Peter invites us to be ready to give an accounting for that hope that is not triumphalist, ostentatious, or identitarian to anyone who demands it from us, not aggressively or defensively, but "with gentleness and reverence," both for the other person and for that delicate hope itself. Ethics is ultimately a public matter, one of modest but rigorous debate and argument. Believing something is right and just, "simply because my heart tells me so," could be dangerous, since "heart" can mean so many things. To be sure, moral conscience, what Scripture often calls "the heart" or our "visceral innards," is a sacred thing, and we need to listen to a conscience that is clear and reasonably certain of what it deems prohibited or mandatory. But we also need to test it to see whether it is vincible or not, that is, whether after serious dialogue with others, our conscience will remain *con-vinced* of its moral appraisal of what should be done or avoided, or whether it can be easily won over by other people's honest and profound counterarguments.

We can be sure we are actually dealing with our moral conscience—and not with some superego, rationalization, intellectualization process, or delusional thinking—only when we expose the dictates of our conscience (and of our intimate moral discernment practices) to the test of public exposure and to explicit interrogation regarding the cogency of the argumentation provided and the authority of the sources adduced in our judgment.

All this brings us to the topic of the current chapter. This public, explicit, and argumentative dimension of ethics implies that Christians—and other moral agents who claim that the Christian Bible is a major source inspiring their rational moral action and thought—will want, at some point, to bring Scripture into this dimension of ethics. As noted in the previous two chapters, we are often able to provide convincing warrant justifying our hope and our action without explicitly mentioning Scripture. But Scripture is an important normative source for Christians, and we cannot and should not always bracket or hide this source behind secular philosophical argumentation. Let us recall the basic tripartite scheme proposed in chapter 2 for bridging Scripture and ethics explicitly:

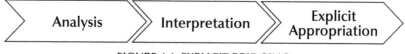

Analysis ⟩ Interpretation ⟩ Explicit Appropriation

FIGURE 4.1: EXPLICIT BRIDGING

Peter's text evokes the adversarial kind of argumentation typical of a courtroom; this challenging locus takes us out of the protected space of private and communal prayer and personal discernment, making us vulnerable at times. Yet herein lies the power and richness of explicit, public, argumentative bridging between Scripture and ethics. In this encounter with true otherness—something that is not just a "clone" of ourselves, like the "otherness" created by social media "friendship bubbles"[5]—our understanding of why we do what we do becomes more robust. We learn from the beliefs and practices of people with different faiths and reasons for hope, and we spread hope and build a wider community of hope. Such a community then convinces us and motivates us further to do what is right consistently and to develop best practices to habituate the community's members to act justly in a stable manner (training in virtue).

For centuries, many Protestant theologians felt that linking ethics (just and virtuous action) to hope could lead to a form of Pelagianism, and therefore relegated ethics to the realm of philosophy, separating it from the "authentic" theological disciplines that received constant biblical nourishment. In the United States in the twentieth century, authors like James Gustafson and many of the Protestant members of the Society of Christian Ethics worked hard to overcome this fear and rehabilitate theological ethics within their churches and institutions. To be sure, most faithful and mature Christians are aware that the follower of Jesus does not act justly so as to buy his ticket into heaven and to hold up her actions to claim an entitlement that supposedly a fair God cannot fail to honor without going against God's own just nature. Business transactions rely on some form of immanent hope in the other party's bona fides, and their ability to deliver what was promised, but our relationship with God is not a business transaction. Theological hope acts in far more profound and delicate ways than a *do ut des* ("I give that you might give") exchange. Mature Christian moral agents act justly because (a) they recognize that they are daughters and sons of a holy Father who acts in an accomplished and wholehearted manner, and desire to act like their Father (Matt 5:48; 1 Pet 1:15–16), (b) they believe that acting so is in "obedience to the Lord's command" (1 Peter 1:14), and (c) they seek to give witness by their actions to their hope in God's redeeming and sanctifying love, confident that such hope can be contagious and can allow them, together with all people of good will, to make God's reign already inchoately manifest in history.

Some Major Concerns among Catholics

As a Catholic, I appreciate Protestant contributions to theological ethics since most authors are serious in wanting to bring Scripture into current debates. This makes sense given that their theological traditions have taught them to use the Bible as a major source for theological knowledge. When Catholic theologians discuss moral issues, they are often more comfortable quoting medieval authors like Aquinas, who used ethical concepts from antiquity—mainly those of natural law, virtue, and conscience—to reframe, build upon, and expand the fragmentary or nonsystematic elements of ethical thought found in Scripture and in the church fathers. Of course, the fathers based their reflections on Scripture, though often read through a Platonic, Stoic, or Neoplatonic lens, so at the end of the day, much of Catholic moral thought is directly or indirectly influenced by Scripture. The problem is that over the centuries many moral discussions in Catholic theological ethics have taken on a life of their own. Thus, their roots in biblical, patristic, and scholastic texts are hard to trace underneath the Salamanca-school interpretations of Aquinas, the post-Tridentine manuals' presentation of Salamanca-school authors,[6] nineteenth- and twentieth-century neo-Scholasticism, and post–Vatican II texts full of references to contemporary Continental and analytical philosophical schools.

Catholics fear that the Bible can easily be misinterpreted if not read holistically as a complex and self-correcting worldview and in the company of other believers rooted within a church tradition, as handed down through a hierarchical interpretive authority. Reading single biblical texts alone, taking them out of context, approaching them with no hermeneutical tools, no authoritative guidance, and no community to challenge or fine-tune our reading, and then proceeding to act "as if inspired by the Bible" can lead to serious immoral actions.

One extreme example of such reading is the case of Joseph Kony and the Lord's Resistance Army, active in Uganda and central African countries since 1987, and responsible for many atrocities and acts of terrorism supposedly committed in an effort to create a theocracy based on respect for biblical ethics. A less extreme form of Christian biblical fundamentalism was that which shaped the belief, common among some Christian supporters of apartheid in South Africa, that just like the Canaanites in the Bible, the autochthonous "black" peoples of Africa were culturally and racially inferior and needed to be conquered and subdued by the white "chosen people of God."[7] Another example from within a Catholic context is that of the Dominican friar Girolamo Savonarola, whose religious and popular leadership shaped many of the policies of the Republic of Florence that existed between November 1494 and May 1498. Savonarola sought to transform Florence into a New Jerusalem and has been accused of shaping an intolerant theocratic regime driven by young zealots and vigilantes who went around "cleansing the city from vice." He has also been praised for his fight against corruption and social injustice. The autocracy implied in the policies he promoted was probably not much worse than the despotism of the former Medici rulers of Florence, but his literalist and hence problematic use of Scripture to sustain autocracy is what history has remembered of this political experiment.[8]

Catholic scholars' concern over unmediated and, especially, fundamentalist use of Scripture to guide action rests on two key points. Some biblical passages present actions and behaviors that most people today (even Christians) deem immoral as normal or even praiseworthy. Other passages denounce actions and behaviors that we would deem neutral or even good. Moreover, what may have been the best course of action in an agrarian subsistence economy two thousand years ago may be completely ineffective or actually harmful if mimicked mindlessly in our contemporary social context. The PBC claims that fundamentalism "invites people to a kind of intellectual suicide. It injects into life a false certitude, for it unwittingly confuses the divine substance of the biblical message with what are in fact its human limitations" (*IBC* i-F).

On one hand, in the absence of a respected authority able to reconcile such interpretations or declare certain positions as unacceptable, conflicting interpretations lead to another problem: divisions within the church, and hence schisms. On the other hand, this fear of misinterpretations and schisms incurs the risk of reducing ethical debates in Catholic theological ethics to discussions about "natural law," "virtue," and "conscience," with no direct nourishment from Scripture. Scripture becomes purely decorative when theologians quote it as window dressing and then move on to the "real" ethical debate, cherry-picking biblical quotes to prove their point without seriously engaging Scripture on the matter.

The Modernist Crisis and a New Openness to Scripture

In light of this background, it is not surprising that the application of critical and historical approaches to the study of Scripture, especially during the nineteenth and early twentieth century, led to a crisis. The crisis was exacerbated by the fact that some authors who were daring enough to challenge traditional readings of Scripture passages often did not limit themselves to the field of exegesis. They also dared to propose iconoclastic moral and political ideas favoring "liberal" human rights doctrines and "socialist" social reform programs, thereby challenging the political and economic status quo. Within Protestantism, the fundamentalist movement was born among conservative Presbyterian theologians at Princeton Theological Seminary and then spread to many denominations. The movement reacted vigorously against liberal theology and historical criticism as an exegetical method, insisting on the strict adherence to five "fundamental" tenets of faith.

The Catholic Church also reacted strongly to the ideas of authors like Alfred Loisy, George Tyrrell, and Ernesto Buonaiuti, all of whom defended historical and critical approaches in the exegesis of Christian sources and the idea of the development of Christian doctrine. Church authorities were fearful that they would scandalize the faithful and provoke social strife. The Roman curia labeled and condemned their ideas as "modernism" and hunted down authors believed to harbor modernist ideas, while encouraging academics, clergy, seminarians, and educated laypersons to report any suspicious-sounding authors, preachers, or lecturers. Meanwhile, in places like Tübingen (considered the most prestigious university in Germany for theological studies, at least until the 1960s), Protestant theologians felt free to experiment with modern exegetical methods, while Catholics observed and quietly supported their efforts. Slowly, after several decades, fear of modernism began to subside and in 1943, Pope Pius XII published an encyclical letter, *Divino Afflante Spiritu*, allowing the use of historical criticism within Catholicism. After experiencing the horrors unleased by unchecked right- and left-wing totalitarian regimes in Europe during the first half of the twentieth century, the Holy See also warmed to the idea of "liberal" human rights (hitherto seen as a corollary of modernism), and a list of fundamental freedoms was officially incorporated in Catholic theological ethics with the publication of Pope John XXIII's 1963 encyclical *Pacem in Terris*.

The Second Vatican Council (1962–1965) sought to take this further and published major documents encouraging Catholic scholars and pastors to rediscover the importance of Scripture and bathe their thought and preaching with the light of God's word (*Dei Verbum*). The Council exhorted scholars and pastors to engage with the world by reflecting on the major social and cultural issues of our time (*Gaudium et Spes*). This implied the need to question and reform pre–Vatican II approaches to biblical and ethical research, and to include the results of that research in the formation of the priesthood and the laity. The change of attitude is most succinctly and clearly stated in the Decree on Priestly Training, *Optatam Totius*, which we mention at the beginning of this chapter, and which establishes that "students are to be formed with particular care in the study of the Bible, which ought to be, as it were, the soul of all theology" and that the scientific exposition of theological ethics, being "nourished more on the teaching of the Bible, should shed light on the loftiness of the calling of the faithful in Christ and the obligation that is theirs of bearing fruit in charity for the life of the world" (16).

Of course, the consideration of ethical matters, especially complex political and social issues, is nourished by two main sources: it is best done "in the light of the Gospel and of human experience" (GS 46). The latter source, "human experience," is recounted and listened to through pastoral contact with people of good will. It is also observed through empirical scientific research (for example, via the Observe-Appraise-Act methodology developed by Catholic Action), and is found sedimented in texts pertaining to philosophy, history, and jurisprudence.[9] The former source, the "good news," is heard echoing through the whole deposit of faith (depositum fidei), which includes Scripture and its authoritative interpretive traditions. In the present book we deal mostly with the first (the evangelical or biblical) source of theological ethics, leaving the more explicit, interdisciplinary, and cross-disciplinary integration of "human experience" into debates concerning the stranger as a task for our readers (VG 4). The two sources cannot be strictly separated, and as we have seen in the previous chapter, Scripture can serve as a mirror and a window through which we can encounter and frame the human experience of the self and of the other.

What, then, does "nourishing" ethics with Scripture (OTE 16) entail? There are at least three different approaches to answering the question.[10] We can (a) propose a series of models, or analyze the texts of famous biblical scholars and ethicists, to classify and showcase best practices and highlight the strengths and limitations of each model or type of usage (taxonomic approach), (b) list the possible traps, hoping that our readers will find their own way of using Scripture appropriately in ethics by avoiding them (negative approach), or (c) we could boldly make a proposal for the best way that explicit Scripture-ethics bridging can be accomplished (constructive approach). Let us start by considering the taxonomic approach.

4.2 Taxonomic Approaches

Spohn's Typology

We have already presented Spohn's more recent book, *Go and Do Likewise*, but his most influential book is probably an earlier text, *What*

Are They Saying About Scripture and Ethics? In it, Spohn has sought to identify various ways in which the Bible is brought into dialogue with other areas of theology.[11] The five models discussed in the second edition (1995) of Spohn's book are summarized in table 4.2.

TABLE 4.2 SPOHN'S FIVE MODELS FOR USING SCRIPTURE IN ETHICS		
Model	Characteristics	Example
1. Scripture as God's command	The reader prays with the Bible and discovers in the text a *series of commands* or vocational imperatives that she believes God addresses to her and her immediate community. The reader seeks to obey those commands.	Dietrich Bonhoeffer, Karl Barth
2. Scripture as a reminder pointing to an intercultural morality	The Bible witnesses to and reminds the reader what it means to be truly human. It points to *moral standards shared by every human person* that shape their lifelong response to the calling of their Creator. Its morality is universal, and not simply the peculiar cultural ethos of a cohort of people living in the ancient Levant. Thus, at the level of general norms and principles, the Bible doesn't offer us something very different from what tradition has referred to as "natural law."	Josef Fuchs, Richard McCormick
3. Scripture as a call to liberation	The Bible speaks principally of salvation in the integral sense, hence liberation from personal and social sin (and oppression). One may therefore look for motivation and inspiration in the Bible to *fight against the structures of the sin* of our world, as companions of a liberator God.	Gustavo Gutierrez, Jon Sobrino, Elisabeth Schüssler Fiorenza

4. Scripture as a call to discipleship	Beyond the content presented in legal form (imperative phrases, apodictic phrases), the Bible invites us to *follow Jesus*. It is a call or vocation that reaches us both personally and as members of a faith community and invites us to use our imagination to continually discern ways of being disciples in our everyday lives, today.	Stanley Hauerwas
5. Scripture as the basis for a response to God's love	Similar to (4), but possibly more universal and less "communitarian." We are all capable of *responding to love* in our way, but Christians see Jesus as the "concrete universal" whose entire story is normative for Christian ethics.	William Spohn (further developed in *Go and Do Likewise*)

Spohn's "taxonomic" approach helps us to identify the elements that different theologians choose to highlight in their use of Scripture, but it presents two main problems. First, it doesn't clearly distinguish between the implicit and the explicit channel. Model 4 seems more implicit since it focuses on a discipleship of commitment within a close-knit Christian community. Model 5, which promotes a more cosmopolitan discipleship of loving service of the greater common good and of creation, seems more outward-looking in its fruits, but not necessarily in its use of Scripture. Spohn admits that "in the final two models [he turns] to the moral agent and [highlights] the use of Scripture in transforming the 'moral psychology'" of the agent, and hence he proposes models of implicit bridging. Model 1 also seems to go in that direction. Spohn's mixture of explicit and implicit bridging models risks confusing the reader.

Second, this taxonomic approach risks being reductive and forcing authors into narrow categories. For instance, Spohn places in model 2 (which he calls "Scripture as a moral reminder") authors like Josef Fuchs and the "autonomous theonomy" school in post–Vatican II Catholic theological ethics. Such authors, however, generally set out reforming Catholic moral theology following the recommendations in *OTE* 16 mentioned above and hence see the moral life as the *response to a call* that entails bearing fruit in charity for the life of the world. This clearly overlaps with models 4 and 5.[12] Authors in this tradition distinguish between a "categorical" and a "transcendental" dimension of moral life. Their best-known publications deal with the categorical dimension, which is more public and argumentative, and implies an explicit bridging between Scripture and ethics, as described in model 2. However, authors such as Klaus Demmer also discuss the "transcendental" dimension of moral life, which caters to implicit bridging and to a discipleship shaped by love at the more personal level, and they develop this dimension considerably, using the notions of Fundamental Stance, Preferential Option, and Option of Life.[13] Many of these authors practiced Ignatian Spirituality, which had a profound impact on their life and publications, and were good examples of the kind of bridging described in Spohn's other book (see section 2.4). Furthermore, the concept of a fundamental stance or option through which our action as a whole is oriented toward responding positively or not to God's calling allows these authors to frame the person's action, taken as a whole, as an existential response to an existential call, and hence something more radical than the optional practices we usually associate with the term *spirituality*.[14]

Other Typological Approaches

Other authors have adopted a taxonomic or typological approach similar to that of Spohn or have analyzed the use of Scripture in the work of theological ethicists they deem important or influential. For instance, Jeffrey Siker presents eight "portraits" of ethicists who use Scripture seriously in their reflections.[15] Similarly, Richard B. Hays analyzes the use of Scripture by five important twentieth century American theologians (Reinhold Niebuhr, Karl Barth, John Howard Yoder, Stanley Hauerwas, and Elisabeth Schüssler Fiorenza[16]) using a diagnostic checklist with four main elements (that also form the structure of his book). These are the descriptive, synthetic, hermeneutical, and pragmatic tests. The descriptive test focuses on the adequacy of the textual analysis provided by the theologians being analyzed. The hermeneutical test can be split into two: as regards the Scripture passages being used, it seeks to identify the device used by the theologian to bridge them to an ethical debate (rules, principles, paradigms, or a symbolic world); and regarding the rest of the theologian's discourse, it seeks to identify the other sources used in the interpretation of the texts (tradition, reason, or experience). The synthetic test appraises the range of Scripture passages used by the theologian in his work, and the rationale underlying his choice of a particular set of texts. Finally, the pragmatic test seeks to identify what is being appropriated from Scripture through this process. The checklist can be linked to our basic tripartite scheme (figure 4.1) and is schematized below in figure 4.2:

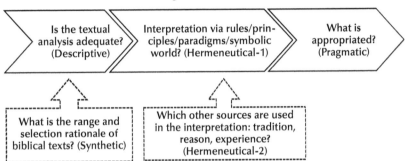

FIGURE 4.2: HAYS'S DIAGNOSTIC CHECKLIST, SCHEMATIZED BY AUTHOR

Lúcás Chan uses a double typology in his book *Biblical Ethics in the 21st Century*, analyzing four bridging attempts by biblical scholars (Richard Hays, Frank Matera, Sandra Schnieders, and Rasiah Sugirtharajah) and four by theological ethicists (Bernhard Häring, Gustavo Gutiérrez, Rosemary Radford Ruether, and William Spohn). He concludes that the works of the first group are often found wanting in ethical hermeneutics and the latter in biblical analysis. Chan asserts that both elements should be given equal importance so as to reach the pragmatic (appropriation) phase in a balanced and helpful manner, using a virtue ethics approach.[17]

4.3 Negative Approaches

Negative approaches differ from taxonomic ones in teaching us what not to do, hoping that by avoiding the major pitfalls, we will find a way of using Scripture appropriately in ethics.

A Historical Note

In the years immediately after Vatican II, various forms of historical-critical biblical scholarship flourished within the Catholic

Church, promising the reconstruction of the historical evolution of Scripture texts and the scientific corroboration of factual claims made by the texts using extrabiblical historical and archaeological data. Concurrently, Bible groups sprouted in many parishes, and Christian "base communities"—nourished by regular prayer, debate, and action rooted in Scripture—spread throughout the developing world. The removal or relaxation of some of the academic shackles and overbearing oversight mechanisms developed during the Modernist crisis increased academic freedom and stimulated research. This also enabled some authors to take risky or doctrinally problematic positions on some exegetical and ethical issues. Church authorities and fellow lecturers eventually became concerned about the use of controversial or highly conjectural conclusions from historical criticism in the formation of seminarians and of the laity for ministry.

In the late 1970s and during the 1980s, doubts started to spread about the ability of scholars to accurately date documents and to precisely reconstruct the historical events and realities of the ancient Near East (ANE). Historical criticism became less fashionable within certain academic circles. A new generation of scholars felt that the historical research it entailed was stifling, imposing a method that chops the Bible into lifeless bits. Furthermore, historical criticism tended to locate meaning uniquely in the past—hence bracketing or denying contemporary relevance—and to become an end in itself.[18] New "synchronic" approaches (that disregard historical antecedents) and "hybrid" styles of exegesis (that mix the synchronic approach and the diachronic, historic approach) started to gain traction. Many authors adopted synchronic approaches of a literary kind, inspired by the Anglo-American New Criticism movement and hermeneutics debates in Continental Europe, namely rhetorical, narratological, and semiotic analysis. I will explain and illustrate the use of some of these approaches in the following chapters. Other scholars espoused nonliterary forms of synchronic exegesis, focused on the texts' interpretation history, dialogue with the social sciences, or the contexts in which contemporary readers and communities are embedded as they seek guidance in Scripture. These approaches continue to enrich our understanding of Scripture even today, especially by introducing elements of Marxist or postcolonial social analysis, psychology, feminism, gender theory, or social theory in biblical analysis in an intelligent and critical manner. Admittedly, some scholars have also shocked more pious readers when seeking to unveil structural social injustice or psychological disorders in the thinking and behavior not only of biblical villains but also of major biblical heroes.

Most of these approaches take note of the results of textual criticism (also called "lower criticism") but tend to bracket those of the more secular diachronic approaches (also called "higher criticism"), such as source, form, and redaction criticism. The most popular methods and approaches are summarized in figure 4.3 below. I will not present higher criticism methods and nonliterary forms of synchronic exegesis in detail in this book; there are already many books that do this competently.[19]

Diachronic Methods		Synchronic Approaches	
		Literary	*Other*
Source Criticism	Textual Criticism	Rhetorical Analysis	Interpretation History Approaches (Patristic, Rabbinic)
Form Criticism		Narrative Analysis	Human Sciences Approaches (Sociological, Psychological...)
Redaction Criticism		Semiotic Analysis	Contextual Approaches (Liberationist, Feminist, Queer...)

FIGURE 4.3: DIACHRONIC METHODS AND
SYNCHRONIC APPROACHES IN BIBLICAL EXEGESIS

Many Christian leaders and seminary formation directors distrusted the nonliterary synchronic approaches and steered clear of them. However, the literary approaches proved popular. They were deemed less shocking to the uninitiated and better suited to the early theological formation of seminarians, vowed religious, and lay pastoral workers than higher criticism. Given that such approaches systematically avoid raising doubts or questioning the factual truth of the text, their popularity continued to rise in many seminaries and theological faculties in the 1990s. In recent decades, as more postmodern converts or faith returnees with a history of nonbelief, nonpractice, or agnosticism seek to strengthen and deepen their newfound faith, theological tools that offer clear doctrinal guidelines and allow the construction of a clear-cut religious identity have flourished.

In some cases, the new exegetical approaches were not introduced with the intention of serenely complementing and enriching the results of historical criticism, but in a polemical way, seeking rather to supplant it completely. This explains the 1993 reaction of the PBC, which welcomes the new approaches while insisting that historical criticism is there to stay (*IBC*). In some countries and centers of formation, ideas and texts pertaining to diachronic exegesis were phased out of syllabuses before they could have any real effect on the teaching of theological ethics. As warrant for this radical reform of the biblical studies curriculum, some used the aforementioned doubts regarding dating, as well as philosophical claims based on oversimplified versions of complex hermeneutical theories, such as that of Paul Ricœur. However, our discussion in chapter 3 showed that we cannot honestly invoke Ricœurian hermeneutics to approach Scripture with the first-level naiveté of someone unfamiliar with its worldview and internal logic, and then proceed to project onto the text whatever comes to our minds and claim this to the be meaning of the text. In the new millennium, some Catholic thinkers, pastors, and religious movements took the methodological skepticism of 1980s even further, abandoning all dialogue with the exegetical sciences, and claiming that the Holy Spirit's assistance suffices for the virtuous and devout Christian. Similar attitudes are present within Protestantism, especially in some evangelical and pentecostal churches.

Over the last hundred years, some of the exegetical debates and trends detailed above and in section 4.1 have bred ideologies and provoked extreme reactions to opposing trends, leading to practices that have been detrimental to the explicit bridging we seek. As a result, we can distinguish four improper ways of using Scripture in ethics:[20] (a) instrumental misuse, typical of pre–Vatican II ethical scholarship, (b) legalistic misuse, (c) attitudes close to fundamentalism, and (d) secularist misuse, which is often a reaction to the previous three misuses. In this last case, some scholars, wary of turning back the clock to the time of the Modernist crisis, double down on critical and iconoclastic forms of exegesis, oblivious of faith, theology, and membership in a Christian community.

An Official Document on Biblical Exegesis and Hermeneutics
In 1993, the Pontifical Biblical Commission published a rich and complex document seeking to address these matters, entitled *The Interpretation of the Bible in the Church*.[21] *IBC*

(i-B to i-E) lists a whole range of "new" approaches to exegesis, discussing the strengths and limitations of each, and encouraging the discerning use of practically all synchronic approaches, but avoids calling them exegetical methods. *IBC* i-A also discusses the merits and weaknesses of historical criticism.

The attitude promoted by the document is freedom to use whatever approach is helpful. Except for fundamentalism, even approaches linked to ideologies deemed questionable or problematic by many bishops and theologians can provide food for thought. "Catholic exegesis freely [literally "without ulterior motives"] makes use of the methods and approaches which allow a better grasp of the meaning of texts" (*IBC* iii-Introduction). The point is that there is no hidden agenda to promote or ostracize any particular approach. We should, rather, train ourselves to engage otherness; we may learn much from what may seem strange to us. Exploring the results of an approach does not mean adopting any questionable ideologies lying behind it.

IBC wisely teaches us that the "new" approaches are not in themselves problematic and should be used and taught freely. Yet we should not let ourselves be seduced by their novelty or by their accessibility to scholars bereft of the thorough classical training in the identification and dating of archeological artifacts and ANE documents in several languages. Historical criticism should not be abandoned, and though we should be wary of some of its claims, we should also appreciate its desire to understand the context in which the texts were written, and to confront their claims with the historical facts we can reconstruct reasonably well.

Instrumental Misuse

Notwithstanding the Gadamerian doubts about the truth obtained through rigorous scientific methods, proponents of higher criticism insist that their methods allow us to uncover the truth about the history of the text and its original meaning. Christians should not be afraid of truth. "The truth will make you free" (John 8:32).

Taking the biblical citation in the previous sentence as a case in point allows us to discuss the instrumental use of Scripture in ethics. To be sure, my use of John 8:32 seems innocent enough; who would deny that the Bible promotes truth telling? Yet, by using this passage to conclude an observation on historical criticism without seeking to understand what it means within its context, namely, what kind of truth and freedom John is speaking about and to whom the "you" is referred, I engage here in the instrumental use of Scripture mentioned above. This is also known as "proof-texting," "cherry-picking," "eisegesis," or the "regressive approach." Our decontextualized commentary of 1 Peter 3:15–16 at the beginning of this chapter runs this risk (despite passing the textual criticism test in table 4.1); readers should revisit it critically after exploring the setting of 1 Peter at the end of chapter 8 of this book.

Used instrumentally, Scripture could become a mere database of citations that I can use out of context to "prove" or shine an aura of divine authority on whatever point or claim I feel like making, without ever nourishing my thoughts and claims with the deeper culture, wisdom, worldview, or spirituality of Scripture or bothering to use any serious method to find out what the text is trying to say, or at least, what it definitely is not trying to say.

The instrumental approach was commonly used within Catholicism before Vatican II and still dominates some conversations in Catholic and Protestant ethics. Whenever an ethics text is richly decorated with biblical citations but avoids any real engagement with whole Scripture passages and with the theologies and the worldviews that give meaning to the citations, a trained eye will immediately become suspicious and ask whether the author's thinking is truly biblical or whether he is simply paying lip service to Scripture.

The dependence of the meaning of text on the larger context is more pronounced in the case of the Bible, since the punctuation and the division into verses, paragraphs, and chapters in our printed Bibles (which may disagree with each other) do not simply replicate the ancient manuscripts upon which they depend. In some of those manuscripts, the text divides words and paragraphs, but multiple ancient manuscripts of the same text often do not agree in this respect, and some may contain one flowing sequence of letters. The very idea of a self-contained, standalone biblical verse that can be readily cited without knowing what comes before and what comes after it is a deceptive one indeed. Simply citing Leviticus 19:34, "You shall love the alien as yourself," out of context, to promote philoxenia (love of the stranger) is not so different from citing Psalm 137:9, "Happy shall they be who take your little ones and dash them against the rock," out of context, to promote xenophobia.

Proof-texting can be innocuous, well-intended, or even enter-taining (for example, in biblical jokes). Yet it can also be "diabolical," as Scripture itself indicates when it depicts Satan asking Jesus to show off his power and to adore him (Luke 4:1–13; Matt 4:1–11), while using biblical citations to claim that what he was suggesting was God's will, based on commands derived from "inerrant" Scripture itself. Intellec-tually dishonest theologians are not the only ones who engage in the instrumental use of Scripture. Sometimes politicians and government officials do so, too. A popular example is Romans 13:1–7, where Paul asks Christians to submit to public authorities. His point here, given the context, is that his incipient Christian community should avoid behav-ing as yet another seditious messianic sect, drawing unwanted attention and unnecessary persecution. They should act on the assumption that social order is better than disorder for the spread of the gospel, while waiting for the imminent end times. Moreover, they should assume that God's purpose, will, and authority can and will shine through flawed (and often oppressive and corrupt) human authority, even within the totalitarian Roman Empire of his day (which probably was the most benevolent and decent political regime Paul could think of). In 2018, US Attorney General Jeff Sessions famously used this text to justify novel policies that he instituted to separate migrant families at the border and to imply that the many Christian leaders from various denominations who critiqued his policies were disobeying Scripture.

Legalistic Misuse

The legalistic approach resembles proof-texting in its arbitrary selectiveness when citing Scripture. Waldemar Janzen develops the paradigmatic approach described in chapter 2, in part as a reaction to the effects of scriptural legalism on ethics debates within his Mennonite community. Typically, a legalistic reader opens the Bible and proceeds to systematically ignore or bracket all biblical passages that do not have the grammatical form of a command or imperative, that is, almost all of Scripture. They also toss out all biblical commands that they deem outdated or no longer valid. Finally, they convert what is left into a list of "divine" laws, supposedly mandated as such by God.

Let us put aside for the purposes of this book the complicated issue concerning the use of the concept of *jus divinum* (divine law) to ground certain positive laws in the Catholic canon law tradition and focus solely on moral theology. On one hand, Christian ethics is neither a Newtonian system made of universal laws (as in Spinoza's geometrical ethics), nor a codified hierarchical system of positive exceptionless norms (as enthusiasts of the Napoleonic Code might hope). We cannot reduce Christian ethics to a moral-legal system deemed to apply uniformly and universally by virtue of its divine origin. This would vilify the epistemological status of ethics as a practical science, one requiring discernment, prudential judgment, and the obedience to the dictates of a clear and honestly convinced conscience, since the same Spirit that inspired the biblical authors and editors inhabits our conscience (*Gaudium et Spes* 16). On the other hand, modern legalism is at odds with the Bible's premodern worldview, where truth is complex and multifaceted and is expressed in a motley array of literary genres. These include historical or genealogical narratives, parables, aphorisms, legal prescriptions, rousing speeches, poetic verses, cryptic prophesies, and descriptions of ritual practices. To take all these at face value as self-contained claims promoting or decrying specific values or behaviors would be unreconcilable.

The Jewish Bible and Christian Bible are replete with tensions, contradictions, and contrasting views that legalistic misuses of Scripture cull, paper over, or resolve in the direction the scholar deems fit. Behind such misuse lies a modern legalistic worldview that coherency and clarity are paramount and that the moral agent should be provided with simple, memorable commands to obey, rather than with a complex system of texts within a biblical dialogue that teaches the believer how to think practically. Hence, legalism seeks to a distill a superficially "biblical" legal code, a scrapbook normative "bible," which then serves as an arsenal that the scholar may use to proof-text their claims or attack any opposing views. The idea of a series of clear norms definitively promulgated by the Creator within the Holy Bible is a conversation stopper, used to shut down any debate or discussion. "This is what God commands: you can't argue with that!"

Biblical authors do provide some collections of norms, whether for conduct in general or for rituals, but most of their ethical reflection is transmitted in texts pertaining to the motley of literary genres just mentioned, which are not easily converted into clear universal prescriptions telling us what to do and what to avoid. The first norm in Scripture addressed to humans is "be fruitful and multiply" (Gen 1:28), but Jesus chose to be celibate. The freedom that the early Christian church exercised regarding the 613 normative formulas (*mitzvot*) of the Jewish

Bible should be instructive: "It has seemed good to the Holy Spirit and to us to impose on you no further burden than these essentials: that you abstain from what has been sacrificed to idols and from blood and from what is strangled and from [*porneia*]" (Acts 15:28–29). The final norm concerns *porneia*, a word that is hard to translate accurately in modern languages, and is rendered as "unchastity," "fornication," and "sexual immorality" in three different editions of the NRSV. The first three norms,[22] despite being NT laws promulgated solemnly by the early church, were rapidly bracketed, as successive generations of Christian leaders discerned what the Spirit asked of them and exercised their freedom and authority.[23] Some may try to argue that the *porneia* rule is of permanent value since it an outlier in the list, an ethical norm among cultic norms, but this is a forced and anachronistic distinction. Arguably, all four norms deal with "kosherness" (the duty to keep dangerous and unmixable things separate).[24] Rather, it is possible that the fourth rule's permanence is linked to the breadth and ambiguity of meaning of *porneia*, which invites ecclesial and cultural interpretation as well as ongoing discernment on matters of sexual morality.

These observations on legalism are not intended to promote antinomianism in ethics. In a society where technology and pluralism constantly give us the impression that everything is possible, we urgently need moral norms and rules that are easily memorized and help to set boundaries. But picking up phrases from the Bible and proposing them as timeless, exceptionless norms simply because they have been lifted off a divinely inspired text is not a mature and effective way of helping people discover the importance of norms in today's moral theology.

The Moral Normativity of Scripture

Many complex questions have been raised regarding the moral normativity of Scripture, and of the words of Christ in particular. Some terminological distinctions can help us navigate the issues discussed in the last fifty years or so.

Inerrancy: Some scholars understand this in a fundamentalist sense to be applied at the level of single texts and content: every formula that has a grammatical structure typical of apodictic norms is thus deemed free of error. However, our discussion of Augustine's "crime and vice" rule in section

117

2.2 shows that this is a flawed approach. Rather, Scripture is ethically inerrant as a whole body of works, in its ability to communicate to us the mystery of Christ. Scripture-mediated encounters with this mystery serve in a myriad of ways to set moral standards for the readers.

Permanence: Many theologians agree that some concrete moral rules inspired closely by the words of Jesus and important OT texts like the Decalogue have permanent value, but few would consider them absolute or exceptionless.[25] James Childress suggests we consider them as moral presumptions that establish a prima facie case for or against a certain type of action (for example, killing or lying).[26] An agent acting in ways incompatible with such rules and claiming his action is morally right would have to bear the burden of proof.

Absoluteness: Many theological ethicists have debated the existence of concrete and exceptionless moral norms in recent decades, and the possibility of using Scripture to ground such norms, especially after the publication of *Veritatis Splendor* in 1993. The history of moral theology recommends great prudence in this matter. It is much safer to claim that exceptionless norms exist at a more abstract level, such as the commandments to "act justly" or to "love one another." It would seem logically impossible to find meaningful exceptions to these rules, since the notion of justice and love are intimately related to the very notion of morality and such commandments ultimately mean "act morally." Similarly, "do not commit murder" may be understood as exceptionless if we define murder as "killing unjustly."[27] "Do not kill," however, does not immediately imply acting unjustly, and so cannot be considered exceptionless.

Authority: Other recent debates have focused on the authority of the Bible, distinguishing its authoritarian use in certain Christian communities from its being authoritative for Christians. I believe that within the bounds of our discussion of the use of Scripture in contemporary ethics, the authority of Scripture should mainly be understood as disclosive, following a series of distinctions made by Sandra Schneiders, which I adapt and summarize below.[28] Authority can be unilateral and absolute (coercive) or dialogical and relative (noncoercive). Both kinds of authority exist within speculative and practical contexts. This allows four combinations:

- Apodictic Authority (coercive and speculative) requires the agent's assent if she is to maintain her intellectual integrity. For example, you are obliged to accept the results of a simple algebraic calculation (1+1=2), unless you want to be absurd.
- Compelling Authority (coercive and practical) requires the agent's assent if she is to maintain her physical, psychological, or (practical) rational integrity. For example, you are obliged to hand over your wallet to a dangerous-looking assailant pointing a loaded gun at you, unless you wish to risk death or serious bodily harm. In general, if you are a rational being that is programmed to seek and grasp certain goods and avoid certain evils, you will be compelled by your practical reason to grasp a good that makes itself available, and avoid an evil, unless there is a greater good or evil at stake.
- Evidential Authority (noncoercive and speculative) solicits the agent's assent when he is exposed to evidence that shores up non-self-evident claims. For example, after thousands of empirical observations (that include no sightings of albino ravens), the inductive inference that "all ravens are black" is deemed substantiated and hence authoritative.
- Disclosive Authority (noncoercive and practical) solicits the agent's assent when he is exposed to existential or experiential stimuli (uniting reason and affect) that provide warrant to non-self-evident claims regarding ethical, aesthetical, or spiritual realities. For example, witnessing the suffering of an innocent person is an experience that elicits a compassionate response; the beauty of a sunset makes a claim on us to recognize it and enjoy it; the loving reprimand of a caring friend draws us to recognize and mend our errors.

Our preference for certitude leads us to associate God and God's Word to unilateral and absolute (coercive) authority, but God prefers to exercise God's authority toward us humans, God's own children, in a dialogical way, leading us toward the truth without compulsion, hence through disclosive authority. According to Schneiders, "Scripture is normative for **theology** because it is a primary symbolic mediator (not the only one) of God's self-revelation. This self-revelation has all the complexity and ambiguity of any personal self-disclosure."[29] Scripture is also normative for the Church's mission (announcing and fostering God's reign in history) and for the faith life of individual Christians, which is intimately linked to their actions, and hence to morality.

Fundamentalist Misuse

We have already mentioned that the PBC takes issue with one particular form of improper use of Scripture in the church, and hence also within theological ethics: fundamentalism (*IBC* i-F). It claims, "Fundamentalism is right to insist on the divine inspiration of the Bible, the inerrancy of the word of God and other biblical truths included in its five fundamental points." Yet, for the PBC, the way in which fundamentalists present these truths stems from an ideology that is not biblical, even though fundamentalists would claim otherwise:

> [Fundamentalism] demands an unshakable adherence to rigid doctrinal points of view and imposes, as the only source of teaching for Christian life and salvation, a reading of the Bible which rejects all questioning and any kind of critical research. The basic problem with fundamentalist interpretation of this kind is that, refusing to take into account the historical character of biblical revelation, it makes itself incapable of accepting the full truth of the Incarnation itself....For this reason, it tends to treat the biblical text as if it had been dictated word for word by the Spirit....Its relying upon a non-critical reading of certain texts of the Bible serves to reinforce political ideas and social attitudes that are marked by prejudices—racism, for example—quite contrary to the Christian Gospel. (*IBC* i-F)

The PBC concludes that the fundamentalist approach is dangerous because it seduces good people who sincerely but naively look to the Bible for ready answers to the problems of life. "It can deceive these people, offering them interpretations that are pious but illusory, instead of telling them that the Bible does not necessarily contain an immediate answer to each and every problem" (*IBC* i-F).

We can distinguish fundamentalism proper from a similar kind of mindset that—as a reaction to secularization and the spread of other religions—seeks in the Bible something particular, esoteric, exceptionalist, or completely countercultural, obsessed by the idea of Jewish or Christian distinctiveness and determined to bring out this element at all costs. Often this is the result of an identitarian mindset that arises when the reader feels that either her identity is not serenely rooted in tradition, or it is threatened and needs ostensibly ancient and powerful identity markers; ancient religious texts often are sourced to cater for this personal and sectarian need. In chapter 1 we argued that the "total otherness" of Scripture is not to be understood in terms of sociological identity markers, which once again tend to collapse that otherness into something mundane and more palatable, yet inauthentic (see pp. 4–5).

Secularist Misuse

Modern exegesis, especially higher criticism, includes a healthy methodological "secularism," but there are three kinds of problematic "secularism." Historical criticism is methodologically "secular" in that it applies to Scripture the methods used to analyze secular literature and seeks not to censor or "correct" its conclusions, even if they are not in line with the tenets of mainstream theology or tradition. In itself this is not a problem; the factual and historical "is" that can be determined to some extent by the critical exegete is separable from both the metaphysical "is" and the practical "ought" that dogmatic and moral theologians are mainly concerned with. Such methodology, when used wisely, is healthy. It pushes theology out of its comfort zone, challenges self-referential thinking, and facilitates a credible formulation of a certain type of claim of factual truth, tested by a community of critical experts, who should be vigilant and exacting in evaluating one another's claims and conclusions, and keen on questioning unfounded or debatable claims.

Yet, the "secular" nature of the methodology does not justify a disrespectful attitude when presenting the results of such analysis either to the general public or within academic circles. Such an attitude, sometimes called "secularist" or "secularistic," ignores the fact that the text being analyzed is sacred to many readers who deem it to provide indications of how to live a good life that are normative to believers. Hence, one kind of problematic secularism concerns the public behavior of exegetes and the way they communicate their claims to their readers, that is, whether or not it is respectful of the religious beliefs of others.

A second kind of secularism concerns theological ethicists and the process whereby they reach their conclusions after seriously and rigorously engaging with Scripture. While a "pure" exegete might be a nonbeliever or might adopt a very skeptical and critical mindset when analyzing a text, a theological ethicist cannot afford to go immediately from exegesis to the formulation of ethical claims without dealing with mainstream theology and Christian tradition. To be sure, an exegete and a moral philosopher who are both nonbelievers could collaborate with one another, treating Scripture as a great human classic and together think through many moral issues. Their conclusions might even be identical to those of an exegete working with a theological ethicist, both practicing believers. Yet there is a difference in attitude when one believes one is in front of a divinely revealed text. Such an attitude does influence the process through which one goes about reading the text and applying it to concrete ethical situations today, even if the barebones conclusions appear identical on paper to those arrived at by nonbelievers. In some cases, such a process might influence the results themselves.

A third kind of secularist attitude consists in ignoring Scripture when engaging in theology or intraecclesial ethics debates or intentionally choosing not to use it. Here we are talking about disuse, rather than misuse. There may be many different reasons behind such an attitude. The Bible may be seen as "outdated," a product of a bygone culture and economic system, or "irrational," since it contains claims regarding supernatural phenomena that cannot be scientifically proven. It may also be considered "particularistic," since many of its claims are closely linked to a particular place and time and may seem unsuited to universalist moral reasoning. Moreover, it may be regarded as merely "informative" and "devotional," a book that informs us about God and God's relationship to humans to stimulate faith and devotion in individuals, having no bearing on action and decision-making concerning other persons.

This final case leads us to the debate on whether Scripture contains a revealed divinity, a revealed morality, or both, or rather a revealed divine-and-human reality that has moral implications. Vatican II, in *Dei Verbum* (2), insists that God primarily reveals Godself to us, and only secondarily reveals information about Godself that can be formulated into doctrines. Within that second level, Scripture primarily provides information about who God is and who we are in the face of God, so as to deepen our relationship with God. This relationship ultimately is the "good life" and the final end of human existence, and hence it is eminently "ethical," though not in the secular, universalist, and normative sense that the word *ethics* has acquired in Enlightenment philosophy.

Heuristic and Evaluative Questions Inspired by *The Bible and Morality*

Since 1993 the PBC has published additional texts on biblical interpretation, including a 2021 document called *What Is Man? A Journey through Biblical Anthropology*, which touches on many moral issues and brings some sound biblical scholarship and nuanced answers to debates on issues like divorce and homosexuality.[30] In 2008 it published a more pastoral text, *The Bible and Morality* (*BM*), which skirts the complexity of some of the debates in *IBC*, while providing criteria for using the Bible in ethics that can help us complete our present overview.

The PBC refers to Christology and integral anthropology as the two fundamental criteria for the interpretation of the Bible, namely conformity to the biblical vision of the human being and conformity with the example of Jesus (*BM* 94–103). It also indicates six specific criteria, connected to fundamental ones: an openness to diverse cultures, hence a certain ethical universalism (convergence); a firm stand in the face of incompatible values (contrast); a refining process of the moral conscience observable in each of the two Testaments, but especially from the one to the other (progress); a rectification of contemporary moral subjectivism (community dimension); an openness to a definite future of the world and of history, capable of shaping the ends and motivations of moral behavior (finality); and lastly, a careful distinction, in every case, between the relative or absolute value of biblical principles and moral precepts (discrimination or discernment) (*BM* 93, 104–54).

It is useful to keep this list in mind when analyzing, interpreting, and appropriating biblical texts from an ethical viewpoint. However, a simple list that contains contraries (like convergence and contrast) does not provide a method, and risks being used instrumentally or employed in petty apologetical discourses. It might, however, be used heuristically if converted into a series of questions, whereby we ask ourselves,

---

123

for instance, whether our interpretation is too individualistic or overly communitarian (community dimension), too eschatological or devoid of an eschatological horizon (finality), and so forth. The fundamental criteria allow us to construct the following tests, which appraise both the text itself (exegetical step) and the interpretation we are adopting (hermeneutical step):

1. Integral Anthropology test:
   a. *Exegetical step:* Does this text conform to the overarching biblical vision of the human being, or does it seem somehow anomalous?
   b. *Hermeneutical step:* Does my moral-theological reading of the passage conform to this vision or not?
2. Integral Christology test:
   a. *Exegetical step:* Does this text (the actions of the main characters, the teaching expounded, the poetic imagery used, the commands imparted, etc.) conform with the example of Jesus Christ (in the canonical Gospels)?
   b. *Hermeneutical step:* Does my moral-theological reading of the passage conform to a reading that the traditional "Jesus movement" (nourished by the canonical Gospels and mainstream Christological doctrines) has adopted in history or might coherently adopt today?

If the results of the tests are "no" or "maybe not," one must proceed with great caution, and avoid constructing moral-theological theses based solely on this passage or reading (or proposing these theses as "biblical" tout court).

4.4 A Constructive Approach

While taxonomies and classifications, as well as a list of things to avoid, are useful in bridging Scripture and ethics, we should provide some indication of what one should do, a constructive approach. I will summarize below, as a series of rules, a procedure for a responsible explicit use of Scripture in ethics, which will serve as a conclusion of the theoretical part of this book. To some extent, the rest of this book will be an illustration of how I believe one ought to proceed.

Rule 1: Create Opportunities for a Scholarly Personal Exchange between Exegetes and Ethicists

Cross-disciplinary teamwork is commonplace in the natural and social sciences, but scholars in the human sciences have traditionally been trained to work and publish alone. We need to rethink this way of proceeding, and proactively create opportunities for a scholarly exchange between exegetes and ethicists, not only by reading one another's texts but also through personal encounters, face-to-face and online.

The PBC, while claiming that ethicists have a right to ask questions of exegetes to simulate their research, recognizes that often the exegetes may respond that the issues are not addressed as such in any scriptural text (*IBC* iii-D3). Nevertheless, the PBC asserts, "the witness of the Bible, taken within the framework of the forceful dynamic that governs it as a whole, will certainly indicate a fruitful direction to follow" (*IBC* iii-D3). The overarching "witness of the Bible" is not something easily summarized in a book; hence, rather than working in silos, exegetes and ethicists need to truly collaborate and propose together a "direction to follow" guided by such a witness. Lúcás Chan proposes some interesting ways to practice such collaboration in our theological schools today, for instance through team teaching and team publishing.[31] The prologue of the recent pontifical document on ecclesiastical universities and faculties, *Veritatis Gaudium* (2018), promotes a stronger and more committed form of interdisciplinarity, which it calls cross-disciplinarity (or transdisciplinarity), wherein scholars from different disciplines truly interact and challenge one another, rather than passively read and cite each other's publications while working alone.

Rule 2: Cast Your Net Wide

In section 1.4, we presented an exploration exercise to seek biblical texts that may be relevant to an ethical debate, but are unfamiliar and do not immediately come to mind. We suggested leafing through a Bible and scanning section headers, using concordances and Bible dictionaries, and looking up headwords in a Bible with the help of digital Bible study tools. The idea is that we need to venture beyond the world of clichéd texts, and cast our net wider.

The process I recommend in this book entails curiosity, patience, generosity, and a certain gratuity or liberality in the use of the individual texts. We might spend time with a passage, hoping it will help us reflect deeper on a particular ethics issue, only to discover that it does not really deal with that issue, or it does so in ways contrary to what we expected when selecting the text. If we feel compelled to produce something simply because we have taken time to analyze a text, we lack the internal freedom to use Scripture responsibly in our moral thinking. Rather, what we propose in this book is an experience of *scholē*, that is, a restful, uncommercial use of reason that is not dictated by the necessities of life (including career advancement). Figure 4.4 schematizes the process for using Scripture in ethics with the necessary freedom or gratuity.

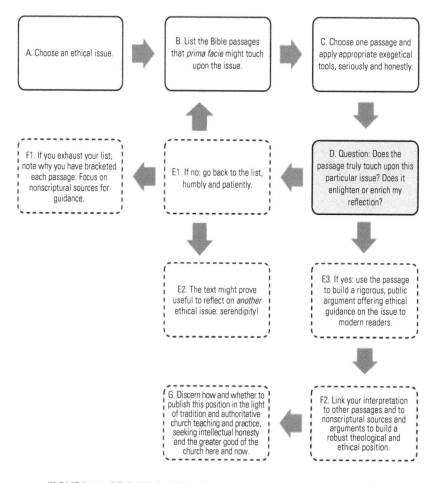

FIGURE 4.4: PROCESS FOR USING SCRIPTURE FREELY IN ETHICS

Rule 3: Become Aware of the Conceptual Differences between Your World and the World of the Text

In section 2.2, we discussed three major models that shape our understanding of the moral life—consequentialism, deontology, and perfectionism—which Thomas Ogletree presents as important preunderstandings when approaching Scripture. It is helpful to become aware of the preunderstandings that help and hinder our access to the biblical text, especially those concerning the moral issue we are investigating.

Our preunderstandings take center stage in the following chapter, where we propose a mapping exercise in which the readers are asked to list and connect the concepts they associate with the ethical issue they are interested in, so to frame an area of moral concern, and then to take time to assess which concepts, if any, within the world of Scripture can be associated with that area of moral concern. The idea is to map and compare two constellations of concepts, those of our world and of the world of the Bible, to see if dialogue is possible. This exercise should be done concomitantly with the exploration exercise used to list Scripture passages of interest (Rule 2). The exploration exercise and the mapping exercise are linked through the reflective equilibrium we described in section 1.4.

Rule 4: In the Analysis Phase, Attend to the Results of Historical Criticism and Approach the Text Using Literary Analysis

Once we have chosen a series of texts that, prima facie, seem to be relevant to the ethical issue we are exploring, and made ourselves aware of any significant differences between our way of conceptualizing that issue and linking it to others, and the way Scripture frames the area of moral concern related to that issue, we may start analyzing one of the texts.

> Step 1: Any serious use of Scripture in ethics should start by attending to the results of textual criticism (lower criticism); both diachronic and synchronic approaches depend on these results. Preferably, this should be done by consulting the apparatus of a critical edition of the

Bible in the original languages, but the footnotes of a good study Bible in English should flag the most relevant issues. In table 4.1, we presented a simple test with two questions: "Is the original text clear and grammatically consistent?" and "Are there textual differences among the major sources that could raise serious doubts on the meaning of the phrases I intend to analyze and discuss?" This can be corroborated using a second test in which one compares various translations of the same text, possibly in different modern languages, and asks, "Do most other translations provide a text similar in meaning to the one I am working with?"

Step 2: A basic level of form criticism is often necessary to distinguish genres and delimit a pericope for analysis, unless we are analyzing a psalm or a short book (such as Ruth). It may be helpful to use the results of form criticism to figure out the life setting (*Sitz im Leben*) in which the sentences that seem more ethically relevant to the reader might have originally been pronounced. The subheadings and footnotes of a good study Bible often include the results of such scholarship. Scholarly texts containing detailed form-critical disassembly of the passage should be avoided until the ethicist has had a chance to spend time with the text and attempt a literary exegetical approach on his own.[32]

Step 3: One should attempt an analysis of the text, using some of the synchronic approaches, preferably two or more, before reading a commentary or consulting a scholarly exegesis of the passage, which can overly condition our understanding of the text. In this book, we have chosen some exegetical tools that do not require a great deal of technical know-how to illustrate how this can be done. In chapter 1, we show how a critical form of allegorization, "allegorical permutations," can stimulate ethical reflection, and in chapter 7, we discuss and illustrate the rhetorical analysis of biblical and Semitic texts. In chapter 8, we deal with narratological analysis and also with a form of sociological analysis. Certain tools are more suitable for the analysis of certain texts by certain readers. The fact of being a straight, white, European, middle-aged man with no formal training in psychology keeps me from attempting liberationist, feminist, postcolonial, queer, or psychological readings of biblical texts. Readers are encouraged to consult books on non-literary synchronic exegesis if they would like to discover and practice these approaches.

Step 4: At this point, the ethicist should acquaint herself with some of the results of higher criticism, such as redaction criticism, source criticism (where available), and detailed form critical analyses (ones that are more deconstructive than what was required in step 2). She may also integrate the results of various kinds of literary and non-literary synchronic analysis.

Rule 5: In the Interpretation Phase, Seek Ethically Relevant Dynamic Encounter Experiences

In our minds and in our hearts, we interpret texts while we are analyzing them methodically. However, explicit bridging between Scripture and ethics requires that we provide a public, argued interpretation that is available to be critiqued by others, and this usually means an interpretation that takes shape as another text. When writing such a text, the ethicist might seek to extract from the Scripture passage (or set of passages) certain rules, principles, paradigms, or elements allowing her to perceive and reconstruct a biblical "symbolic world." However, it is often only possible, or more helpful, for the ethicist to construct her interpretation based on her ethically relevant dynamic experiences of encounter with the text or texts (see p. 83, section 3.1). Here, the elements of consonance and dissonance, similarity and contrast, emerging both from within the text and from within the reader placed in front of the text, are given pride of place in the interpretation.

In moving from interpretation to the phase of explicit appropriation in ethics, the ethicist will need to bring in other sources of moral reasoning: tradition (including its interpretation by the church magisterium), experience, reason, and prudential judgment. The PBC asserts that exegesis has the task assisting moral theologians by assessing the significance of the motley of biblical genres relevant to ethics, and it explains:

The Bible reflects a considerable moral development, which finds its completion in the New Testament. It is not sufficient therefore that the Old Testament should indicate a certain moral position (e.g., the practice of slavery or of divorce, or that of extermination in the case of war) for this position to continue to have validity. One has to undertake a process of discernment....The New Testament itself is not easy to interpret in the area of morality, for it often makes use of imagery, frequently in a way that is paradoxical or even provocative. (*IBC* iii-D3)

Rule 6: In the Appropriation Phase, Introduce Extrabiblical Sources

While dialogue between exegesis and ethics is helpful to interpret a text and bring it into wider ethics debates using other sources, the point of the exercise is to reach the third phase, appropriation, a pragmatic phase, when the ethicist proposes something to contemporary believers and to society at large, inspired and enriched by scholarly encounters with Scripture texts. The PBC calls this phase "actualization" when it refers to appropriation in a different time from the text and "inculturation" when it happens in space, across cultures (*IBC* iv-A, iv-B).

In this book, we will analyze and interpret several biblical texts that are relevant to today's debates on immigration and asylum, framing them within the area of moral concern surrounding the topic of identity and alterity, which can be linked to a constellation of concepts present in Scripture. Given space limitations, we will not complete our interpretation by explicitly bringing nonbiblical sources into our reflection or proceed to the appropriation phase proper. This means that we will not propose a concrete ethics for migration policymaking that Christians should advocate for in a particular country or region of the world. We will leave that task to our readers.

This discussion concludes the more theoretical part of this book. Let us now proceed to apply these concepts and rules to the question of strangerhood in Scripture.

PART 2

A CONGREGATION OF METICS AND TRAVELING PEOPLE

BRIDGING THE DIVIDE BETWEEN KIN AND STRANGER

5

MAPPING THE CONCEPTS

Metics and traveling people, kin and stranger. The second part of this book (chapters 5–8) is inspired by the various metaphors of alienage and itinerancy found in the NT. Often presented in pairs, such metaphors describe the experience of the Christian community or the patriarchs, for instance, *paroikoi kai parepidēmoi* (1 Pet 2:11), *xenoi kai parepidēmoi* (Heb 11:13), and *xenoi kai paroikoi* (Eph 2:19). *Paroikoi* (long-term resident aliens) and *parepidēmoi* (short-term sojourners, traveling people) are considered strangers (*xenoi*), as we shall see in section 8.4. Part 2 will guide readers through a series of biblical texts focused on Israel's relationship with strangers, hoping that a scholarly encounter with such texts may inform our ethical stance on hospitality, integration of immigrants, and immigration policymaking in general.

In this chapter, readers will realize to what extent our understanding of statehood, citizenship, nationalism, patriotism, and cosmopolitism are shaped by modernity and the system of nation-states formed after the Peace of Westphalia (1648). They will actively seek to gain awareness of their preunderstandings as they approach biblical texts that they tend to associate with these notions, and to shore up their ability to effectively encounter the world of the text by ensuring that what the text presupposes of them as readers is well in place (see chapter 3).

Readers will first learn techniques, such as the use of word clouds and the construction of a table of opposites, to map out the concepts in the "world of the reader." The use of these techniques will lead to a more lucid discussion of identity and difference in the following chapters, and hence of the "we-and-they" mentality that shapes our understanding of issues like migration or relationships with strangers. Readers will then be led to the second step, where we ask ourselves what related concepts can be found in antiquity and especially in the ancient Near East during the period when the main books of the Old Testament were composed and edited. This will ensure a more responsible use of Scripture in ethics as we analyze texts dealing with strangerhood in the rest of the book.

In the process, readers will explore the notion of the distinctiveness of Israel as a "nation" and survey its cosmological and historical aspects while critically appreciating Israel's sense of being the "Last-Born among Nations." They will delve into the narrative construction of such a notion of distinctiveness, with wandering and migration as markers of national identity, as well as the presence of different voices and complex stances that challenge and enrich the mainstream narrative of Israel's origins.

5.1 Mapping Our Conceptions of Selfhood and Otherness

In my early attempts to find ethical criteria to appraise migration policymaking, I read many official Catholic texts produced by organs of the Roman curia and by conferences of Catholic bishops. Some moved very quickly from biblical citations to modern concepts such as nationalism, nation-states, subjective rights, sovereignty, national identity, and modern democratic citizenship. While such hermeneutical operations and forms of appropriation may be adequate for implicit bridging between Scripture and ethics, on the explicit channel—where our reflection is exposed to critical appraisal—we need to be very careful of anachronism. It is necessary to take time to map both our concepts and those of the text, and to bring the two maps together. Above, in section 2.2, we noted that preunderstandings can become prejudices and warp our understanding of the text, but they can also provide a useful and privileged access point into the world of the literary work. They are also the "selling point" that makes us undertake a fascinating but possibly costly and risky travel adventure or journey (*safari*, in Swahili) into the world of the text. They advertise a text coming to us from antiquity as relevant to our social and existential problems, rather than simply a fascinating artifact or museum curiosity. You may think of the following chapters in this book as a "biblical safari."

What I propose to my readers is a two-step process. In step 1 we will list and connect the concepts we associate with the ethical issue with which we are dealing, so to frame an area of moral concern. In step 2, we take time to assess what concepts, if any, within the world of Scripture can be associated with that area of moral concern. This will allow us to map and link the two constellations of concepts. We can then keep these two constellations at the back of our mind while we read each text. This will allow us to note the differences, tensions, or lack of true parallelism, and to come to a healthy "fusion of horizons" (*Horizont-verschmelzung*), as Gadamer would say. I believe that in the case of rigorous ethics research, in-person contact with biblical scholars (besides direct contact with their work) may be helpful, and in some cases even necessary, to obtain an updated and adequate bibliography for step 2. This interaction allows us to explain to our colleagues in the biblical sciences what we are looking for precisely and what knowledge we already possess, and hence obtain a tailor-made answer. In the process we may build a cross-disciplinary network of collaboration that is a very useful and common feature of research in the natural and social sciences, but less so in religious and ecclesiastical academia. Of course, using a theological library and looking up concepts in a collection of exegetical and historical dictionaries and encyclopedias of the Bible and the ANE, in different languages, can also be a great place to start, followed by going through some of the references in those articles and seeking updated materials through online article databases. After concluding this methodological introduction (5.1), this chapter will next map the first (our own) constellation of concepts or horizon (5.2). We will then move on to the second step, which will help us map and connect the concepts of selfhood and otherness in Scripture (5.3).

Nations and Polities after Westphalia

The operations exemplified in this chapter are based on materials that are not hard to obtain. However, for a reader to realize that they might be required reading before embarking on textual analysis, interpretation, and appropriation, she must have a certain sensibility honed by years of reading between the lines, asking hard questions, being inquisitive, and building up a modicum of general culture. She needs to be able to get a whiff of something that might be amiss, in her reading, in the translation, in the text itself, or that might require further investigation, and then have the determination to hound it persistently until she gets to the bottom of the matter.

The Treaty of Westphalia inaugurated our notion of the nation-state and modern national sovereignty, which is the lens through which we conceive the political order.[1] It is important to be aware of this preunderstanding of politics that we bring with us to the Bible as readers, and to realize that biblical authors had a very different political landscape in mind when writing. In Jesus's day, Judaea and Samaria were not sovereign nations, but were united in one province within the Roman Empire, ruled by a governor, while Galilee and the upper district of Caesarea Philippi were two regions governed by tetrarchs, quasi-kings who were clients of Rome. The political realities that the OT records as comprising ancient Israel and its neighbors had autonomy at times, but often they were situated in systems of vassalage within the ANE. In this chapter I will focus mainly on the OT, since the community of the followers of Jesus in the NT never considered itself a political entity of any kind. Some NT texts might be helpful to remap discourses about inclusion and exclusion within the church, but they are less suited to reflect on political and juridical issues and thus to appraise ethically the discourses on migration and strangerhood of our time.

Using Word Clouds

There is no easy way of mapping and questioning the concepts we take for granted. One strategy to stimulate critical distancing (nothing very precise is required here) could be to use word-cloud generators on the Internet, which have recently become quite popular. Into such a generator we can feed the text of a new law on immigration, a speech by a political leader, a philosophical or sociological paper, or a synodal or papal document, to obtain a table with headwords and their frequencies. After pruning from the table the most common and banal prepositions, verbs, and nouns used in English writing, we are left with a shortlist containing terms that are frequently used in the text, indicating the more particular words people associate today with the topic at hand. Due to the power of visual cues, a word cloud can be more effective in helping us map out concepts than the simple list of word frequencies in the spreadsheet used to generate it. Below is a word cloud generated from words in Pope Francis's encyclical *Fratelli Tutti*, featuring only words used twenty or more times:

There is, of course, a certain subjectivity to the exercise, but when I scan the word cloud for the most important concepts we use in official Catholic Church discourse to talk about kin and stranger—the topic of the encyclical—what strikes me are notions like human dignity, human rights, peace, dialogue, development, love, countries, fraternity, peoples, solidarity, justice, church, neighbor, community, and universality.

I have done the same with the Dublin III Regulation of the European Union (Reg. no. 604/2013) using software that groups compound words together. What strikes me are terms like international protection, (charter of) fundamental rights, regulations and procedures, residence document, unaccompanied minor, stateless person, third country national, crisis management, asylum system, parliament, member state, territory, national law, competent authority, visa, and personal data.

We cannot discuss all these concepts here, but they can serve as a checklist to formulate questions like, "Can we talk about rights in antiquity?" "Were there immigration crises?" "How did they conceive of borders and political membership?" "What did the people in the ANE think about ethnic kinship and hospitality?" We can then use these questions to leaf through some dictionaries, encyclopedias, and specialist literature that help us familiarize ourselves with the political and social realities of antiquity.

5.2 A Table of Opposites

One way of mapping concepts without overly systematizing them, which has been transmitted to us by antiquity, is the construction of a table of opposites (*sustoichía*). The secretive Pythagoreans and other presocratic philosophers favored the use of this approach; Aristotle famously attributes one such table to Pythagoras himself (*Metaphysics* I 986a).[2] Semiotic approaches use an analytical tool called the Greimas Square to analyze biblical texts using contrary and contradictory terms, but here we are mainly interested in opposites as a heuristic tool.

Let us proceed to construct tables of opposites with the terms surrounding our notion of kinship and strangerhood. What follows is not a series of simple or "neutral" distinctions, but a lens through which we can look at our political and social reality. I will not try to imagine what my average reader understands when contrary notions listed below are invoked. Rather, I will share what comes to my mind as reader as I place myself in front of the biblical text seeking wisdom to reflect on contemporary ethical issues. I am aware that I may be an atypical reader: I have lived abroad for many years and during those years, I have cultivated an interest in political philosophy and sociology that has allowed me to challenge and reshape the preunderstandings of political sameness and otherness I had when I first left my country. I am also aware that my reading is based on the Catholic Social Thought tradition, hence a rich and metaphysically encumbered reading rooted in a full theory of the good.[3]

In-Group versus Out-Group

According to a well-accepted theory in sociology based on the research of British anthropologist Robin Dunbar, we can only really maintain about 150 interpersonal connections at once. This limits the dimension of the main group or groups of which we are members (our in-group social bonds) and effectively places most other humans in an out-group. When we think of a parish, a social movement, a cultural community, an ethnic group, a nation, or a body politic of a modern nation-state we are thinking of numbers far greater than 150 persons. We often try to convince ourselves for many reasons that we share some kind of intimate link with all members of these groups that could justify considering the whole group a "we," in contrast to other groups we consider as "they." However, this larger pool of belonging is mostly a product of our social imagination, and having such an imagination is arguably one of the most salient characteristics that distinguishes humans from other animals.[4]

Let us push this sociological discussion into the realm of political philosophy. In the first chapter of his 1951 book *Man and the State*, Jacques Maritain distinguishes between communities and societies. *Communities*, on one hand, are considered primarily products of nature, social facts. We are born into a certain family, and we share genes and physiological traits with our biological ancestors; we grow up in a certain culture. We do not choose our starting community and its identity. *Societies*, on the other hand, exceed what is natural and are deemed products of reason, and hence ongoing tasks to accomplish. We can get married or start a business partnership: we thereby create societies through our reason and will. At a later stage, marriage can give rise to a clan that is once again a community for the descendants of the couple; hence, societies can spontaneously become communities. Communities, however, cannot naturally become societies since the introduction of human reason and will implies a jump to a different order of things.[5]

(Ethnic) Nation versus Body Politic

Maritain then takes his distinction a step further and uses it to discuss nations. Maritain sees communities as the bases of nations: he understands *nation* etymologically in the natural sense. Societies, on the other hand, constitute bodies politic, which are products of human reason and will, and hence not merely natural. Other authors prefer using the term *ethnic nations* in the first case (Maritain's natural nations) and *demotic nations* instead of bodies politic; the distinction is based on two different words for nation used in ancient Greek, *ethnos* and *demos*, which are conflated in many modern languages. Maritain notes that over extended periods of time, bodies politic tend to cohere biologically and culturally, and give rise to nations in a secondary sense, just like marriages may give rise to clans. We may say that they start to appear more and more like ethnic groups, though they are originally demotic. People from different ethnic nations (for example, Tanganyikans and Zanzibarians) can come together to build a single body politic (Tanzania) that slowly gives rise to a new people with a Tanzanian identity.

A short discussion of my sociopolitical identity may help the reader to better understand Maritain's distinctions. As a Maltese citizen, I am a member of the (modern) Maltese body politic, which is an ongoing political project, resulting from a series of willed and planned political decisions, including the granting of a constitution in 1921 to the Crown Colony of Malta, which allowed limited self-government, followed by full independence from Great Britain in 1964. My will, together with that of the other members of the Maltese demotic nation—including several new citizens naturalized this year who may not speak Maltese— shapes the present and future of this political project. I can, however, apply for Italian citizenship and renounce my membership in this group.

By contrast, many people would consider me "ethnically Maltese," but what constitutes an "ethnic group" or *ethnie*, especially in the case of tiny port-nations such as Malta, is subject to debate in contemporary cultural anthropology.[6] When I reached a certain age, I was taught to feel part of a group of people who—without making any conscious choice—happen to speak Maltese as their first language, have European light skin pigmentation, grew up in a Mediterranean culture mainly shaped by southern Italian Catholicism (which nonetheless contains some British and Maghrebi elements), and have ancestors who were born in the Maltese archipelago and shared the traits above. Probably there are many third-generation Australians and Canadians who feel more ethnically Maltese than I do, though a nativist might be angered by this claim, since I was born and schooled in Malta and the Micallefs are among the oldest known inhabitants of the Maltese islands, with records going back to the 1400s.

Maltese ethnicity is hard to delimit. The Maltese are too few to be considered a full-blown ethnic group, so they have been defined in the past by reference to larger groups. However, they have always been hard to place (a phenomenon called "liminality")[7] and in different contexts were considered Italian Brits, Arab Italians, Westernized or Latinized Orientals, Catholic Maghrebis, European Semites, Mediterranean blacks who pass for white, papist gentlemen corsairs, and so forth, until independence created a Maltese demotic nation in 1964. The absence of significant immigration to the islands until recent years allowed the Maltese to conflate their newfound demotic identity with an ethnic identity. Most other Europeans are traditionally less insecure about their ethnic identity. Through modern mass movements like Romanticism, majority groups and some minority groups in large European nation-states have been constituted, based on certain recognizable biological and cultural features, and their members were taught to feel they belong in a single, large "ethnic nation."

Dunbar's number should help us understand that though some of the listed traits are real, the large ethnic groupings posited as social facts by nationalist movements in the 1800s and the 1900s are not as "natural" as they seem. Maritain's distinctions avoid this complex debate on the origins of nationalism. His point is that as such, a natural community or small *ethnie* is not a political entity and cannot become a society, since true politics for Maritain (following Aristotle and Aquinas) is a question of rational orientation of a group toward a good end, which is called the common good. The physical and biological proximity of persons who find themselves enmeshed in a web of relations through instinct and hereditary linkages can produce culture and be studied by sociologists and anthropologists. But for politics, we need a *society*, a group of persons brought together to accomplish a task, having a common end, and a society does not "happen" naturally.

Maritain invites us to make a further distinction between bodies politic (demotic nations) and states. The state "is only that part of the body politic especially concerned with the maintenance of law, the promotion of the common welfare and public order, and the administration of public affairs."[8] Bodies politic are much larger realties than states. They include what many authors today call "civil society" (the "third sector of society" distinct from government and for-profit business, that is, the aggregate of nongovernmental and not-for-profit associations such as churches, universities, trade unions, and clubs) plus the large social group comprising all families and private citizens (which I do not include in the term *civil society*, though some authors do). We may also consider "resident aliens" to be part of the body politic, to some extent, insofar as their reason and will can help shape the ongoing project of the body politic (its search for the common good through concrete political choices). Noncitizen residents may shape political debates through civil society movements, and in some countries, they have a right to vote in local elections.

By contrast, the (ethnic) nation is "a community of people who become aware of themselves as history has made them, who treasure their past, and who love themselves as they know or imagine themselves to be, with a kind of introversion."[9] Maritain avoids linking nations to *countries*, another ambiguous and burdened term. Though nations are usually associated with *soil* or a *land*, in this context *land* is not a "territorial area of power and administration but a cradle of life, work, pain and dreams."[10] By abolishing the distinction between bodies politic (demotic nations) and ethnic nations, some populist movements in modernity have created an undifferentiated notion of nationhood, called "The People," *Das Volk*, or *La Patrie*. Some of these movements morphed into totalitarian governments, using state organs to exclude, harass, and persecute minorities, leading to the modern "plague of nationalism" or what we may designate more precisely as "ethno-nationalism." The horrors perpetrated by National Socialism in Germany and by the Vichy Government in France (which was allied with the Nazis during World War II) were still fresh in Maritain's mind when in 1949 he gave the series of lectures in Chicago that became *Man and the State*. Maritain's distinctions, however, do not exclude the possibility of a healthy patriotic nationalism at the level of the demotic nation, what contemporary authors would call "civic nationalism."[11]

Maritain's distinctions are helpful, but his insistence on reason, freedom, and a common telos (ultimate purpose) seems too one-sided. Most people find themselves belonging to a body politic simply by being born in a certain place and risk total political disenfranchisement (and possibly social exclusion, misery, and even death at the border) were they to try to leave that bounded physical space. Though, as Habermas insists, we should not conceive modern polities as "communities of fate" (*Schicksalsgemeinschaften*) in the prepolitical sense (as in German Romanticist thinking, for example, Herder's theory of the *Volksgeist*),[12] and we cannot forget that a modern polity is a human rational project of social construction, superimposed on the physical fact of a territory that must be (and is already being) inhabited and managed.

This brings us to another important notion: whereas ethnic nations are tied to a "soil" symbolically, in modern polities after Westphalia, bodies politic exercise material and legal control over a tract of land on the surface of planet Earth, usually in an exclusive manner. Surely, modern polities are human associations (products of human will and reason that have a beginning and end in history), but they are more than simple clubs or associations that rent or occupy physical space as subjects of laws made by a higher authority. There is of course no higher authority that rents out territories to modern polities, and evicts them when they use it in ways detrimental to the human society as a whole, to future generations, or to other creatures. However, this does not mean that we may conceive modern polities to be the exclusive and undisputed owners of the land they control: polities are stewards, not owners, of the land. The territory or "country" in question existed and belonged to humanity long before these societies were constituted, and long before the very idea of exclusive territorial control was invented at Westphalia. Modern polities can control and occupy tracts of land exclusively simply because other polities allow them to do so, in exchange for the recognition of these others' title to the land they control.

This discussion implies that from an ethics point of view, modern polities, being territorial stewards and not merely clubs, do not respond only to the will of their members, but are also bound by duties toward the whole of humanity (including future generations), and toward creation. If they desire to keep their moral title to the stewardship of the land entrusted to them by humanity, they cannot continually and systematically refuse to welcome new members if their economies can support them. When wealth accumulates in certain territories due to their polities' luck and to advantageous power differentials among countries generated by that wealth, they cannot indefinitely hoard the resources of humanity, keeping members of poorer bodies politic from having access to them. Furthermore, given that the planet Earth is a sphere and its surface a finite expanse of land,[13] and there is no "empty land" left to colonize, exclusivist Westphalian sovereignty over land imposes—within certain limits—a moral duty on wealthy bodies politic to welcome new members from burdened and destabilized polities, especially if the wealthy polities contributed to current predicament of the latter societies. The moral alternative—unpalatable and unthinkable for most people today—would be giving up land[14] or reverting to a pre-Westphalian notion of nested and overlapping territorial sovereignties.

Ethnic Nationalism versus Civic Nationalism

At this point we can introduce a first point of contact between our modern constellation of notions that frame our area of moral concern (selfhood and strangerhood) and the world of the Bible. Historians like Shaye J. D. Cohen argue convincingly that Jewishness is an imagined identity, not underpinned by any "empirical, objective reality to which we can point."[15] We will discuss this further when we move to the other notions in the constellation. Yet the idea that there was in antiquity a distinctive ethnic group—the "Jews" or the "Israelites"—that was oppressed or exiled multiple times, and that fought to have a land of its own, has inspired many ethno-nationalist movements in modernity.

For instance, "Va, pensiero" or the "Chorus of the Hebrew Slaves" from Verdi's *Nabucco* has a central place in the history of the Italian Risorgimento. No matter what the intention of Verdi's librettist was (that is, whether he was truly committed to the nationalist cause), and whether or not the chorus was actually encored on the premiere night,[16] there is no doubt that the text soon took on a life and meaning of its own in Italian political history. Based on Psalm 137, the chorus speaks of Israelite slaves in Babylon in antiquity. It allowed the Italian-speaking spectators of the nineteenth century to wonder whether they, like the Babylonian captives, were being held captive by foreign rulers in the Italian peninsula, and so to appropriate the biblical image and become romantically conscious of their ethnic identity as the "Italian people." Arguably, a vague idea that there was such a thing as an Italian nation, split among petty kingdoms and lands ruled by "foreigners," may have existed since the 1300s, but this was understood as one of many overlapping ethnic identities a person born in Sicily or Florence possessed, and rarely stood out as a very important one. However, the idea that such a nation could be clearly defined, and that it was entitled to possess and rule a certain contiguous tract of land alone and as one group was what drove the Italian liberation and unification movement. Important Italian politicians like Massimo Taparelli, Marquis of Azeglio, came to admit upon unification that while the movement had succeeded in creating Italy (as a sovereign territory), one still had to "create the Italians."[17]

The Risorgimento is considered by most scholars to be "nationalist" in the proper sense of the word or as that word has come to be understood in light of the events of the twentieth century. Modern nationalisms, as Walker Connor argued in the 1990s, are mass political phenomena, the products of mass cultures, which can develop only in modern states.[18] Yet, the biblical texts that modern nationalist movements often used and referred to in their rhetoric hint at a premodern sense of national belonging. In antiquity, we can find politically assertive discourses and movements based on the ostentation of real or imaginary ethnic ties and sentiments seeking to define and promote the interests of a particular human group, but they are not products of mass cultures and hence are not "nationalisms" in the proper sense of the word.

Anthony Smith argues that nationalism does have premodern incarnations that he classifies under three paradigms: "hierarchy," "covenant," and "republic."[19] Three corresponding forms of nationalism (hierarchical, covenantal, republican) are already present in some of the political arrangements of antiquity. Empires, such as those in Mesopotamia and Egypt, emphasized hierarchy and presented themselves as divinely mandated. Tribal confederations and ethnoreligious kingdoms, such as biblical Israel, emphasized the idea of a covenant with God and among tribes. (Biblical Israel also showcases elements of hierarchical nationalism promoted in times of centralized monarchic rule.) Among city-states, such as those in ancient Greece, some promoted republican nationalism, while others developed ideologies supporting hierarchy, always in accordance with the supposed political propensities of their respective city gods.

Given these rudimentary elements of nationalistic thought, at the end of the Middle Ages and in early modernity, the Bible, alongside Roman legal texts and Greek philosophical writings, had a central role in shaping the proximal precursors of what we call "nationalism," which nevertheless were different from today's nationalisms, heavily influenced by Westphalia and Romanticism. Of course, even modern nationalist movements, starting with the Risorgimento, make ample use of the Bible, as we have hinted above. Moxnes, for instance, traces how the various versions of the historical Jesus resulting from the different quests in the nineteenth and twentieth centuries often mirror the nationalist ideals of the different exegetes.[20]

Any polity sufficiently large to have the governance structure required by modern economics and diplomacy is of course much greater than a group of 150 persons and has a history of migration and mixing of peoples, whether or not this is taught to children at school and admitted by historians and politicians. There is little need to map mitochondrial DNA and Y-chromosome haplogroups to realize that even tiny island polities like Malta are multiethnic. Yet ethnic nationalism in its biological and cultural simplicity is powerful and seductive and has been historically beneficial by allowing human politics to evolve beyond tribalism and warlord rule. It is not easily superseded by a healthier civic nationalism or patriotism. Patriotism, too, can become discriminatory, excessively exclusive, hysterical, or expansionist. There is a long debate on how citizens of modern polities today can espouse a balanced form of patriotism and become "cosmopolitan patriots" in a globalized world.[21] Yet, many recognize the importance of a healthy patriotism, for instance in Europe. The European Union is a body politic, but it can function well only if its citizens feel they belong together, rather than simply possessing European passports and being represented in the European Parliament.

In-Group Solidarity versus Out-Group Solidarity

This brings us to the notion of solidarity, a ubiquitous term in moral and political discourse, especially within Christian churches, yet laden with ambiguity.[22] First, we need to distinguish between solidarity as a social fact that can be observed and studied (such as Durkheim's *organic* and *mechanical* solidarity, both of which are mainly descriptive notions) and solidarity as a call to do something (a prescriptive notion). In the latter case, the moral agent is invited either to choose solidarity as a good (value) or to engage in a series of solidary practices that become stable habits when repeated consistently over time (virtue). Second, we need to figure out how our solidarity extends in fact, or not, and how it should extend, or not, beyond the most immediate concentric social sphere around the self, for example, the 150 people in Dunbar's theory.

The question "Who is my neighbor?" which we discussed extensively in chapter 1 when dealing with the parable of the good Samaritan, can be rephrased as "With whom should I be solidary?" The parable "presupposes" (in Eco's sense) that we have duties toward people in biological and cultural proximity to ourselves, people belonging to our family, clan, nation, culture, or closely-knit religious group. It invites us, however, to take a step beyond that, and to be solidary with people who are physically close and in need, though ethnically distant (I here understand "ethnically" in a wide sense to include cultural, biological, and religious components). Hence, one dimension along which we build concentric spheres around the "I" has a mix of physical and ethnic closeness/distance. The other dimension is the time dimension, regarding whether the relationship (and hence closeness/distance) is short-term or long-term. This allows us to distinguish among different types of solidarity, as in table 5.1.

TABLE 5.1: TYPES OF SOLIDARITY (PRESCRIPTIVE)

Solidarity		*How permanent?*	
		Short-term	*Long-term*
With whom?	Family, friends, neighbors, peers	In-group Hospitality	In-group Kin-bonding/Fraternity
	Strangers nearby	Outreaching Hospitality	Outreaching Kin-bonding/ Fraternity
	Strangers far away	Philanthropy	Humaneness, Global Justice, & Peace

The table brackets discussions of solidarity that are purely descriptive. We have discussed Dunbar's number, which points to a very restricted sociological circle of solidarity around the self, but the flip side of this theory is the notion of "six degrees of separation" popularized in the "small-world" experiments of Stanley Milgram and more recently Columbia University's Small World Project.[23] All humans are six or fewer social connections away from each other, especially today with the advent of modern forms of communication, and this allows us to adopt a wide-raging notion of human solidarity from a descriptive viewpoint.

The table focuses on solidarity as a prescriptive notion. Religious leaders like Pope Francis and Grand Imam Al-Tayyeb have recently promoted the notion of universal "human fraternity," even though we are conscious that there are sociological limits to the imaginary social extension of kinship-bonding, and that group boundaries are an essential feature for the functioning of human groups.[24] I may not feel I am the brother or sister of every other human, unless we are using these kinship terms in a very loose and figurative manner. Nevertheless, I may be moved by a war or famine video clip to send money or aid to the other side of the world (in the short term) and eventually to strive more consistently for global justice and peace, developing the virtue of humanity or humaneness (in the long term) that roots humanitarianism.[25] This constitutes the bottom row of our table.

Above this row, we deal with a shorter-term form of solidarity that we usually call *hospitality* (though it may be constant, risky, and radical, as in the case of the good Samaritan),[26] or a longer-term form that we call *fraternity* or kinship bonding (here we use the term *kinship*, not in a biological sense, but in the figurative and social sense of membership in a political family). Both hospitality (welcoming the other) and kinship bonding (integrating the other) can be limited to people who are ethnically close (members of the same clan, culture, religion) or extended to people who are ethnically distant (at least initially) but physically close.

Hospitality versus Kinship Bonding

In chapter 1 (Allegory 5) we mentioned the Kew Gardens Principle. David Hollenbach argues that

> reflection on the Kew Gardens case suggests that an agent has a positive ethical responsibility to respond when four conditions are present: (a) there is a critical need; (b) the agent has proximity to the need; (c) the agent has the capability to respond; and (d) the agent is likely the last resort from whom help can be expected. These criteria cannot be applied mechanically, but they are useful in thinking about the scope of responsibility in the face of the suffering [of refugees].[27]

Hollenbach is describing what we have called *hospitality* in the previous section; it is not always a supererogatory duty or a virtue that we may or may not habituate ourselves to pursue and excel in, but it can at times become a strict moral duty. At other times, hospitality is optional, in the case of individuals, but consistently bracketing this virtue will eventually make us unhospitable and risks irreparably fouling our moral character.

Let us compare and contrast hospitality, amply treated in our discussion of the parable of the good Samaritan in chapter 1, to the notion of "civic kinship bonding." The two can be seen as related concepts lying on a continuum, but also as contraries, in the sense in which "temporary," "occasional," and "extraordinary" (hospitality) are contraries of "permanent," "constant," and "ordinary" (kinship bonding). Many people welcome refugees and vulnerable migrants, but they may at the same time be hostile to the idea that such foreigners should be allowed to stay permanently in the country, obtain citizenship, benefit from the welfare state, and enjoy all the rights of "ordinary" citizens.

A helpful criterion to determine "whom should I treat as my civic kin" is the notion of interdependence, not merely understood as a sociological fact, but as a reality that can and should be shaped morally. For example, David Hollenbach reflects on the poverty present in US core cities, and on the moral and political wall that keeps their inhabitants from fully sharing in the goods visibly available in the affluent suburbs. He argues that the problem is not so much one of dependence (that is, the dependence of the poor on welfare, or the dependence of the rich on the systemic exploitation of the lower classes), but one of unequal interdependence.[28] The opposite of this is "interdependence in solidarity," which Hollenbach elsewhere describes as a reciprocal relationship among equal partners, set in the context of "a transformed institutional framework that supports a more equal and reciprocal relationship with the larger society."[29] Unequal interdependence, conversely, is "the kind of relationship that exists between persons who hold very different amounts of power, both power which enables them to influence the shape of the larger society they live in and power to influence each other, whether directly and intentionally or indirectly and unintentionally."[30] In such a relationship, "one of the partners has the power to make things happen while the other partner lacks such power."[31]

Hollenbach links his distinction to that made by Pope John Paul II in *Sollicitudo Rei Socialis* 26 between de facto interdependence and moral interdependence. The positive (solidary or moral) form of interdependence is one that "enhances the agency and well-being of all who are part of it,[32] and in this process, greater respect for the human dignity of all is attained. Enhancing agency and increasing respect for human dignity are common goods, shared achievements, rather than goods up for grabs in a zero-sum game. This is why John Paul II defines the virtue of solidarity as a "firm and persevering determination to commit oneself to the common good" (*SRS* 38).

In the context of the relationship between core-city dwellers and suburbanites who must live together permanently, one would hope that such solidarity would grow beyond mere hospitality into kinship solidarity. When speaking of the relationship with immigrants, however, this depends on the length of their stay and on the depth of the interdependence that develops. However, both in the form of hospitality and in the form of kinship, solidarity has a transformative property that seeks to reduce or compensate for the power differentials that exist in the relationships between inner-city poor and wealthy suburban residents, and between citizens and migrants—whether they are sojourners or long-term immigrants wishing to become fully integrated into the polity. In this way, rather than posit a conflict between justice and love, solidarity demands that we love the other justly. In other words, we are to practice a *caritas* that does not overlook the dignity of the other or suppress her agency, a love that does not perpetuate power differentials that cannot be morally justified, as traditional forms of "philanthropy" and "charity" often do.[33]

Here again, there is a point of contact and contrast between our constellation of notions and those in Scripture, and we will explore this briefly. Hospitality is an important moral virtue in antiquity, but, as Elias Bickerman notes, "Oriental civilizations had no concept of naturalization,"[34] and so we must take special care when we project our notions of integration and societal fraternity (or societal kinship bonding) onto Scripture. Antiquity tolerated a permanent underclass of metics or denizens, given the feudal nature of society in general, which made of most residents a politically disenfranchised underclass whether they were autochthonous or not (unequal interdependence). The poverty that subsistence agriculture imposed on most residents, the relative simplicity and repetitiveness of their occupations, and the mentality of the day made many of the civil, political, and economic rights we take for granted today simply inconceivable. By contrast, modern societies cannot function healthily—and indeed risk destabilization—if they allow a permanently disenfranchised underclass of denizens to subsist and grow. Several factors account for this difference. Modern societies are complex, their political systems encourage and depend on representation and political participation, and their economies offer education and create free time for their citizens to get them engaged in political activism and deliberation.

Nevertheless, the lack of formal, legal procedures for naturalization or for permanent integration of the other into one's social group does not mean that there is nothing to be sought in Scripture beyond notions of occasional or temporary hospitality when reflecting on how a human community and society should shape its relationship with the non-threatening resident alien.

Identity versus Difference

The basic set of opposites underlying all the notions above is identity/difference (or, in other words, selfhood/strangerhood, or sameness/otherness). In real life, people often have multiple overlapping identities that modern nationalism and our heuristic use of opposites tends to obscure, and the tension between these opposites is often internal to the self. One way of resolving this tension, in many nationalist and religious ideologies, entails selecting one identity as predominant and linking it to faithfulness (that is, faithfulness to one's people or to one's God lived out as a faithfulness to a received identity). This is then used as a rationale to exclude the "other," discriminate against her, or treat her with hostility, including the "other" present within ourselves. The "other," especially when she comes too close or when we are stressed or not completely serene in our self-understanding, is seen as a threat to our identity and hence to the faithfulness we feel called to. Her tantalizing otherness is perceived as a temptation that may lead to contamination, disunity, syncretism and even betrayal of our origin, our being, or of the image we have built of ourselves. Identity faithfulness is these cases is based on a latent fear that haunts fragile selves, a fear of losing oneself; it therefore leads to exclusivist or closed notions of kinship and minimal displays of hospitality that I shall call *timorous identity faithfulness*.

The opposite of this phenomenon is *trusting identity faithfulness*. At some level, these two opposites constitute a matter of choice, which can result from constant training in the virtue of hope or be a product of faith in a just and generous God. Still, there are a lot of social and historical factors involved that limit and condition this choice, this training, and the kind of faith (and image of God) we carry with us in our lives. In people or communities who have been deeply hurt and feel vulnerable, a pervasive fear may shape their notion of identity and of faithfulness. Some, however, are embedded in contexts and cultures that, combined with their personal action, allow them to experience sufficient resilience so to become beacons of hope, surprisingly capable of trusting strangers.[35]

As we shall see, there are times when biblical authors seem tempted to think in terms of timorous identity faithfulness, believing that the exclusion of the other is necessary to avoid idolatrous contamination and remain faithful to YHWH, and thereby avoid being exiled and losing the land once again. Ironically, in the process, they risk letting themselves be "contaminated" or "influenced" negatively by an idolatrous image of a mistrusting, petty, narcissistic God. The revelation of the biblical God points to a very different use of the idea of identity faithfulness, one based on trust, as we shall see in the following chapters.

To be sure, Israel is asked to live out her faithfulness to God by remaining faithful to her God-given identity, but that identity is best understood as one that is solidary with the nonhostile stranger and open enough to welcome him. This initial solidarity, first lived out as hospitality, can then lead to an open understanding of kinship that implies the gradual inclusion of the others permanently residing in our midst as part of our very self, without necessarily or completely extirpating their otherness.

5.3 Mapping Some Biblical Concepts of Selfhood and Otherness in the Old Testament

Now that we have mapped out and linked some of the major concepts that we use today to reflect on group identity and strangerhood, on setting the boundaries of nations and opening them for immigration, let us turn to sound historical and archaeological scholarship to help us understand what purchase our concepts have in the world of the Old Testament. Though we will not stop to analyze particular texts at this point in the book, I believe the conceptual differences we will discover will give us much food for thought in ethics.

Compassion and Equity versus Mixability

Let us start with a general note on the notion of right and wrong, fair and foul, since this is ultimately a book about ethics. Modern ethics texts and catechisms offer various distinctions between sinless/sinful, right/wrong, and good/bad, inspired by authors such as Plato, Aristotle, Aquinas, and Kant. They are not always helpful to navigating Scripture and antiquity. The word *ethics* in English is derived from two similar Greek words (*ēthos* with an eta, already found in Homer, and *ethos* with an epsilon, first attested in Aeschylus) both referring to customary behavior deemed wise because of its customariness. Table 5.2 provides a more suitable rough compass for our remapping exercise.

TABLE 5.2: MODERN AND PREMODERN NOTIONS OF ETHICAL/UNETHICAL		
	Premodern notion of fair/foul (sinful)	Modern notion of right/ wrong
Objective dimension (relational)	Violation of standards of mixability, ancestral valor and vitality, equity, and sometimes, compassion	Violation of standards of equity and compassion
Objective dimension (cosmic)	Some concomitant impact on cosmic order/ chaos (entropy) is often assumed, with material impact in this universe	Besides direct mechanical causality from the external act, no direct material cosmic impact is assumed (only theological impact, in a spiritual realm)
Subjective dimension	Unintentionality combined with nonnegligence may attenuate culpability but do not always exonerate. Ethics and positive law are not clearly distinguished	Unintentionality combined with nonnegligence exonerates in ethics, though some strict liability torts persist in positive law

When we think about why it is wrong to lie, to steal, to hurt or kill someone, we usually see these actions as violating the values of truth, property, and life, including bodily integrity. As indicated at the top right corner of the table, most of us intuitively link these evil acts to unfairness or callousness (lack of empathy/compassion), notions that have deep biological roots, and hence are transcultural and intuitive.[36] We rarely think in terms of virtue in the archaic sense (*aretē*, *virtus*), which refers to the maintenance of a clan's ancestral prowess and vitality, rather than equity or compassion. Neither do we think in terms of unmixability or "defilement" (purity/impurity, "kosherness"), which were very important notions in antiquity and were not a question of hygiene or microbial density. (Germ theory wasn't widely popularized until the early twentieth century). Yet the Torah is a double-Decalogue system, one Decalogue leaning more to the modern sense of "ethical," the other (Exod 34:14–26) dealing more with kosherness.

The core idea of kosherness is that there are certain things that do not mix or that pertain to separate realms; mixing them is dangerous and should be avoided.[37] The reason why they do not mix is usually not intuitive, and it is not always logical (though there might be partial sociological and medical warrant for some of the taboos). A story or myth is generally used to make some sense of the unmixability rules. Mixability rules are learned through socialization; some are subtle and sophisticated and help distinguish social classes.[38] We moderns, too, have similar notions (food in a restroom, sandals on a desk or coffee table, prayer during a sporting event or political rally) but often they are more muted and less noticeable than in antiquity.

Furthermore, in some contexts and texts there is also the idea that mixing the unmixable, and violating basic fairness (and, to a lesser degree, acting callously, without compassion) can have not only a social impact but also a cosmic impact. Human action may stir up the supernatural forces of chaos and order into action in the celestial realm, in tandem with what is happening on the ground between human groups. The two realms are seen as intimately linked and materially linked, and what happens in the celestial realm might have a direct, visible impact on the terrestrial one. In our modern societies, we do have some notion of "miracle" and of "existential" threats, but most mainstream religions tend to avoid this kind of cosmology. Fundamentalist sects often don't, and certain terrorists read reality using this kind of mentality.[39]

Finally, in antiquity the fact that an act might not be willed or intentional does not fully exonerate the agent from a moral or theological standpoint, even when the agent cannot reasonably be accused of negligence. A person may "sin" (offend the deity) unconsciously or may inherit culpability from her parents (though Jer 31:29–30 and Ezek 18:1–4 challenge this). Of course, we do have a legal and moral notion of culpable negligence in modernity (and of "sins of omission"). Nonetheless, medieval debates after Peter Abelard led to a distinction between a morally irrelevant "act of a human" (*actus hominis*) and a morally relevant human act (*actus humanus*), which is consciously controlled and deliberately willed, allowing us to attribute responsibility for the act and its effects more fairly to the agent. This distinction shapes modern thought, but is not clear in many Scripture passages about sin.

Communitarian Grouping versus Territorial Grouping

We cannot touch on all notions that might need remapping, so let us focus on those most central to the topic of this book. The title of Cohen's book, *The Beginnings of Jewishness*, indicates that we are dealing with an imagined identity, like most other national identities.[40] Yet, when we consider the text of the Jewish Bible, there is clearly a "we" that is assumed. We often use different terms in English to speak of this "we": the Jews, the Hebrews, the Israelites. Whatever term we decide to use, we necessarily and implicitly invoke at least two dimensions of this political "we," as in most cases when we speak of human groups: (a) distinctive cultural, religious, or biological traits that allow the members to join together and exclude others considered "different," and (b) a link to a tract of land.

The first dimension, distinctiveness (key to communitarian grouping), invites a series of questions we need to explore before reading biblical texts about strangerhood. Were Israelites in antiquity a distinct human group? Was there an Israelite "ethnicity," and if so, in what sense? Can we project modern notions of ethnic identity onto Scripture? If we let what we think about the modern state of Israel and its citizens or the members of Jewish communities whom we might have met or are present in our countries excessively determine the "we" of the Hebrew Bible, our reading risks being anachronistic. Distinctiveness in Scripture is linked to *holiness* (separateness in general), both on the mixability axis (separateness qua kosherness, which we as moderns tend to bracket) and on the equity-compassion axis (separateness from what we deem "moral evil").

The link with a territory brings us to the second dimension, land (key to territorial grouping). The Romanticist notion of an ethnic nation-state created a veritable monster by fusing together the notion of an ethnic nation (a community, with a symbolic relationship to land, as described by Maritain) with the notion of a body politic, a post-Westphalian political society based on a territorial grouping of humans. Here, a demotic nation, represented by the institutions of the state, is allowed by other such nations to exercise total economic, social, and political control over a geographical portion of the planet Earth. This conflation of human groupings has given rise to centuries of persecution of minorities, ethnic cleansing, and genocide, as powerful ethnic nations present within territories they came to control insisted that different ethnic nations should not exist in "their" space, even if the latter had been there for decades and centuries.

As readers of the Bible, we therefore need to ask ourselves to what extent the editors of canonical Scriptures had a sense of Israel as an "ethnic group" in the modern sense and of the promised land as a territorial area where power and administration is subjected to the monopoly of one single organ called the state (in the post-Westphalian sense, as intended by Maritain). Conversely, we need to ask to what extent the Romanticist "monster"—for example, the dream of an Italian nation-state projected onto the sighs of the Hebrew slaves of *Nabucco*'s "Va, pensiero"—is an anachronistic modern reappropriation of a dispute between Judean/Israelite groups in Persian and Hellenistic Syria-Palestine, which the Bible only fragmentarily preserves.

To illustrate the problem, let me note that in antiquity, even the notion of "possessing land" was quite different from today. The real owners were the gods, and the secondary owners (or primary lessees) were kings or powerful nobles or clans. (The shifting notions of royal ownership of land are illustrated in the case of Naboth's vineyard, 1 Kgs 21.) The commoners working and living on the land were never considered "owners" in the modern sense, but rather lessees subleasing from higher-tier lessees. In some Mediterranean countries, like Malta, we still have a sense of this, having to inherit and deal with complex medieval contracts, leases with no eviction clause and with symbolic ground rents, usufructuary rights, and perpetual emphyteusis. There are different types and layers of *dominium* (control) over property. Absolute property rights where all levels of *dominium* are collapsed into one are mostly a modern simplification, but we often project them onto texts from Antiquity dealing with control over expanses of land.

Observable Distinctiveness versus Discoverable Distinctiveness

The awareness and polemic assertion of distinctiveness of one's people (*'am*) from among the nations of the world (*gôyim*) is indeed characteristic of the Hebrew Bible, so much so that it has shaped the understanding of ethnicity not only in Italy (as we have noted above) but also in relatively modern polities such as the United States. Roger Waldinger observes that what the early scholars of sociology had in mind when speaking of "ethnicity" was the Hebrew notion of *gôy*, rendered in modern scientific jargon through derivatives of *éthnos*, following the Septuagint rendering of *gôy*.[41] Romanticism and modern notions of ethnicity have an impact on our reading of Scripture, but the reverse is also true, as noted above regarding "Va, pensiero."

Observable Distinctiveness?

What is this awareness founded on? Was an ethnic group of Israelites in Old Testament times clearly distinct from other nations in the ANE? Israel's distinctiveness (in premonarchic times, at least, and possibly until Hezekiah or until the exile) is not easily observable using material artifacts and empirical scientific methods. It is very hard and maybe impossible to determine a trait that clearly distinguishes preexilic Israel from the other peoples of the Near East. Monotheism, aniconism, and other characteristics have been tried, but they did not exist in pure form at the time and were not exclusive to YHWH religion in the biblical Levant.[42] You cannot single out a distinctive culture or group from among a series of bordering groups on the basis of material artifacts alone, without texts that define the group, its boundaries, and its features.

Nevertheless, the Old Testament is written and edited in a way that seeks to convince the reader that such a distinctiveness is obvious and indubitable. The process of editing and canonizing the Bible was "part... of a wider struggle to articulate and propagate national-cultural identity during a period when such identity was threatened with major change and even extinction."[43] As we shall see below, Israel's awareness of its distinctiveness led it to shaping a very peculiar notion of national identity that may be challenging (and hence morally interesting) to modern-day readers, in contrast with modern ethno-nationalist ideologies that, ironically, were themselves inspired by a certain reading of Scripture.

Peter Machinist lists 433 "distinctiveness" passages in the Old Testament.[44] Scholars explain this insistence on distinctiveness, which cannot be easily corroborated by archeological and historical data, to a concern of the biblical editors before, during, and especially after the Babylonian exile. It probably became clear to the groups involved in these historical processes that gave us the Hebrew Bible that it was futile to try to reestablish a relatively independent Israelite or Judahite kingdom with clear territorial borders in a world of multicultural and multireligious grand empires. Thus, a normative narrative text was put together that served as an ideological wall around the Palestinian clans that subscribed to the YHWH worship considered "orthodox" in Jerusalem in the postexilic period.

Machinist draws two important conclusions from his survey of "distinctiveness" passages in the Old Testament. First, given their quantity and ubiquity, "distinctiveness…seems to have been an established and not unpopular preoccupation in Israel well before the advent of the canonical organizers in the sixth century BCE."[45] Therefore, this concern about Israel's uniqueness is not merely postexilic, but has deep roots in the old literary and cultic traditions of YHWH religion. Second, given that they focus mainly on the distinctiveness of the people of Israel (and of her God, who is the source of such uniqueness), it is presumed "that this people has a beginning within already known time: the Exodus from a long established Egypt."[46]

Discoverable Distinctiveness

Let us start by considering Machinist's first conclusion that the distinctiveness idea is too ubiquitous in the Bible to have been invented ex nihilo. In some way it is "invented," not so much in the sense of "fabricated," but more in the etymological sense of the word (*invenire*), hence "discovered" or "found." There are certain things in our childhood that we may have considered irrelevant, ignored when recounting our life story in the past, and displaced from our memory for many years. Later, at a certain point in our lives, after reading a particular novel or watching a movie or opening a family album, these details may have come back to mind powerfully. The "me" at that point in its history began to see them as key events necessary to make sense of a certain part of its past, present, and future. Some elements of these recollections may have been vivid, while other things are fuzzily remembered and are in part imaginative reconstructions. In the past they were ignored and deemed marginal, and they may still be considered marginal by many friends who may have lived through them with us. But for us, once rediscovered, they may become a key part of our identity. Our identity depends greatly on what we remember, how we remember it, and how we use it in the way we recount our story.

The plot of the narrative that is told to make sense of most biblical assertions of Israelite distinctiveness—the exodus-wilderness-conquest narrative—is not, in itself, a distinguishing feature, since other nations in the Mediterranean that also emerged in the Late Bronze to Iron I transition seem to have told similar stories about their origins.[47] Yet that common plot (successful infiltration or invasion of foreign lands, foundation of new cities by strangers, etc.) may have helped Israel stand up and say, "I too have a similar story to recount! My forebears weren't born on this land!"

The history of prestate Israel is told, in the Bible, as a three-part exodus-wilderness-conquest narrative. The exodus-wilderness part of the narrative, in its essence, is not impossible to conceive from an archaeological and historical point of view. One can assume that small groups most probably did migrate in and out of Egyptian-controlled areas and in and out of Palestine at the time, as has always happened throughout the history of the Near East.[48] The "conquest" part of the narrative, however, is much more problematic. In the past, three scenarios have been proposed concerning Israel's presence in Palestine in the prestate period: (a) conquest from outside (the narrative as presented in the Bible, defended by W. F. Albright and his disciples); (b) infiltration of pastoral nomads (proposed by A. Alt and M. Noth, and their disciples) and (c) indigenous revolution (proposed by G. Mendenhall, and in a modified version, by N. Gottwald). All are rejected today by most archaeologists and historians,[49] yet a strong consensus has formed around the claim that Israelites have emerged largely from the indigenous population of Canaan.[50]

In around 1200 BCE, villages appeared in the previously unpopulated Levantine highlands, in areas associated with the emergence of biblical Israel; there are no clear signs of violent conquest or peaceful infiltration by groups originating from outside Syria-Palestine. How these settlements arose is still a hotly debated issue; authors like Israel Finkelstein claim the process was started by pastoral nomads who already were living in these areas but now settled and started tilling the land (sedentarization); others give a greater role to poor laborers leaving the coastal city-states after years of economic decline, given the introduction of city-state agricultural technologies (ruralization).[51] This scenario does not completely discount the "exodus" part of the biblical narrative. Claiming that Israel arose largely from indigenous peoples in Iron I Syria-Palestine does not exclude the possibility that small groups of immigrants from the outside (such as from convict forced-labor camps in Egypt) may have mingled with the families and clans who fled the cities and colonized the hill country of Palestine and contributed their own inspirational family and clan narratives to the bigger group originating in Syria-Palestine.[52]

As an analogy, let us consider the claim that most US-Americans are descendants of English colonists, Louisiana French Creoles, Spaniards from what was formerly northern Mexico, and millions of West-African slaves and poor nineteenth- and twentieth-century immigrants (from Ireland, Germany, Italy, China, Japan, Eastern Europe, and so forth), often scorned and ill-treated by the former groups upon arrival. By accepting this claim, we are not saying that the pre-Columbian peoples simply disappeared or were completely exterminated, and hence shouldn't be considered as the ancestors of contemporary US-Americans in some sense. Nor are we saying that the Pilgrims were such an insignificant and peripheral group that they cannot be considered the ancestors of current US-Americans, not even in a symbolic and mythical sense. The claim in question makes a generalization based on the biological ancestry of the bulk of current US-Americans. Through the analogical imagination, however, we can see ourselves the descendants of people who are not biologically related to us, or whose actions were insignificant when they were alive, but came to inspire others and shape history years after their deaths. The Pilgrims were a tiny and marginal group, but their migration story was adopted by the larger group who felt "anamnestically solidary" with them (see box below). Their story allowed the others to make sense of their being in the United States. The pre-Columbian peoples, after many struggles, were slowly reintegrated into the land that had been theirs and woven into a new multiethnic nation that took shape via a long confrontation with their nations. Their story was never adopted by the whole modern nation, as that of the ancient Gauls in French Romanticism. This is, of course, no apology for the horrors of colonialism, but simply a helpful analog allowing us to understand how Israelites could adopt the foundational narrative of a small, marginal group.

Anamnestic Solidarity

Anamnestic solidarity means being associated and united with people in the past through the use of memory. Christian Lenhardt uses this concept to speak of the debt owed by a "liberated" generation to its oppressed and marginalized predecessors.[53] A liberated generation is one that finds itself living in a reasonably just political society thanks to the liberation struggles of previous generations, though these generations may be ethnically or culturally distant. Though inspired by Marxism, this concept challenges traditional Marxist taboos regarding the ritualization and idealization of the past and the future.

The idea behind this term probably comes from Walter Benjamin, who argued that Jewish and Christian theology can be of great help to historical materialists (Marxists) in their quest for social justice.[54] It has been adopted in theological ethics by William O'Neill.[55] The theological underpinnings of the notion are obvious: reflection on the ecclesial value of liturgical anamnesis abounds in sacramental theology, inspired by Pauline theology: "The cup of blessing that we bless, is it not a sharing in the blood of Christ?" (1 Cor 10:16). We also commemorate the Christian martyrs, whose sacrifice sanctifies our churches today and allows many Christians to live in polities shaped by many Christian values, where they may practice their religion freely. In such commemorative exercises, an Asian-American Lutheran is united with Christ in his passion, and with several martyrs, including, for example, the monks of Iona (Scotland) whose sweat and blood are emblematic of the arduous and momentous spread of Christianity in Great Britain and Scandinavia.

Some historians indirectly associate the word *Hebrew* to *ʿapiru* (Akkadian: *ḫāpiru*) a term found throughout the Fertile Crescent in second-millennium BCE texts, roughly meaning "dusty person, vagabond, traveler"—which in some literary texts became clearly pejorative ("outlaw, raider, robber")—to refer loosely to members of a motley and fringe social group.[56] It is posited that some of these traveling people may have mingled with ruralized Canaanites and that the whole group appropriated the term of abuse to describe themselves (cf. Deut 26:5, "A wandering Aramean was my ancestor").[57] Thus, what may have been a term indicating lifestyle and social class may have slowly morphed into an indicator of ethnic belonging as some persons associated with this group slowly settled lands and became more sedentary. Other scholars connect term Hebrew (*ʿibrî*) to the idea of "coming from across [the river]," hence to mean roughly "migrant." The two etymologies are probably reconcilable since the root 'br means, in various forms, to cross over, transgress.[58]

The distinctiveness question, nonetheless, is not completely settled if we accept that the prestate Israelites were mostly descended from Syro-Palestinian sedentary and seminomadic indigenous people. In the hill country of Palestine, before the establishment of a monarchy that called itself and its faithful client tribes "Israelite," was there an Israelite "tribe" or "people" or "tribal amphictyony," distinct from other populations? Diana Edelman claims that, "given the present state of textual and artefactual evidence, nothing definitive can be said about the ethnicity of premonarchic Israel."[59] Not much can be deduced from Joshua and Judges or from the Mernaptah Stele,[60] and even less from the Mesha Stele[61] and other archeological finds.[62] Even as regards the monarchy, we have little to go by to identify the "united" Davidic and Solomonic monarchy, or the early dual kingdom until the reign of Omri (ca. 885– ca. 874 BCE).[63]

Thus, in Palestine before the monarchy, there might have been a group of people clearly distinct from others, or who thought of themselves as clearly distinct and coterminous with the prestate Israel referred to in the Bible, but we have no reliable historical or archaeological evidence of that today. Though there may be some premonarchic elements of historical truth staying the biblical claim about Israel's distinctiveness, the claim owes much to a desire of some intellectuals, both in the late monarchic period and during and after the Babylonian exile, to present Israel's history as emphatically distinctive. They sought to portray Israel as a people with a clear beginning in history, and to claim the stories of the exodus group and of the wandering patriarchs for all the peoples integrated into the Israelite identity during the monarchy and after, including to some extent those living in the Babylonian, Alexandrian, and Antiochian Jewish diasporas.[64]

Cosmic Origins versus Historical Origins

Let us now examine Machinist's second conclusion concerning the "historical consciousness" of Israel. The Jewish Bible portrays Israel as a nation that has a beginning in time; its origins are not lost in history. At some point in time such a nation did not exist; then it came to be. This way of presenting things is not as obvious as it sounds. Most modern forms of ethnonationalism hint at a mythical origin and assume that the ethnic group has always existed and always lived on a certain tract of land. When an ethnic group acknowledges having been born in time, centuries after most arable lands on Earth were occupied by one tribe or another, it implicitly admits not having an ancestral "autochthonous" title to any land the group ends up occupying. A "latecomer" nation, a last-born son, starts off disinherited, a migrant, or "resident alien" at birth.

The great civilizations of the ANE preferred to trace their origins outside of time, using "classical" cosmogonic narratives. They presented themselves as firstborn among nations, created and settled since time immemorial on the land where they built their oldest and most sacred city, as instructed by the gods who blessed that land and its original inhabitants with power and prosperity. For instance, in Mesopotamian cosmogony, the god Enlil when creating order from chaos founded the city of Nippur at the center of the world and placed his throne there; all order radiates out of this center.[65] I call this way of reconstructing one's national origins the "cosmic" way; it is hidden in the mist of time and related to an act where cosmic ordering was implanted on a chaotic Earth by the gods. From the point of view of Egyptian or Mesopotamian cosmogony, while "new" peoples may be created through separation from a sacred and well-ordered origin, such peoples will be only dysfunctional peoples, barbarians, severed from the divine wellspring of order and harmony that a center of civilization provides. Distinctiveness through novel creation is tantamount to decay.[66]

When we read the first chapters of Genesis with this conceptual framework in mind, we get to see many things that could previously have been invisible to us. The creation narratives are often called "myths"—in the positive sense of symbolic stories that unveil a deeper reality to us.[67] However, the Bible (in the Book of Genesis, but also indirectly in its distinctiveness texts) does not create a parallel cosmogony (understood in the classical sense) to directly dispute the idea that the ancient inhabitants of the earth may have been Egyptians, Mesopotamians, or Canaanites. Nor does it deny that Israel's ancestors may indeed have been born of such "ancestral peoples." Rather, the Bible simply claims that the Israelites were separated from their ethnic and cultural roots by YHWH's salvific action within history and constituted into a new people, starting with the story of Abraham, and that this separation and novelty was a "very good thing." Such a claim probably would have sounded preposterous to the intelligentsia of the grand civilizations of the time. It is a claim asserting the creation of an originary order *within history* and challenging a certain notion of cosmic ordering of space where the great deities are tied to shrines and theophanic sites at fixed geographic coordinates. How can a migrant people and their migrant God birth civilization?[68]

If we bracket Genesis 1—3, biblical sources also readily concede (mostly for the sake of the argument) that while other peoples may have been created on their own land and have a prima facie title to the land they reside in (cf. Deut 32:8–9), Israel's ancestors were removed by YHWH from their ancestral lands and then ordered to invade and take for themselves the land "belonging" to other peoples. This means that the Israelites have no real originary title to the land; they have simply been stationed there as stewards by YHWH and can be removed by YHWH at any moment. It also means that Israel, as a nation, can exist apart from the land.

Indeed, Old Testament prophetic theologies concur that this precarious link to the land is what YHWH uses to chastise and purify Israel when it tries to copy the decadent ways of its older and more powerful neighbors. Leviticus 25:23 insists that "the land is mine [YHWH's]; you [Israel] are nonnationals and residents [gērîm wətôšābîm] with me" (my translation). Richard Clifford argues that even in the cosmogonic priestly creation narrative of Genesis 1, when humankind is ordered to "fill the earth and subdue it" (1:28), the text is not intended to give humans license to exploit nature (as some anachronistic modern interpreters would have it), but is rather projecting backward Israel's "historic" exodus narrative.[69] According to the vision of the exilic and postexilic Priestly sources, Israel needed to fill and conquer "Canaan" to have a land of its own (Num 32:21–22; 1 Chr 22:17–19; cf. Gen 10:1—11:9; Deut 32:8–9), where they would no longer be subjected to subservience, barrenness, or being crowded out.[70]

Even so, Adam and Eve are not only the ancestors of Abraham but also of all nations. Hence, in a way, the cosmogonic setting of Genesis 1 universalizes the experience of Israel, implying polemically that other nations, despite their claims to have been born and settled since the moment of creation on the land they claim as "theirs," are simply bluffing; they are most probably the sons of migrants, created like Israel at some point in history, just a few centuries older. All peoples have been constituted or reconstituted in the course of history and have had to conquer the land they now claim as their own.

Indeed, after this creation narrative, the Bible presents a series of cosmogonic myths, integrated within a genealogy and laid out as quasi-historical narratives:[71] Adam and Eve (the banished founders of the first family), Abel and Cain (the fugitive founder of the first city), Noah and his family (the migrant founders of the first human settlements after the flood), and the Babel story (where peoples spread out from a dysfunctional and uninhabitable city to found all the known nations away from it). All these stories repeat the same theme that nobody was created on the land they are living in, and so all are daughters and sons of migrants, and no nation has an absolute right to the land it is occupying. Without resorting to a classical cosmogony in competition with that of older nations, the Bible subtly demolishes the territorial claims of peoples who consider themselves autochthonous or "native born."

A United Yet Diverse Humanity

Enrique Sanz Giménez-Rico proposes a framework for OT ethics based on two linked groups of fundamental concepts: gift and limit, on the one hand; and sin, mercy, and justification, on the other. Relationship and law are both gifts and limits.

When discussing the relationship between nations as both gift and limit, Sanz notes that in the Genesis origins narratives (Gen 1:27–28; 9:1–10) God does not create the different nations as separate hominid species, but as one diverse race.[72] Hybridization between nations is not prohibited. In the biblical worldview, all nations are united through common ancestry in Adam and Noah, but they are also distinguished and carefully listed (Gen 10). Sanz interprets this listing as a blessing in the light of God's gifts of land (Gen 9:1; 10:31–32) and of the Babel narrative (Gen 11:1–9).

Various elements of the Tower of Babel story point to a totalitarian project, seeking to unite humans and abolish their diversity through subjugation and violence.[73] Thus, God gives different languages and cultures to the nations not only as a limit to totalitarian and nationalist hubris (overreach, defiance of one's finitude), but also as a gift (Gen 11:7–9). The nations are scattered, but God does not condemn them to living apart: the rest of Genesis presents stories of migrants who defy neat separations between nations, and who are blessed by God. Rather, God reacts against the summary and violent abolishment of the differences among peoples and cultures.[74]

Furthermore, as Machinist argues, Israel turns on its head the traditional claim made by the ancient empires (Egypt, Mesopotamia, China) that to be an "outsider" is to be a barbarian, member of an inferior people.[75] Rather, for the Bible in its polemical rhetoric, to be a "native" (such as the oppressive Egyptians in the exodus narrative, the Canaanites in the conquest narratives, and the Babylonians in the exile narratives) is to be contaminated, while to be separated and constituted as a people beyond the borders of "civilization" is a virtue. Novel distinctiveness, in the biblical worldview, is not decay, but rather a call to excellence in worship, social justice, and the use of political freedom in a world dominated by old, idolatrous, and oppressive nations.

6

TRACING A KEY TERM

The Gēr

We will now focus on one Hebrew term used to express strangerhood in Scripture: the *gēr*. Readers will learn that it is difficult to reconstruct a single historical referent of this term since it may refer to different groups of vulnerable people in different parts of the OT, for instance, in the three main legal collections in the Torah (Covenant Code, Deuteronomic Code, and Holiness Code). Readers will also discover the rights accorded to the *gēr* in each of these legal collections, while noting that our idea of "rights"—qua individual liberties and entitlements—cannot be easily applied to ancient texts. Finally, this chapter explores the duties of autochthones toward people deemed as foreigners (and hence the "rights" of the latter, in a sense) recognized in the Deuteronomic and Priestly sources.

6.1 Strangeness and Otherness: Who Is the *Gēr* in the Bible?

In the second step of our bridging methodology, we propose fine-tuning the mapping (outlined broadly in the previous chapter) by focusing on some particular words in the biblical texts we will use in our ethical reflection. The problem is that words change their meaning even within the same language. When I studied medieval English history at school in Malta, my teacher had to explain that King Æthelred the

Unready was not "unprepared"; *unready* meant "ill-advised" or "poorly counseled" in older forms of English.

Using texts like the OT presents two orders of difficulty regarding particular terms: (a) some evolve within the ancient language itself, and hence within the texts, and (b) to discuss them today, we need to translate them with simple words or short (two- or three-term) expressions into contemporary vernacular languages. The term *gēr* is an excellent example of this problem, and it is central to our discussion on strangerhood. In the first part of this chapter, our terminological investigation focuses on strangerhood in ancient Israel and the words used to express it, and the *gēr*, or nonintegrated resident, is probably the most important concept discussed below.

Discovering and Exploring Biblical Terms That Are Hard to Translate

How can an ethics student discover and explore terms like *gēr* that are particularly hard to translate, and yet important to link Scripture texts to the ethics topic on which he is working? When analyzing a verse considered important for interpretating and appropriating Scripture, the ethicist can detect such terms by comparing different translations of the Bible. For instance, he can scan different renderings, listed in parallel, of that verse. (Googling a Bible verse usually brings up websites like biblehub.com that allow listing of different translations in this manner.) If an important term is hard to translate, translators will have to select a word in modern English (or French, etc.) that approximates one of the possible meanings for that term, but different translators will probably adopt different translation options, resulting in renderings which are patently different. Furthermore, in some study Bibles, there may be footnotes to indicate other possible translations.

Such translation discrepancies will indicate to the ethicist that she needs to look up the original term in a Bible dictionary or a lexicon of biblical Hebrew or Greek. She will then be able to appreciate some of the complexity of the term and avoid building moral arguments based on a partial and possibly anachronistic translation. If the dictionary indicates that the term's interpretation is particularly complex, the discussion should then turn to specialized articles and books, sometimes indicated in the bibliography provided by the dictionary itself. Much of the discussion in these dictionary articles and specialized texts is based on a comparative analysis of how the term is used in different contexts in Scripture. Yet an ethics student cannot simply use a Bible concordance to figure out by herself the different meanings of a term without proper training; scholarly definitions are often reinforced with philology and epigraphy and the use of historical and archeological materials.

In the following pages, before exploring the different terms, we anticipate some of the results of our investigation and sketch the framework in which the terms are used. This will make things clearer at the beginning. In a nation like biblical Israel, aware of its distinctiveness and its peculiar identity, and uncomfortable with the notion of integration, resident strangers tend to stand out and could easily end up being marginalized and oppressed. In the Pentateuchal law codes, Israel is asked to take special care of the *gērîm* (plural of *gēr*), which is unusual in ANE legal systems. The Israelites are called to love the stranger, remembering that they were strangers in the land of Egypt. Yet xenophobia and hostility toward the foreigner are also present in the OT, and when one looks more closely at who exactly is designated by the term *gēr* and why Israel needs to be reminded not to exploit the *gērîm*, a very complex world of interethnic relations and structural injustice starts to emerge.

Being Israel versus Becoming Israel

The different voices and groups that contributed to the final canonical text of the Jewish Bible all adopt the same narrative of the people's origin; they tell the same story of exodus, wilderness, and conquest, but often for different reasons. Some of these groups were isolationist or hostile toward certain kinds of strangers, and their voice is in the canon. However, we should avoid associating these voices and groups too quickly with xenophobic tendencies present in our societies today, lest we stereotype and oversimplify the various stances included in the Bible. The exodus-wilderness-conquest master narrative is found in the first four books of the Bible (Tetrateuch), but also in a second block of texts that includes Deuteronomy and a series of books placed after it in our Bibles (Joshua, Judges, 1 Samuel, 2 Samuel, 1 Kings, and 2 Kings), collectively called the Deuteronomistic History. I start by making some observations on the Tetrateuch, though it is useful to keep in mind that this version of the master narrative was probably put together and edited after the one found in the second block, as a fresh way to retell the story.

The Tetrateuch narrative starts with the following words: "Now there arose a new king over Egypt, who did not know Joseph" (Exod 1:8). Two sets of introductions precede this important verse. The first is the origins of the nations stories in Genesis 1—11 (briefly discussed in the previous chapter). The second is a series of wandering patriarch narratives featuring the sons of Israel as resident strangers first in Canaan, and then in Egypt.[1] Exodus 1:8 is important since it marks a shift: in the narratives before it, Israel is a *gēr* in Egypt and Canaan, able to cohabit with the autochthonous peoples in relative comfort, despite the obvious disadvantages of been seen as a stranger in a foreign land (we will discuss this in the following chapter). In the narratives after it, Israel is presented as a slave, existentially threatened by the peoples who live alongside it, who needs to respond in kind to their hostility, aided by YHWH, to survive. These are probably two very different narrative traditions, and two alternative political views regarding the relationship between Israel and its immediate neighbors, spot-welded through this little verse that makes both traditions appear true and compatible to the reader by placing them in separate time periods.

What is relevant for us is that the "*gēr* in Egypt" tradition, which indicates that cohabitation with strangers can be tolerable and even prosperous and beautiful, despite the vulnerability of the weaker groups in the mix, is recognized by the editors of the Tetrateuch, but then set aside. The exodus-wilderness-conquest master narrative—whether in the Tetrateuch, Deuteronomy, or the Deuteronomistic History—focuses on possible conflict and on the need for peoples to be separated. It becomes the standard way of retelling Israel's story. Many scholars claim that this way of reading Israel's past may date back to the reign of King Josiah (ca. 640–609 BCE) and the so-called Josianic (Deuteronomic) reform movement, but it became consolidated and predominant during and after the exile. The exodus-wilderness-conquest narrative makes two main assumptions:

(a) The first, in the words of Peter Machinist, is that "the land that the Bible understands as home *has to become* Israel," and this partly explains why there is a "sharp differentiation between Israel and other inhabitants of the

170

land, whether understood as autochthonous or also as outsiders....Contamination, thus, is a basic fear, perhaps most pervasive in, but by no means exclusive to, the Deuteronomic corpus."[2] In other words, there is a transformation going on, and the isolationist or hostile voices are afraid it might be hijacked by "outsiders" or people who sympathize with the outsiders. This fear creates an "us-against-them" mentality.

(b) The second assumption—which can be seen as a corollary of the first and ironically also as a nod to some elements of the "*gēr* in Egypt" tradition—is that "the community of Israel can exist apart from the land, as its experience in Egypt and the wilderness demonstrates."[3] This reminds the various Jewish diasporas during and after the exile that no loyalty is due to the city gods of the places where they have been transplanted. Their Israelite ancestors were *gērîm* and their God too was a *gēr* (Lev 25:23; Ps 39:12; 1 Chron 29:15). Owning and controlling territories, and the promised land in particular, is a great gift, but not essential to the group's identity and persistence in time.

Part of the process of becoming Israel is set in motion with the Josianic reforms, which established a clear theological, political, and liturgical framework toward a national identity: "one God, one king, one Temple."[4] The reforms also contemplated some social measures, probably less successful, countering the oppressive excesses of monarchic rule.[5] The theological and liturgical aspects of this identity-consolidation process progressed significantly during the exile and after, as distinctiveness fended off the risk of being assimilated and never "becoming Israel." As we shall see, the land to which the descendants of the exiles returned did not look like the Israel they had pictured during this reform process, and so even the land had to become Israel.

Strangers in "Their" Space

Having presented this framework, let us start dealing with terminology.

The Hebrew language uses a number of different expressions to refer to people who do not belong to the majority, however the latter might be defined. Some of these expressions are generally used in a more negative sense, always emphasizing the otherness of those persons and their separateness from the majority, such as *nokrî* (e.g., Deut 17:15) or *ben-nēkār* (e.g., Exod 12:43), and *zār* (e.g., Isa 1:7). In other cases, the difference is not as evident and not always emphasized, as with *tôšāb*, which is often used together with *gēr* (e.g., Gen 23:4), the latter being the most frequent among these expressions.[6]

The terms *nokrî, bẹn-hannēkār/ben-nēkār* (son of a *nokrî*), and *zār* belong together;[7] some scholars understand them to refer generally to "those who occupied what was taken to be essentially gentile space."[8] There are, of course, exceptions to this rule. In 2 Samuel 15:19–20, we find a case of a foreigner (*nokrî*), Ittai the Gittite, occupying Israelite space. Nevertheless, "the story underscores the fact that he is not really at home among the Israelites, that he has come 'only yesterday' and is an exile from his own home who by all rights should return home."[9] The foreigner (*nokrî*) in 1 Kings 8:41–43 could refer to visiting foreign dignitaries or diplomats, who are not seen as hostile or dangerous, but clearly are not "in their space" in Israel.

In general, the *nokrî* was to be avoided, or simply suffered, by Israelites who had to enter his space as merchants, diplomats, or captives. Insofar as *nokrî*-occupied territory was not perceived as promised to Israel by God, we could say that Israel recognized these foreigners' right to territorial integrity. However, this way of framing things anachronistically betrays a Westphalian notion of sovereignty rights, and it fails to recognize that the Hasmonean kings of Judea did engage in expansionist wars.[10]

The *nokrî* was often seen as a potential enemy and hence treated with suspicion and hostility, sometimes being referred to with strong hate language, for example in Psalm 137:8–9:

> O daughter Babylon, you devastator!
> Happy shall they be who pay you
> back what you have done to us!
> Happy shall they be who take your little ones
> and dash them against the rock!

Given the psalm's explicit setting during Babylonian captivity, the "little ones" here probably are to be seen mainly as the historical extension of an oppressive people rather than foreigners tout court. The resentment and hatred is directed toward the demographic expansion of the oppressor, and not so much toward the "little ones" as individual infants. The use of such violent language is seen by some exegetes today as a therapeutic exercise of release of rage by trauma victims,[11] but it also conveys some of the more widespread attitudes toward the *nokrî*.

One text that rekindles painful memories of Israelites inhabiting the land of the *nokrî* is the Book of Esther.[12] The desire for vengeance builds up along the narrative, and when we reach the denouement, we could find ourselves hating the Babylonians, at least the "bad" ones, and applauding the words, "The Jews struck down all their enemies with the sword, slaughtering, and destroying them, and did as they pleased to those who hated them" (Esth 9:5). Nevertheless, not all uses of emotive language in the Bible function as actual expressions of emotion, as they do in modern literature since Romanticism; sometimes they are standardized legal or commercial formulas implying tort or satisfaction, distancing or rapprochement.[13]

Strangers in "Our" Space

The terms *gēr* and *tôšāb* also belong together: they mostly designate people classified as "strangers" or "others" who occupied what was seen as Israelite space. Some were permanent residents and others were foreigners passing through Israel, such as wayfarers. In general, all these others, being often poor and defenseless, were not seen as a threat and hence were treated with less hostility than the *nokrî*. Their vulnerability invited hospitality, and at times brotherly love. Found mostly in the singular in the OT, *gēr* has no feminine form; it is more an indication of a precarious state of things, and less of ethnicity in the modern sense.

As Jobling claims, "some uses suggest persons living in a place not their own, even a foreign country, but *gēr* should probably be defined in class rather than ethnic terms. Landlessness seems fundamental to the meaning."[14] The accent is on nonintegration, while alienage is invoked as justification, but the term *gēr* does not necessarily entail a biological or cultural difference from the self-group (a different *ethnie*, in the modern sense), but a de facto difference on the ground, underwritten by local tribal authorities and upheld by law. Scholars like Christoph Bultmann have sought to *completely* exclude any identification between *gēr* status and alienage or migratory status, but this view is probably overstated.[15]

The word *tôšāb* seems to indicate a landless resident. It is sometimes associated with *gēr*, especially in Leviticus 25, which unites the two terms in the hendiadys *gēr-we-tôšāb* several times to indicate "nonintegrated resident," who is probably also landless. Possibly the hendiadys is used to indicate long duration.[16] At other times *tôšāb* is associated with *śākîr* (hireling/journeyman). "[The distinctions in Lev 25:39–46 give] the impression of a certain social hierarchy: *gēr-tôšāb-śākîr*-slave, whereby the first three groups can be differently juxtaposed. But this hierarchy does not mean that the *gēr* will always be the wealthiest of these groups."[17] The slave (*'ebed*) stands, of course, at the lowest social rank.

The term *gēr* is by far the more commonly referred to "proximal other" in the OT, and, following the reasoning above, some authors understand it to mean simply "non-integrated resident." Novak, for instance, defines the *gērîm* as "those people living among the people of Israel in a subordinate capacity, although one having definite rights and duties and enjoying the protection of the due process of law."[18] However, at different moments in Israelite history, and in different situations, *gēr* referred mainly to particular groups of nonintegrated neighbors.

Revealingly, in the context of the Septuagint, the notion was split into two: *pároikos* (nonintegrated permanent resident, metic, denizen) is used to translate texts where the *gēr* is treated differently from the *'ezrāḥ* (native), while *prosēlutos* (proselyte) is adopted for those where legal equality between the *gēr* and the *'ezrāḥ* is taken for granted.[19] The latter texts are usually associated with the Priestly source in the Pentateuch, but understanding *prosēlutos* as convert is anachronistic, since the idea of conversion and formal integration probably dates back only to the Hasmonean Period (140–37 BCE).[20] It is unclear whether some ritual was developed during that period to mark the beginning and completion of the Judaization process, but after the Roman destruction of the temple in 70 CE, the need to have such a ritual and to eventually standardize the text and rubrics was clearly felt. The text of the ritual currently included in the Babylonian Talmud arguably is derived from a *beraita* (text of Palestinian origin) from the second or early third century CE.[21] In any case, the Septuagint realizes, centuries before Julius Wellhausen and the modern documentary hypothesis, that *gēr* means different things in different OT texts.

José Ramírez Kidd notes that the noun *gēr* developed from the verbal root *gwr* (to linger, sojourn, abide) in a special way; it is not identical to *gār*, the participle of that verb, but emerged as a form of legal jargon to designate different realities that needed to be regulated in the OT legal codes.[22] Table

6.1 helps us navigate the uses of *gēr* in these codes. When *gēr* designates a collectivity, it usually refers to Israel (as a historical or symbolic sojourner or resident alien in a foreign land). When referring to an individual, it indicates persons residing within Israelite space; we need to see to whom the law is addressed to figure out the term's referent. If the law is addressed only to the sons of Israel (as is typical in the Deuteronomic sources), then it considers the *gēr* as someone outside of Israel, to be treated as a protégé of the Israelite community. If the law obliges both the "seed of Israel" (*'ezrāḥ*) and the *gēr* (as is typical in the Priestly sources), then the *gēr* is seen as having one foot inside and one foot outside the community, similar enough to the "pure" Israelite to be encouraged to participate in the same rituals (and hence to be assimilated), yet different enough to be tagged as a possible source of defilement for the community.

TABLE 6.1: DIFFERENT MEANINGS OF *GĒR* IN THE OT LEGAL CODES		
Reference to a group	Reference to an individual	
	Laws addressed to Israelites for protection of the gēr	*Laws compulsory for both ('ezrāḥ + gēr) to preserve the holiness of the community*
gēr ≈ Israel	gēr ≈ protégé of Israel	gēr ≈ partially assimilable other, yet possible source of community defilement
	gēr linked to "orphan/ widow": Deuteronomist sources	*gēr linked to "native": Priestly sources*

In the following sections we further explore the complexities of such a seemingly simple concept, attempting a diachronic reconstruction of prime lexical referents of the term *gēr*, and we include a discussion of the rights of strangers in Israel. Let us first explain some of our translation options. We shall assume as a rule of thumb that the lack of integration was mostly due to landlessness and should be understood more in terms of class difference than ethnicity, though the landlessness may be linked to immigration many generations prior or to the pauperization of autochthonous ancestors. "Immigrant" is therefore not a very good translation.

Similarly, "temporary resident" or "sojourner" does not properly convey the reality of persons who were permanent residents and, in some cases, culturally and religiously indistinguishable from the native Israelites. "Resident alien" is American immigration legalese, with Latin roots traceable to the Norman conquest of Britain.[23] However, referring to nonnationals as "aliens" sounds odd and possibly offensive in everyday language in many non-US English-speaking countries. In many of the "totalitarian" regimes of antiquity that did not have a robust notion of citizenship rights, denizen status and autochthonous status were not as different as we would imagine them today from the perspective of an egalitarian modern democracy such as the United States.

"Nonnational resident" comes closer, but the words *nation* and *national*, when used to translate biblical concepts, are problematic, as noted in the previous chapter, and should be understood as premodern references to the social "we," rather than prefiguring the modern ethnocultural or civic sense of "nation." We thus resort, in this book, to the seemingly tautological term "nonintegrated resident," mostly for lack of a better term.

6.2 The Referent of *Gēr* in the Legal Codes of the Torah

The *Gēr* in the Covenant Code

Who is a *gēr*? How should she or he be treated? After reviewing the different law codes in the Torah, Christiana van Houten[24] argues that there is a development:

> The laws dealing with the alien developed and became more inclusive. What began as an appeal for justice for the alien in the Covenant Code (Exod. 23:9), comes to be understood as a legal principle in the Priestly laws: "There shall be one law for the alien and native-born." This then opened the door for the inclusion of the alien into all the rights and privileges of Israelite society....The inclusive tendency is the working out, in the legal tradition, of God's purpose to include and save all.[25]

Such a simplistic progression toward greater openness and inclusiveness is frowned upon by other scholars such as Smith-Christopher.[26] The problem here is twofold. How do we determine the sociopolitical referent of the word *gēr* as it occurs in the different codes, accounting for their different social contexts? How do we navigate the current dispute among scholars as to when to date those codes? We will have to bracket the second question for the purposes of our present discussion and rely on estimates we deem "mainstream."[27]

Let us start with what is called the Book of the Covenant, or Covenant Code (Exod 20:22—23:19). Traditionally, it has been deemed the oldest collection of laws in the Bible, possibly dating from the prestate period. Many scholars today consider this code as an early stage of the Deuteronomic law tradition, even though it is incorporated into the Tetrateuch, which was composed as a corpus much later.[28] Rainer Albertz, for instance, has argued that Exodus 20:23—23:19 is not necessarily older than the Hezekianic reform, and may actually have been the basis of this reform:

> A dating in the eighth-century situation which I have assumed is supported by [several arguments, including] the fact that the Book of the Covenant pays quite special attention to the protection of the alien (20:20; 23:9), which could well be a reaction to the increasingly serious refugee problem which Judah faced after the fall of Samaria.[29]

If Albertz is correct, the word *gēr* in the Covenant Code refers to a very particular type of nonintegrated resident in the Southern Kingdom: landless Israelites from the destroyed Northern Kingdom. Archeologists note that around 700 BCE, the area occupied by Jerusalem tripled or quadrupled in size, pointing to the massive influx of urban refugees from the North, as well as others coming from territories that Sennacherib transferred from Judah to the Philistine cities.[30] After investigating the oldest usages of the noun form *gēr* in the Pentateuch, Ramírez Kidd concurs that the emergence of this form "as a legal term is related to the need for a generic nominal term to designate, in the laws, the status of immigrants settled in Israel [referring here to the Southern Kingdom, Judah] after the fall of Samaria in 721 BC."[31]

The *Gēr* in the Deuteronomic Code

If we assume that the Deuteronomic Code (Deut 12-26) was the basis of the Josianic reform (ca. 640–609 BCE), *gēr* in this code could refer, in part, to a specific group of people, namely unemployed Levites (see Judg 17:7; 19:1–2); such persons may, at least, have been considered as the archetypal *gērîm* of the day.[32] It might also have included people descended from refugees who arrived in 721 BCE, but who were not completely assimilated.

In the first case, as has been shown by the investigations of A. H. J. Gunneweg and H. Schulz,[33] the ethnological tribe of Levi seems to have perished early on in the history of Israel and was then replaced by a religious "clanless clan" of Israelites who distanced themselves from their ethnic groups (thus becoming landless) to live with no ties to clan or tribe (cf. Exod 32:29; Deut 33:9), entrusting themselves uniquely to YHWH's protection (Deut 33:11; cf. Judg 20). In Deuteronomy 26:12 the Levite and the *gēr* (as well as the fatherless and widows) are listed as beneficiaries of charitable tithes. The Levites and the *gērîm*, though mentioned separately, are classified together.

Scripture presents the destruction of temples outside the official borders of Judah (cf. 2 Kgs 23:15–20) after 628 BCE as one of the main features of the Josianic reform, but there is no conclusive archeological evidence of this.[34] Those temples were probably destroyed earlier during the invasions of Pharaoh Sheshonq I and of the Assyrian kings Tiglath-Pileser III, Shamaneser V, and Sennacherib; the YHWH cult was de facto concentrated in Jerusalem when Samaria fell.[35] Yet, it is plausible to assume that many of the shrines passed into Philistine-controlled areas and that "the provincial priests ('Levites') who had [been forced out and] lost their jobs became a significant social problem [and that] attempts were made to cope with it by charitable measures."[36] If this thesis is correct, in the last years of the monarchy, such Levites became a prominent and visible group of resident aliens, probably refusing to seek "normal" employment, and living on alms. However, this problem most probably disappeared after the exile,[37] and *gēr* came to mean something else in postexilic texts (and in the exilic additions and postexilic edits and reappropriations of Deuteronomy).

Ramírez Kidd claims that in the law codes,

> [the noun *gēr*] functioned, on the one hand, as an internal boundary between the native members of the Israelite community and those newly accepted and, on the other hand, as a sort of external boundary of the community in relation to

other immigrants, whose religious practices were commonly perceived as a threat to their own material security and religious purity.[38]

If the *gērîm* in Judah before the exile were a mix of former refugees from the Northern Kingdom and uprooted Levite groups, then making laws to protect them would have made sense. However, a modern reader would expect an eventual integration and assimilation, given that they were not so different from the Judahites. Cultic laws that applied to both these *gērîm* and to the autochthonous Judahites would also have made sense, since the various YHWH-Sabaoth cults in the Levant before the exile were not extremely different from each other. There would have been little need of "conversion" or "religious assimilation" and no need to force or even provide official permit for such a process to take place.

Given that considerable sections of Deuteronomy are considered exilic, and the final editing of the Deuteronomic code is postexilic, we need to ask whether and in what sense Ramírez Kidd's claim is still true during the exile and after the return from Babylon. For instance, he considers "You shall also love the stranger" (Deut 10:19a) a postexilic text (here, the noun *gēr* is separated from widow/orphan and from economic issues). In his reading, it must have been formulated by non-Palestinian postexilic Jewish communities willing to accept new members and inviting the Palestinian postexilic group to do likewise.[39] Postexilic Israel was arguably a *multicentered religious community*. It would have included, on one hand, a Jerusalem group governing a tiny self-governing Persian province, Yehud Medinata, feeling threatened by foreigners outside its borders and within its land, and on the other hand, Alexandrian, Babylonian, and Antiochian groups who had accepted their diaspora situation and were more cosmopolitan and open to the stranger.

This command's justification, "for you were strangers [*gērîm*] in the land of Egypt" (10:19b), is seen by Ramírez Kidd as an addition by the Egyptian diaspora, who during the exile had had a long dispute with the Babylonian diaspora regarding who was the true remnant of Israel (cf. Jer 44:19; 43:4–7).[40] This kind of operation is typical of historical criticism and may help us reconstruct theologies and debates that might stimulate ethics discussions today. Yet we should remain skeptical as regards the ability of exegetes to accurately cut up single verses and reconstruct redactional operations. Critical readers will be able to interpret a text more fruitfully if they constantly ask themselves whether their exegetical sources are using a particular diachronic method too zealously, and whether these historical analyses need to be integrated with a synchronic reading to benefit from a different and broader perspective.

Similarly, Ruth Ebach distinguishes between the sections of the Deuteronomic code which she considers preexilic, exilic, and postexilic. Preexilic materials do not see the individual *gēr* as dangerous. Exilic materials, written by exiled elites outside the land, use the nations as a literary foil, a negative standard against which Israel's goodness or holiness (its obedience of the Torah) is to be weighed. If the exiles are found lacking, any attempts to return to the land will fail.[41] For instance, they may become too "contaminated" by the mentality of the "other" and not be obedient enough to YHWH and his will expressed in the Torah, which establishes how to become and remain "distinctive."

In postexilic texts, as we shall see, traditional alienage terms are recycled to refer to Judeans who were not exiled and remained in the land. Though these "people of the land" call themselves Israelites, they are not considered so by the returnees who end up governing Yehud Medinata. The returnees see them theologically as foreigners: they have not been purified by the exilic experience and have not subjected themselves to the Torah.[42] More concretely, they have not adapted to the YHWH cult as reformed during the exile (based on the practices of Jerusalem élites immediately prior), and so they are seen as religiously dangerous remnants of a primitive YHWH cult that led to the exile, a cult that should be discarded. Other foreigners, who do not see themselves as Israelite, but who accept the Torah and the exilic YHWH cult and identity markers seem to have a better chance of being integrated, according to Ebach.[43]

As we shall see when dealing with the Ezra and Nehemiah texts in chapter 8, the tension was exacerbated by at least two factors. Firstly, these other "primitive" YHWH-Sabaoth worshiping Israelites had occupied the lands of the returnees' ancestors. Secondly, the returnees were themselves a puppet government representing the interests of a foreign power, who in many ways looked very "Babylonian" or "Persian" to the other YHWH worshipers in the Levant. Imagine the fall of the communist regime in Cuba, and then Washington sending and propping up a group of Cuban-descent businesspersons and intellectuals from Miami to form a US-leaning regime in a new "democratic"

Cuba, and the kinds of conflict that could arise between the returnees and the locals.

The idea of a "mass return" or a return of the few to an "empty land" are ideological inventions promoted by some historians, retrieving theologized notions present in Scripture (e.g., 2 Chr 36:21). Jeremiah 52:28–30 notes that a total of 4600 "souls" (*nepeš*) were deported in three phases. This is a realistic number (probably counting only the *patresfamilias*), but the land could contain many thousands more, so these were only the elites. Most people (probably more than 75 percent of the population) had remained in the Judean territories where they were born. The empty-land thesis is thus untenable.[44] Similarly, the exiles couldn't have grown to a huge mass of people in less than fifty-eight years, and most descendants of the exiles probably did not return to Yehud Medinata, so the notion of "mass return," too, is implausible.

Ezekiel presents the claims of nondeported Israelites remaining in the land, the majority, whose voice is rarely heard in the final version of the Bible:

[Son of man], the inhabitants of Jerusalem have said (as) to your brothers, your kinsfolk, your fellow exiles, and the whole house of Israel: "Distance yourselves from the Lord; to us this land is given for a possession." (Ezek 11:15; my translation)

In the view of those who remained, it was the sophisticated city-dwelling élites who sinned, who were punished by exile, and who should remain in exile. Those still in Judea were the descendants of the "good" folk, the peasants who needed no punishment and were never exiled in the first place. They are Abraham's multitude of descendants, now pruned by God from the "evil" elites.

The response of the other group can be found in Jeremiah's vision of the figs (Jer 24:1–10); the basket with the very good figs (the elites) was taken to Babylon to be preserved, while the basket with the very bad figs (the countryfolk) was left in the field to rot and to be destroyed. The idea is that the land should, ideally, be completely burnt to remove any traces of the roots and seeds of the bad plants. Then, the seeds from the good figs in Babylon should be brought back to reseed the field with grade-A crops. Extending this logic, any remaining fig plants around the field should not be allowed to pollinate the new plants, hence the Ezra-Nehemiah intermarriage crisis (discussed in chapter 8).

The *Gēr* in the Holiness Code

Many scholars today consider the Holiness Code (Lev 17—27) to be mostly postexilic,[45] written in a political context quite different from that of the Judahite monarchy, one in which the referent of the word *gēr* has changed once again. Van Houten claims that, more so than the Deuteronomic laws, the Priestly laws seem more inclusive toward those they call *gērîm*. For instance, according to the Holiness Code, the *gērîm* are to be treated as "the children of your people" (Lev 19:18), and Israel is commanded to love the foreigner "as yourself" (Lev 19:34). But here again, whom do these texts refer to when using the word *gēr*?

Recent scholarship, as noted above, tends distinguish the descendants of those who remained from the returned offspring of those who were exiled; in the initial postexilic years, *gēr* is usually a term recycled from the past by the latter group to designate the former. However, over time, some of these "peoples of the land" (*gôyē-hā 'āreṣ*), together with other foreigners, including *nokrîm*—in the Jewish diasporas, in Hellenistic Judea, and among some of the neighboring Syro-Palestinian populations—start accepting the returnee theology, obeying the Torah, and asking to join Israel. Ramírez Kidd notes a variety of verbal forms used to designate these people, who will later be called proselytes: *gôyim rabbîm* (many nations; Zech 2:11), *ben-hannēkār* (son of a stranger; Isa 56:3.6); *gēr* (unintegrated resident; Isa 14:1); *kol-hannilwîm* (all-who-would-join; Esth 9:27); *rabbîm mē 'ammê hā 'āreṣ mityahădîm* (many of the people of the land who Judaized, declared themselves Jews; Esth 8:17); *episteuse/perietemeto/prosetethē pros ton oikon Israēl* (believed; was circumcised; joined the house of Israel; Jdt 14:10).[46]

Ramírez Kidd notes that the peculiarity of the late additions to the Holiness Code and to the Priestly sources is that they present laws that apply equally to the *gēr* and the *'ezrāḥ* (native, though here implying returnee), and that "the fundamental common element to all these laws is their primary concern with the matter of holiness."[47] The reader will recall that holiness is a matter of respecting mixability rules, and not uniquely or primarily of moral probity, in the modern sense. Most of these laws are prohibitions intended to avoid the defilement of both groups. They help to define the indispensable conditions for admission of the *gēr* to spaces deemed to belong to the returnee Jew, in Palestine or in Jewish diaspora communities, and for his coexistence with Jews. However, in Leviticus 19:33–34, we find:

> When a *gēr* resides with you in your land, you shall not oppress the *gēr*. The *gēr* who resides with you shall be to you as the autochthon (native) among you; you shall love the *gēr* as yourself, for you were *gērîm* in the land of Egypt: I am the LORD your God. (NRSV, slightly modified by the author)

This complex formulation, which in part mirrors Deuteronomy 10:19, is seen by some scholars as the result of a process of theologizing the notion of *gēr*. The passage theologizes in two directions: backward, whereby Israel is imagined as a *gēr* before the monarchy and exile; and forward, whereby Late-Persian and Hellenistic-period *gērîm* are identified as persons in the process of becoming Jews, who should therefore be treated as members of the Jewish religious community, in Palestine and in the diaspora cities.[48]

6.3 What Rights Did the *Gērîm* Enjoy?

Given what we have said above, let us start this section with a gentle warning. First, we shouldn't think of "rights" as actionable, subjective rights in the modern sense; unlike many of the other laws, the biblical laws protecting the *gēr* from oppression have no sanctions. They designate minimum standards for decent treatment of the other, rather than define the "freedoms and entitlements" of the *gērîm*. Second, by translating *gēr* as simply "nonintegrated resident," we are probably being much more inclusive than the biblical law codes ever intended. The *gēr* is more precisely the other who is practically indistinguishable from the autochthone but who has not been legally integrated, despite many generations of residence within Israel. By discussing the problems of the *gērîm* in a text intended to spur ethical reflection on immigration and otherness in the twenty-first century, we might be assuming too quickly that the otherness of the biblical *gērîm* can be compared to the otherness of contemporary immigrants. As Jobling has it,

We should not entirely deny a connotation of alienness to *ger* in Deuteronomy. Perhaps the existence of the class of *gerim* was rationalized, with whatever degree of truth, in terms of their having originated elsewhere than where they live. Perhaps *ger* was an available legal category for people who continued to arrive as refugees. But the simple definition of *ger* as "resident alien" is not viable.[49]

Does this mean that our long and laborious terminological investigation has been in part a failure. If so, this is fine, given the method described at the end of chapter 4. It is all a part of a patient process, and we are not anxious to obtain quick results. We have learnt a lot about social inclusion and exclusion in the Bible. Some of the above reflection on the *gēr* may enlighten political debates in countries that still today generate social exclusion and statelessness by refusing a path to citizenship to persons born to noncitizen parents, even after many generations of residence. It is less relevant, or only indirectly relevant, to debates on immigration in countries with birthright citizenship like the United States, and many EU countries that have laws facilitating the obtaining of citizenship by persons who were born and educated there. This is why our approach to the question of otherness in the Bible does not place the legal texts at the center, as many theological ethicists tend to do in similar works on immigration. We cannot, of course, completely ignore the classical discussion of the legal rights of the *gērîm* in a work like this, and so we cover this material briefly, and critically, at this point of our discussion.

Some authors claim that nonintegrated residents living in preexilic Israel and Judah are persons having "definite rights and duties and enjoying the protection of the due process of law."[50] To be sure, this is how things are presented in the final (postexilic) edition of the Pentateuch, though the actual legal structures in historical (both pre- and postexilic) Israel, especially in rural areas, were weak.[51] As the wealth gap between the rich and the poor widened during the monarchy and in Yehud Medinata, poor and marginalized persons often found it very hard to have their rights upheld by local tribunals, who were easily corrupted or co-opted by the wealthy landholders.[52] The *gērîm*, it seems, were easily and routinely exploited (cf. Mal 3:5; Ps 94:6).

Rights Recognized in the Deuteronomic Sources

In the Deuteronomic sources, "gerim are separated rhetorically from Israel in that they are not part of the 'you' to whom the law is addressed; they are referred to as a separate group in the third person."[53] Even in ideal situations where justice could be obtained by the non-integrated resident, his[54] rights—as recognized by biblical law—were very limited: if he was a slave, he was entitled to little more than bodily integrity (he could not be raped or mutilated), while if he was a free person, he could, in theory, avail himself of the legal structures (mainly arbitration by elders) which sought to somehow redress criminal and civil injury (Deut 1:16–17; 24:17; cf. Deut 27:19). Generally, a *gēr* could do this when "exploited" (cf. Exod 22:20), which could include having wages withheld (Deut 24:14) or being forced to work without any days of rest or Sabbaths (cf. Exod 23:12).[55]

Israelite law codes, especially Deuteronomy, do not offer a path to integration (except possibly to *gērîm* of Egyptian and Edomite descent; cf. Deut 23:2–8[56]) and simply assume that the *gēr* will be a marginalized other, to be listed with the two other traditional *personae miserabiles* in the ANE, the widow and the orphan.[57] For this reason, given their inescapable misery, they are to be given "special treatment" in the form of charity; they may glean after the harvesters (Deut 24:19–22; cf. Lev 19:9–10) and benefit from the proceeds of the voluntary third-year tithe for the very poor (Deut 14:28–29).

Several historians believe the Josianic reformers and the early postexilic reformers were concerned with what we modern readers call social justice, and not just with theological orthodoxy (promoting monotheism and combatting idolatry), cultic purity, and mixability rules. We would expect them to use their creative imagination (which was not lacking) to develop concrete ways to legally and politically resolve the social structures that marginalize the *personae miserabiles*. They did not.[58] They saw possession of land linked solely to ancestral rights and could hardly envisage the *gēr* as anything but a metic, a person out-of-place. Eventually the idea of religious integration started to be considered, as well as annexation of nearby lands (and their populace) during the Hasmonaean Period. Hence, the more enlightened social justice projects of the Josianic and early postexilic reformers automatically excluded nonintegrated, and especially non-Israelite, residents.[59] Some authors, such as Donald Gowan, however, suggest that we should not overemphasize the poverty of the *gērîm* and be too critical of the reform movements' failure to offer them better means to social and economic integration; their lot was similar to that of many natives in a subsistence agrarian economy.[60]

Rights Recognized in the Priestly Sources

The Holiness Code (e.g., Lev 24:22) makes the claim that there is a single law for the *gēr* and the socially and politically integrated Israelite (*'ezrāḥ*). The *gēr* is seen here as a more or less equal subject of the priestly law, meaning that he is not normally exempt from observing purity rules and religious laws, or from exhibiting the Jewish identity markers developed mostly during the Exile (Lev 17:15; 18:26; 24:16). Thus, the *gēr* is here assumed (or forced) to be culturally and religiously assimilated to the Jewish identity developed during and after the exile. He is mostly "other" not in terms of culture, religion, or ethnicity, but in terms of class, and as noted above, roughly equated to the "people of the Land" in Ezra–Nehemiah. The projection of alienage onto non-exiled Israelites, implicit in the recycling of the term *gēr* in the context of foreign domination, and the resulting distinction between *gēr* and *'ezrāḥ* established by the returnees, "satisfied their sense of being the only authentic Jews and justified their economic privilege."[61]

In the priestly laws, such *gērîm* have gleaning rights (Lev 19:10; 23:22) similar to those of the *gērîm* in Deuteronomy 24:19–21, and have the right not to be oppressed (Lev 19:33–34), as in the Deuteronomistic sources. They may keep the Passover and participate in certain public religious rituals (and why would anyone stop them, if there are Israelites?—cf. Num 9:14). They are to be loved "as though they were kin" (and why would they be loved in a different manner, if they actually were kin?—cf. Lev 19:34) but this does not mean they should be emancipated from their subordinate social condition. The rights of these *gērîm* do not go much further than that.[62]

6.4 Some Takeaways for Theological Ethics

Many theological ethicists writing on immigration focus on the biblical term *gēr* as used in the legal materials, reading synchronically,

186

and they generally cite verses like Deuteronomy 10:18–19 and Leviticus 19:33–34, which insist on "loving the *gēr.*" However, they generally avoid drawing the more socially problematic consequences of an intellectually honest, exegetically informed approach centered on the Law Codes as a block. Were they to do so, they would have to recognize that some of the unresolved tensions that we face today existed in biblical times, albeit in a different social context. Since Scripture does not resolve those tensions, it is especially useful to ethics in the formulation of the questions modern ethicists should try to resolve.

As formulated, the land laws in the Bible (e.g., the Jubilee laws), emphasize the value of protecting the rights of poor Israelites. These laws implicitly deny poor *gērîm* the right to hold property (at least permanently) in an agricultural society, condemning them to being a permanent social underclass, while recognizing this as an unavoidable fact and providing some meagre legal remedies.[63] It is doubted that Jubilee land laws were ever enforced as formulated, given the enormous risks of implementing radical property reforms in a volatile preexilic situation or under Persian or Greek rule. However, this case shows that, in the Bible, the conflicting needs and vulnerabilities of different groups of poor persons remain in tension, resonating with many debates about immigration today. The fact remains that in antiquity, the elites were the literate persons who administered justice and wrote laws, and their ability to imagine a different world order wherein their entitlements and privileges risk being eroded was limited, even when they were inspired by God's spirit to write down God's Law. God's pedagogy takes its time, and divine inspiration is not brainwashing or dictation.

In general, rights were limited and poorly enforced. Laws concerning the peculiar social rights of the *gēr* have no sanctions; they function primarily as moral imperatives, deontological indications, or "soft law." Similarly, the *Universal Declaration of Human Rights* (1948) and *Global Compact on Refugees* (2018) and the *Global Compact for Safe, Orderly and Regular Migration* (2018) are more exhortatory than normative, advice rather than stricture; yet one cannot discount their historical impact.[64] By singling out the particularly vulnerable groups in society, Covenant Code and Deuteronomic law preempt our tendency to think in terms of slogans like, "We take care of our poor; others take care of theirs." As in the parable of the good Samaritan, physical proximity, urgency, and intensity of need are the major moral criteria to consider when helping the vulnerable, not culture and biological relatedness.

When the law codes are analyzed diachronically, to track their changes over time, one also starts to see that the different layers may be referring to different social groups designated by the term *gēr*. This is important for us too; some experts consider 1973 a watershed moment in global economics and invite us to distinguish mass migration before and after this year, though we should not exaggerate the differences between the migrants involved. Similarly, we need to understand and appreciate the differences between various types of vulnerable migrants: refugees as defined in the 1951 Refugee Convention, victims of internal conflict and climate displacement, and poor migrants produced by the darker side of globalization. Some members of the middle classes of polities marred by violent crime, nepotism, and kleptocracy may also be considered vulnerable, though in a broader sense. All of the above need to be distinguished from many other expatriates who cannot honestly be considered vulnerable in any particular way, for instance, those who choose to seek better opportunities abroad or are recruited for their skills.

A diachronic reading indicates some awareness in the Bible that the social reality of who is considered a "stranger" changes with time, requiring laws to be kept up to date. From a modern ethical viewpoint, it is hoped that laws concerning strangers would be continually updated to adequately respond to changing realities. In polities like the United States, sensible comprehensive immigration reform has stalled for decades, creating a huge metic class. While premodern authoritarian and totalitarian polities could tolerate residence without citizenship for centuries, modern representative democracies are not designed to function with huge, marginalized underclasses.

Finally, our research on the referent of *gēr* in the OT led us to conclude that the *gēr* status, seen in historical perspective, is better understood as a problem of class rather than of ethnicity or race. The takeaway, here, is that when a society excludes certain groups of people for a long period of time, citing cultural, racial, or religious differences, we need to ask ourselves whether those differences are still relevant and whether this justification simply masks the creation of a new exploitable underclass with no social mobility. A hermeneutics of suspicion can be helpful in analyzing many political discourses on immigration today. A powerful or stressed social group that deems itself more autochthonous than others could exaggerate the cultural, religious, or ethnic differences of certain poor or under-educated groups to justify and increase their marginalization. Though we cannot deny the existence of racism and xenophobia toward immigrants and refugees today, it is important not to overemphasize racial and cultural differences, and to remember that many of the problems of the integration of immigrants today boil down to problems of class. Indeed, marginalization is often linked to poverty and lack of education among migrants, and to consumers' lack of will to pay what is necessary for certain goods and services to be produced in decent work conditions which offer social mobility to the workers and their children.

7

HOSPITALITY

This chapter starts by mapping out the concepts that moral theology seeks to explore using Scripture as a source of inspiration: identity faithfulness, hospitality, and kinship bonding. These concepts can be grouped together in a stratified notion of solidarity.

Readers will first learn the importance of hospitality in antiquity. Our discussion will help them distinguish between hospitality offered during the transit of a stranger and during a longer sojourn. Readers will then explore the hospitality diptych in Genesis 18—19, comparing Abraham and Lot, as each welcomes the strange yet fascinating "messengers." A note on the Deborah story adds some complexity to the debate.

In the second part of the chapter, readers will survey and appraise the uneasy hospitality in the encounter between Jesus and the Syrophoenician woman in Mark 7, and in the process learn how to use a simplified form of rhetorical analysis particularly adapted to biblical and Semitic texts.

7.1 Hospitality in Sodom, Mamre, and Gibeah

Hospitality: Transit and Sojourn

We have presented our notion of hospitality as a temporary or occasional form of solidarity in our table of opposites (chapter 5, section 5.2), distinguishing it from civic kinship bonding (fraternity) and humanity or philanthropy for far-away strangers. We will focus here on hospitality shown toward people who are physically near but ethnically (biologically, culturally, religiously) distant.

The first level of hospitality in the Hebrew Bible concerns the right of safe transit (*ma ʿăbār*) of the nonresident (*nokrî*) through one's land. Refusal of such a right is deemed by the Bible as a grave evil, as can be seen in Numbers 20:14–21 and 21:21–35. In these two texts, the Israelites request to pass unharmed through the land of the Edomites and Amorites without looting. First the Edomites and then the Amorites refuse, behavior that the Bible considers abominable, unacceptable. In the first case, Israel turned back, but in the second case the Israelites decided to pass through all the same. They were attacked and while defending themselves, ended up conquering the land (according to the text). In the rabbinic Midrash, this text is seen to argue that refusing the right of transit in times of peace (especially to persons or groups who do not pose a threat of invasion or conquest) is ethically unacceptable.[1]

The second level of hospitality, which is to be shown toward wayfarers or temporary sojourners, is one step further than the mere right of transit. Biblical Hebrew does not have an abstract noun for "hospitality," opting instead for expressions like "to lodge a sojourner" or "to open one's doors to a traveler" (Job 31:32). Though in most cases, the host is not obliged to take in a guest (unless they are dying of thirst in the desert, for example), once she does, violation of hospitality is considered a grave evil in the biblical worldview, as illustrated by the sin of Sodom in Genesis 19, which we will explore below.

Lot's Hospitality in Genesis 19
Justification of the Choice of the Text

"The sin of Sodom was not homosexuality, but inhospitality," argues a friend in a Facebook post. In the commentary below the post, another friend writes, "No, hospitality in the Bible is not a very important value: just read the Jael story!" There are some interesting moral issues to investigate here, so let us take a closer look. I'm obviously less interested in the topic of homosexuality in this book, but as we shall see, Genesis 19 is a classic text where we might go to find a reflection on a topical moral issue, and instead find something different, but equally topical. We shall start our quest using the instruments provided in two good study Bibles lying in my office: *The Catholic Study Bible* (2nd edition) and *La Bibbia—Via, Verità e Vita* (revised edition), which I will call the "American" and the "Italian" study Bible, respectively.[2] Study Bibles are not a bad place

CONGREGATION OF METICS AND TRAVELING PEOPLE
A CONGREGATION OF METICS AND TRAVELING PEOPLE

to start investigating a question like this, as a scholar and friend has recently taught me. Even when your office is a few meters away from one of the largest theology libraries in the world, as is my case, detailed exegetical texts may not be the most helpful place to start, though they may prove useful later.[3]

Parceling the Text + Textual Criticism

Both study Bibles separate Genesis 19:1–29 from the rest of the chapter on the origin of the Moabites (which, however, may be of interest to understanding our analysis of the Book of Ruth later). The Italian study Bible further divides the passage in two: *The Two Angels and Lot in Sodom* (vv. 1–11) and *The Destruction of Sodom* (vv. 12–29). My Zondervan NIV Bibles[4] keep them together, which makes sense, but the Italian subeditors, Rita Torti Mazzi and Federico Giuntoli hint at the reasons for specifying 19:1–11 as a unit by repeatedly noting the parallels between 19:1–11 and 18:1–15 in their notes. The hospitality part of the narrative can be separated from the destruction part of the narrative.

We will focus on 19:1–11, for which there are no particular manuscript or translation problems noted in the study Bibles.[5] Yet, though we might separate 19:1–11 from 19:12–29, the notes in these Bibles make us wonder whether we can separate 19:1–11 from 18:1–15. Though these texts are not contiguous in our canonical Bibles, they clearly are written as a hospitality diptych. The rest of the verses in Genesis 18 and 19 seem to function as digressions and expansions of these two blocks, but at least these pericopes, if not the whole two chapters, should be read in parallel.

Chapters 18 and 19 combined form a continuous narrative, concluding the story of Abraham and his nephew Lot that began in 13:2–18. The mysterious men visit Abraham in Mamre to promise him and Sarah a child the following year (18:1–15) and then visit Lot to investigate and then punish the corrupt city (19:1–29). Between the two visits, Abraham questions God about the justice of punishing Sodom (18:16–33). At the end of the destruction of Sodom, there is a short narrative about Lot as the ancestor of Moab and the Ammonites (19:30–38).[6]

Let us take note of this invitation to read the two pericopes together, but stick to Genesis 19 for now.

Intertextuality and Diachronic Considerations

Are there any other parallel texts to consider? In the cross-reference system, the Italian study Bible lists several (Gen 19:5 ‖ Judg 19:22; Gen 19:6 ‖ Judg 19:23; Gen 19:8 ‖ Judg 19:24). Three references to the same chapter in Judges (part of the Deuteronomistic History) should be enough to draw our attention to that chapter, which might be older than our text from the Tetrateuch, and which deals with lack of hospitality between Israelite tribes. Curiously, though, the editors seem to ignore these cross-references in the notes, preferring instead to link the text to ones on abominations and on male homosexual intercourse. They write,

> Just like in the case of Abraham in Gen 18, hospitality is a sacred law for Lot. Indeed, the inhabitants of Sodom violate this law and their sin—expressly condemned in Lev 18:22 and punished by death (Lev 20:13)—is thus also of a theological and social nature, and not only sexual.[7]

The second sentence starts off confirming the first, and telling us that the *violated law* is lack of hospitality, but then the incidental implies that the *sin committed* is "that other sexual sin" that the editors assume we are already projecting onto the text (while ignoring what they just said on hospitality), and finally the sentence concludes, commenting that the "sin of Sodom" is not just sexual but also includes other aspects (presumably including inhospitality). This is a good example of a markedly Catholic attitude of keeping everything together. The main phrase points to where the serious exegesis (including the cross-references in the same Bible) is taking us. Then, an incidental bit is included that seemingly brackets the results of that exegesis and upholds the traditional stereotypes of the Sodomites and the reader's preunderstandings, using ad hoc cross-references brought in surreptitiously. Finally, the main phrase concludes in a way that attempts to fuse everything together. My point, here, is not so much to criticize the editors of this Bible, but to show readers how to read the notes of their study Bibles with a critical mindset. The editors are subtly telling us that the passage requires a much longer note that they cannot afford to write, and that the reader should pursue the issue using better study tools.

Admittedly, the text is complex and allows for a conflation of several moral issues. These include (a) *sacrilege* (attempt to touch and have sex with God's messengers), (b) *violation of hospitality*, (c) an attempt to *humiliate and violate* the physical integrity of adult independent males through rape (probably the worst conceivable insult to an esteemed gentleman in antiquity), and (d) the *sexual* issue regarding intercourse between adults who might appear as males (angels are traditionally deemed asexual beings). For a theological ethicist who is willing to bracket the meaning of "sodomite" in English and Italian, and focus on what the text is actually saying, the mention of the Leviticus texts by the Italian editors is surprising. The sexual sin here is intended or attempted homosexual rape, not consensual homosexual intercourse; the two things are completely different moral acts, from a contemporary Catholic ethics viewpoint.

One may argue that Leviticus 18:22 speaks about homosexual rape, and not homosexual intercourse, by saying that in antiquity it was hard to conceive the act as a consensual one, since "lying with a male as with a woman" was seen as something so humiliating that a reasonable self-respecting male would not freely consent to it without being manipulated or coerced by a superior. I am less confident, though, that we can read this much into the text of Leviticus, and more confident that we should not assume a clear link between these texts.[8] A lot of mixability norms are involved in what we see as sexual ethics issues in Scripture. What is obvious to me is that this is a case of rape, traditionally considered a type of sexual sin and concomitantly, a violation of the dominium rights of the paterfamilias (in societies where women and children were seen as protégés and dependents of their husbands or fathers). Many Catholic ethicists today would tend to link it more with the violation of the bodily integrity of the victim, hence placing it in the "thou shalt not kill" category (traditionally called "fifth commandment" sins) that includes hurting and maiming others unjustly. There are some texts in the OT that clearly condemn or punish some forms of heterosexual rape (Deut 22:23–29; cf. Gen 34; 2 Sam 13:1–39) and the word used for "rape" is usually "humiliation" (Gen 34:2; 2 Sam 13:12, 14, 22, 32). There are no texts that deal with male homosexual rape in a clear, explicit manner.

All this suggests that avoiding any conjectural links to Leviticus and following the clear intertextual leads to Judges that the Italian editors provide, which are expressly noted in the American study Bible.

"The passage resembles Jgs 19:15–25, which suggests the dependence of one story on the other."[9] As noted above, Judges 19 might be the older text, while Genesis 19 could be a later midrash built upon it, though dating is always a very complex issue. It is helpful to remember that the OT was built a bit like the *Star Wars* movies: the oldest books are not the ones placed at the beginning and listed as first in the series. This would lead us to suspect that Judges 19 is the base text, which is then reworked in Genesis 19, and to which a parallel is added in Genesis 18, as can be seen in the following synopsis:

Judg 19 (Gibeah)	Gen 19 (Sodom)
[20] The old man said, "Peace be to you. I will care for all your wants; only do not spend the night in the square." [21] So he brought him into his house, and fed the donkeys; they washed their feet, and ate and drank.	[2] He said, "Please, my lords, turn aside to your servant's house and spend the night, and wash your feet; then you can rise early and go on your way." They said, "No; we will spend the night in the square." [3] But he urged them strongly; so they turned aside to him and entered his house; and he made them a feast, and baked unleavened bread, and they ate.
[22] While they were enjoying themselves, the men of the city, a perverse lot, surrounded the house, and started pounding on the door. They said to the old man, the master of the house, "Bring out the man who came into your house, so that we may have intercourse with him."	[4] But before they lay down, the men of the city, the men of Sodom, both young and old, all the people to the last man, surrounded the house; [5] and they called to Lot, "Where are the men who came to you tonight? Bring them out to us, so that we may know [have intercourse with] them."
[23] And the man, the master of the house, went out to them and said to them, "No, my brothers, do not act so wickedly. Since this man is my guest, do not do this vile thing. [24] Here are my virgin daughter and his concubine; let me bring them out now. Ravish them and do whatever you want to them; but against this man do not do such a vile thing." [25] But the men would not listen to him.	[6] Lot went out of the door to the men, shut the door after him, [7] and said, "I beg you, my brothers, do not act so wickedly. [8] Look, I have two daughters who have not known a man; let me bring them out to you, and do to them as you please; only do nothing to these men, for they have come under the shelter of my roof." [9] But they replied, "Stand back!"

Continued on next page

	⁹ᵇAnd they said, "This fellow came here as an alien, and he would play the judge! Now we will deal worse with you than with them." Then they pressed hard against the man Lot, and came near the door to break it down.
So the man [the Levite guest] seized his concubine, and put her out to them. They wantonly raped her, and abused her all through the night until the morning. And as the dawn began to break, they let her go. ²⁶ As morning appeared, the woman came and fell down at the door of the man's house where her master was, until it was light.	¹⁰ But the men inside [the divine messenger guests] reached out their hands and brought Lot into the house with them, and shut the door. ¹¹ And they struck with blindness the men who were at the door of the house, both small and great, so that they were unable to find the door.

The irony of Judges 19:22–28 appears in two ways. While the crowd initially intends to rape a man, they end up being quite satisfied with raping a woman to death—it seems they were not very picky on the gender, but were primarily interested in the narcissistic thrill of humiliation, physical injury, and violent abuse of a defenseless person. Moreover, the abusers were not members of pagan nations from whom the ancient audience might have expected such abominations (Lev 20:23), but fellow Benjaminites. The text seems to suggest that had the Levite not refused to stop in Jebus, "a city of foreigners, who do not belong to the people of Israel (Jgs 19:11–12)" he might have avoided the murderous inhospitality of his fellow Israelites. It is tempting to suspect that the editor of Genesis 19 intentionally reshaped the Judges 19 text to accentuate the homosexual element and cast the blame once more on foreigners, expunging the antinationalist candor in the older text, but upon close examination neither of the texts can be easily hijacked and used to support contemporary "culture wars"; we will return to that below.

Before engaging in a detailed comparison of the texts, however, let us try to figure out the relative dating to verify to the extent possible our thesis above. For this purpose, we need a more scholarly tool than a study Bible. Wenham's commentary on Genesis considers Genesis 18—19 as a narrative text based on an earlier tradition with respect to postexilic composition of the Tetrateuch, but claims that "attempts to reconstruct earlier forms of the tradition are quite speculative."[10]

Butler's commentary on Judges takes us a step further, noting that many scholars, including Stuart Lasine, Daniel I. Block, Susan Niditch, and Philippe Guillaume have argued convincingly that the two texts are linked, with the latter two scholars claiming that the Judges texts is the older of the two, for a variety of reasons, which we will not list here.[11]

Returning to the narrative of the destruction of Sodom (Gen 19:12–29) and all the cities of the plain (except Zoar, following Lot's plea), which we separated from the in-house hospitality pericope, this unit mirrors the Judges story (Judg 20—21), which ends with a fratricidal war. In that war not only Gibeah, but "all the [Benjaminite] cities they came upon" are destroyed by fire (Judg 20:48). Genesis 19:12–29 can also be read in parallel with the Noah story in Genesis 6—7.[12]

When the in-house hospitality parts are read in parallel, two differences come to the fore. First, we have the insistence in verse 9b that Lot is a gēr (alien), hence, a guest of the Sodomites. What is clearly implied is that he cannot be a good host unless they let him be a good host, since his hospitality is subject to theirs. This has no parallel in Judges 19, since the old man (the host) is not presented as a gēr; the reader is led to assume he is a Benjaminite. If we assume the Genesis text is the newer text, a midrash on the Judges text, this addition reinforces the hospitality theme. The xenophobic insult is interesting to note: the assailants are claiming, either as a jibe or in rage, that Lot the powerless gēr is under the delusion that he himself is an authority figure possessing rights, a "lawgiver" or "judge."

Second, the old man does not leave the house to negotiate with the assailants, as Lot does, so he doesn't need to be pulled back in. Hence, in the first case, the guest (Levite) *pushes out* the concubine (but not the old man's virgin daughter), while in the second case, the guests (messengers[13]) do not *push out* Lot's daughters, but rather *pull* Lot inside. They obviously have the power to blind and stop the assailants. The supposedly powerless guests of the powerless guest overpower the hosts! In the Gibeah story, the Levite does not have such power to curb their violence, and his host is equally powerless (not because he is a gēr, but because he is an *elderly* man, and they are a crowd).

Composition / Rhetorical Analysis

Let us now get back to our original Genesis text. Wenham considers Genesis 18—19 as a literary whole and proposes the following palistrophic (concentric) scheme of scenes for the second part of the text.[14]

| TABLE 7.1 PARALLEL SCENES IN GENESIS 18—19 ||
Scene	Parallel Scene
1. Abraham's visitors look toward Sodom (18:16).	11. Abraham looks toward Sodom (19:27–28).
2. Divine reflections on Abraham and Sodom (18:17–21)	10. Sodom and Gomorrah destroyed (19:23–26)
3. Abraham pleads for Sodom (18:22–23).	9. Lot pleads for Zoar (19:17–22).
4. Angels arrive in Sodom (19:1–3).	8. Departure from Sodom (19:15–16)
5. Assault on Lot and his visitors (19:4–11)	7. Lot's sons-in-law reject his appeal (19:14).
6. Destruction of Sodom is announced (19:12–13).	

The composition of the first part of the text (Gen 18:1–15) uses a parallel structure, probably building an icon of Abrahamic hospitality as the photographic positive of the inhospitality of Genesis 19, as can be seen in this synopsis.[15]

Gen 19 (Sodom)	Gen 18 (Mamre)
[1] The two angels came to Sodom in the evening, and Lot was sitting in the gateway of Sodom.	[1] The LORD appeared to Abraham by the oaks of Mamre, as he sat at the entrance of his tent in the heat of the day. [2] He looked up and saw three men standing near him.
[1b] When Lot saw them, he rose to meet them, and bowed down with his face to the ground.	[2b] When he saw them, he ran from the tent entrance to meet them, and bowed down to the ground.
[2] He said, "Please, my lords, turn aside to your servant's house and spend the night, and wash your feet; then you can rise early and go on your way." They said, "No; we will spend the night in the square." [3] But he urged them strongly; so they turned aside to him and entered his house.	[3] He said, "My lord, if I find favor with you, do not pass by your servant. [4] Let a little water be brought, and wash your feet, and rest yourselves under the tree. [5] Let me bring a little bread, that you may refresh yourselves, and after that you may pass on—since you have come to your servant." So they said, "Do as you have said."

³ᶜ And he made them a feast, and baked unleavened bread, and they ate.	⁶ And Abraham hastened into the tent to Sarah, and said, "Make ready quickly three measures of choice flour, knead it, and make cakes."
	⁷ Abraham ran to the herd, and took a calf, tender and good, and gave it to the servant, who hastened to prepare it. ⁸ Then he took curds and milk and the calf that he had prepared, and set it before them; and he stood by them under the tree while they ate.
⁴ But before they lay down, the men of the city, the men of Sodom, both young and old, all the people to the last man, surrounded the house;	
⁵ and they called to Lot, "Where are the men who came to you tonight? Bring them out to us, so that we may know them."	⁹ They said to him, "Where is your wife Sarah?" And he said, "There, in the tent." ¹⁰ Then one said, "I will surely return to you in due season, and your wife Sarah shall have a son." [But Sarah was infertile.]
¹⁴ᶜ …[Lot warns his sons-in-law to leave.] But he seemed to his sons-in-law to be jesting.	¹² …So Sarah laughed to herself, saying, "After I have grown old, and my husband is old, shall I have pleasure?"

This brings us to expand our pericope and discuss Abraham's actions at Mamre.

Abraham's Hospitality in Genesis 18

Much can be said about the details of this text. Authors like Luigi Di Pinto scrutinize every detail of every one of Abraham's gestures to build a sort of phenomenology of hospitality.[16] Offering a calf and curds, not just bread and water, implies going above and beyond what desert hospitality usually requires; these extra details remind us of Gideon's welcoming of the angel (Judg 6:19). Lot, too, appears to be very hospitable. Both Abraham and Lot place themselves in a liminal space, a threshold between different types of spaces (e.g., public/private or rural/urban): Abraham at the tent entrance and Lot at Sodom's gateway. This in-between position is particularly suitable to welcome others, as well as to quickly detect approaching threats; it aptly emblemizes their being *gērîm*.

Interestingly, in the Mamre story, the inside and outside spaces are inverted, as are the times of day: Abraham and the messengers are under the tree, enjoying the shade and the breeze "in the heat of the day" (18:1), while Lot and the messengers are inside the house "in the evening" (19:1). Given this setting, Sarah is the person standing outside the welcoming space ("listening at the tent entrance behind [Abraham]," 18:10). She is the one jesting and laughing, refusing to take the situation seriously, like Lot's sons-in-law in 19:14.

Though there is no rape or intercourse in the Mamre scene, Sarah becomes pregnant soon after, and the text presents this as a desired outcome linked to the kind and hospitable encounter. Thus, the sexual/procreative element of the scene is also present here, but inverted (another similar text is Judg 13). Hospitality is generative *for the host*. Lot's hospitality, though it starts well, ultimately fails, since it rests on the shaky hospitality of an evil city; the result of this overshadowing inhospitality is death and destruction (of the Sodomites, the greater host), and incestual generativity (of Lot's family, the hosted host) from which the Moabites and Ammonites are born (Gen 19:30–38). Abraham's hospitality, based on the more solid hospitality of the kings of the wilderness and hill country (Gen 14), succeeds, and his gift is returned by the guests who kickstart the fulfilment of the promise of a progeny; the result is life and prosperity.

Some Loose Ends
A Dangerous Guest (Gen 20)

There are three loose ends in our discussion that we need to deal with. First, before we conclude that Abraham is a paragon of virtue, and that his situation is much safer than that of Lot, let us extend our pericope a bit further, and adopt a more synchronic and narratological approach to the whole Abraham cycle of stories in Genesis. (We will discuss narratology more in detail in the following chapter; for now, we adopt a beginner's approach).

We may be used to the NT image of a good and faithful Abraham (Rom 4; Heb 6:13–15; 7:1–10; 11:8–19). However, the Abraham we find in the Tetrateuch is a much more complex character: he is

200

also a cunning and devious figure. Unlike Lot, Abraham can offer safe hospitality to his guests because he has found a way preemptively and constantly to manipulate and threaten his hosts. He does not need to be reminded of the precariousness of his situation as resident alien in Egypt and Canaan to act.

In the chapters of the Abraham story preceding the Mamre passage, we see him—an anxious and fearful *gēr* in Egypt—taking the initiative of offering the sexual services of his wife-cum-half-sister to ingratiate himself with his hosts. He then notes the effects: YHWH punishes the hosts with plague (Gen 12:10–20). After Lot's experience in Genesis 19, Abraham weaponizes this strategy. Sojourning in Gerar, he deceives and seemingly tempts King Abimelech of Gerar to sleep with his attractive (though elderly, at this point in the narrative) wife. On the one hand, Abraham seems to be doing this to deal with the anxiety of his vulnerable status as *gēr*. On the other, he must be aware that he is tempting his host to commit an unintentional evil, and he seems to desire and plot the ill that will befall his host due to God's wrath (Gen 20:1–18). He seems to be using God (and God's dependable wrath in the face of sexual misconduct) to make his host, Abimelech, fear him. In this way Abimelech will never dare renege his hospitality in Gerar and violate Abraham's space when he is welcoming guests, as the Sodomites did to Lot. Abraham can now welcome God and God's messengers safely, should they visit him again.

Abraham seemingly rationalizes his actions with the usual "she is also my sister" excuse (20:12), simply assuming he is a powerless sojourner and that "there is no fear of God" among strangers (20:11), but of course, the most scandalous aspect of this story is that God seems complicit in Abraham's actions. To be sure, God takes pity on the poor Abimelech and warns him in a dream to keep him from falling into Abraham's trap, but God still places Abimelech at Abraham's mercy by giving him the impression, without exactly saying so, that returning Sarah might not be enough for him to avoid death. He might also need to ask Abraham to pray for him (20:7). While Abimelech confronts Abraham (20:8–10), fearfully accusing him of playing dirty, he ends up feeling obliged to pay handsomely (presumably for the intercessory prayer), even if Abimelech did nothing intentionally wrong. Much of the OT retains a premodern notion of unintentional sin linked to the notion of purity with which contemporary Christian ethics has to struggle.

If a modern virtue ethicist were to seek a paradigm of justice and virtue in this text, a person with a clear conscience (20:5–6), who could it be? Obviously, it would be Abimelech, who seems to truly fear God, and this helps us challenge an overly nationalist reading of the Sodom narrative. Genesis 19 highlights that "some" foreigners are inhospitable and evil (the city dwellers of Sodom and Gomorrah), just like Judges 19 insists that "some" Israelites are inhospitable and evil (the Benjaminites). By contrast, Genesis 20 warns us not to conclude that "all strangers" are evil, be they in a position of power (*nokrîm* like Abimelech) or in a position of weakness (*gērîm* like Abraham). Vulnerable strangers can be dangerous not simply because of their picaresque deviousness and craftiness, but because, as the Abraham stories show, God often champions the cause of the underdog. Such stories imply that God understands the anxiety that vulnerability causes and the tendency to cunningly shore up one's defenses, and allows the weak—the last-born son, the *gēr*, the orphan and the widow—to get away with a lot. God calls Abraham a "prophet," while explaining to Abimelech that he has been conned by this man (v. 7); I believe this shows us God's sense of humor. God's wrath is usually reserved for the powerful who get used to abusing their position of power.

A Dangerous Game: Needless Mass Killing

A second loose end can be found in an honest comparison of the ending of the Genesis 19 story with Judges 19—21. Such a comparison raises the complex question of the needless killing in both texts. At the end of Genesis 19, God uses his enormous blowtorch like a refiner's fire (Mal 3:2–3) to draw out the dross of the Jordan valley—including the humans—and burn it away. Obviously, from a modern ethics perspective, the effects are identical to genocide. Why does God resort to mass killing to purify nations and punish evil? Is there no other way? Scripture is aware of the uneasiness that readers feel in front of scenes of needless slaughter, even readers in antiquity who were used to close encounters with death and dead bodies. The Genesis text goes to great lengths to justify God's destruction of the cities of the Jordan Plain, with Abraham trying to haggle God out of it (Gen 18:20–33) and the author insisting four times that nobody was innocent ("the men of the city, the men of Sodom, both young and old, all the people to the last man" 19:4). Even so, such a manner of understanding God's mind and God's justice is not fully satisfactory. In Genesis 1:29–30, the author takes a step back and shows us a very different image of God, who creates a universe where humans and other animals are herbivorous. This God seems averse to any kind of slaughter.

By contrast, other images of God in the OT permit or encourage humans to engage in needless mass killing. A particular case is the ban (*ḥērem*): the consecration (especially of land) to God by total annihilation of anything evil or impure lying on it. Many scholars have attempted to make sense of the ban from a cosmological, juridical, liturgical, rhetorical, psychosocial, sociological, and philosophical perspective.[17] For instance, Susan Niditch sees the ban serving a psychosocial function: by situating mass killing in a cultic framework, it alleviates the innate human difficulty of killing other humans by encouraging the Israelites to see their actions as ones that permit the killed enemy to be dignified as the "best sacrifice" for God.[18] Others have argued, referring to the ban and to other cases of mass killings in Scripture, that these passages should not be read as an account of what happened historically; in many cases the story clearly presents itself as a saga-like exaggeration and is not borne out by archeological evidence. Rather, these passages may work as a therapeutic game of imagination whereby a vulnerable people convinces itself that threats to their dignity internalized as a result of violations by enemies have lost power over them, the "internalized enemies" being defeated through the drama of divinely sanctioned destruction.[19]

Even so, the moral problem is not so easily avoided. The end of the Book of Judges provides a critical perspective on the issue. It recognizes the existence of practices of mass killing in ancient Israel, sometimes rationalized theologically and placed in a cultic framework, but seems to argue against these practices by showing the reader how they lead to absurd and untenable consequences. After the horror of Gibeah, the other tribes unite to seek justice and attempt to annihilate Benjamin, but after losing two battles, they start doubting that God is on their side (Judg 20:26–28). They then use a ruse to obtain the victory to which they feel entitled, but instead of being content with Benjamin's humiliation, they turn their victory into needless mass murder of their Benjaminite brothers. When they realize this extreme punishment is unwarranted, they resolve to leave some Benjaminites alive, while they vow not to give their daughters in marriage to any of them (21:1). But even this solution risks becoming a form of annihilation unless they provide wives for the surviving Benjaminites. When this proves difficult, they encourage

Benjamin to kidnap and rape the daughters of the inhabitants of Shiloh (the central Israelite shrine at the time)[20] with the excuse that it lies "in the land of Canaan" (Judg 21:12). If the Benjaminites marry the girls after raping them, the girls' fathers would not be able to reclaim them, so the Benjaminites can now reproduce while the other tribes avoid breaking their oath not to give their daughters to Benjamin.

The result is that the "purified" Benjamin is encouraged by the confederated tribes to repeat the abominable behavior that their war of punishment sought to extirpate after Gibeah. Furthermore, the status of the shrine of Shiloh starts to be downgraded, eventually to be replaced by Jerusalem (Jebus), the "pagan" shrine that the Levite should have stopped at in the first place to avoid this chaos, but didn't due to his fear of the stranger (Judg 19:12). The irony and absurdity of this story reveals a voice in Scripture that contests the logic of other biblical narratives that assume mass killing is the only reasonable option available to God and God's people to mete out justice and root out widespread evil. The cycle of violence needs to be broken through mercy and forgiveness; the demonization of the "other" and the fear of the stranger should be conquered by hope.

This is neither the only voice in the OT on the matter, nor necessarily the predominant one, but it is simply included alongside other voices. For the Christian, Jesus's death on the cross—while mysterious and paradoxical in its own way—provides a convincing way of fitting together God's justice and mercy, and of distancing God from the human rage and fear that generate cycles of needless mass killings in history, while placing God's saving power in God's own nearness to the victims.

A Dangerous Host (Judges 4—5)

The final loose end is the Jael story. Recall that our reflection on Lot and Genesis 19 started from a Facebook debate on the value of hospitality in the Hebrew Bible that mentioned Jael (p. 191, section 7.1). Vulnerable persons, if they win God's favor, can be dangerous hosts as much as they can be dangerous guests. I believe that Jael's actions in Judges 4—5 should be read through this prism. The prose version (Judg 4:17–22) may sound chilling to the modern reader, but the ironic levity of the poetic version in Judges 5 gives it a flavor of saga, helping us root for the underdog much more readily.

[24] Most blessed of women be Jael,
the wife of Heber the Kenite,
of tent-dwelling women most blessed.
[25] He asked water and she gave him milk,
she brought him curds in a lordly bowl.
[26] She put her hand to the tent peg
and her right hand to the workmen's mallet;
she struck Sisera a blow,
she crushed his head,
she shattered and pierced his temple.
[27] He sank, he fell,
he lay still at her feet;
at her feet he sank, he fell;
where he sank, there he fell dead.

Women's songs after a battle are typically moments of cathartic relief for those who usually have to bear the brunt of male intransigence and bellicosity (Exod 15:2–21), but this stereotype is doubly challenged in the song of Deborah. The song is intoned by Deborah, a bellicose woman who needed to incite the reluctant men to battle (Judg 4:8; 5:8). The grief of the stranger women who lost everything at the end of the story, in particular the mother of the enemy general, Sisera, is callously converted into an object of jest and ridicule.[21] In contrast, the femme fatale stereotype is introduced here as Jael, together with the idea that deception is an essential weapon in the arsenal of the underdog.[22]

The trap that the reader needs to avoid here, as above, is facile moral identification with the heroes of the story. This is not easy, since on the one hand, the narrative strategy of these texts leads us quite naturally to identify with the heroes, and on the other, the typical modern churchgoer in North America—after being bombarded throughout childhood and adolescence with moralizing heroism by supposedly wholesome traditional comics and children's movies—may find it hard to deal with ambiguity and moral flaws in biblical heroes. Readers in Semitic antiquity did not conflate heroism and moral probity as easily as we do.

Jael is undoubtedly a great heroine—a woman who kills an enemy general, up close, in cold blood, with a tent peg, while he is fleeing. That is the greatest humiliation of an enemy we can think of in this context. Yet this does not necessarily imply moral virtue. Readers have been told she is the wife of a Kenite, a *gēr* and a descendant of Cain (who murdered his brother). This casts a doubt on her loyalty to Israel, or her willingness to support Deborah's war, and this is probably why Sisera trusts her and shelters in her tent. While YHWH does not require of her the violation of hospitality or the murder of a fleeing general, her action is probably dictated by anxiety regarding her vulnerability, or a desire to prove her loyalty to Israel and YHWH, and God willingly tolerates it.[23] Like Abraham and Gideon, Jael goes over and above in her hospitality, giving her guest milk in a luxurious bowl, not just some water as he asked, but then she kills him. This prompts the other women to declare that she is blessed, likely meaning that she is recognized favorably as a loyal member of YHWH's people, in contrast to those tribes who are cursed because they did not come to help the warring tribes in their time of need.[24] However, we should not mistake this blessing for a positive ethical appraisal of her act. Neither can we condemn it too easily: for instance, applying a late medieval or modern understanding of the Principle of Noncombatant Immunity from the *Jus in Bello* tradition to his case would be anachronistic.

As a final note, it is important to realize that there is a clear cosmic dimension to the Song of Deborah (which we will not explore) that lends existential import and an aura of exceptionalism to Jael's actions.[25]

Some Takeaways for Theological Ethics

Many countries with rapidly aging populations, especially in Europe, are known for their restrictive immigration policies and for harsh anti-immigrant political parties.[26] The Lot story reminds us of the cost of inhospitality and ethnocentrism: incestual generativity. To be sure, even Abraham's promised son is born of his wife and half-sister Sarah, a very close degree of blood relation; the fact that Isaac could be born, survive, prosper, and give birth to a multitude despite all this one of Mamre's "miracles."

In his 1953 Christmas radio message to the whole world, Pope Pius XII claimed that in his day,

> the natural right of the person not to be impeded when emigrating or immigrating [was not being] recognized or [was being] practically annulled with the pretext of an ill-intended or an ill-applied notion of the common good sanctioned and validated by law and administrative protocols,

Hospitality

[and that similar demographic and social engineering can be found in] public birth-control policies.[27]

Pope Pius saw overly restrictive immigration policies as a form of eugenics.[28] Of course, the "natural right not to be impeded while immigrating" is not an absolute right and can be restricted somewhat, but only when its restriction truly serves the common good. The Catholic Church has since developed an impressive body of teaching on migration and the respective rights and duties of migrants and autochthones, suggesting that when borders are left porous and integration is well-managed, the presence of the migrant "other" can be life-giving to local churches, political communities, and civil society.[29]

The texts we have analyzed offer much food for thought. Lot's hospitality depends on the fact that he is a guest in an inhospitable city. This limits and finally destroys his capacity to welcome others. We may be shocked to see him offer his daughters to be raped rather than expose his divine guests to such abuse, but this shows us how important hospitality is in Scripture. Jael's actions do not cancel or relativize this fact. If we welcome migrants, they will in turn welcome others and welcome us; hospitality can be contagious and self-sustaining. Hostility reduces everyone's capacity to welcome the other. Inhospitality ends up harming not only strangers but also has a way of coming back to haunt us and harm our kin, as the experience of the Levite in Judges 19 and its horrible aftermath aptly demonstrates.

Guests—and immigrants—can also play dangerous games, especially if they feel too vulnerable. A text like Genesis 20:1–18 can help us look more kindly upon the behavior of certain migrants who, knowing they are in a very disadvantageous situation, feel entitled to take dishonorable shortcuts and even to exploit their own family members. We may rightly question some of their decisions and the strategies they use to rationalize them, but we should also appreciate the underlying courage, hope, and initiative that brought them to where they are today.

At the level of the whole cycle of Abraham narratives, the character Abraham can be seen as a paradigm of the good head of a family, in Janzen's sense, and his story can hone our moral sense though the analogical imagination, as understood by Spohn (see chapter 2, above). A dialectical approach is useful when approaching single narratives and passages in this cycle, but we cannot lose sight of the foundational fact that Abraham took a huge risk when he obeyed God and left his homeland for good, making himself vulnerable to the whims of foreign kings. Whatever trouble he gets into, the storyteller cannot allow a powerful king to kill him to steal his beautiful wife, and hence endanger God's promise, after going through all that. At the end of the day, what "God" (the character in the narrative cycle) seems to care about is that Abraham is God's chosen vessel and that he trusts God enough to say yes to God's plan.

Yet, the sacred author counterbalances this simple and unilateral take on the divine by dedicating ample space to the virtue of King Abimelech and his appeal to Abraham's conscience: the readers are surprised by the goodness of the lord of the land, who remains a powerful and dangerous stranger in their eyes. The author arguably does so to confound the readers, keep them from idealizing Abraham and stereotyping God's moral reasoning, and make them react personally to the text and dig deeper into certain moral issues, without providing a ready-made solution. Abimelech is a "God-fearing" king; he stands in awe of God and of Abraham, seeing in this cunning migrant something holy to be respected. We are invited to stand in awe of the sacred dignity of each migrant and refugee today. We should, of course, learn how to sapientially, fraternally, and frankly, but productively, question and discuss with strangers and migrants any dangerous actions and behaviors bred by mistrust that might erode the rule of law. Yet while doing so, we should reject stereotypes that equate the migrant with the criminal ("crimmigration"),[30] and keep us from seeing the other as a possible vessel of God's grace for our society.

7.2 The Faith of the Syrophoenician Woman (Mark 7)

Is hospitality just an OT virtue, or can it also be found in the NT? Vatican II (*OTE* 16) and the PBC (*BM*) invite us to look at Jesus as the model of virtue and insist that Christian ethics should be christocentric. NT texts portray Jesus, his disciples, and early Christian missionaries as guests, at times demanding guests (Mark 5:39–40; Luke 5:4; 7:44–46), dangerous or inconvenient guests (Mark 1:45; 5:14–17; Acts 9:10–19; 13:48–52; 14:1–7), or guests who accepted the scandalous hospitality of tax collectors, prostitutes, Samaritans, and uncircumcised foreigners.[31] But was Jesus hospitable? Lot welcomes his guests within his house, Abraham, under a tree outside his tent, and Jael, inside her tent. "Foxes have holes, and birds of the air have nests; but the Son of Man has nowhere to lay his head" (Matt 8:20). Can an itinerant preacher be hospitable?

James Keenan answers this question by pointing to the parable of the good Samaritan and distinguishing between the in-house hospitality of the innkeeper ("Benedictine hospitality") and the on-the-road hospitality of the Samaritan ("Jesuit hospitality").[32] But is Jesus truly welcoming while on the road? We have already noted above (p. 74, section 2.5) that a quick scan of the way Jesus treats strangers in real life (outside of the parables) indicates an initial attitude of indifference, if not haughtiness and hostility, toward non-Jews (Matt 15:21–28; Mark 7:24–30; John 4:1–42; 12:20–23), with some notable exceptions in the case of Romans (Luke 7:1–10; Matt 8:5–13). Let us focus on the Syrophoenician-woman story in Mark 7. A traditional way of analyzing this text is by using a Gospel synopsis to compare Mark 7:24–30 with Matthew 15:21–28.[33] Assuming that Matthew and Luke are both based on a version of Mark's Gospel and on one or more other sources—the prevalent view among scholars today—it is interesting to note that Luke omits this story. A synoptic reading indicates that Mark's version is heavily rewritten in Matthew, leaving little of the original text; each of the resulting versions has a theological consistency of its own. We have already done ample comparative work in this chapter, so it is time to try something different. Let us explore biblical Semitic rhetorical analysis.

Rhetorical Analysis of Biblical and Semitic Texts: Overview

The best-known forms of rhetorical analysis are those developed to study the composition of Classical Greek and Latin texts. Semitic texts (and biblical texts written in Koiné Greek, mostly by Semitic authors) do not obey the same rules; until a particular form of rhetorical analysis was developed for such texts, most scholars assumed that the literary works contained in Scripture were not well composed, but rather resembled a patchwork of small texts strung together almost at random. Form criticism before World War II, with its practice of breaking texts into small units, reinforced this impression, and redaction criticism in the second half of the twentieth century did not dispel it altogether.[34]

However, committing text to paper was a costly and erudite job in antiquity, not a task to be done carelessly or left to chance. In most cases, it is reasonable to assume there is a structure and logic that explains why

parts of texts were assembled in a certain manner, and how pericopes fitted together in an opus, but the structure and logic are neither intuitive
nor indicated by formal linguistic cues in the text. Often, structures that
reveal the meaning of the whole become evident when we analyze the
meaning of the parts, hence tagging words belonging to similar semantic
fields is helpful. Tagged words can be used in attempting to rewrite the
text using blocks and indentation to discover possible patterns indicating
its composition. For instance, words having to do with sleeping or waking
up might be arranged concentrically around a core phrase to underline
its importance (wake up...slumber...*rise*...doze off...quicken), indicating that the sense of the whole composition is to be found in that phrase,
rather than in the final sentence of the speech, poem, or story.

As understood by Roland Meynet in his *Treatise on Biblical Rhetoric*, biblical rhetorical analysis "is uniquely descriptive and not prescriptive; in fact, it is limited to the study of texts in a book written long
ago and fixed."[35] It corresponds only to the *dispositio* or "arrangement"
part (the orator's organization of arguments) of a typical classical treatise of rhetoric, which taught and analyzed this and four other "canons" of public speaking (the orator's search for convincing arguments or
"invention," his mastery of style, his stimulation of his own memory and
of the recall of the listener, and the delivery of his viewpoint through
an effective speech).[36] For Meynet, biblical rhetorical analysis is not an
exegetical method proper, but rather an operation, "one of many stages
in exegetical work, alongside textual criticism, lexicographical research,
grammatical and syntactical analysis, research on the history of the text,
determination of the literary genres, and so forth."[37]

In his *Treatise*, Meynet describes in detail a number of "rewrit-
ing rules" and various techniques that allow us to search effectively for
structure in biblical passages, sections of works, and whole works.[38] We
will not discuss these techniques in detail here. Members of the International Society for the Study of Biblical and Semitic Rhetoric (RBS) have
analyzed many books of the Bible and published the results in various
languages; the society's website offers various resources for beginners.[39]

Applying Rhetorical Analysis to Mark 7:24–30

Let us see how Meynet applies this form of analysis to the NT
passage we have selected. A more detailed analysis of the pericope, in
French, can be found in Meynet's work on Mark's Gospel, in a section

entitled *The Faith of a Syrophoenician Woman* (Mark 7:24–30).[40] Here
I have retranslated the text (from Greek) and simplified that analysis,
which uses various fonts and a complex system of tabulation, with the
help of Prof. Meynet. The delimitation of this pericope is justified by an
extreme term (verse 24) followed by a concentric structure, as can be
seen below.

²⁴ From, having risen, he went away to the region of Tyre.
And having entered a house [he] did not want anyone to
know. Yet he could not escape notice.

²⁵ But immediately, having heard—a woman—of him,
whose LITTLE DAUGHTER had an **unclean spirit**,
fell down, having <u>come</u> at his feet.
²⁶ And the woman was Greek, Syrophoenician by birth.

And [she] was begging him
that he *cast* the *demon* out of her DAUGHTER.

²⁷ And he said to her:
"Let first be sated the OFFSPRING,
for it is not fine to take the food of the OFFSPRING,
and to little dogs throw [it]."

²⁸ But in reply she said to him:
"Lord, even little dogs under the table,
eat of the crumbs of the CHILDREN!"

²⁹ And he said to her:
"For this reasoning go. [It] *has exited*,
from your DAUGHTER, the *demon*."

³⁰ And having <u>come away</u>, toward her house,
she found the CHILD lying on the bed
and the *demon gone*.

The passage is presented here in a peculiar way: we use a literal translation, we identify and differentiate the semantic fields (using italics, bold,
underline, etc.), and we organize the text using blocks (drawn based

on those differentiations) to make its rhetorical structure visible. This allows us to note several features, and doing so helps us interpret the text more fruitfully. For example, after the introductory verse (v. 24), we can trace the existence of two bookends of the narrative text that mirror one another (verses 25–26; 29–30), sandwiching a central part (verses 27–28). A concentric structure with a central core often points to a main theme contained in that core. In the core of this text, Jesus implies that the Jews are "the offspring" (*tekna*, 27b.d). This word primarily indicates natural children, rather than dependent minors who could be adopted, born of one's slaves, or under one's temporary care. Natural children are intimate with the paterfamilias, and the term presumably hints at the Jews' claim of having God as progenitor. By contrast, the pagans ("Greeks" here means non-Jews[41]) are "the little dogs" (*kynarioi*: 27e; the term denotes domesticated canines allowed around children).

The woman accepts and assumes the canine slur (28b), but she uses a more generic word for children (*paidia*, 28c) which emphasizes young age, immaturity, and dependence. The Jews may be called God's children because they resemble infants cared for by the paterfamilias, due to their young age, not so much because of their pedigree. The house-dogs (non-Jews) too are being cared for by the paterfamilias—in some cases, as we know from experience, housedogs are treated like natural children or even better—so the difference between the two groups is not as big as it sounds, even if we accept Jesus's unsympathetic metaphor. After Jesus accepts her claim/saying/reasoning (*logos*), the narrator goes even further and swaps the term "little daughter" (*thygatrion*, 25b) in the first bookend, for "child" (*paidion*) in the conclusion (30b). Healed (exorcised) by Jesus, neither the child nor her faith-filled mother can any longer be deemed a "little dog," notwithstanding their perduring strangerhood. Pagans are God's children, even though they may not be considered God's offspring.

Meynet notes that in verse 25, the woman is portrayed throwing herself at Jesus's feet just as soon as she hears about him: she is quickly convinced that he has the power to free her daughter from the evil spirit possessing her.[42] The encounter between her and Jesus in the house where Jesus was hiding mirrors the separation of the demon from her daughter in her own house, presumably located in some other part of the city. Though translating *Kyrios* as "sir" (as in the NRSV translation, "Sir, even the dogs under the table eat the children's crumbs") probably conveys better the ambiguity between a stranger's formal tone of protest and a hint of tongue-in-cheek, we have used the theological term *Lord* in our translation since, the woman is the only character in the Gospel of Mark who calls Jesus *Kyrios*, thus recognizing him as Lord.[43]

Does Mark intend her use of this title to convey faith in Jesus's divinity, or to portray her as merely flattering him by using an exaggeratedly flowery form of address? There are no intonation marks or emoticons in the text that can help us resolve this ambiguity. Jesus's use of a canine slur may be understood here as an effort to curb and test her messianic zeal (in line with the Messianic Secret motif in Mark), or else as an impertinent response to a slightly sassy or affected request. In any case, the woman retains her composure.

To be sure, Jesus might leave the contemporary reader perplexed or offended. Though he uses the diminutive form "little dogs" (*kynária*), which might function as a term of endearment (small housedogs are not stray and dangerous dogs), it is certainly not polite or "politically correct" toward non-Jews to compare them with animals. Jesus's audience (and Mark's original readers) would have noted the harsh tone, but it was common to speak in this way to strangers traditionally scorned by one's culture, and it would not have seemed very shocking at the time.[44] Jesus's insistence on the priority of the progeny of the paterfamilias ("let the offspring be sated first") seems to indicate that afterward, it will be the dogs' turn to eat. Yet his assumption that the offspring should not only eat first, but be *sated*—in a subsistence economy where children often do not eat their fill—leaves us wondering if anything will be left over.

It is worth noting that the traditional interpretation, which underlines the fact that Jesus is the Lord and is intimately attuned to the Father's voice and wisdom, refuses the idea that he might have something to learn from this pagan woman or that his ethnocentric view of the world might need to be challenged. In this reading, which Meynet does not discard, Jesus feigns hostility and unwillingness or lack of authorization to heal the daughter to put the woman's faith to the test.[45] Indeed, Mark's Jesus likes testing people. For instance, in the narrative of the calming of the storm, Jesus remains conspicuously asleep in the boat and then rebukes the disciples for their lack of faith (4:38–40; see also 9:19, 23–24). Yet Meynet also provides a more modern interpretation, which I prefer, that fully acknowledges Jesus's humanity, and hence recognizes that he shared the worldview of any "normal" Jewish man of his time, with its stereotypes and ethnocentric notions of salvation. As such, he could not have accepted the idea that the Gentiles could partake of God's covenant without first overcoming a certain cultural resistance. Read in this manner, the foreign woman changes from a marginal disciple to a key person in Jesus's life journey, nudging him to discover his own calling and the breath of his salvific mission, which at this point is seen to include the gentiles.[46]

Looking at the Subsequence (Mark 7:17–30)

However, both the traditional and the modern interpretation will seem incomplete if we zoom out of the passage and look at a slightly larger unit of text, which Meynet calls the "subsequence." This zooming-out exercise is justified for two reasons. First, Jesus was in Bethsaida in the previous verses, and now he is several miles away in present-day Lebanon; before we conclude that the editor of Mark's Gospel just inserted this story here at random, we need to ask ourselves if it is linked to what Jesus was doing or saying in Bethsaida. Secondly, a rapid rhetorical analysis of the verses prior to verse 24 reveals a parallelism that points to a larger text unit going from verses 17 to 30.[47]

---

[17]When he had left the crowd and <u>entered</u> the **HOUSE**, his disciples **asked** him about the parable. [18]He said to them, "Then do you also fail to understand? Do you not see that whatever goes into a person from outside cannot *defile*, [19]since it enters, not the heart but the stomach, and goes out into the sewer?" (Thus he declared all foods *clean*.) [20]And he said, "It is what COMES OUT of a person that *defiles*. [21]For it is from within, from the human heart, that evil intentions EMERGE: fornication, theft, murder, [22]adultery, avarice, wickedness, deceit, licentiousness, envy, slander, pride, folly. [23]All these evil things EMERGE from within, and they *defile* a person."

---

[24]From there, having risen, he went away to the region of Tyre and having <u>entered</u> a **HOUSE** he did not want anyone to know. Yet he could not escape notice. [25]But immediately, a woman, having heard of him, whose little daughter had an *unclean* spirit, having <u>come</u>, fell down at his feet. [26]And the woman was Greek, Syrophoenician by birth, and was **begging** him that he CAST OUT of her daughter the demon. [27]And he said to her: "let them first be sated, the offspring, for it is not fine to take the food of the offspring, and throw it to little dogs. [28]But in reply she said to him: "Lord, even little dogs under the table eat of the crumbs of the children!" [29]And he said to her: "for this reasoning go, the demon has EXITED from your daughter." [30]And having <u>come away</u>, toward her **HOUSE**, she found the child lying on the bed, and the demon GONE.

Hospitality

We find three instances of "exit/emerge/come out" (*ek-poreuomai*) in the first pericope, which match three uses of synonymous verbs in the second pericope. In both units, we are in a house where Jesus takes refuge from unfamiliar faces, and discourse is centered around the question of purity/impurity ("what defiles;" "a defiling spirit"). Read together, we note, on the one hand, that by declaring all foods "clean," Jesus removes a major barrier separating Jews from Gentiles (which, however, continued to be a source of division in the early Church between Jewish Christians and pagan-born Christians). What makes people clean or unclean, according to Jesus, is something we find inside: vices and intentions coming from the evil heart. On the other hand, the Syrophoenician woman, even though she doesn't follow Jewish dietary rules, is "clean"—clean enough to recognize Jesus as *Kyrios*. She may well eat mixtures of food that Jews do not deem "pure," just like the little dogs eating mixed scraps under the table, but that no longer matters for Jesus; what matters is what is in her heart.

Regarding the daughter, the issue is more complex. She is impure because she is possessed by an "impure" spirit. That could mean two things. On the one hand, it could point to an unidentified physical ailment or psychological syndrome, something that she is not responsible for or in control of, and which ANE cultures linked to spiritual impurity, just as they linked certain foods or food combinations to alimentary impurity. Jesus is not challenging the psychology and physiology of his day here. It will take yet many centuries for Christians and others to realize that people suffering from severe psychological syndromes are not spiritually "impure," and to learn to distinguish between the psychological *psyche* and the spiritual/moral "heart" or conscience.

On the other hand, despite her being called a "child," we cannot completely exclude the possibility that the girl might be an adolescent rather than an infant, harboring an evil (natural or supernatural) seed in her heart. If left untouched, this seed could corrupt her moral character and lead to some of the vices that Jesus mentions in the first pericope— fornication, theft, murder, adultery, avarice, and so forth—when the daughter grows up. For all these vices to be considered moral (culpable) vices in the modern sense of the word, the daughter would need to be free enough to say no to the compulsions she finds within, and to be able to start disentangling herself from the vicious cycle in which she is trapped. Yet sometimes the agent's will is so weakened that the help and

215

intervention of others, in this case, her mother and Jesus, to break them out of the cycle is practically indispensable.

Some Takeaways for Theological Ethics

As an ethicist, the first observation I feel I should make is that in all cases considered in these texts—psychical/psychological ailment, corruption of moral character, demonic possession—impurity is unlinked from ethnicity. One of the first manifestations of Jesus's saving power in Mark (1:21–28) is the cleansing of a "possessed" Jew. Indeed, evil spirits, ailments, and vices don't distinguish between the circumcised and the uncircumcised, between those who regularly visit synagogues and make pilgrimages to Jerusalem and those who do not, or between those who carry in their veins the blood of Abraham and those descended from the other descendants of Adam.

Many Christian and agnostic citizens in secularized countries think that their worldview is free of any ethnocentric notions of purity that exclude strangers for "irrational" or "obsolete" reasons, like those invoked to justify norms of alimentary purity or flesh cuttings in traditional cultures. Yet we do well to question the rationality of many reasons invoked today to exclude refugees and forced migrants: "they steal our jobs," "they carry diseases," "their religion and culture predisposes them to crime," "they are incapable of understanding freedom and democracy and hence cannot be integrated," "they have nothing to contribute." Most of these "reasons" are in fact myths, disproven by serious and unbiased research,[48] but they are not easily debunked since they serve to rationalize and whitewash deeper convictions rooted in "secular" notions of purity and defilement that cannot be voiced freely in liberal democracies without using explicitly racist language.

Sociologists like Sophie Krossa, who studies conflict and tension between social groups, have shown that even left-wing cosmopolitan Germans, like those who championed "welcome culture" in 2015 and opened their homes to Syrian refugees, often end up distinguishing between "clean" and "unclean" residents. They do this, for example, based on the thoroughness of waste separation practices and routines—hence linking strangers to some form of "impurity."[49] In Italy, a salty or spicy breakfast and the odors it produces could be linked to lack of civilization and to other forms of "uncleanliness," since purity is not mainly a question of sanitary hygiene and germs, but a question of social ordering.

216

Notions of what is and is not proper are often created and constantly adjusted or rendered more sophisticated by an upper class, or even a middle class, that wants to remain exclusive and privileged and seeks to stop the poor and people who look different from climbing the social ladder en masse, even if they are rich or famous or very intelligent. The use of peculiar features of language or a particular accent that is hard to fake is another key factor used to distinguish "old money" from "new money."

The dynamism of Mark's text pushes readers, even today, to identify notions of purity used to exclude others in their society, and to ask themselves to which of these notions they subscribe—even unwittingly—to unfairly maintain their privileges. Foreign-born residents or second-generation immigrants may have cultural norms that are strikingly different from those of the dominant cultural group. Such differences do not imply that strangers are "unclean," or that they contaminate or imperil our culture. Immigrants, in their "hearts," are not morally better or worse people than native-born people: most of the visible differences that fascinate, shock, or annoy us are to be situated outside their human core (Mark 7:19) and are morally irrelevant.

Evidently, when seeking to know the heart of the stranger, rather than focusing on his exterior self, we may also discover evil, even in the most likeable and integrated immigrants, who are indeed human just like everybody else. We might even notice peculiar tendencies toward crime and vice in certain geographical areas or groups, but any generalization needs to be studied sociologically, and any remedy must seek and build on the wisdom and goodness already present in the strangers' communities. An intellectually honest scientific approach will help us to better understand what triggers certain behaviors we deem antisocial, and whether our current laws unfairly criminalize certain actions deemed acceptable in minority groups, while possibly tolerating more harmful acts deemed acceptable in the majority group.[50]

8

KINSHIP BUILDING

What guidance can Scripture provide regarding the just integration of refugees and migrants in today's societies? This chapter explores this issue by taking a step further than hospitality and discussing kinship building, or fraternity, in the Bible. Readers will first be introduced to the concept of kinship building, or kinship bonding, and will gain awareness of the ethical and theological issues it raises in the OT.

In the second part of this chapter, readers will explore the hostility toward the other that is manifest particularly in the Books of Ezra and Nehemiah. This is required by an intellectually honest approach to biblical inquiry on a topic such as immigration, an approach that doesn't avoid dealing with those pages in Scripture that might fuel xenophobia in some contemporary readers. Ethnological and political approaches are used to understand some of the issues involved, and the theology used to justify such hostile attitudes is examined. Readers will learn to identify the historical demographic and psychological stress factors that bring about this situation, seeking to draw some lessons from this experience that may help them see that even texts they might find unpalatable and xenophobic could enrich modern ethics debates. At the end of this part of the chapter, readers will map some postexilic views in contrast with that of Ezra and Nehemiah, notably in some of the final chapters of Isaiah. This will allow them to observe how Scripture often records and presents to us several sides of a complex debate without resolving the tensions. Consequently, we cannot read Scripture as a univocal text and simply say that "the Bible teaches x" on any complex moral issue, without also noting the diverse voices and the outliers.

In the third and central part of the chapter, readers will be led in a narratological analysis of the Book of Ruth. We will explain this exegetical approach and show how it can be applied step-by-step in a simple but effective way by an ethics student. Stories are a prominent literary form in Scripture and are very useful in shaping action and ethical reflection, as we saw in chapters 2 and 3. Narratology is a very useful tool for ethics students wanting to approach Scripture analytically and use it explicitly in their reflection. We dedicate considerable space to this approach since it can be used effectively even by readers that have little training in ancient languages, history, archeology, and higher criticism techniques, and so it can help overcome many resistances experienced by ethicists wishing to use Scripture critically and responsibly in their work. It can help them moderate their tendency to use ready-made professional exegetical works excessively or uncritically, works often written by persons with little knowledge or interest in ethics. I believe ethicists should be encouraged to approach many biblical texts freshly, yet rigorously and methodically, bringing to each passage their concerns and expertise as ethicists, before reading commentaries and technical analyses by exegetes.

Finally, readers will explore the notion of kinship building as it is understood in a particular NT text, 1 Peter. They will learn to use some sociological tools to reflect on the in-group versus out-group relations of early Christian communities in the first century CE. Some takeaways for theological ethics are provided at the end of each of the three major sections of this chapter, pointing to ways in which readers might appropriate the texts in their current contexts, integrating extrabiblical sources of inquiry on human realities and human experience.

8.1 Kinship Building in the Bible

In the previous chapter, we discussed hospitality, whereby the other is welcomed but remains clearly an "other." Integration implies taking a step further and including the other within the self, while not completely or immediately abolishing her otherness. We can apply this logic metaphorically to the relationship between Scripture and ethics, but for now let us focus on human persons and societies.

As we have seen in chapter 1, we can make ourselves neighbors though a choice we make (Luke 10:36). We build societies and demotic nations through our reason and will, as we have seen can when discussing Maritain's distinctions (see p. 139, section 5.2). Hence, we can adopt the other and make them our kin, in a process we call kinship building (when underlining the intentionality of this process) or kinship bonding (when simply noticing it happening as a fact). In this book, we extend the notion of "kinship" beyond the biological relatedness of siblings or members of a clan, in an effort to use a more gender-inclusive term than "brotherhood" or "fraternity." *Fraternity*—a term that evokes medieval Christian associations and the grand nation-building value of the French Revolution—is a central notion in Pope Francis's theology, one that extends siblingship beyond biological relatedness or ethnicity. Its etymology points to the fact that Latin and classical Greek distinguish the *frater/phrater* from purely consanguine notions of brotherhood (*germanus/adelphos*). But does the Bible discuss fraternity or kinship building?

To be sure, Scripture is fully aware of the fact that some strangers simply want to pass through, others may require hospitality for a few days or weeks as wayfarers or sojourners, and still others stick around. This is where things start to become more complicated, when the *gēr desires* to become an *'ezrāḥ* (native), or at least a proselyte, to enjoy better social and legal protections or bind himself to YHWH, or when it makes sense for Israel, for the sake of its cultural and religious cohesion, to integrate the *gēr*. Scripture struggles to deal with these scenarios and to offer a clear framework for kinship building. This is probably a good thing for the modern reader who has more to gain from pondering the disputes preserved in the Bible than from copying a ready-made model of kinship building from an agrarian premodern society. As we shall see, one part of the Bible's difficulty with kinship building comes from societal resistances due to economic, political, cultic, and theological reasons, and the widespread tradition of maintaining resident aliens as metics in antiquity. Another part comes from the dual dimension of integration—religious conversion and social integration—in premodern polities, making assimilation seem too demanding a process for all involved. Undoubtedly, the call to practice costly hospitality and kinship building echoes through the pages of the Bible. Yet, those pages also attest both to the difficulties and resistance that this call provokes in otherwise pious believers and devout communities, and to the complexity of designing laws and social institutions that strike a fair balance between openness to the other and protection of one's own identity. We have already mentioned a triple notion of the *gēr* in the legal codes— the other needing protection, the other requesting integration but who might defile the group, and the theologically constructed originary

220

self—when discussing Ramírez Kidd's analysis of the use of this term (see table 6.1). The first two senses (where *gēr* is the other) make kinship building seem problematic; hence, biblical law assumes fatalistically that there will always be in Israel an indigent underclass of *gērîm*. It insists on loving them "as" brothers and sisters, "as" our native-born (Lev 19:34), but proposes few and limited means to removing the "as." At the same time, however, and regarding the third sense (the *gēr* as the idealized originary self) we find a national-religious narrative exalting the status of the *gēr*. Both the Lord God and the original Israelites are depicted as *gērîm* (Lev 25:23; Ps 39:12; 1 Chron 29:15). Additionally, the Bible critiques the prerogatives of autochthonous peoples in a way that suggests the rejection of slogans such as "this land is ours," which are popular expressions of ancient and modern ideologies of absolute sovereignty. In the Old Testament, therefore, we find a body politic and a nation that claims it is special because it has been birthed by a traveler God through traveler ancestors. "Traveler" points to the integration of the *gēr*, but "special" entails election and separation from what is foreign.

The "traveler" part of that formula implies that a particular compassion and care for other strangers, sojourners, and nonintegrated residents lies at the very heart of Israel's self-understanding. The "special" part, however, implies a certain fear of contamination by the "nonspecial" peoples living in the vicinity and by the members of such peoples living within the land given to the Israelites by their traveler God. Indeed, letting foreigners come too close may mean letting their ideas about the divine (including idolatry) and about lucrative and efficient agronomics (including land grabbing from the poor) lead Israel to commit acts of unfaithfulness toward God, and this carries the risk of losing the land and becoming landless exiles ("travelers" in a very real sense, *'ibrî*) once again.

We can restate this more forcefully by saying that the exilic and postexilic OT editors were concerned with a major dilemma. On one hand, how could Israel afford to integrate non-Israelite *gērîm* without becoming contaminated with their autochthone mentality and losing the Land due to unfaithfulness to YHWH? On the other hand, how could Israel afford not to integrate non-Israelite *gērîm* without implicitly forgetting her past as *gēr/ 'ebed*, adopting the arrogant autochthone mentality of the *nokrîm*, and losing the land due to unfaithfulness to YHWH? If the returnees and diaspora communities become too welcoming of the *gēr*, they risk running into mixability issues, while if they aren't welcoming enough, they risk becoming callous and unjust toward the vulnerable (see table 5.2). In both cases, transgression of the kosher-ness and ethical dimensions of holiness might be punished by a new traumatic event that once again makes them landless, destitute *gērîm*, themselves. Seen through this lens, integration is indeed a very tricky balancing act.

Preexilic and Early Postexilic Considerations

Historically, biblical Israel not only welcomed unhostile strangers, whom it calls *gērîm*; over time it integrated them within the "people" of the covenant. There are some narrative traces of this in Scripture. In Joshua 9:3–27 the Gibeonites (Hivites), one of the nations of Canaan, cunningly ask to join Israel pretending to be a destitute band of travel-ing people, and they are eventually accepted and integrated. Similarly, many *gērîm* appear in the entourage of important biblical figures, clearly indicated by their demonyms, and seemingly well integrated, like the famous Uriah the Hittite (2 Sam 11). In general, however, while biblical texts speak clearly about the importance of hospitality, they often skirt the more delicate issue of integration.

One possible exception is Deuteronomy 23:2–8, which speaks of the possibility of integrating Egyptians and Edomites in the "assembly/troop of YHWH" (*qəhal-YHWH*) after the third generation, but not castrated persons, illegitimate children, Ammonites, or Moabites (that is, offspring of incest, see Gen 19:30–38), "even to the tenth generation." The text has recently been read by Mark Awabdy as referring not to participation in a liturgical assembly or military troop, but to an ethnic, geographical, or theological integration process.[1] To be sure, participat-ing in certain assemblies entails a certain degree of integration. There-fore, assuming an exilic or postexilic setting, *qəhal-YHWH* can be seen theologically to mean "the assembly of YHWH's people privileged to hear YHWH's word, affirm [the] covenant, [and] participate in cultic gatherings," while the integrable *gērîm* are the residents descended from the *nokrîm*-blessing-you (symbolized by Egypt and Edom) and the nonintegrable *gērîm* are those descended from the *nokrîm*-cursing-you (symbolized by Moab and Ammon).[2] The conclusion is that strangers who "bless" Israel can be integrated after three generations of *gēr* status. As noted above on p. 206, section 7.1, "to bless" is best understood here as "to recognize relationship to someone favorably."

Awabdy's proposal is well argued, though still quite speculative,

222

given the data available. However, even if such a framework for integration really existed within biblical law, for most *gērîm* the only real means of political integration into Israel was to let the sands of time obscure their origins and then claim to be linked by blood to one of the "tribes" of Israel, probably derived from a "canonical" list of clans that supported the Davidic dynasty and its wars of conquest in the Levant. Genealogical lists are also useful for this purpose (Gen 1—11), and some are constructed backward (by positing and adding ancestors common to more groups) to integrate new groups a posteriori. If that is not possible, the *gēr* could attempt intermarriage to claim kinship through daughters and grandsons.[3]

After the exile, when the mixing of populations became the inevitable reality in a world of transnational empires, a dominant group of returnees to the Persian province of Yehud sought to block the access of people they considered foreign to integration by the only available means, intermarriage. They preached divinely mandated endogamy. In this chapter, we explore their claims. We also examine some of the voices of protest against this group found in biblical texts considered "secondary," such as Ruth and Jonah. At the level of ideas, these "secondary" voices were probably drowned by those of politicians, religious leaders, and intellectuals supporting strong identity markers and "ethnic purity." Still, pragmatic solutions were found on the ground by officials and community leaders, driven by magnanimity, common sense, or opportunism.

Late Postexilic Period

We have noted above (7.2) that in the late postexilic and intertestamentary periods we find several verbal forms used to designate "foreigners who wanted to join Israel" or to "Judaize," for whom the term *proselytes* will eventually be coined. We shall not discuss this period, except for the following remarks that are helpful to understand the reality that Jesus and the authors of the NT would have had in mind were they to discuss kinship building in a more political sense (which they didn't, as far the canonical text goes).

During the Hellenistic Period, benefiting from a period of internal strife among the Seleucids, the Hasmonean rulers of Judea (the dynasty born of the Maccabee rebellion) managed to obtain a certain degree of independence, and then proceeded to progressively conquer and annex Perea, Idumea, Samaria, parts of Philistia, Galilee, and Iturea, increasing their territory more than ten times in size. To ensure cultural and religious cohesion in this extensive Levantine kingdom, in some strategically important areas they offered the inhabitants two options: convert (circumcise your males) or leave.[4] Eventually, given this urgent political need to integrate the stranger, a *giyyûr* process (basically a baptismal ceremony) was developed to mark the end of the conversion-cum-naturalization process and the rebirth into God's people of Israel.

However, even in this period, the word *gēr* and the notion of integrating strangers are seen as increasingly problematic in some Jewish contexts. Cardellini shows how the vocalization (pointing) and letter separation of many biblical manuscripts is cunningly altered in this period in some communities to remove the word *gēr* and mask biblical references to the equal treatment or integration of *gērîm* or to the marriage of Israelites with foreign wives (often without touching the unpointed script).[5] For example, in Genesis 38:2 (cf. 1 Chr 2:3), Judah marries Shua, "the daughter of a certain *Canaanite*," which in certain manuscripts becomes "the daughter of a *merchant*," ("Canaanite" could also have this extended meaning), while in others "a proselyte" is added to the name Shua. Some verses down, in Genesis 38:12, Judah's "*friend* Hirah the Adullamite" becomes Judah's "*herdsman* Hirah the Adullamite." The natural ambiguity of unpointed Hebrew script allows such reinterpretations. Furthermore, in various Targums, the Cushite (Ethiopian) wife of Moses (Num 12:1) is glossed to say "Cushite" means "beautiful" or to note that Moses married her when in Pharoah's court, but then repudiated her. Smith-Christopher also notes how terms like "son of Canaanites" becomes a pejorative slur in this period (Dan 13:56).[6]

8.2 Repudiation of Foreign Wives in Ezra and Nehemiah

Disputes in the Texts

The hostility found in the Books of Ezra and Nehemiah toward people labeled as "foreigners," and especially women considered "foreign wives," immediately conjures the image of ethnocentrism and xenophobia in the mind of the modern reader. We must proceed with caution here. Some exegetes with more apologetic tendencies rush to dismiss such readings as anachronistic, and may have a point in some cases. Yet others reply that, though we should be aware of our tendency to project our modern intercultural moral standards onto a biblical text, we should not be afraid of noting and discussing what we deem ethically problematic in Scripture: being overly defensive of the text often implies playing games of intellectual dishonesty.

To be sure, some authors note differences between the two positions. Ezra seems to be mainly protesting against marriage between postexilic and nonexilic Jews/Israelites (despite tagging them as old Northern Kingdom Israelites and then as old Canaanites, etc.). Nehemiah attacks mainly Jewish marriage to those perceived as non-Jews (or non-Israelites).[7] In any case, Ezra and Nehemiah adopt a particular reading of old lists of hostile nations and of the Josianic (Deuteronomic) reformists' texts to block the social mobility of persons in Persian Yehud who were not of exilic extraction, seeing them as a "contaminated/contaminating" presence or a menace to the "holy" oligarchy, who are using the wiles of their daughters to subtly open up access to administrative positions for people whose ancestors did not experience the Babylonian exile.

The first dispute concerns the building of the temple. The "peoples of the land" ('*am-hā 'āreṣ* or *gôyē-hā 'āreṣ*) claim to worship the same God.[8] But the returnees, without denying this, claim that the temple is for their God, and the others cannot help build it, since the king (the blessed *nokrî* whom they must obey), Cyrus of Persia, did not envisage their help.

> When the adversaries of Judah and Benjamin heard that the returned exiles were building a temple to the LORD, the God of Israel, they approached Zerubbabel and the heads of families and said to them, "Let us build with you, for we worship your God as you do, and we have been sacrificing to him ever since the days of King Esar-haddon of Assyria who brought us here." But Zerubbabel, Jeshua, and the rest of the heads of families in Israel said to them, "You shall have no part with us in building a house to our God; but we alone will build to the LORD, the God of Israel, as King Cyrus of Persia has commanded us." (Ezra 4:1–3)

The passage invokes the quintessential bureaucratic excuse, typical of byzantine administrations ("Sorry, federal rules don't allow this"), and reveals the foreignness of the returnees. Moreover, the references to "adversaries of Judah and Benjamin" and to Assyria depict the "strangers" who wish to build and share the temple with them as Israelites of the Northern Kingdom (before the fall of Samaria), not sons of non-deported Judahites as they most probably were. Yet, according to Ezra, returnees should remain strictly separated from them (Ezra 6:21; 9:1; 10:8–11). In Nehemiah, however, there may be a more noticeable ethnic difference (cf. Neh 9:2; 10:28; 13:3). Further along in the Ezra story, the problem becomes the issue of intermarriages:

> After these things had been done, the officials approached me and said, "The people of Israel and the priests and the Levites have not separated themselves from the peoples of the lands with their abominations, from the Canaanites, the Hittites, the Perizzites, the Jebusites, the Ammonites, the Moabites, the Egyptians, and the Amorites. For they have taken some of their daughters to be wives for themselves and for their sons; so that the holy race has mixed itself with the peoples of the lands. And in this faithlessness the hand of the officials and chief men has been foremost." When I heard this, I rent my garments and my mantle, and pulled hair from my head and beard, and sat appalled. (Ezra 9:1–3)

> Then Ezra the priest stood up and said to them, "You have trespassed and married foreign women, and so increased the guilt of Israel. Now then make confession to the LORD the God of your ancestors, and do his will; separate yourselves from the peoples of the land and from the foreign wives." Then all the assembly answered with a loud voice, "It is so; we must do as you have said." (Ezra 10:10–12)

Wives deemed "foreign" are to be repudiated. Presumably, they must be thrown out of the house with their children and abandoned. Whoever among the returnees was involved in such marriages is named and shamed publicly in a long list included at the end of the book, probably intending that they be berated for posterity and so that their contaminated children would be easily identified and kept out of positions of power (Ezra 10:10–44). Interestingly, in Ezra 9, the "people of the land" are no longer simply non-Judeans, but become members of peoples who supposedly lived outside the two Israelite kingdoms, ranging from Canaanites (a wide-ranging term that could designate all the peoples of the Levant, and their "Phoenician" colonies overseas) to Jebusites, the original inhabitants of Jerusalem who were integrated into Judah centuries before. From a historical point of view, there is little warrant to believe the "peoples of the land" weren't simply nonexiled Judahites: some Edomites may have moved into what was southern Judah during the exile, but there is little evidence of significant population shifts in the area around Jerusalem that constituted Persian Yehud.[9]

Even if we were to take Ezra's and Nehemiah's ethnic retagging of peoples within Yehud Medinata and immediately outside its tiny territory as authentic, their interpretations remain problematic. Most narrative passages in the Jewish Bible do not seem to have a problem with such intermarriages (Gen 16:3; 38:2; 41:45; Exod 2:21; Num 12:1; 2 Sam 3:3; 1 Kgs 11:1–2). Some risk of dangerous contamination (and syncretism) is involved in such marriages and is sometimes noted (Gen 24:3; 28:6–9; Exod 34:15; Judg 16; 2 Sam 3:3; Prov 5). Such unions risk preventing YHWH from definitively driving out before Israel "the Amorites, the Canaanites, the Hittites, the Perizzites, the Hivites, and the Jebusites" (Exod 34:11) and the Girgashites (which Deut 7:1 adds, probably to round it up to seven nations). Yet, the idea that there was an established Jewish law prohibiting such unions comes from a tendentious reading of such texts by Ezra and Nehemiah.[10] It is a textbook case, within Scripture, of instrumental misuse of Scripture in political discourse and action, which we analyzed above (see p. 113, section 4.3).

As in the case of Abraham and Jael, Ezra and Nehemiah are national heroes, but Scripture does not ask us to consider them as unimpeachable paragons of moral virtue, or to take their interpretation of other Scripture passages as evidently authoritative. A careful reading of the other texts in the canon shows that their understanding of Jewish intermarriage law is anomalous, notwithstanding the fact that, historically, it was preserved and followed for many generations after their time and is included in the canon.[11]

Different Hermeneutical Approaches

Several authors have studied the Ezra–Nehemiah texts and provided interpretations using a panoply of analytical approaches.

227

Ethnological Reading and Political Realism

Neil Glover brackets ethical considerations as irrelevant here and doesn't see anything particularly xenophobic or exclusionary in the "high ethnological walls" built by Ezra and Nehemiah around their social group. Their "policies are not born out of prejudice or paranoia. They are born of necessity. No *ethnie* can survive if it fails to police its ethnic boundary, and ethnic boundaries are policed through attention to kinship, commensality, and religious cult—precisely the areas of life dealt with by Ezra and Nehemiah."[12] They were afraid that the Israelite *ethnie* (or its authentic remnant, purified by the exilic experience) was dying out and intervened forcefully to preserve it. This reading, however, ignores that even pure political realism, especially in a theocratic regime, cannot indulge with impunity in unfair and callous policies, and that the *Sitz im Leben* of the texts (fifty-nine years of separation during exile) does not justify the ethnic differential Glover presupposes.

Demographic and Psychological Readings

Katherine Southwood uses various exegetical tools and insights from social sciences to analyze Ezra 9—10 in a book dedicated to the issue.[13] As noted, according to recent research, the ethnic difference between the returnees and the people of the land (nonexiled Judahites) may be more a question of perception than reality. Nevertheless, Southwood contends that these texts are best analyzed when situated in a context of heightened awareness of one's in-group identity, coupled with a context of a real or perceived imminent threat to that identity which elicits fear.[14]

Southwood differs from Glover by focusing on the stressors driving this perception: demographic inferiority and return migrant psychology. Smith-Christopher develops the reflection on demography by comparing the text with the fear of extinction present today in some Native American communities, while Jobling notes the small size of the community; their minority status was a sure motive for fear of the other.[15]

Southwood investigates the social psychology stressors and uses the notion of "hybridity" from Homi Bhabha's postcolonial theory to help us understand that the returnees were cultural hybrids who felt they did not really belong, either in Babylon, or in Yehud. This hybridity resembles that of many postcolonial intellectuals and revolutionary leaders in the late twentieth century who absorbed a great deal from their Western-style education and from their colonist friends, and inhabited an ambivalent cultural space, but were often reluctant to admit it (with some exceptions like Senghor in Senegal, Bourguiba in Tunisia, or Houphouët-Boigny in Ivory Coast). The returnees couldn't go home to Zion, which they pine for in Psalm 137, since this preexilic place existed no more, and never existed as such to some extent; it was a product of nostalgia.[16] Yehud was not Zion, it had to become Zion, to the extent possible when having to negotiate between ideals and reality.

Their identitarian interpretation of tradition and their obsession with recreating an archaic prestate Israelite world was mostly an effort to prove to themselves that they belonged and were "more native than the natives." In this way, they showcase many of the identity issues seen among forced migrants and return migrants today, who seek to prove they belong through the ostentatious and aggressive promotion of mummified versions of the traditions of the people who remained in the land, often interpreting any developments in their ancestors' village as "corruption," "decay," or "syncretism."[17]

This reminds me of the Italian Americans or the Maltese Australians who come to Italy or Malta and tell us, "You don't cook like our ancestors did anymore!" They are oblivious of the fact that what they deem ancestral traditions were the product of ingenious adaptations and rubrications—within the orthodox diaspora cookbooks and "grandma's tales"—of much more heterogenous and flexible culinary traditions practiced by people who had remained in the homeland and had nothing to prove regarding their identity, and who continued to develop and modernize these living traditions over time.

Economic and Political Readings

Given their hybridity, the returnees are a "collaborator" minority placed in positions of power by an imperial power,[18] as Anglo-Indians in the Indian Raj or Tutsis in Belgian Rwanda-Urundi. They fear losing their grip on power and being "punished" or discriminated against in the event of a political destabilization that transfers power to the majority group, and reasonably so. However, while the political situation is stable, they do not want to lose their privileges and their grip on power, and tend to ostracize those who marry out of the group (and hence "marry down"), providing footholds for ambitious social climbers from the majority group to "marry up." Smith-Christopher mentions studies in "hypergamy theory" that can shed light on the text.[19] Sociologists also note, however, that the relationship between returnees and nonexiled is particular and more complex; it is not simply competitive but also symbiotic.[20]

If power and wealth are the main issues at stake, then presumed or minor ethnic or theological differences used to define the out-group mostly mask what we would call "class" issues. We can imagine that the returnees, descendants of the elites, wanted to expropriate and gain control of their ancestral farmland and city dwellings, but it is hard to determine what real power the returnee administration had to expropriate such properties; some of those lands lay outside the boundaries of tiny Yehud Medinata in provinces administered by other governors, some probably sons of non-exiled Judahites. Thus, it is not clear who was the richer group, the nonexiled or the returnee Judahites.[21]

This discussion leads us to widen the geographic area beyond Yehud. The issue of political power is clearly central to the Nehemiah texts (especially Neh 13:23–31), which are to be distinguished from Ezra 9—10, especially since they seem to perceive the threat coming from outside Yehud, according to Smith-Christopher.[22] In Nehemiah, the returnee administrator class is threatened not only by the "people of the land" (who probably loathed being lorded over by their "Babylonian-ized" kin imported as a new ruling class by the Persians), but also by the rulers of neighboring Persian provinces.

These political neighbors are angered by the concessions and preferred treatment that the "new" rulers of Yehud are obtaining through their contacts in the imperial court. Tobiah "the Ammonite," and Sanballat "the Horonite"—both probably Israelites, despite Nehemiah's labeling[23]—opposed Nehemiah's rebuilding of Jerusalem (Neh 2:19; 4:7). They believed the Persians were making a big mistake by giving political semiautonomy to what they saw as the most rebellious and traitorous region in the Levant. The rebuilding of the temple, a lucrative pilgrimage site, is not just a question of piety but a potential source of great and lasting wealth and political influence for Jerusalem and its new rulers.[24] Seeing that they could not beat the rise of their Jerusalem power rivals, these neighbors who had accumulated wealth and power under the previous regime probably decided to "join them," by giving them their daughters in marriage.

Theological Approaches

The hermeneutics of suspicion applied above may give the impression that the theology of the dominant group of returnees was mostly a cynical use of religion to establish and maintain power, concentrating wealth in the hands of a few—the descendants of an elite who claim that their lands had been unfairly occupied by the countryfolk and exogenous *gērîm*. It is, however, probable that some of these dynamics of power and exclusion were not conscious and that many returnees genuinely feared that Israel risked contamination by the unorthodox or idolatrous religious practices of the stranger, especially when subjected to foreign influence. We have discussed above (6.2) the dispute between different theologies of the exile regarding who is the true remnant of Israel (Ezek 11:15; 33:24; Jer 24:1–10).[25]

The modern reader will note the irony that, despite the admissions of guilt and penitential liturgies that abound in Ezra–Nehemiah, the returnees are also tempted to seek a "Canaanite" scapegoat outside their group to blame for the unfaithfulness of Israel and their vulnerable political situation, which is one of total dependence on the good will of the foreign king of Persia. Isolationism is a good theopolitical strategy to solve the kosherness dimension of the holiness equation, but can the equity and compassion dimensions of holiness be simply ignored? Can one separate the *gērîm* from the widows and orphans and proceed to treat them in ways that provoke the ire of YHWH? The answer to this theological question will come from reading different Bible texts. In modern academic texts, we usually include dissenting opinions and comments on different approaches in footnotes and endnotes, or in different sections of a text (*videtur quod/sed contra*) with an introduction and a resolutory conclusion (like the *respondeo* in Aquinas). Antiquity didn't have these editorial tools, but simply appended and collected different opinions on the same and on additional scrolls.

Views in Contrast with Ezra–Nehemiah: Postexilic Isaiah

Other groups in postexilic Yehud/Judea had very different attitudes toward foreigners. Smith-Christopher distinguishes two types of nonexclusionary attitudes: transformation and inclusion.[26] The "dangerous" foreigner (inside or outside), rather than being fought, subjected, or destroyed, may be transformed into a nonhostile or even amicable "other," with God's help. This is a leitmotif in the court narratives in Daniel, as well as in the Book of Jonah. The "nondangerous" resident alien, on the other hand, should be integrated; the authors here probably assume they are speaking to "reasonable" Judeans, who are not afraid of an imaginary, treacherous "fifth column" of "Canaanites" or "Jebusites" arising from among the populations integrated many centuries prior to remove the returnee Judeans from power.

In the final chapters of Isaiah (Isa 56—66), we find a surprising claim that everyone who binds himself to YHWH, native or foreigner, can be included in the people, and can become a servant of YHWH:

Do not let the foreigner joined to the LORD say,
"YHWH will surely separate me from his people"....
The foreigners who join themselves to YHWH,
to minister to him, to love the name of YHWH,
and to be his servants,
all who keep the sabbath, and do not profane it,
and hold fast my covenant—
these I will bring to my holy mountain....
Thus says the LORD YHWH,
who gathers the outcasts of Israel,
I will gather others to them
besides those already gathered. (Isa 56:3, 6, 7a, 8)

Interestingly, the term for "foreigner" in verses 3 and 6 is *ben-hannēkār* (literally son-of-a-*nokrî*). Recall that *nokrî* is used to designate foreigners living in non-Israelite space (in foreign lands), hence potentially powerful, dangerous, and hostile; yet good King Cyrus, who is as *nokrî* as you can get, is seen as chosen by God (Isa 41—48). He and his successors are the political guarantors of Yehud Medinata's semiautonomy.

There is a long build up to this claim in Isaiah 56. Most probably Isaiah 40—48 (with its constant references to Cyrus) is of Babylonian origin (hence an exilic text), while chapters 49—55 were written after the Babylonian exile, in or around Jerusalem.[27] Isaiah 42:19-21, when linked to 43:8-10, gently introduces the novel idea that one who abandons blindness and deafness can be God's servant (singular) and God's chosen one, a term that in this context refers to Cyrus and to the exiled

Judeans. Chapters 49—54 alternate passages that speak of God's servant with ones referring to Zion/Jerusalem, indicating that God's servant is primarily the community of the returnees. However, from 54:17b onward, "the figure of the servant (singular) is consistently replaced by the servants (plural...)": if the *nokrî* Cyrus could be a servant by abandoning his blindness, then the returnees were not necessarily the only servants, since foreigners could join God's service as well.[28] This theme is further developed in Isaiah 55—66, traditionally called the Trito-Isaiah (following Bernhard Duhm's tripartite division of the book in 1892) and dated at the time of the restoration of the temple (515 BCE) and in the successive years under Nehemiah's rule (given the many cultic references).[29] The text cited above (Isa 56:3–8) from the beginning of this section is mirrored in the final verses of the book (Isa 66:18–24), which envisage a mission to the nations.

The contrast between Trito-Isaiah and Nehemiah and Ezra's view of strangers is striking, even though all these authors belong to the returnee community and agree on many other theological and cultic issues.[30] The authors of Trito-Isaiah (possibly Levitical singers and poets whose voices can be found in some of the Psalms)[31] seem to counter the scaremongering of the isolationist returnees—for whom every *gēr* is a potential *nokrî*—by inverting the argument, and claiming that every *nokrî* can be a potential "servant of YHWH," and hence a more authentic member of God's people than the Judahites who remained in Babylon.[32] Berges, following Christoph Bultmann, concludes that in this context, *gēr* was used to designate a circumcised person who was not a member of the returnee community in Yehud, while *ben-hannēkār* was used to designate a person who wasn't circumcised as an infant, or couldn't be circumcised (for instance, due to defects in the genitalia), and wasn't a member of the returnee community.[33] Isaiah 56:1–8 aims to overrule Deuteronomy 23:2–8 (the basis of the above discussion regarding Awabdy's integration scheme), to assert that both circumcised and non-circumcised "people of the land" can be included in the community of the servants of YHWH.

The condition for access to this new and very generous prophetic "integration scheme" was the observance of standards of "justice and righteousness" (56:1), which refer to previous sections of the Book of Isaiah (e.g. 1:21, 27; 5:7, 16; 9:7 and 45:8; 46:13; 51:5–8) that deal with issues we would consider "ethical" in the modern sense.[34] In general, the Trito-Isaiah sees the previous chapters of the Book of Isaiah as the

"Prophetic Torah" that should be observed after the exile (bracketing most of the Pentateuchal Torah): this is the new "covenant" that returnee and nonreturnee Judeans are expected to observe (56:6). The enduring validity of the cultic rules of the Pentateuchal Torah are challenged in a particular way here since the idea of the uncircumcised *ben-hannēkār* not only participating in temple rituals but also bringing offerings and sacrifices to the altar (56:7) is in clear conflict with Numbers 18:4.[35]

Trito-Isaiah's proposal was probably scoffed at and ignored by the political and temple officials of the day, but arguably, from a pragmatic point of view, at some point in time the tensions between the returnees and "the people of the land" (showcased in Ezra and Nehemiah, and possibly in the fourth Song of the Servant in Isa 52:13—53:12[36]) must have eased. If the *nokrîm*, total strangers with no ancestral roots in Israel or pagan friends of the diaspora communities, could be partially integrated, then it made no sense not to offer some integration to the Judahite, YHWH-worshiping "people of the land." The concrete conditions for integration, one would assume, were the result of a complex compromise between the various voices in the returnee community. Probably complete or quasi-complete assimilation and submission to all the laws of the Torah was asked of most proselytes, hence pushed to renege any differences in cultural identity. Proselyting and Judaizing texts written in the later postexilic years and in the intertestamentary period offer different interpretations of what conversion to Judaism entails. Cohen, referring to Judith 14:10, claims that they typically required these "three elements: practice of the Jewish laws; exclusive devotion to the god of the Jews; and integration into the Jewish community."[37]

Trito-Isaiah's proposal of a more universal, more ethically minded and less cultically demanding process of integration into YHWH's people starts to be seriously explored for Christian "servants of YHWH" of pagan origins, in the NT and especially in Paul's writings.[38] Eventually it will be considered also in Rabbinic Judaism for marriage partners and people feeling "ethnically, but not too religiously Jewish," in medieval times and more intensely in the last two centuries.[39]

Some Takeaways for Theological Ethics

The transition from offering hospitality to offering kinship or fraternity through integration and naturalization is clearly a difficult one. In preexilic Israel, integration simply "happened," but the texts, as edited by postexilic Judeans, do not provide narratives, rituals, or clear administrative procedures to illustrate how it happened in the case of male heads of household, either before or after the exile.

In the case of Ezra and Nehemiah, we note that the major problem of the receiving community—the handful of Babylonian returnee families to whom the Persians had entrusted the administration of Yehud—was one of integration capacity. The returnee community had a low integration capacity, especially due to (a) demographics (the community was small and needed to be built up slowly), (b) psychological reasons (they had to wrestle continuously with all the complex hybrid identity issues faced by typical return migrants), and (c) political reasons (they were collaborators with the foreign colonizer, and felt they had to continually and radically prove that they were "Jews" not "Babylonians"). All these stresses made it difficult to develop the literary, legal, and ritual tools necessary to incorporate others into the community.

Yet, these difficulties gave rise to several different attitudes toward the "other" in the postexilic community, as we can see by comparing Ezra and the later chapters of Isaiah.[40] These attitudes, present in the biblical text, are not different shades of a single theological movement; they are at times contradictory and are kept together without a clear resolution in the canon, as part of an ongoing process of normative discernment and development. This dialectical plurality within Scripture brings to mind Jürgen Habermas's communicative action theory and some of its implications for the ethics of immigration policymaking explored by authors like Seyla Benhabib. Habermas and Benhabib describe how different social actors challenge one another in communicative processes that generate right and rights (jus-generative processes), and the texts we analyze in this chapter can be seen as acts of communication within one such process.[41]

Jus-Generative Processes and Immigration Policymaking

A legally recognized right (an element within a formalized and promulgated system of subjective and collective freedoms and entitlements) as well as "right" (that is, a positive system of laws) is called *jus* in Latin. Unlike natural right/s or human rights, positive right/s are generated through social processes of opinion and will formation of elites (in an oligarchy) or of citizens (in a democracy), which we call *jus-generative* or *juris-generative* processes. From a moral standpoint, positive right and rights should conform to ethical standards that are universally valid and hence cannot be created and destroyed in these sociopolitical processes. However, in democracies such standards cannot be introduced from the outside and imposed against the will of the people; rather, one hopes that they will be discovered gradually in these processes if the communication is rational and allows all concerned parties to participate and make their case convincingly. As can be seen by the current debates on abortion, gun ownership, and socially harmful self-expression (for example, misinformation and hate speech on social media), legal rights may be successively expanded and restricted and expanded again during ongoing historical jus-generative processes, as each new generation reiterates the process and reaches a new equilibrium between the rights and duties of minorities and majorities ("democratic iterations").

Benhabib shows how these processes are slowly challenging and transforming ethno-nationalist notions of citizenship within modern political societies. The rights of refugees and vulnerable migrants are sometimes expanded slowly, with legal provisions taking two steps forward and one step backward in these iterations.[42] The lack of "integration capacity" is often used in these processes to block the expansion of migrants' rights. I am of course skeptical when arguments of insufficient "integration capacity" (of migrants or receiving communities) are too liberally invoked in my country, Malta, let alone in large and wealthy polities such as the France, the United States, or the United Kingdom, but I believe that these claims are best challenged and debunked by reinforcing the communication ethics within immigration jus-generative processes, rather than claiming that vulnerable migrants are entitled to certain rights simply "because the Bible says so" or because "Kantian moral theory says so."

One final note concerns the Jewish process of naturalization-conversion (*giyyûr*), which allowed "others" to become part of the Jewish "corporate self." The beauty of *giyyûr* lies in its powerful ritual element;

naturalization is not simply a bureaucratic process. The problem, however, is that it does not respect Maritain's distinctions between nation and body politic, community and society. Thus, *giyyûr* highlights some serious problems that arise in many countries around the world that don't have a healthy separation between church and state, between religious belonging and political membership. Even within countries like the United States, whose First Amendment to its constitution has been a boon rather than a threat for religious liberty and the flourishing of faith and spirituality, other quasi-religious dimensions of the majority culture might be unfairly imposed on migrants, not necessarily by law, but by social pressure.

Similarly, in Malta, we celebrate the ability of the Maltese diaspora in Australia and Canada to keep many traditions alive even after three generations, while we expect Somalis and Eritreans to give up their cultural identity after five years in our country to "truly" integrate themselves. This is hypocritical and counterproductive: cultural integration and hybridization takes time and must not be forced, beyond the bare minimum to establish social trust and friendship. Trust and friendship will help the "other" choose what, how, and when to absorb from our culture's richness and may help our culture to grow and develop in contact with hers.

8.3 Strangerhood in the Book of Ruth

A Protest against Xenophobia?

The Book of Ruth, upon a naïve first reading, seems to promote the integration of at least certain strangers, though it dares not propose anything besides complete assimilation. Ruth is introduced as a Moabite (Ruth 1:4) and on six subsequent occasions (1:22; 2:2, 6, 21; 4:5, 10) in four short chapters, we are obsessively reminded of her origins. Only at the end, after she becomes Boaz's wife (4:13) does the text stop insisting, or even claiming, that she is a Moabite. Neil Glover proposes three possible interpretations based on three schools in anthropological theory: primordialism holds that ethnic identities are given, natural, ancient, immutable, and mutually exclusive; constructivism sees them as a product of a slowly evolving social collaborative consensus and hence as constructs that can be gradually shaped and affected by politics; and situationalism gives great importance to circumstances and social context in determining human decisions and the resulting social realities.

> (1) Unilateral Situationalists may suggest that Ruth becomes an Israelite upon her pledge of allegiance to Naomi [Ruth 1:16]. (2) Sympathetic Constructivists may argue the welcome Ruth receives from the Bethlehem assembly meets the necessary criteria for ethnic membership [Ruth 4:11]. (3) Hard Primordialists will resist any of the above: ethnicity is immutable; neither speeches of allegiance nor community welcomes can do anything to erase the Moabite gene. Ruth never becomes an Israelite.[43]

Glover excludes (1) since the idea that a person may choose a different ethnicity unilaterally and at will, without the recognition of those who are deemed to possess that ethnicity, sounds absurd from an anthropological point of view. Constructivism (2) cannot be easily dismissed, but it is more plausible to assume that some element of primordialism (3) is at play, since in anthropology, ethnic actors are generally seen as tending toward primordialist thinking, though exceptions might be made at times. Glover, however, suggests that the final genealogy (Ruth 4:18–22) might be "a satirical move, with the dull mechanics of the primordial genealogy being exposed by their juxtaposition alongside the literary élan of what has gone before."[44]

The story's positive portrayal of the Moabite Ruth stands out over against the Torah's hostility toward Moabites. Glover notes that this hostility rests on three stories. That Moab was conceived when a drunken Lot is seduced by his daughters (Gen 19:30–38) paints his progeny as incestuous. The Moabites' refusal to give Israel bread during the exodus (Deut 23:3–4) makes them stingy and inhospitable. Their use of the services of the sorcerer Balaam to curse Israel (Num 22:1–7) denotes them as idolatrous.[45] Ruth challenges these stereotypes. She marries a Judahite (Ruth 1:4), selflessly provides Naomi with bread (2:18), pledges faithfulness to Naomi's God (1:15; 2:12), and leaves Moab to remarry outside of her clan, even though Naomi suggests that to do so, she must leverage a Moabite stereotype—the "seduction of a drunken elder relative"—to get Boaz thinking about marriage.

The Ruth story does not, of course, promote an easy integration of the other, but it seems to place the household and its interests and dynamics over and above those of the larger ethnic group or nation. This starkly contrasts the positions of Ezra and Nehemiah. Whether it can be seen as a direct critical response to these positions has been debated; a lot depends on the dating.

Until the 1970s, there was a consensus among scholars, based on some Aramaisms and theological themes, that Ruth is a postexilic text posing as a premonarchic novella.[46] Between the mid-1970s and the mid-1990s, some authors maintained that dating,[47] while others questioned it.[48] Fredric W. Bush provides a clear analysis and methodologically sound solution of the issue, based on the study of its written Hebrew features.[49] The text in general has features both of Standard Biblical Hebrew and of Late Biblical Hebrew, and hence should be dated as pertaining either to the period immediately prior to the exile, or immediately following the return. Ruth 4:7–8, however, has several features that point to a postexilic dating, though a few scholars who insist on an earlier dating dispute the relevance of these two verses in resolving the dating issue, claiming them to be a gloss added by a later hand.[50] In conclusion, most scholars now locate the writing of the book in the Second Temple period, though few still see the possibility of at least a kernel of the story dating back to the monarchic period.[51]

If the book is indeed a sort of response or protest against the "nativist" thinking of the returnees, supported by authority figures like Ezra and Nehemiah, the strategy of writing a seemingly innocent story about women and love, posing as a short story from the premonarchic era, makes a lot of sense. The practice of writing texts that pretended to come from earlier periods of history or to be penned by famous writers was quite common in antiquity. It may be frowned upon in our day, with our modern notions of intellectual property, artistic uniqueness, literary genius, subjectivity, and so forth. But in antiquity, a strong preference for past tradition prevented commoners or "subversive" intellectuals from voicing their opinions as their own. People did not believe in "progress" and were not enthusiastic about anything new, but instead often saw the present as a time of decadence and regression in comparison to the past. In that context, making one's texts sound archaic was an effective strategy for convincing a skeptical audience.

María Elisa Estévez López argues that "the book of Ruth is not simply a story concerning some women, but rather a metaphor of the collective construction of a people."[52] In the postexilic context it challenges the idealized "us" brandished by the returnees while seeking to make the book's message receivable to its intended audience. For this reason, whether its proponents during the postexilic period conceived the story from scratch or worked with some prior material, we can assume them to be a minority group. They proposed a story situated in the prestate period to argue that what was needed in their society was not restoration (of the social structures and social fabric of the late monarchy, the "true we"), but reconstruction (of a new and inclusive social fabric, a "new we").

This historical background will be of help as we interpret this text as ethicists today, but let us first approach it analytically. The Book of Ruth is a fascinating and well-written story, it is brief enough (four chapters) to be analyzed as a whole, and it is thus a great candidate for the application of narratological analysis.

Narratological Analysis: Overview

Robert Alter's *The Art of Biblical Narrative*, published in 1981, inaugurated formal and methodical narrative criticism of Scripture. The nature of this kind of biblical analysis is pragmatic; it seeks to understand the function of the text, that is, what it is trying to do, how it is trying to have an impact on its readers. As explained in past chapters, we do not see exegetical approaches like narratology as stand-alone methods of biblical analysis but as tools within a larger methodological toolbox. My presentation of this method of analysis will follow two French-speaking authors, Jean-Noël Aletti and Daniel Marguerat, whom I have found particularly helpful, though many guides to narratology can be found in English.

Narrative analysis, according to Marguerat, "attempts to determine *by which procedures the narrator constructs a story which, upon being read, will free a narrative universe.*"[53] This analysis of narration procedures applies, of course, to stories, which are texts (or speeches) where events are linked together using the flow of time (chronologically) and positing some events as being the effects of some antecedent. Narratives have a timeline and usually follow an intensity curve, starting with the exposition of a situation, going through different levels of rising action to reach a climax (when all the knots and twists of the plot are combed up to the surface), and then descending again toward the resolution or denouement (unknotting). In longer and more complex stories, there may be various episodes and subplots, each with their catalysts, miniclimaxes, and partial resolutions.

As a synchronic, not a diachronic (e.g., historical-critical) approach, narratology does not analyze the context or referents that root the message, so it cannot say anything about the historical truth or fictitiousness of the message. Its main objective is to focus on the receiving end and discover the effects that a text (a written message) exercises on the reader and how the author touches and transforms the reader indirectly, via the text. Marguerat refers to Umberto Eco's notion of presupposition or "cooperative interpretation by the reader," discussed above (see p. 93, section 3.3).[54] The author of narrative texts creates a sort of "sleeping siren"; for the siren song to be heard, she needs to be constantly reawakened with the collaboration of another person's operation of reading and interpretation, their "prince's kiss." Hence, the same story (e.g., end of a marriage) can be told in different ways (e.g., in a courtroom, blog, pub, or therapy session), and the effect on the reader can depend greatly on the rhetoric of the narrative or narrative strategy being used; this is why we distinguish the information content (the "story") from the narrative mold in which it is cast (the "discourse").[55]

At the sending end, narratology assumes there is an "author," but it is not particularly concerned with getting to know the real sender. It may analyze the implied author—the author as he appears in the text to the reader—which may be very different from the real author. A socialist (real author) can write a story to subtly convince libertarians to pay more taxes, using right-wing language and arguments while continually berating socialism: the implied author is so quintessentially libertarian that it is practically impossible for the reader to figure out the true political views of the real author. Furthermore, the real author may interpose between the implied author and the reader a character called the narrator who is so staunchly socialist and so ridiculous in his running commentary on the other characters that the reader is led to believe the author is mocking socialism by vilifying the narrator, and so cannot possibly be a socialist himself.

Narrators may be constructed as ignorant, omniscient, or partially informed characters (regarding the external world of the narrative and its past and future, or regarding the personal feelings of the other characters, or both). They may use "internal focalization" to home in on the subconscious or hidden feelings of a character, "external focalization" to step outside this zone and observe features like facial expressions or gestures, or they may watch the events of the story unfold from a distance as though seated in front of a stage; this

241

is "zero focalization." Stories may have an "extradiegetic narrator," situated outside the plot of the story, or else the narrator might be yet another character in the narrative, an "intradiegetic narrator," for instance in an autobiographical narrative. Furthermore, a narrator can tell us things explicitly ("Ben was happy") or else show them to us by inviting us to observe elements in the scene and make inferences from our observations ("Ben had a broad smile on his face"): we therefore distinguish between "telling" and "showing."

Not all real authors are skilled in constructing narratorial characters or telling stories without a narrator. Kind and gentle people sometimes write angry rants about what happened during their day, or innocently tell stories that readers interpret as racist, and that unintentionally go viral on social media, leading readers to picture them as aggressive, bitter, and bigoted (since the implied author appears to be so). All these considerations explain why narratology thus limits itself to analyzing the narrator and the implied author.

If we move once again to the receiving end, we will note that narratives have an implied reader (the persons whom the author has in mind as recipients when writing the text, say, a Jewish diaspora community in the first century CE), which may be very different from the real reader (say, an astronaut floating in the International Space Station in 2022 and praying with the Mass readings). Furthermore, in some cases, the narrator may be narrating to a hearer character set within the story, the narratee. Figure 8.1 helps us to schematize this.

FIGURE 8.1 INTERPOSED AUTHOR AND READER FIGURES

The above diagram, however, does not include another important element in the case of texts we consider "revealed": the divine author. Jews and Christians write and transmit stories because they believe their God acts in history and God's action can be told and retold through narratives. God is not a ghost writer or muse and does not write or dictate the text to the real author. Rather, God is the protagonist of many of the stories told in Scripture or the underlying presence or agent they ultimately seek to make known to us. We believe God guided the real author (and this also includes the various editors, as the text progressed to its final canonical form). The authors were divinely guided as they chose the stories to tell, molded them into a narrative discourse, and composed them into a canonical opus—spiritual inspiration—while God's Spirit in history continues to guide the community of real readers when constituted as a church or people of God—spiritual assistance.

Developing what we have discussed above, narratology provides a toolbox to analyze stories; we do not need to use every tool in the box, but only those we find helpful regarding the text at hand. Marguerat mentions six analytical concepts we work with in narratology: (a) characters and their actions, (b) plots, (c) narrative frameworks, (d) time and causality (transformation), (e) narratorial perspectives, and (f) focalization. We shall present most of these tools below, using methodological text boxes adapted from Aletti's narratological commentary of Luke–Acts.[56]

Aletti's Method of Narratological Analysis

Step A: *Split the text into episodes and scenes*
Step B: *Analyze the internal (intradiegetic) elements*
  • The characters (incl. narratorial character if intradiegetic)
  • The actions
  • The plot
  • The transformations of space and time
Step C: *Analyze the external (extradiegetic) elements*
  • Narrator (if extradiegetic) and implied author
  • Reader (implied and real)
Step D: *Place the episode(s) in context*

Split the Text into Episodes and Scenes

Keeping in mind the timelines of narratives and their intensity curve, our first operation is to divide the narrative into episodes (major units of the text) and scenes (divisions of episodes).

How It's Done: Splitting the Text

1. **Episodes:** the following criteria are used to split the whole text into episodes: presence or change of actors, changes in time and/or space, changes in theme, etc.

> **2. Scenes:** the same criteria are used to split larger episodes into small scenes. Scenes may be labeled according to their respective role in the narrative (e.g., presentation of the characters, actions, complications, plot twist, climax, resolution).

Let us now apply this operation to the whole book of Ruth. Of course, there is no one single way to divide the text; different criteria might be used by different interpreters, and different levels of detail and complexity sought.

TABLE 8.1: EPISODES AND SCENES IN THE BOOK OF RUTH		
Four Episodes Divided into Scenes		**What Defines the Scene**
Background		
1:1–5	*Elimelech and Naomi Leave Bethlehem and Settle in Moab: Weddings and Deaths*	Movement to Moab
1:6–18	*Choices and Partings*	Decision to return
1:19–22	*The Journey to Bethlehem*	Movement to Bethlehem
Catalyst		
2:1–3	*Ruth the Gleaner*	Ruth moves from the city to the fields
2:4–7	*The Return of Boaz*	Boaz moves from the city to the fields
2:8–17	*A First Encounter with Boaz*	Encounter
2:18—3:5	*Ruth Talks to Naomi (1)*	Ruth moves back and forth; encounter
Climax		
3:6–15a	*Ruth Lies Down with Boaz*	Ruth moves to threshing floor; encounter
3:16–18	*Ruth Talks to Naomi (2)*	Ruth moves back to city; encounter
Resolution		
4:1–8	*Boaz Negotiates with the Other Relative*	Boaz moves to gate; private encounter

4:9–12	*The Agreement Is Approved by the Elders*	Encounter becomes public
4:13–22	*Marriage, Birth, Genealogy*	Return to private space (newlyweds)

Analyze the Internal (Intradiegetic) Elements

Once the text is divided into subunits, the analysis of the characters can begin. The order and level of detail of the following operations—action analysis, plot analysis and transformational analysis—may vary.

Characters

How It's Done: Character Analysis

1. **List the characters:**
   - **Single and collective characters:** Note names, descriptions, lifestyle traits; create a detailed "dramatis personae."
   - **Protagonists and their supporting/contrasting characters:** Note the key roles and those characters that serve to provoke some sort of response or reaction from the protagonists.
   - **Narratorial character:** If the narrator is intradiegetic, they should be included here.
   - **Other characters:** Note if there are typical or stereotypical characters, and if there are absent characters (mentioned by real characters in their speeches or mentioned by the narrator).
2. **Note which ones are likeable** (the "goodies"), dislikeable (the "baddies"), or leave the implied reader indifferent.
3. **Analyze their transformations** along the timeline of the narrative:
   - **Entry and exit:** When do the main characters appear and disappear?
   - **Transformation or unveiling:** Which characters have a constant identity or palette of values? Which ones have different identities or values in different parts of the narrative (due to transformations or to the unveiling of a different self)?

- **Agreement and disagreement:** Are there instances of opposition or conflict between the characters and at what level (ethical, physical, religious)?
- **Characters and events:** *Before the events*: Which characters prepare or announce the major events in the narrative, and which are those most affected by such events? *After the events*: Which characters react, and how? How do they interpret such events?

The main character in our case is, of course, Ruth, while Naomi and Boaz are supporting characters. The narrator is extradiegetic and will be considered later. Naomi's husband Elimelech ("my God is king") is an antihero figure. His situation is scandalous: there is famine in Bethlehem ("House-of-Bread," where "bread" can broadly denote "food"), possibly hinting at a situation of bad governance by the judges, and he seeks bread in Moab, the territory of a "bad" people, implicitly, a cursed land. This solution proves to be a serious error for him that brings about his death and that of his male lineage. Yet this encounter with the "other" brings into his house a Moabite daughter-in-law who then ventures to the House-of-Bread with Naomi and becomes a gleaner, living off the grain missed or left unharvested by the Judahite harvesters, and hence bringing bread to the House-of-Bread. Ruth is not described as pretty, but rather as loyal, obedient to Naomi, hard-working, and resourceful.

Naomi is pragmatic, wise (2:22), and at times shrewd (3:1–4). Twice she pushes away her Moabite daughters-in-law when they ask to return back to Judah with her (1:8–13), possibly testing whether they are just being polite or whether they are really willing to accompany her to a land where Moabites have a bad reputation. She might also be concerned that they will become a burden for her. She seems self-absorbed and doesn't react or reciprocate when Ruth powerfully expresses her great filial devotion and love toward her (1:16–18), merely accepting her company rather reluctantly. This might be due to Naomi's sorrow and bitterness (1:20–21), but as the story unfolds, she slowly seems to warm up to Ruth and chooses to mentor her (2:20–22; 3:1–5, 16–18).

Boaz is a just and kind man; he is quickly presented as rich and generous (2:1), potential husband material for a destitute woman in a premodern society, whose safety, well-being, and self-esteem are socially tied to her marital and maternal status. This is not a "romantic" story. Ruth uses a ruse to help Boaz realize she is desperately seeking someone, possibly in her extended family, to take care of her as her husband.

An unnamed next of kin (4:1–6) voices interest in acquiring a field that Naomi wants to sell, but upon being told that buying it is somehow linked to "acquiring" Ruth the Moabite, he claims that he cannot redeem land for himself without damaging his inheritance (4:6). In any case, he is easily convinced to transfer to Boaz the responsibility for the redemption of land and for Ruth.

The elders and people of Bethlehem serve as witness to both the transfer of the land inheritance to Boaz and his taking Ruth as his wife (4:11–12). Somehow transformed in the process, the witnesses end up blessing Ruth with a very "Israelite" blessing: "May the LORD make the woman who is coming into your house like Rachel and Leah, who together built up the house of Israel" (4:11).

The final "character" is King David, whose name brings the narrative to a close (4:22). Less important characters include Mahlon and Chilion (Elimelech's sons), and Orpah (the Moabite wife of Chilion). None of the characters presented is a true "baddie"; rather, the contrast is made between excellent examples of virtue (like Ruth and Boaz) who follow their good desires to the very end, no matter the cost, and good persons (like Orpah and the unnamed kinsman) who are less radical or keen on living the main values of the story to the full. They are willing to give up on what the reader is led to believe might be the better option (namely, sticking with Naomi, marrying Ruth) when it becomes too hard.

Actions

How It's Done: Action Analysis

1. **Analyze significant verbs and other important words:**
   - **Powerful verbs:** Which verbs indicate desire, knowledge, or action?
   - **Performative words:** Which are those words through which things happen or are made? Note the words expressing judgment, well-wishing, command, inauguration, evaluation, and so on, in the most central episodes and scenes of the narrative.

- **Nuanced action:** Note the modal verbs (*can, must, may, might, will, would, should, had to* + other verb; e.g., *Mary could not eat, John had to study*). Do they hint at or nuance something important in the narrative?
2. **Analyze complex actions:**
   - **Transformative actions:** What transformations are set in motion (at the start, in the middle, and toward the end of the story)?
   - **Contact between characters:** On which occasions is such contact *easy* and natural? When is it difficult, tricky, awkward?

A limited analysis geared to our purpose focuses on obvious places containing powerful verbs and performative words. First, the verbs used by Ruth in 1:16–17 are emotionally charged and performatively transformative:

> Where you go, I will go;
>   where you lodge, I will lodge;
> your people shall be my people,
>   and your God my God.
> Where you die, I will die
>   —there will I be buried.
> May the LORD do thus and so to me,
>   and more as well,
> if even death parts me from you!

A second touching moment is 2:15–16, where Boaz instructs his young men, "Let her glean even among the standing sheaves, and do not reproach her. You must also pull out some handfuls for her from the bundles, and leave them for her to glean, and do not rebuke her."

Another tender moment, yet marked with a resolute decision, happens at night on the threshing floor. In 3:13, Boaz asks Ruth to remain the night, and declares to her, "If [your more-closely related kinsman] is not willing to act as next-of-kin for you, then as the LORD lives, I will." Finally, after convincing the other kinsman to let him act as kinsman-redeemer, Boaz declares to the elders and all the people at the gate,

Today you are witnesses that I have acquired from the hand of Naomi all that belonged to Elimelech and all that belonged to Chilion and Mahlon. I have also acquired Ruth the Moabite, the wife of Mahlon, to be my wife, to maintain the dead man's name on his inheritance. (4:9–10)

The words and actions pertaining to the more complex and subtle parts of the text are best studied in Hebrew, but in most decent English translations we may find cues to transformative action and intriguing contact among characters in the following passages: (a) Naomi's repeated attempts to convince Orpah and Ruth to stay in Moab (1:8–18); (b) Ruth's plan (supported by Naomi) to glean behind someone in whose sight she might find favor (2:2), and her humble but eloquent discourse when she first meets Boaz, "Why have I found favor in your sight, that you should take notice of me, when I am a foreigner?" (2:10); (c) Naomi's subtle and shrewd suggestion that Ruth should limit her gleaning to Boaz's field and avoid gleaning behind other men (2:22); (d) Naomi and Ruth plotting the threshing floor ruse (3:1–5) and Ruth's putting the plan into action (3:6–9) by "[coming] stealthily and uncover[ing] [Boaz's] feet" and then asking him to "spread [his] cloak over [her];" and finally, (e) Boaz's delicate negotiation with the other kinsman at the gate (4:1–6), which we will deal with in further detail below.

Plot

How It's Done: Plot Analysis

1. **Determine the Plot Type:** Is the plot focused on (a) the characters and their character (as social types/individual heroes/paradigms of virtue), (b) values, (c) the situation, or (d) some form of knowledge or unveiling of the truth?
2. **Determine the Plot Structure:** What are the moments or components of the plot? Is there a five-part scheme: (a) beginning, (b) complications, (c) breakthrough, (d) climax (transformation/gain/loss), (e) resolution?

Having identified four episodes in our first step (background, catalyst, climax, and resolution), we can determine the plot structure relatively easily. Many stories have a five-part scheme, and this can be found here;

249

the "background" episode includes the first two parts (beginning and complications).

- Beginning: A Judahite migrates to Moab with his family in a time of crisis and finds wives for his sons there.
- Complications: the men die and the women become destitute, yet a Moabite daughter-in-law decides to cling to a Judahite widow and to her God, and hence to migrate to Judah with her.
- Breakthrough: The Moabite meets a rich and kind kinsman who might be able to give her a son (and progeny to her father-in-law), while redeeming the family field.
- Climax (including the transformation of the relationship between Ruth and Boaz): The Moabite uses a ruse to convince the rich kinsman to give her what she and her mother-in-law desire, but there is another kinsman who needs to be dealt with first possibly due to levirate-like obligations (see box on levirate marriage).
- Resolution: The issue regarding the other kinsman is resolved, the Moabite and the rich kinsman marry, the property of the deceased migrant Judahite is redeemed, and a male heir is given to him; the grandson of the heir is revealed to be a great future king, promising to rule Judah wisely and avoid a repetition of the original crisis.

Levirate Marriage and the Book of Ruth

Levirate marriage involves the legal or social obligation of an unmarried man to marry the widow of his deceased clan member. The best-known cases of levirate marriage in the Hebrew Bible (Gen 38; Deut 25:5–10) involve brothers or very close kin. Boaz is only distantly related to Elimelech (and to Mahlon, Elimelech's son and Ruth's former husband), hence he is not a *levir*; neither is Ruth's other unnamed, but closer kinsman. Frederic Bush conjectures a moral levirate-like obligation rather than a strict legal one. He follows other interpreters who assume (as is customary) that the pointed version of Boaz's speech in 4:5 is correct when it reads, "The day you acquire the field from the hand of Naomi, you acquire Ruth the Moabite as well." However, the unpointed version ("you acquire the field...I acquire Ruth") makes sense: it implies a more complex, nonlevirate tribal obligation, unknown to the scribes who pointed and corrected the text later, or simply invented by the author who is asking us to suspend judgment on the legal technicalities. "Acquiring" a Moabite wife can be socially demanding, but "acquiring [the ownership title and tribal duty to manage] the field" can also be a burden (rather than a gift) if someone else (for example, a money lender) currently possesses the usufruct, and a costly redemption process is required. It would make sense for Boaz to cunningly offer to "relieve" the kinsman of the "burden" of Ruth if there is no levirate-like obligation. It is more sensible to assume that the pointed text (mistakenly) projects a levirate-like obligation onto the text since scribes during the Hellenistic Period could not imagine a Judahite wanting to marry a Moabitess unless constrained by a levirate-like obligation. The scribes, less keen on the text's openness to strangers than the original author, may have pointed to the text according to their preunderstandings.[57]

Determining the plot type is less obvious. Given the delicate issues involving the integration of a stranger from a reviled or mistrusted people, different readings have been adopted in the history of its interpretation, at times to skirt what would seem to be the main issue. The text itself seems constructed to allow a certain ambiguity regarding what the story is primarily about, possibly to gain acceptance among a wider audience.

1. If we focus on the first words, "In the days when the judges ruled, there was a famine in the land," and on the last one, "David," we can read the text as an apology for the Davidic monarchy; by inheriting the loyalty, industriousness, and shrewdness of Ruth the gleaner, the monarchy brings bread to the House-of-Bread (Bethlehem) and hence guarantees a just and prosperous rule. Here, we can find elements both of a *value-driven plot type* (Ruth's character) and of an *unveiling plot type* (the surprising revelation in the final verses that the whole novella is about David's great-grandmother). In both cases readers are subtly led to the realization that the Davidic line has what it takes to provide Judah with

virtuous future rulers who will redeem and aggrandize it.[58] However, while the Christian ordering of OT books (placing Ruth between Judges and 1 Samuel) reinforces this reading, the Jewish ordering (Ruth is the second of the Five Scrolls—*Megillot*—which are part of the Writings—*Ketuvim*) does not.

2. A similar option is the *ḥesed* (lovingkindness) reading whereby we see the *plot focused on the moral character of main characters*, seeing them as models of what is arguably the most important virtue in Scripture.[59] *Ḥesed* is a love of benevolence, done out of one's supererogatory goodness or kindness, not out of obligation. There is, of course, a general obligation to practice such love, at least with some people, as best we can in our lives; what is not obligatory is the choice of the recipients or of the acts by which it is expressed (and this is the point that distinguishes *ḥesed* from justice).[60] *Ḥesed* does not necessarily mean a completely selfless love, since it naturally invites the recipient to reciprocate, and the lover might consciously or unconsciously desire such reciprocation, or at least some form of recognition of their love by the beloved. While the word appears only three times in Ruth (1:8; 2:20; 3:10), it drives the narrative from death and despair to life and joy. Ruth's *ḥesed* is contagious and it enlivens and transforms Naomi and Boaz.[61]

3. We can look at the characters in themselves, at how Ruth and Naomi bravely and intelligently figure a way out of a complex and unpleasant situation, and how the good Boaz comes to their rescue. This *character-driven plot type* with strong, assertive characters seeking their self-realization and pulling themselves out of poverty by their bootstraps is probably what many modern readers read into this story, given that they are immersed in a world where most narratives (in bestseller novels and blockbuster movies) function that way.

4. Other readers could focus on the *situation* and see the characters as types. The vexed question here is whether Ruth primarily typifies widows, vulnerable women, poor persons, or wives hailing from a reviled foreign nation.

252

Let us concentrate on such a *situation-driven plot type*. Focusing more on Ruth's widowhood, vulnerability, gender, or class, and less on her foreignness, many authors home in on two narrative features: property redemption and levirate-like marital unions (discussed above, in the box "Levirate Marriage and the Book of Ruth"). The details of both are not clear to a modern reader. The debates among the rabbinic sages have apologetic overtones, while modern exegetes have engaged in very complex and inconclusive juridical debates. Such exegetes, however, sometimes assume too easily that the Jewish laws on marriage and property as we see them today, codified in the texts included in Jewish biblical canon, were perfectly known, promulgated, and enforced at the time when Ruth was written.[62] Yet anyone who has ever lived in the Mediterranean and had to deal with property transfers will doubt this, knowing how legal matters in these areas tend toward the byzantine, how staunchly attempts at codification, simplification, and standardization are resisted, and how custom sometimes trumps written law, even in a tiny modern democracy like Malta after 150 years of British colonialism.

For example, Boaz's claim (4:3) that Naomi is selling land that belonged to Elimelech surprises the reader, who was led to think by the story that Naomi and Ruth were destitute. Some law experts and historians may be even more surprised because they doubt that widows in ancient Israel could inherit or alienate property. These surprises lead us to assume, from a narratological viewpoint, that the author is not very concerned with the legal technicalities and is asking the reader to suspend judgment and take him at his word.[63] Alternatively, there may be an ancient kernel of text that assumes the reader is knowledgeable about peculiar premonarchic Bethlehem-clan traditions, which the postexilic author integrates without bothering to fully explain them to his readers.

In any case, the point of the plot—as I see it—is that the son of a Moabite woman is somehow allowed to legally inherit Judahite land. This claim cannot easily be squared with a system of laws redacted during and after the exile with the intention of prohibiting such a thing (e.g., Nehemiah's obligation to repudiate foreign wives). In 4:5 (following the unpointed text: "you acquire the field...I acquire Ruth," as discussed above) Boaz seems to want to separate the tasks of redemption of land (which implies a financial burden on the other man) and protection of Ruth. Arguably, he is seeking to spare the closer next of kin (*gō'ēl*) a frowned-upon marriage with a Moabite he doesn't know or love, or to warn him that Ruth might not die childless and his half-Moabite heirs might end up ostracized by the community. The closer next of kin does not welcome the separation, wary that if Ruth bears a son by the prominent man Boaz, that son or his descendants might become powerful enough to lay claim on Elimelech's ancestral title, even if it had been lawfully redeemed within the clan. King David, the reader will recall, laid claim not only to Elimelech's land, but to the whole of Judah, and well beyond. Rather than spend money (e.g., by selling other land and "damaging his inheritance," 4:6) to redeem land that may become a cause of conflict between heirs, the closer *gō 'ēl* asks Boaz (who seems to have ample financial means) to acquire both the land and Ruth. In doing so, he also presumably keeps his inheritance "undamaged" by refusing to introduce Moabite blood in his progeny.

The resolution of the narrative thus hinges on the closer next of kin's refusal to marry a Moabite, presumably for ethnocentric reasons, and fear of loss of land to the sons of an unintegrable foreigner, *ben-hannēkār*, and the denouement revels in the irony by ceremoniously indulging us with the illustrious genealogy of Boaz's "damaged" inheritance. Many recent commentators, in an overzealous attempt to produce something new, seek to distance themselves from older commentators who read Ruth too easily as a response to Ezra–Nehemiah. The newer commentators intentionally seek a plot type that is not focused on Ruth's foreignness. They may be missing this irony and bracketing the most obvious interpretation, which, in my reading, is not an ethnological projection of our modern migration debates onto the text, but leaps out of the text at any reader with some knowledge of biblical and Mediterranean culture who sits with the story long enough.

The Transformations of Space and Time

How It's Done: Transformational Analysis

1. **Observe transformations in space:**
   - **Physical space:** Are there an inside and an outside? Is there movement between these spaces?
   - **Symbolic space:** Are there values related to space (e.g. public/private, sacred/profane, familiar/hostile)?
2. **Observe transformations in time:**
   - **Chronological order:** What is the relationship between the timing of the narrative (i.e. the sequence of the

scenes presented to the reader) and the timeline of the events lived by the characters (days on their "calendar")? Are there any *analepses* (literary flashbacks) or *prolepses* (literary projections of events in the "future" of the narrative)? Where do they originate (from a character, symbol, or happening inside the narrative, or from the narrator)?

- **Narrative speed:** Is there any extension or compression of real time in the story (e.g., ten calendar years reduced to a sentence, ten seconds inflated into a whole chapter)? Are there any ellipses (literary time jumps; e.g., "They reached Jericho; and as he left Jericho..." [Mark 10:46])?

Regarding topological transitions, Bethlehem is at the center of a series of to and fro movements: Bethlehem ⟶ Moab ⟶ Bethlehem ⟶ the field ⟶ Bethlehem ⟶ the threshing floor ⟶ Bethlehem ⟶ the city gate ⟶ Bethlehem. The most significant movement, physically and culturally, is that between Bethlehem (in Judah) and Moab.

For the reader, typically understood to be a Judahite, Bethlehem is the "inside," "familiar," and "sacred" space. Symbolically, Bethlehem/House-of-Bread is the place of plenty, but somehow it has become a land of famine "in the days when the judges ruled" (Ruth 1:1). From the point of view of Ruth, the Moabite woman who adopts the identity of her mother-in-law Naomi (1:16), Bethlehem is desired as a "home space." But reality is not always what we want it to be, and to a woman resident alien coming from a hostile-stranger space outside the promised land, Bethlehem (and the surrounding fields) presents itself initially as a hostile space, reducing her to barely surviving through gleaning, a condition of misery. Given her situation at the very bottom of the social order, she would not normally have been allowed to glean among the standing sheaves, but Boaz instructs his "young men" to make an exception for her (2:15). Naomi instructs Ruth to stick with Boaz's female workers, or else she risks being "bothered" (2:22). As for Boaz, he seems quite at home and in control, be it in the city, in the fields, or at the gate. The only place that momentarily seems hostile to him is the threshing floor, at midnight (3:8) when he wakes up from a drunken sleep to find a woman lying at his uncovered feet.

As regards chronological transitions, the story is quite linear, without obvious flashbacks (prolepses) or anticipated scenes (analepses). The narrative speed starts out fast with the events in Moab and the return to Bethlehem of Naomi; it decelerates as Ruth settles down as a gleaner, to the point of the slow-motion encounter at the threshing floor and the complex negotiation at the gate. The pace picks up following the marriage, and the final genealogy spans four generations from Ruth to David in one sentence.

Analyze the External (Extradiegetic) Elements
Narrator (or Narrating Author)

How It's Done: Narrator Analysis

1. **Determine the type of narrator:** If the narrator's voice is external to the narrative (extradiegetic), and it hasn't already been fully analyzed above (among the characters), the following steps are useful to understand the narrator's storytelling techniques.
2. **Distinguish between telling and showing:**
   - When does the narrator provide information by "telling" us things (i.e., presenting the relevant facts directly, e.g., "Anne was angry")?
   - When does the narrator use "showing" (i.e., making the relevant facts pop out indirectly through descriptions, speeches, gestures, e.g., "Anne's face turned red as she banged her fist on the table and shouted, 'Enough is enough!'")?
3. **Distinguish different kinds of focalization:** How does the narrator help us to see things?
   - From within the character's consciousness ⟶ Internal focalization (e.g., "Anne thought, 'What a disgusting mess, covered with flies!'")
   - From the point of view of external characters ⟶ External focalization (e.g., "The vendor saw Anne look at the fish on display in the market, covered with flies, and smiled as she turned away with a look of disgust on her face.")
   - From far away ⟶ Zero focalization (e.g., "Since time immemorial, visitors and tourists have visited the colorful fish markets of Zanzibar. Even Anne, when visiting the island, took a trip to the buzzing

Darajani market on the edge of Stone Town, but was
not thrilled by the sight of fish outside a freezer.")
4. **Determine the depth of knowledge of the narrator:**
Does the narrator know more than the main characters (omniscient narrator)? Does he or she know just as
much as they do? Or does he or she know less than the
characters (ignorant narrator)?

The narrator in this story is extradiegetic and omniscient, though
stingy with details, expecting readers to fill in many blanks with their
"presuppositions" (in Eco's sense). His focalization is mainly zero focalization, both as regards temporal and spatial width, especially at the
beginning and end of the story—"In the days when the judges ruled,
there was a famine in the land" (1:1); "Now these are the descendants of
Perez..." (4:18–22)—and regarding psychological depth into the inner
feelings and thoughts of the characters. We only get a sense of Naomi's
grief (1:20–21) and of Boaz's surprise (3:9) through dialogue, not narrative telling. Some narrative showing of the depth of Orpah and Ruth's
love of Naomi can be found in the 1:6–18, but during the rest of the
story, the characters and narrator appear stoic and almost incapable of
expressing or describing their feelings, while we are nevertheless deeply
touched by their words and actions.

Reader

How It's Done: Reader Analysis
1. **"Implied reader": Try to reconstruct the "ideal" or
"implied" reader intended by the author.** What would
a reader able to understand what all the nuances, the
complexities, the cultural references, the silences of the
narrative look like?
2. **"Real reader": Note the limitations of "real" readers,
today.** You may also imagine typical readers in pastoral
settings you are familiar with: people reading Scripture
in parishes, schools, seminaries, and so on. How can
we attempt to overcome such limitations?
3. **Identification:** Does the story favor the identification of
the reader with a particular character?

> **4. Effects on the reader:** Are there any other effects that the narrative seeks to provoke in the reader through the literary phenomena used (e.g., scandal, surprise, confusion, profound sadness and tears, joy, rage)?

The implied readers are expected to know something about Judahite norms regarding clan territory inheritance and redemption, and about social protections for widows. They are expected to know the importance of the Davidic dynasty in Judah (4:22) and hence of Bethlehem, David's town of origin (1:1), as well as the stereotypes regarding Moabites and foreign women in general which prevailed in Judah/Yehud before and possibly immediately after the exile (given the obsession of the text with reminding the reader of Ruth's origins). Assuming, from a synchronic perspective, that the commentary in Ruth 4:7–8 is not a later addition, the implied reader is not expected to know all the ancient customs that accompanied business transactions in preexilic Judah.

To go further in our reconstruction of the implied reader, we need to bring intertextuality and historical criticism into the picture. We can assume that Ruth was written later than Deuteronomy 23:4–6 and its author is familiar with this text. Furthermore, given the story's incessant mentioning of Ruth's Moabite origins, the implied reader is probably expected to know the sons of Moabites cannot be integrated (see p. 222, section 8.1). Though the rabbinic sages tend to dismiss this link, saying that this law only applies to males, modern exegetes note that *Moabite* (in Deut 23) is a collective noun referring to an entire people.[64] That the Book of Ruth might be a protest against Deuteronomy 23 (and possibly against Ezra and Nehemiah's hostility toward foreign wives) should come as no surprise. Read synchronically, even the Book of Deuteronomy holds tension on this issue. Many scholars see the argument in 23:4, excluding Moabites permanently, as a part of a preexilic core. Deuteronomy 2:26–29, seen as occurring in the frame added to the book during the exile, paint a diametrically opposite picture of Moabites as a people that is generous and hospitable toward Israel.

Furthermore, given mention of Tamar and Perez in Ruth 4:12, 18, the implied reader is probably expected to know their story in Genesis 38, in which another desperate woman seeking to give birth to a child dresses seductively and uses a ruse to get what she wants (and what she is owed) from the patriarch Judah. Tamar, too, attracts the sympathy of the reader despite both her deception and the probability that she is a foreigner, given the place where Judah was staying and the fact that he himself had married "the daughter of a certain Canaanite" (Gen 38:2) who bore him a son, Er, for whom he took Tamar as a wife.[65]

The implied reader is hereby challenged to identify with a destitute foreign woman within a story in which women take the initiative and Boaz—seemingly the only important man in their lives who doesn't die or isn't facilely bought out and dismissed from the scene—ends up dancing to their tune. Real readers today may need to acquire some of the above knowledge to better profit from the narrative experience.

Regarding the effects on the reader, noting Ruth's industriousness, bold initiative, and resourcefulness, certain commentaries see this text functioning as a defense of the Davidic monarchy, and as an antidote to the political incompetence of the last judges, as noted above on p. 203, section 7.1. All of this might have fired up the Judahite reader with royalist enthusiasm. I am more convinced, however, that both in antiquity and in our day the text seeks to confound and challenge readers who do not recognize complexity, especially those who naïvely accept attitudes and policies that are wantonly and indiscriminately hostile toward strangers. At the same time, the text comforts other readers who are more skeptical of such attitudes and policies, even when presented by legitimate religious leaders as coming from YHWH. This dialectic dynamic, in fact, helps readers and their communities confront complexity, especially when dealing with true otherness, and become more mature in their ethical judgments.

Place the Episodes in Their Context

Given the brevity of the text and the sociological and historical introduction provided before our narratological analysis, we will consider this step as already complete. Our detailed narratological work has produced a lot of insights, many of which will not be used in our discussion below. We have thoroughly explored the exegetical tools offered by narratology since we believe they can be particularly helpful to the ethicist; we did not seek to censor our exegesis in advance by reducing it to what we considered useful for our ethical reflection already while analyzing the text. The narratological work can and must be pared down, in a purely ethics-oriented publication, to what is most relevant to the final reflection of the ethicist, but this trimming process should be done after having freely and patiently completed the above steps, to avoid any instrumentalization of exegetical tools.

Some Takeaways for Theological Ethics

My first instinct, as a theological ethicist, is to apply a virtue ethics reading to the text. Ruth lends itself well to this operation; it is a powerful text showcasing the virtues needed for the process of integration, on both the side of the migrants and of the receiving society. Lovingkindness (*ḥesed*) is first on the list. Courage, hope, ingenuity, and perseverance are highlighted as well. Ruth's presence brings food and life to a barren place. The rapid integration of a Moabite in Judahite society is scandalous, but it shows how hate and mistrust of the stereotyped other can be dismantled and how the foundations of kinship bonding can be laid.

In Ruth 2:12–16, Boaz blesses Ruth and is generous with her, but he does not justify this by invoking kinship ties, although if he knows so much about Ruth already, he must know they are related. Instead, he attributes his actions to Ruth's labor of love and care toward Naomi (2:11). He seems amazed that someone would come over from Moab to take care of his kin. Even today, we may greatly admire the dedication of migrant women who take care of our children and our elderly relatives as their own, for more than the money, yet we may speak ill of their children as future social problems who should be kept out of the country. We doubt that the children will have their mothers' work ethic, and we reduce debates on migration to how useful migrants may be to us. Though Ruth's industriousness is painted in bright colors in this chapter,[66] Boaz moves beyond appreciating her productivity and work ethic and sees Ruth's intrinsic value as a lovable being, a "person."

The alternative possibilities of reading the plot type offer interesting stimuli for theological ethics, which we cannot fully explore here. The monarchic reading, which presents the benefits of the outbreeding of the Davidic dynasty, can help us challenge modern forms of ethnonationalism and segregation.

8.4 A Missive to Metics and Traveling People: 1 Peter

Politics and the New Testament

We have spoken of the dilemma in the OT regarding integrating non-Israelite *gērîm* (see p. 221, section 8.1): doing so would risk becoming contaminated with their autochthone mentality and losing the land due to unfaithfulness to YHWH; not integrating them would risk implicitly forgetting Israel's past as *gēr*, adopting the autochthone mentality of the *nokrîm*, and losing the land due to unfaithfulness to YHWH. A similar paradox can be found in the New Testament, even though the Christian community does not control a polity of its own, and the Jewish communities through which Jesus traveled in his mission years were provinces within a cosmopolitan Roman Empire.

The New Testament does not develop a political ethics proper because for most of the authors, the idea of establishing a polity shaped by Christian values was a nonstarter. Indeed, the authors were marginal citizens, denizens, or social outcasts with little access to political power. Many believed, at least in the first decades, that the second coming of Christ (Parousia) was close at hand, implying the end of history as they knew it, so political thinking in the classical sense (i.e., focused on long-term order and justice within earthly kingdoms) was seen as a waste of time or even a sign of nonbelief in the imminent irruptive establishment of God's definitive reign. This doesn't mean, however, that all we can find in the NT is a disincarnate spirituality, an intracommunitarian personal ethics, or a public ethics of convenience (demanding Christians to obey the authorities, and not to cause trouble for the missionaries spreading the good news, see p. 115, section 4.3), suitable only for the interim period until the Parousia. There are indeed some elements that we can use to reflect on more structural and long-term social issues. Gratuitous hospitality is widely practiced with everyone in need (leading to many free conversions), though fraternity or kinship bonding in the NT texts is mostly limited to membership within the church.

What does this kinship bonding entail? On the one hand, the church was called to be a host. Most Christians today have pagan ancestors and tend to assume that making membership in the Christian community easily accessible to non-Jews would have been an obvious choice for the disciples of Jesus, but many New Testament texts indicate considerable resistance to welcoming and incorporating non-Jews. On the other hand, the church was also a guest. As we read through the New Testament, we cannot help noticing that in many ways Jesus and his disciples were foreigners and travelers. They traveled to preach, they were mostly Galileans and diaspora Jews (cultural hybrids), they were progressively marginalized by the Jewish authorities (who held a modicum of local power), they announced and belonged to the kingdom (of God) that was (and is still) not yet politically visible on earth, and most of their converts hailed from ethnic diasporas, migrant worker families, and posted Roman soldiers and civil servants. In this context, faithfulness to Jesus and his Jewishness made the opening up of the early church toward "foreigners"—firstly Samaritans, then pagans in general—quite a difficult process.

A Communitarian "Home" for the Denizen

First Peter is an interesting text for exploring some of these issues. John Elliott approaches the epistle with a particular attention to its social setting, using an approach he calls "sociological analysis."[67] Referring to the research of Leonhard Goppelt, Elliot notes that 1 Peter "is the only New Testament writing which systematically and thematically has addressed the issue of Christian alien residence within the structures of society."[68]

The letter starts by calling the addressees the "elect visiting strangers of the diaspora"[69] (*eklektois parepidēmois diasporas*) of Pontus, Galatia, Cappadocia, Asia, and Bithynia (1:1), and it ends by claiming that the sender is the sister church in "Babylon," which is probably a coded reference meaning Rome (5:13). The text indicates a certain distance between the Christian household assemblies (churches) of mixed Jewish and pagan origins,[70] and the Jewish diaspora communities at the time of writing. Thus, the appropriation of terms like *election* and *diaspora*, which were formerly uniquely used by Jews, offers an interesting perspective to understand how Christians saw themselves at the time: a chosen nation dispersed among nations. Terms referring to sojourner (denizen) status and temporary residence status of strangers abound in the text (1:1; 1:17; 2:11).[71] The addressees are called "a chosen race, a royal priesthood, a holy nation, God's own people" (2:9), despite being continually harassed and slandered by their neighbors and reminded that they have no real roots in the place where they live. The term *oikos* (house, residence, abode, dynasty, clan) occurs in 2:5 and 4:17 and is the linguistic paronym of *pároikos* (sojourner, resident alien). The use of *oikos* is seen by Elliot as counterbalancing the unrooted (or home-less) feeling of metics, temporary residents, and traveling people who composed the core members of Anatolian Christian communities, the implied readers of the text.

Elliott argues that the classical reading that sees 1 Peter as espous-ing a clear two-tiered theology involving a "pilgrimage on earth and a home in heaven," possibly influenced by readings that project too much preterism onto NT texts, is not warranted. Preterism interprets the harassment of Christians under Emperor Nero and the destruction of Jerusalem in 70 CE as the historical manifestation (partial or complete) of the biblical prophecies regarding the end times (especially those in the NT, in Matt 24 and parallels). Authors and readers of texts from this period, such as 1 Peter, may have interpreted some of their experiences in this manner, but only to a certain point, since the harassment was probably confined to certain areas and not a full-blown persecution.[72] Christian sojourners do have a home in heaven, but they also possess a home on earth, within the sect-type social structures of early Christian communities. Some English Bibles use imprecise terms like *exile* or *pil-grimage* to translate the Greek legal-demographic terms *paroikos* (resi-dent alien or sojourner), *parepidēmos* (visiting stranger), and *paroikia* (residence as an alien). They do so possibly under the influence of the Babylon reference at the end of the text, but this preference for meta-phor instead of legal precision overly spiritualizes or cosmologizes the text.[73] Such translations imply the risk of missing the text's concern with the social and political problems of concrete historical Christian com-munities in Anatolia, and of interpreting it as a blanket invitation to Christians of all ages to practice a disincarnate spirituality, according to which our only real home as Christians is in heaven, and so we should not concern ourselves with political and social issues here on earth.

To be sure, readers are admonished to respect political authorities and not attract unwanted attention and provoke unnecessary harassment and xenophobia, but also to maintain their distinctive ethic, beliefs, and practices. All of this is a "political" game, rather than a form of escape from what is earthly, a *fuga mundi*. Though these practices were looked down upon by their neighbors, they are important and virtuous in the eyes of God (2:11–17). This sect-type dynamic allows for the creation of clear boundaries with the out-group, and reinforces in-group bonding and internal cohesion. The strategic maintenance of a boundary tension helps to avoid assimilation and the centrifugal breakdown of the sect. Yet if that tension becomes too strong, the group becomes too exclusive to survive and grow, and this centripetal dynamic becomes a target of dangerous and excessive external ostracization. Historically, at the time of writing there was probably no official persecution of Christians in Anatolia, but the authorities may simply have closed an eye to their constant harrying by pagan citizens and well-established Jewish diasporas.[74]

"Membership in an *oikos*, be it in a community of fellow expatriates, fellow immigrants, co-tradesmen or coreligionists, meant the possibility of at least a minimal degree of social security and of a psychological sense of belonging," and this was especially true "in an age of anxiety, turmoil and dislocation such as that of the Hellenistic Roman era."[75]

Some Takeaways for Theological Ethics

My first reaction to this text, as a Catholic ethicist, is to note that, in most countries today, mainstream Christianity is not a sect-like religious group, even though it may be a minority religion or the faithful might feel assailed by aggressive forms of secularism. Christian attitudes of hospitality and the championing of the human rights of migrants by religious leaders like Pope Francis may be frowned upon by politicians and even by many believers in the pews who have let nationalism and other worldly ideologies bracket important parts of their Christian identity. Instead of identifying with "metics and traveling people," many Christians today behave as the well-established pagan and Jewish residents of Anatolia and despise and harry immigrant communities that they see as too sectarian, while insisting on their immediate and total assimilation, or else on their expulsion.

Conversely, some of the sectarian dynamics and "ideology" of 1 Peter is visible among members of migrant diasporas today, who are generally deferential to public authorities to avoid trouble, but cling tightly onto some markers of their migrant identity. Some Christians and other citizens have fallen prey to the lies of the merchants of fear who, after 9/11, have built their political and media careers by blowing the sectarian

264

dynamics of minorities out of proportion and taking them out of context to amplify irrational anxiety in our societies. However, these dynamics can sometimes cause warranted alarm among Christians and other established citizens and residents, even when they are well-informed and do not conveniently conflate immigrant sectarianism and identity politics with crime and terrorism. After all, none of us wants to leave a fragmented, segregated society to future generations. I believe that religions have an important place in civil society as mediators of dialogue. They can sapientially keep smaller religious groups from becoming too sectarian, without necessarily forcing openness using the instruments of administrative coercion. Burka bans may be counterproductive, but a respectful discussion on the respective theologies of the "face of the other," especially after the mask mandates of the COVID-19 pandemic, may be a fruitful exercise for all the persons involved.

CONCLUSION

I n these final comments, I will focus on the book's second part, its last four chapters, where we sought to illustrate its first four "methodological" chapters in practice, applying them to the question of "the stranger in the Bible." The last section of chapter 4 serves as a conclusion for the methodological first part of the book.

We have made several generalizations in the "ethical takeaway" sections of the second part, but we did not present an overarching summary of what "the Bible says" about just and loving relationships with strangers. Our aim was to provide a series of vignettes, with accompanying takeaways that may be woven into larger ethical reflections that include social scientific data, lived experience from church communities, tradition, current church teaching, and contemporary theology. Vatican II (*GS* 46) invites us to consider social and political issues such as asylum and migration "in the light of the Gospel and of human experience." This means that the results of this book are just the first step in a larger process of ethical appropriation and reflection.

Rather than summarize the many issues raised in this book, let me make some final reflections on our theme, bringing together some of the main results of our inquiry on how strangers are seen in Scripture.

A Chorus of Voices

The Bible presents a complex mosaic of ways to see and treat the "other"; part of that complexity comes from the fact that many of the writers and editors of the biblical texts in postexilic Yehud saw themselves as return migrants with a tenuous grip on power. On the one hand, since they are the children of exiles who were *gērîm* in Babylon (cf. Ruth, Isaiah, Holiness Code, pervasiveness of the exodus-wilderness narrative in the postexilic Deuteronomistic editing, etc.), they sympathized with the *gērîm* in Yehud. On the other hand, the postexilic editors were also afraid of the people of the land—the Levantine Israelite majority whose religious and social customs evolved separately from those of the Jews who returned from exile in Babylon. Given their return-migrant psychology, the returnees saw these other residents as religiously impure and ethnically "contaminated"; given their political and demographic weakness, they saw these others as socially and economically threatening.

The receiving society established by imperial decree in Persian Yehud was a small and stressed community, with diminished receiving capacity. This is something to note as we seek to reflect on immigration policymaking today. However, we can go even one step further: we can assume that, when most other Jews stayed abroad, this group returned likely because they found it hard to be integrated in Babylon; they had a low integration capacity as refugees in Babylon, and they now had a low integration capacity as ruling class in Yehud.

Reading between the lines in texts like Ezra and Nehemiah, we can see the sociological and psychological complexes created especially by forced migration and by the return of forced migrants. This helps us relate not only to some of the problems experienced by refugees and asylum seekers, but also to the fatigue experienced by the poorer autochthonous and migrant communities who constantly receive new migrants in burdened neighborhoods. Furthermore, it helps us appreciate some of the problems faced by second- and third-generation immigrants who grow up in marginalized social contexts, are not fully "integrated," and feel they were uprooted from an idealized "homeland" and forced to grow up in a "foreign" country (not fully appreciating the difficult choices made by the parents and grandparents). Whether they stay in the country they call "foreign" or return to the homeland of their ancestors, these persons have particular social and personal needs, and they will require just and intelligent policymaking to encourage them to integrate themselves somewhere. Furthermore, their particular social and psychological issues are not to be projected onto the whole immigrant population.

Identity and Distinctiveness

The existence of a chorus of voices regarding how to relate to the stranger does not remove the desire to define one's identity and distinctiveness. To some extent, Israel's distinctiveness lies in the historical consciousness that a nation's pedigree and claim to antiquity are no guarantee of its holiness, justice, and respect toward the politically marginalized. Nations are not tasked to stay "civilized" as the gods made them in some golden age beyond the front end of history. Rather, Scripture assumes that humankind has a history of sinfulness. It bears a weight of past and present evil that erodes its relationship with the Divine, creating mentalities and patterns of behavior that exert a corrupting influence on our personal and social decision-making. Therefore every nation must struggle in history to become a "civilized" nation. This is not an easy process; even though Israel construed its history as one of marginalized, oppressed, and excluded "others," it did not always treat the "others" in its midst as the Israelites wished to be treated while in exile or as the Israelite slaves of the exodus narrative desired to be treated in Egypt.

We have mentioned (section 5.3) the notion of "anamnestic solidarity," which I find helpful to understand how Israelites in monarchic and postexilic Israel could adopt and continue to transmit the Abraham and Moses narratives, which were associated in past centuries with a vilified social group of vagabonds. Keeping fresh the memory of the suffering or abuse experienced by past generations (anamnesis) and seeking thus to maintain the contact between generations (solidarity) does not erase from human history the scars of genocide, slavery, or xenophobic oppression. However, this active evocation and remembering is necessary to prevent complacency about justice (and the perception that it can be cheaply obtained) in the present, and to prevent vanquished forms of abuse and oppression from resurfacing in the future.

Furthermore, anamnestic solidarity can be a double-edged sword. It can be placed at the service of social inclusion and hospitality to promote justice in the present and spare others the evils suffered by our ancestors, but it can also be used to justify isolationism or hostility. The memory of the suffering of one's forebears can be used to separate oneself from certain persons in the present who have different ancestors. Such people who can be seen as different (since their ancestors "did not suffer like ours") or as people who can be treated as inferior or as legitimate targets of hatred (since their ancestors were "those who made ours suffer"). This distancing from the other may at times be warranted (e.g., to protect one's group from someone who is truly dangerous), but at other times may be simply an expression of xenophobia and/or a form of scapegoating.

The notion of anamnestic solidarity helps us to understand a central feature of Israelite identity. Israel's solidarity with the "exodus group" is not primarily one of blood ancestry and of ethnicity. The historical evidence regarding ancient Israelites, as explored in this book, clearly indicates a situation where persons mostly derived from groups of natives engaged in an exercise of historiography (mainly during the late Judahite monarchy and the early years of Yehud Medinata) wherein a generation that deems itself "liberated" adopts the memory of a minority group of immigrants. We do not know where the exodus-wilderness stories come from, but they are not complete fictions; true stories of abuse, marginalization, enslavement, and liberation abound in the history of humankind, and Israel's link to the oppressed persons in the stories is pervasive in the biblical text.[1] We do no not know to what extent these narratives might be related to some of the blood ancestors of the generations that produced the canonical text of the Bible, but certainly these generations somehow felt anamnestic solidarity with the people in those stories.

As we have seen, however, an "outsider" national narrative does not by itself exorcise the tendency of the oppressed to become oppressors. Nevertheless, every society must face the problem of how far one can integrate another person whose presence and mentality are considered dangerous or contaminating without hurting oneself and without hurting the other. While it can seem like an intractable dilemma, this problem invites creative solutions in each new context and period in history.

Four Final Takeaways

What can we learn from Scripture about how to deal with this tension? To start, two important "deconstructive" ideas resulting from our inquiry challenge some aspects of modern ethno-cultural nationalism and of Westphalian sovereignty.

1. *Autochthony is mostly a fiction, and migration is not a marginal phenomenon in human history.* In biblical times, the idea that nations could be formed outside the lands they presently inhabited, or those where the mythical "father of the nation" was born, surely challenged the way ancient empires looked at outsiders and the myths they used to legitimize their possession of the land they inhabited. The biblical precedent for separating national origin from land of residence can also be used today to help us debunk similar nationalistic myths born in Europe in the Romantic Period, and in some newly independent countries in the 1960s and 1970s, and after the fall of the Iron Curtain in 1989. Political societies, as we saw in chapter 5, have a beginning in history, and are not "natural." They do not sprout out of the land, as autochthonous mythologies and ideologies claim. Groups of peoples move across borders, start new political societies, and, when establishing themselves as polities they have to struggle with political and cultural "others" both within their borders and outside.

2. *Religion is a problematic source of civic national identity.* To be sure, religion in the Bible is a primary shaper of ethnic national identity, but the Bible also shows the serious limitations of this "cultural" approach to the identity of political societies. By insisting on faithfulness to YHWH, even in exile or under foreign rulers, and by proposing YHWH as the God of all peoples, the Bible points to a certain decoupling between religious and political identity. This allows freedom of conscience, which people of faith, when powerless, have often demanded from others, but, when in power, have not always granted to fellow residents. Modernity has helped Christians and Jews become supportive of the religiously neutral state and to respect the right to legitimate religious freedom for all, not only for philosophical reasons, but also out of faithfulness to their own religious tradition. YHWH is not an idol to be co-opted by politicians and used as an ideological device to buttress identities and create social coherence in modern polities. Of course, religion

270

Conclusion

is not the only problematic source of political identity. Imposing certain elements of the majority culture on minorities—language, eating habits, dress codes—can be problematic. Yet perhaps these do not violate freedom of conscience in the same way as imposing a religion or letting social forces present religious practices as a sine qua non condition for integration.

On the constructive side, two important ideas can enrich contemporary immigration policymaking.

1. *National narratives are necessary, but not just any narrative will do.* Mythical national narratives are useful and often necessary in politics, but one must remain critical of such myths. The importance that Israel gives to internal cohesion, to the building of a stable and united community, is instructive. The insistence in the Bible on Jewish distinctiveness to defend Israel's political and religious unity and its cultural identity—even at the risk of becoming xenophobic or segregated from surrounding nations (when the actual differences were not so great)—speak of a nation's need for unity. Though actually offering outsiders few or no formal means of integration, the Bible's insistence on national unity and cohesion can support the claims of theological ethicists and Christian political activists today that integration is crucial. Yet this should be done narratively and imaginatively, not reduced to a mere bureaucratic procedure, be it simple or byzantine. This, in turn, points to the need for an "adoptable" national narrative, one that is not completely assimilationist and that we can reasonably expect resident political others—who do not want to excise their past, but who nonetheless want to become part of the political self of the receiving polity—to adopt. On the other side of the equation, we need "adoptable" immigrants, immigrants who do not refuse to buy into the national narrative and integrate themselves; such attitudes can be cleverly nudged, encouraged, and channeled.

2. *Anamnestic solidarity should be a prime shaper of national identity.* Israel adopts for itself an outsider narrative and

271

STRANGERS in the BIBLE

is adopted by an outsider God; arguably, this helps it to see social outsiders with greater sympathy than its neighbors do. Most polities today can revive memories of oppression, destitution, or wandering in positive ways, to see and sympathize with the oppressed and marginalized in their midst. The opposite of anamnesis is amnesia: forgetting the times when our ancestors were the underdogs, and adopting the self-same attitudes and behaviors of past despotic rulers and colonizers, suffered and denounced by the "mothers" and "fathers" of the polity. Furthermore, as can be seen in the Bible, for instance in the Book of Ruth, national narratives are most powerful and longest lasting when constructed from the perspective of the oppressed and the "outsider," not the from that of the "insider" with an iron grip on power and wealth.

The tension between national identity and strangers is resolved in the Bible, paradoxically, by the notion of being a nation of strangers (1 Pet 2:9–11). Of course, from a Christian faith perspective, the gradually deepening understanding of what this expression actually means forms part of God's pedagogy and can be fully grasped only through the advents of Christ—past, present, and future (in the Parousia)—which illuminate all biblical revelation. It is nevertheless still a struggle, even for Christians today, to truly see the stranger from the loving eyes of a stranger God, to truly understand the implications of being "sojourners" on earth. Doing so challenges us to be ready to live up to our vocation of walking the road to our "Emmaus" (Luke 23:13–34) with a Stranger who is God and with strangers whom, although they are deemed nobodies by others, we recognize as persons created in God's image. As Christians in today's secularized world, we may need to resist the constant temptation to see ourselves mythically as *gērîm* and brandish this "strangeness talk" as a mere banner of distinctiveness and a weapon to fend off those who seem different and strange to us. By doing so, we risk both investing too much energy to defend our Christian identity politically against a real or perceived secularist onslaught, and losing sight of the real *gērîm* in our societies, whom God desires that we welcome and protect, promote their interests, and help their integration.

Conclusion

These four verbs—to welcome, protect, promote, and integrate—summarize 130 years of official Catholic teaching on ethics and human mobility, starting with the encyclical *Quam Aerumnosa* in 1888, and including the groundbreaking apostolic constitution *Exsul Familia* in 1952. They have featured prominently in Pope Francis's discourses on migration ever since his *Message for the 104th World Day of Migrants and Refugees* in 2018 and the Holy See's engagement in the process leading to the signing of two Global Compacts (one for refugees and the other for migrants) during that year. The second half of this book has illustrated to what extent we can find biblical warrant for these verbs and this teaching, which are based on a tradition of theological ethics amply enriched with extrabiblical sources.

In conclusion, Scripture teaches us a lot about hospitality explicitly, but its implicit struggles with integrating the "other" are probably even more instructive as we reflect on immigration today. The many reflections above can serve as a basis for theological ethics to consolidate its discourse on migration, well nourished by the Sacred Page.

NOTES

Foreword

1. Pope Francis, "Homily at the Arena Sports Camp," Salina Quarter, Lampedusa, Italy, July 8, 2013, https://www.vatican.va/content/francesco/en/homilies/2013/documents/papa-francesco_20130708_omelia-lampedusa.html.

2. Pope Francis, "Meeting with the People of Lesvos and the Catholic Community: A Remembering of the Victims of Migration," Presidium of the Coast Guard, April 16, 2016, https://www.vatican.va/content/francesco/en/speeches/2016/april/documents/papa-francesco_20160416_lesvos-cittadinanza.html.

3. See the overview of church teachings provided by the Australian Catholic bishops, "Church Documents on Migration," https://acmro.catholic.org.au/about/church-documents-on-migration/what-the-catholic-church-teaches-on-asylum-and-migraiton, and US Conference of Catholic Bishops, "Catholic Social Teaching on Immigration and the Movement of Peoples," https://www.usccb.org/issues-and-action/human-life-and-dignity/immigration/catholic-teaching-on-immigration-and-the-movement-of-peoples.

4. For reflection on the frequency of the command to love the stranger in the Hebrew Bible, see Jonathan Sacks, *The Dignity of Difference* (New York: Continuum, 2002), 58–60, and chap. 6.

5. See US Conference of Catholic Bishops, "Catholic Social Teaching on Immigration and the Movement of Peoples."

Preface

1. In his recent book, *The Bible and Immigration: A Critical and Empirical Reassessment* (Eugene, OR: Pickwick Publications, 2021), ch. 1, Markus Zehnder has listed many of the pitfalls involved.

2. Julia Kristeva, *Strangers to Ourselves* (New York: Columbia University Press, 1994).

Chapter 1

1. Regarding the use of commonplaces in ethical reflection, see Jonsen and Toulmin, *The Abuse of Casuistry: A History of Moral Reasoning* (Berkeley: University of California Press, 1990), 74.

2. T. S. (Thomas Stearns) Eliot, a poet and literary critic, and Hans-Georg Gadamer, a Continental philosopher, have provided us with important characterizations of what constitutes a "classic"; cf. Tansu Acik, "What Is a Classic according to T. S. Eliot and H.-G. Gadamer?," *The International Journal of the Humanities: Annual Review* 8, no. 8 (2010): 53–64. American theologian David Tracy has used these and other authors to develop a notion of a "religious classic" and a "Christian classic" useful for a contemporary grounding of fundamental, systematic, and practical theology: *The Analogical Imagination: Christian Theology and the Culture of Pluralism* (New York: Crossroad, 1981).

3. Cf. explicit references in *FT* 2, M1997§2, M1999§5, *EM* 3, and implicit references in *GS* 27; William H. Willimon, "An Open Letter to Governor Robert Bentley, Senator Scott Beason, and Representative Micky Hammon," North Alabama Conference of the United Methodist Church, June 13, 2011, https://day1.org/articles/5d9b820ef71918cdf2002e5b/bishop_will_willimon_an_open_letter_on_immigration.

4. Michael Walzer, *Spheres of Justice* (New York: Basic Books Inc, 1983), 33.

5. Joachim Jeremias, *The Parables of Jesus*, 2nd ed. (New York: Scribner, 1972); David B. Gowler, *What Are They Saying about the Parables?* (Mahwah, NJ: Paulist Press, 2000); Klyne Snodgrass, *Stories with Intent: A Comprehensive Guide to the Parables of Jesus* (Grand Rapids, MI : Eerdmans, 2008).

6. *FT* 69, however, notes that "all of us are, or have been, like each of the characters in the parable. All of us have in ourselves something of the wounded man, something of the robber, something of the passers-by, and something of the Good Samaritan."

7. Paul Ricœur, "The Socius and the Neighbor," in *History and Truth* (Evanston, IL: Northwestern University Press, 1965), 98–128.

8. Ricœur, "The Socius and the Neighbor," 105.

9. Ricœur, "The Socius and the Neighbor," 104.

10. Ibn Hishâm, *Sirât Ibn Hishâm (Ibn Hishâm's Biography of the Prophet)*, trans. Înâs A. Fârid (Cairo: Al-Falah Foundation, 1955), 56–60; Ibn Qayyim Al-Jawziyyah, *Provisions for the Hereafter—Mukhtasar Zad al-Maʾad*, ed. Muhammad ibn ʾAbd al-Wahhab (Riyadh, Saudi Arabia: Darussalam, 2003), 261–65.

Notes

11. Kwame Anthony Appiah, *Cosmopolitanism: Ethics in a World of Strangers* (New York: W. W. Norton & Company, 2007), 158–62.

12. John Gerald Simon, Charles W. Powers, and Jon P. Gunnemann, *The Ethical Investor: Universities and Corporate Responsibility* (New Haven, CT: Yale University Press, 1972), 22–25.

13. Melody Young, "The Aftermath of *Peng Yu*: Restoring Helping Behavior in China," *Washington International Law Journal* 22, no. 3 (June 1, 2013): 693. Article 184 of the General Provisions of the Civil Law of the People's Republic of China now states, "A person shall not bear civil liability for acting voluntarily to help another in emergency and thus causes damage to the person being helped," http://www.npc.gov.cn/englishnpc/lawsoftheprc/list.shtml.

14. Pina Francone, "Sea Watch a Lampedusa: ma il 61% degli italiani non vuole che attracchi," *ilGiornale.it*, June 27, 2019, sec. Politica, https://www .ilgiornale.it/news/politica/sea-watch-lampedusa-61-degli-italiani-non-vuole -che-1717463.html.

15. "Two nations my soul detests, and the third is not even a people: Those who live in Seir, and the Philistines, and the foolish people that live in Shechem" (Sir 50:25–26).

16. Geoff Dench, *Maltese in London: A Case-Study in the Erosion of Ethnic Consciousness* (London: Routledge & Paul, 1975).

17. I am here referring to the classical distinction between "is" and "ought" (David Hume/G. E. Moore). Though they need to be distinguished, according to an important but complex debate, every system that proposes "oughts" has an explicit or implicit metaphysical/anthropological grounding. Even those of Kant, Rawls, or Habermas are ultimately based on a system of universal moral reciprocity that the Bible proposes in the famous "Golden Rule." Such systems necessarily leverage some conception of the human good, no matter how "thin" and "procedural" the conception. (Even the Golden Rule implies bracketing the conception of the "good" of sociopaths and masochists!). Hence while the "ought" can and should be distinguished from the empirical/scientific "is," it always presupposes at some point a deeper moral/anthropological "is" (and hence some "moral facts" or "values/goods/capabilities" we assume all moral agents recognize or possess).

18. Ricœur, "The Socius and the Neighbor," 99. This work was originally published in a religious booklet in 1954. See Dirk F. Vansina, "Bibliographie de Paul Ricœur (jusqu'au 30 juin 1962)," *Revue Philosophique de Louvain* 60 (1962): 394–413.

19. Ricœur notes that in the parable, a sociology of the neighbor is shut out in a twofold sense. "First, in the sense that the neighbor is the personal way in which I encounter another, *over and above all social mediation*. Secondly, in the sense that the significance of this encounter does not depend on *any criterion immanent to history* and cannot be definitely recognized by the actors

themselves, but will be discovered on the Last Day" (Ricœur, "The Socius and the Neighbor," 101.) The eschatological reference is built on an intertextual reference to Matt 25:31–46, a text we will explore below.

20. Tracy, *The Analogical Imagination*.

21. Wayne A. Meeks, *The Origins of Christian Morality: The First Two Centuries* (New Haven, CT: Yale University Press, 1995), 45–51; 104–6; Rodney Stark, *The Rise of Christianity* (New York: HarperOne, 1997), 73–94.

22. *AAS* 44 (1952): 681.

23. One of the most extensive, independent, and authoritative reports on these matters is that published by the United States. The National Academies study helps debunk many myths on the economics of migration: The National Academies of Sciences, Engineering and Medicine, *The Economic and Fiscal Consequences of Immigration* (Washington DC: National Academies Press, 2007), chap. 5, 6, 9, https://www.nap.edu/read/23550/chapter/1.

24. Robert D. Putnam, *Our Kids: The American Dream in Crisis* (New York: Simon & Schuster, 2015).

25. Matthew Stewart, *The 9.9 Percent: The New Aristocracy That Is Entrenching Inequality and Warping Our Culture* (New York: Simon & Schuster, 2021).

26. The private sector and small government are not necessarily more innovative and efficient, and less corrupt, than big government. Bigger is sometimes better, since it benefits from economies of scale and from the spread of risk, cost of breakthrough, and slow-to-mature innovation and investment over larger human groups. See Mariana Mazzucato, *The Entrepreneurial State: Debunking Public vs. Private Sector Myths* (London: Penguin, 2018).

27. Ricœur, "The Socius and the Neighbor," 109.

28. Another thought-provoking movie on the topic by the same director is *District 9* (2009).

29. Susanna Snyder, "The Dangers of 'Doing Our Duty': Reflections on Churches Engaging with People Seeking Asylum in the UK," *Theology* 110, no. 857 (2007): 351–60.

30. Stark cites Dionysius of Alexandria, Emperor Julian, and other sources. See Stark, *The Rise of Christianity*, 73–94.

31. Stark, *The Rise of Christianity*, 82–92.

32. *On Christian Doctrine*, 3.16.

33. Riemer Roukema, "The Good Samaritan in Ancient Christianity," *Vigiliae Christianae* 58, no. 1 (2004): 56–74.

34. *De Doctrina Christiana* I:30–31 [67–68]. Cf. Roukema, "The Good Samaritan in Ancient Christianity," 60–70.

35. *CCC* 2247.

36. After Vatican II, some theologians and bishops have been tempted to push popes and ecumenical councils to use their authority to summarily

Notes

"resolve" complex and intractable moral and doctrinal issues. Highly respected theologians have called this attitude "infallibilism," and have criticized such a facile use of the Catholic doctrine whereby certain papal teachings and conciliar declarations are guaranteed by the Holy Spirit to be free from error. Papal and conciliar doctrinal inerrancy is based on the inerrancy of the faith of the whole people of God, and is different from the unappealable nature of juridical authority as used in the resolution of disputes (as in matters of ecclesial discipline). For a better understanding of the issues involved, see "Il ministero del Papa dopo i due concili vaticani," *La Civiltà Cattolica* 3249 (November 2, 1985): 209–21; Francis A. Sullivan, "Recent Theological Observations on Magisterial Documents and Public Dissent," *Theological Studies* 58, no. 3 (September 1997): 509–15; Franco Ardusso, *Magistero ecclesiale. Il servizio della parola* (Cinisello Balsamo: San Paolo, 1997); Bernard Sesboüé, *Le magistère à l'épreuve. Autorité, vérité et liberté dans l'Eglise* (Paris: Desclée, 2001).

37. Alexander Roberts and James Donaldson, eds., *The Ante-Nicene Fathers: Translations of the Writings of the Fathers down to A.D. 325*, American Reprint of the Edinburgh Edition (Grand Rapids, MI: Eerdmans, 1977), vol. 1., https://en.wikisource.org/wiki/Ante-Nicene_Christian_Library/Epistle_to_Diognetus.

38. The text is taken from Chrysostom's *Homiliae in Mattheum*, 50, 3–4 (PG 58, 508).

39. In the Sermon on the Mount, Matthew uses the notion of *plēroō*, which in Greek indicates completeness, completion, and fulfillment, rather than an obsessive or elitist form of "perfection."

40. Daniel J. Harrington, *The Gospel of Matthew*, Sacra Pagina 1 (Collegeville, MN: Liturgical Press, 1991), 355–60; Craig S. Keener, *A Commentary on the Gospel of Matthew* (Grand Rapids MI: Eerdmans, 1999), 602–6.

41. E. P Sanders, *Paul and Palestinian Judaism: A Comparison of Patterns of Religion* (Philadelphia: Fortress, 1977).

42. Noahide commandments constitute the basic laws of morality, according to the Babylonian Talmud (Sanhedrin 56a; Avodah Zarah 64b).

43. Eugene Korn, "Gentiles, the World to Come, and Judaism: The Odyssey of a Rabbinic Text," *Modern Judaism* 14, no. 3 (1994): 265–87; Matthew P. Van Zile, "The Sons of Noah and the Sons of Abraham: The Origins of Noahide Law," *Journal for the Study of Judaism in the Persian, Hellenistic, and Roman Period* 48, no. 3 (2017): 386–417; George Y. Kohler, "Finding God's Purpose: Hermann Cohen's Use of Maimonides to Establish the Authority of Mosaic Law," *The Journal of Jewish Thought and Philosophy* 18, no. 1 (2010): 75–105.

44. Edward de Bono, *De Bono's Thinking Course: Powerful Tools to Transform Your Thinking* (Harlow, UK: BBC Active, 2006), 1–17.

45. John Rawls, *A Theory of Justice* (Cambridge, MA: Belknap Press of Harvard University Press, 1971), 20–22; 48–51; 432–34.

Chapter 2

1. Greg Carey, *Using Our Outside Voice: Public Biblical Interpretation* (Minneapolis: Fortress, 2020), 7.

2. Carey, *Using Our Outside Voice*, 13.

3. Ernst-Wolfgang Böckenförde, "Die Entstehung des Staates als Vorgang der Säkularisation," in *Recht, Staat, Freiheit* (Frankfurt: Suhrkamp Verlag AG, 1991), 112.

4. Jürgen Habermas, "Pre-political Foundations of the Democratic Constitutional State?," in *The Dialectics of Secularization: On Reason and Religion*, by Jürgen Habermas and Joseph Ratzinger, trans. Brian McNeill (San Francisco: Ignatius, 2007), 44–45.

5. His terminology is inspired by Kant's distinction between private and public reason in *What Is Enlightenment?* (1784); the texts included "The Idea of Public Reason" (from the 1990 Melden Lectures), "Reply to Habermas" (1995), and "The Idea of Public Reason Revisited" (1997): John Rawls, *Political Liberalism*, 2nd ed. (New York: Columbia University Press, 2005), 212–54; 372–490.

6. Rawls, *Political Liberalism*, 249–50.

7. Bartolomé de Las Casas, *In Defense of the Indians: The Defense of the Most Reverend Lord, Don Fray Bartolomé de Las Casas, of the Order of Preachers, Late Bishop of Chiapa, against the Persecutors and Slanderers of the Peoples of the New World Discovered across the Seas*, trans. Stafford Poole (DeKalb: Northern Illinois University Press, 1992).

8. John T. Noonan, *A Church That Can and Cannot Change: The Development of Catholic Moral Teaching* (Notre Dame, IN: University of Notre Dame Press, 2006), 3–123.

9. Brian Tierney, *The Idea of Natural Rights: Studies on Natural Rights, Natural Law, and Church Law 1150–1625* (Grand Rapids, MI: Eerdmans, 1997); Roger Ruston, *Human Rights and the Image of God* (London: SCM Press, 2004).

10. *On Christian Doctrine*, 3.16 (my translation).

11. Thomas W. Ogletree, *The Use of the Bible in Christian Ethics* (Philadelphia: Fortress, 1987), 15–45.

12. Ogletree, *Use of the Bible in Christian Ethics*, 17.

13. Cf. Waldemar Janzen, *Old Testament Ethics: A Paradigmatic Approach* (Louisville, KY: Westminster John Knox, 1994), 27–29.

14. Janzen, *Old Testament Ethics*, 8–9.

15. Janzen, *Old Testament Ethics*, 32–33.

Notes

16. Janzen, *Old Testament Ethics*, 88.

17. Gordon Willard Allport, *The Nature of Prejudice* (Cambridge, MA: Addison-Wesley, 1954); Irwin Katz, "Gordon Allport's 'The Nature of Prejudice,'" *Political Psychology* 12, no. 1 (1991): 125–57.

18. William C. Spohn, *Go and Do Likewise: Jesus and Ethics*, updated ed. (New York: Continuum, 2003), 10–11; 31–33.

19. Spohn, *Go and Do Likewise*, 4.

20. Paul Ricœur, *Oneself as Another*, trans. Kathleen Blamey (Chicago: University of Chicago Press, 1995), 172.

21. MacIntyre himself slowly moves to more universalist positions after the mid-1980s; cf. "Relativism, Power and Philosophy," *Proceedings and Addresses of the American Philosophical Association* 59, no. 1 (1985): 5–22; "Colors, Culture, and Practices," *Midwest Studies in Philosophy* 17, no. 1 (1992): 1–23; *Dependent Rational Animals: Why Human Beings Need the Virtues* (Chicago: Open Court, 1999).

22. Spohn, *Go and Do Likewise*, 3; 27–28.

23. Joseph J. Kotva, *The Christian Case for Virtue Ethics* (Washington DC: Georgetown University Press, 1996); James F. Keenan, *Virtues for Ordinary Christians* (Kansas City, MO: Sheed & Ward, 1996).

24. James Clear, *Atomic Habits: An Easy and Proven Way to Build Good Habits and Break Bad Ones* (London: Cornerstone, 2019); Charles Duhigg, *The Power of Habit: Why We Do What We Do in Life and Business* (Toronto: Anchor Canada, 2014); BJ Fogg, *Tiny Habits: The Small Changes That Change Everything* (Boston: Houghton-Mifflin-Harcourt, 2020).

25. Danièle Hervieu-Léger, *Le Pèlerin et le converti. La Religion en mouvement* (Paris: Flammarion, 2001); Danièle Hervieu-Léger, *Religion as a Chain of Memory* (New Brunswick, NJ: Rutgers University Press, 2000).

26. Spohn, *Go and Do Likewise*, 35.

27. Spohn, *Go and Do Likewise*, 36. "Church" and "sect" used in this way refer to a famous distinction associated with the German sociologist of religion Ernst Troeltsch.

28. Cf. Martin R. Tripole, ed., *Promise Renewed: Jesuit Higher Education for a New Millennium* (Chicago: Jesuit Way, 1999); Melecio Agúndez Agúndez, "El paradigma universitario Ledesma-Kolvenbach," *Revista de fomento social*, no. 262 (2008): 603–31.

29. Some of these aspects of Ignatian and Jesuit Spirituality can be found in internal documents that characterize the Jesuit "way of proceeding," for instance, in decree 26 of *General Congregation 34* (1995).

30. In chapter 2, n40, Spohn refers to Alasdair MacIntyre's definition of "practice" in the first edition of *After Virtue*. According to MacIntyre, practices are "coherent and complex form of socially established co-operative human activity through which goods internal to that form of activity are realized in the

course of trying to achieve those standards of excellence which are appropriate to, and partially definitive of, that form of activity, with the result that human powers to achieve excellence, and human conceptions of the ends and goods involved, are systematically extended": see Alasdair MacIntyre, *After Virtue: A Study in Moral Theory*, 3rd ed. (Notre Dame, IN: University of Notre Dame Press, 2007), 187.

31. See Javier Melloni, *Los Ejercicios, en la tradición de Occidente*, Eides 23 (Barcelona: Cristianisme i Justícia, 1998), 14–18. Santiago Arzubialde's scholarly research on the history of the Exercises offers a more detailed picture. Some parts have been published in English: see "The Development of the Exercises: Recognising the Spirit," *The Way* 50, no. 4 (2011): 78–96.

32. John W. O'Malley, *The First Jesuits* (Cambridge MA; London: Harvard University Press, 1993), 43–44; 47–48.

33. Andrés Tornos, "Discernimiento y autocrítica," in *Ciudad de los hombres, ciudad de Dios. Homenaje a Alfonso Álvarez Bolado, S.J.*, ed. Xavier Quinzá Lleó and José Joaquín Alemany (Madrid: Universidad Pontificia Comillas, 1999), 373–95.

34. An insightful comparison of Ignatius's understanding of healthy "emotion-driven" decision-making and modern psychology and neuroscientific data is found in Nicolas Standaert, "What Ignatius Did Not Know about Making Decisions," *The Way* 53, no. 3 (2014): 32–55.

35. Ignatius of Loyola and Luís Gonçalves da Câmara, *St. Ignatius' Own Story*, trans. William J. Young (Chicago: Loyola University Press, 1980), 46–50.

36. Spohn actually says that "the spiritual practice of meditatively reading Scripture…'schools the affections,'" using a less archaic but more ambiguous term in English: Spohn, *Go and Do Likewise*, 120.

37. Martha Craven Nussbaum, *Love's Knowledge: Essays on Philosophy and Literature* (New York: Oxford University Press, 1992); *Upheavals of Thought: The Intelligence of Emotions* (Cambridge: Cambridge University Press, 2001).

38. Spohn, *Go and Do Likewise*, 127.

39. Spohn, *Go and Do Likewise*, 127.

40. Some psychotherapists emphasize the importance of expressing anger in therapeutic contexts (which may integrate spirituality) to address internal wounds sustained in prior trauma. Such contexts must ensure the safety of all concerned, the upholding of the client's values, and truth telling about past violations. See for example, Christopher G. Frechette, "Two Biblical Motifs of Divine Violence as Resources for Meaning-Making in Engaging Self-Blame and Rage after Traumatization," *Pastoral Psychology* 66 (2017): 239–49.

41. Spohn, *Go and Do Likewise*, 18, 58–60, 62, 137.

42. Jon D. Levenson masterfully portrays how this dynamic occurs in the Jewish Bible as a mystery preserving a tension over how people may

approach the Creator God when they experience evil: protesting is legitimate, yet God's love has the capacity to woo people into a stance of awe and submission. See his *Creation and the Persistence of Evil: The Jewish Drama of Divine Omnipotence* (Princeton, NJ: Princeton University Press, 1994).

43. Spohn, *Go and Do Likewise*, 103–6.
44. Spohn, *Go and Do Likewise*, 91. The book was published before the 9/11 attacks, when some groups that occasionally committed acts of terror (such as the IRA or the PLO) were not seen as purely evil, and were even seen sympathetically by parts of the US American public.
45. Spohn, *Go and Do Likewise*, 97n37.

Chapter 3

1. Augustine of Hippo, *On Genesis*, trans. Edmund Hill (Hyde Park, NY: New City Press, 2004).
2. Augustine of Hippo, *On Christian Doctrine*, trans. D. W. Robertson (New York: Macmillan, 1988), bk. 1.36. Unless otherwise stated, citations from this work are from this translation.
3. Richard B. Hays, *The Moral Vision of the New Testament: Community, Cross, New Creation; A Contemporary Introduction to New Testament Ethics* (San Francisco: HarperCollins, 1996), 209.
4. Hans-Georg Gadamer, *Truth and Method*, 2nd ed. (New York: Crossroad, 1989), 438–56.
5. Sandra M. Schneiders, *The Revelatory Text: Interpreting the New Testament as Sacred Scripture* (San Francisco: HarperSanFrancisco, 1991), 16.
6. Ricœur's presentation is much more nuanced than mine. He distinguishes three meanings and functions of both ideology and utopia, which I combine for the sake of clarity and simplicity. See Paul Ricœur, "L'idéologie et l'utopie: deux expressions de l'imaginaire social," *Autres Temps. Les cahiers du christianisme social* 2, no. 1 (1984): 53–64; Paul Ricœur, *Lectures on Ideology and Utopia*, ed. George Taylor (New York: Columbia University Press, 1988).
7. Ricœur, "L'idéologie et l'utopie," 54–60.
8. Ricœur, "L'idéologie et l'utopie," 60–63.
9. Schneiders, *The Revelatory Text*, 20.
10. Paul Ricœur, "The Hermeneutical Function of Distanciation," *Philosophy Today* 17, no. 2 (1973): 129–41. The unpublished original French text was slightly revised and expanded, and published fifteen years later in a collection of articles: Paul Ricœur, *Du texte à l'action* (Paris: Éd. du Seuil, 1998), 101–17. The revised text was then retranslated into English as part of that collection: Paul Ricœur, *From Text to Action: Essays in Hermeneutics 2* (Evanston, IL: Northwestern University Press, 1991).

11. Other authors have used a different and much simpler "mirror and window analogy," adopted from Murray Krieger, to discuss hermeneutics but the simplicity of their analogy has led to misunderstandings and polarization among scholars. See John R. Donahue, "Windows and Mirrors: The Setting of Mark's Gospel," *The Catholic Biblical Quarterly* 57, no. 1 (1995): 3.

12. The original article lists four steps and develops four corresponding sections; the modified French and the retranslated version English version contains five sections, since an excursus on "The Relation of Speaking to Writing in Discourse and in the Works of Discourse" is elevated to a major section.

13. Paul Ricœur, *From Text to Action*, trans. Kathleen Blamey and John B. Thompson, new ed., Northwestern University Studies in Phenomenology and Existential Philosophy 2 (Evanston, IL: Northwestern University Press, 2007), 77–80; Ricœur, "The Hermeneutical Function of Distanciation," 130–34.

14. Ricœur, *From Text to Action*, 80–84 (I am citing the 2007 edition here and in the remaining notes); Ricœur, "The Hermeneutical Function of Distanciation," 134–39.

15. Outside the United States, "structural linguistics" or "structuralism" are associated with authors like Ferdinand de Saussure, Louis Hjelmslev, and Claude Lévi-Strauss (analysis of myths). In the United States, however, the term *structuralism* usually refers to a different school popular in American linguistics before Chomsky, and is associated with authors like Wilhelm Wundt and Leonard Bloomfield. These authors were unfortunately nicknamed "American Structuralists," causing confusion with the standard use of this term outside the United States.

16. Unless otherwise indicated, references to Ricœur in this section point to Ricœur, *From Text to Action*, 83–86; Ricœur, "The Hermeneutical Function of Distanciation," 139–41.

17. Gottlob Frege, *The Frege Reader*, ed. Michael Beaney (Oxford: Blackwell, 1997), 151–80; Schneiders, *The Revelatory Text*, 14–17.

18. Ricœur, *From Text to Action*, 86–88; Ricœur, "The Hermeneutical Function of Distanciation," 141.

19. Ricœur, *From Text to Action*, 86.

20. Paul Ricœur, *Oneself as Another*, trans. Kathleen Blamey (Chicago: University of Chicago Press, 1995), 87.

21. Sangkeun Kim, *Strange Names of God: The Missionary Translation of the Divine Name and the Chinese Responses to Matteo Ricci's "Shangti" in Late Ming China, 1583-1644* (New York: Peter Lang, 2004), 1–4.

22. Umberto Eco, *Lector in fabula: la cooperazione interpretativa nei testi narrativi*, Studi Bompiani (Milan: Bompiani, 1979), 24.

23. Eco, *Lector in Fabula*, 15; 49–51.

24. Eco, *Lector in Fabula*, 54–59.

25. Eco, *Lector in Fabula*, 63.

26. Ricœur, *Oneself as Another*, 87.
27. Tom Deidun, "The Bible and Christian Ethics," in *Christian Ethics: An Introduction*, ed. Bernard Hoose (London: Cassell, 1998), 4.
28. See Xavier Thévenot, *Morale fondamentale: notes de cours* (Paris: Don Bosco / Desclée, 2007), 40–56.

Chapter 4

1. The noun *doctrina* in Latin is possibly a reference to the Latin title of Augustine's treatise *On Christian Doctrine*.
2. The following was used in the case of 1 Pet 3:15–16: Institute for New Testament Textual Research, *Nestle-Aland Novum Testamentum Graece*, 28th ed. (Stuttgart: Deutsche Bibelgesellschaft, 2018), 702–3.
3. Bernard Arthur Owen Williams, "Moral Luck," in *Moral Luck* (Cambridge: Cambridge University Press, 1981), 20–39; Martha Craven Nussbaum, *The Fragility of Goodness: Luck and Ethics in Greek Tragedy and Philosophy* (Cambridge: Cambridge University Press, 1991).
4. Kant's three questions can be found in the *Critique of Pure Reason* (p. 805 of the 1781 German "A" edition, and p. 833 of the 1878 "B" edition).
5. Eli Pariser, *The Filter Bubble: What the Internet Is Hiding from You* (London: Penguin, 2012).
6. Vincenzo Viva, "Bibbia e morale nel contesto dei manuali post-tridentini di teologia morale," in *Etica teologica nelle correnti della storia: contributi dell'accademia alfonsiana al secondo congresso mondiale dei teologi morali cattolici*, ed. Gabriel Witaszek and Vincenzo Viva, Dibattito per Il Millennio (Vatican City: Lateran University Press, 2011), 39–50.
7. J. Alton Templin, "God and the Covenant in the South African Wilderness," *Church History* 37, no. 3 (1968): 281–97.
8. Some modern historians, following the research of Roberto Ridolfi, have sought to defend Savonarola and question the negative image propagated after his death, and in 1997 there was even a formal request to the Holy See to initiate a process for his beatification. See Stefano Dall'Aglio, *Savonarola and Savonarolism*, trans. John Gagné (Toronto: Centre for Reformation and Renaissance Studies, 2010).
9. The Observe-Appraise-Act methodology is also known as See-Judge-Act. See René M. Micallef, "The Method Informing *Laudato Si'* and Its Critical Dialogue with the Empirical Sciences," in *Foundations of Integral Ecology*, ed. Jacquineau Azétsop and Paolo Conversi (Rome: Gregorian & Biblical Press, 2022); Joe Holland and Peter J. Henriot, *Social Analysis: Linking Faith and Justice* (Maryknoll, NY: Orbis Books, 1983).

10. Lúcás Chan offers a good overview of the current debates concerning Scripture and ethics, mainly in Anglo-American scholarship and English-speaking theologians: Lúcás Chan, *Biblical Ethics in the 21st Century: Developments, Emerging Consensus, and Future Directions* (Mahwah, NJ: Paulist Press, 2013).

11. William Spohn, *What Are They Saying About Scripture and Ethics?*, 2nd ed. (Mahwah, NJ: Paulist Press, 1995).

12. Josef Fuchs, "Moral Theology According to Vatican II," in *Human Values and Christian Morality* (Dublin: Gill, 1977), 1–55.

13. Klaus Demmer, *Living the Truth: A Theory of Action* (Washington, DC: Georgetown University Press, 2010), 118 and 146; Klaus Demmer, "La decisione irrevocabile. riflessioni sulla teologia della scelta di vita," *Communio* 16 (1974): 9–17; Klaus Demmer, *Fondamenti di etica teologica* (Assisi: Cittadella, 2004), 311–45.

14. Karl Rahner, "Der Anspruch Gottes und der Einzelne," in *Schriften zur Theologie*, vol. 6 (Einsiedeln: Benziger, 1965), 521–36; Philip Endean, "Moral Theology, Karl Rahner and the Ignatian Exercises," *The Way Supplement* 88 (Spring 1997): 55–65. Unfortunately, the Continental reflection on the fundamental stance or option has often been banalized and hence misunderstood in many Anglo-American theological ethics texts or discarded simply because of its use of terminology originating in Enlightenment philosophy. Actually, it seeks to avoid a Pelagian approach to theological ethics and to place single concrete moral acts within a relationship with God (and is deeply gospel inspired, in that sense). By accepting and responding to a call to holiness, through our actions seen as a whole (rather than through an accounting of meritorious good works), we accept justification freely given through Christ's faith.

15. Jeffrey S. Siker, *Scripture and Ethics: Twentieth-Century Portraits* (Oxford: Oxford University Press, 1997).

16. Richard B. Hays, *The Moral Vision of the New Testament: Community, Cross, New Creation; A Contemporary Introduction to New Testament Ethics* (San Francisco: HarperCollins, 1996).

17. Chan, *Biblical Ethics in the 21st Century*.

18. Greg Carey, *Using Our Outside Voice: Public Biblical Interpretation* (Minneapolis: Fortress, 2020), 93.

19. See, for example, *IBC* and Sandra M. Schneiders, *The Revelatory Text: Interpreting the New Testament as Sacred Scripture* (San Francisco: HarperSanFrancisco, 1991), chap. 4.

20. Cf. Alain Thomasset, *Intérpreter pour agir. jalons pour une éthique chrétienne* (Paris: Cerf, 2011), 63–72.

21. Pontifical Biblical Commission, *The Interpretation of the Bible in the Church* (Boston: St. Paul Books & Media, 1993).

22. Some of the sources lack "and from what is strangled," so the list may actually consist of only three norms. See Institute for New Testament Textual Research, *Nestle-Aland Novum Testamentum Graece*, 433.

23. Carlo Maria Martini, "Il decreto del Concilio di Gerusalemme," in *Fondamenti biblici della teologia morale. Atti della XII settimana biblica*, ed. Associazione biblica italiana (Brescia: Paideia, 1973), 345–55.

24. Édouard Hamel, "Scripture: The Soul of Moral Theology?," in *The Use of Scripture in Moral Theology*, ed. Charles E. Curran and Richard A. McCormick, Readings in Moral Theology 4 (New York: Paulist Press, 1984), 117.

25. Kenneth R. Himes, "Scripture and Ethics," *Biblical Theology Bulletin* 15 (May 1985): 72; Hamel, "Scripture: The Soul of Moral Theology?," 122.

26. James F. Childress, "Scripture and Christian Ethics," in *The Use of Scripture in Moral Theology*, ed. Charles E. Curran and Richard A. McCormick, Readings in Moral Theology 4 (New York: Paulist Press, 1984), 284.

27. Josef Fuchs, "The Absoluteness of Moral Terms," *Gregorianum* 52, no. 3 (1971): 449.

28. Schneiders, *The Revelatory Text*, 55–59.

29. Schneiders, *The Revelatory Text*, 57.

30. The more recent text published by the Commission is helpful here: Pontifical Biblical Commission, *What Is Man? A Journey through Biblical Anthropology*, trans. Fearghus O'Fearghail and Adrian Graffy (London: Darton Longman & Todd, 2021).

31. Lúcás Chan, "Biblical Ethics: 3D," *Theological Studies* 76, no. 1 (March 2015): 112–28.

32. Carey, *Using Our Outside Voice*, 77–83.

Chapter 5

1. Richard Falk, "Revisiting Westphalia, Discovering Post-Westphalia," *The Journal of Ethics* 6, no. 4 (December 1, 2002): 311–52; Daniel Philpott, "Westphalia, Authority, and International Society," *Political Studies* 47, no. 3 (August 1999): 566–89; Daud Hassan, "The Rise of the Territorial State and the Treaty of Westphalia," *Yearbook of New Zealand Jurisprudence* 9 (2006): 62–70; Steven Patton, "The Peace of Westphalia and Its Effects on International Relations, Diplomacy and Foreign Policy," *The Histories* 10, no. 1 (2019): Art. 5.

2. Other Aristotelian references to this approach can be found in *Metaphysics* IV 1004a-b; *Physics* II.2 201b; and *On Generation and Corruption* I.3 319a. See Michel Crubellier, "La beauté du monde : les sciences mathématiques et la philosophie première," *Revue Internationale de Philosophie* 51, no. 201 (3) (1997): 322.

3. Michael J Sandel, *Liberalism and the Limits of Justice* (Cambridge: Cambridge University Press, 1998); John Rawls, *A Theory of Justice* (Cambridge, MA: Belknap Press of Harvard University Press, 1971), 382.

4. Yuval Noah Harari, *Sapiens: A Brief History of Humankind* (New York: Harper, 2015), chap. 2.

5. Jacques Maritain, *Man and the State* (Washington, DC: Catholic University of America Press, 1998), 2–4.

6. Cynthia K. Mahmood and Sharon L. Armstrong, "Do Ethnic Groups Exist? A Cognitive Perspective on the Concept of Cultures," *Ethnology* 31, no. 1 (1992): 1–14; Kay Deaux, "Ethnic/Racial Identity: Fuzzy Categories and Shifting Positions," *The Annals of the American Academy of Political and Social Science* 677 (2018): 39–47.

7. Andrea L. Smith, *Colonial Memory and Postcolonial Europe: Maltese Settlers in Algeria and France* (Bloomington: Indiana University Press, 2006).

8. Maritain, *Man and the State*, 12.

9. Maritain, *Man and the State*, 5.

10. Maritain, *Man and the State*, 6.

11. David Brown, *Contemporary Nationalism* (London: Routledge, 2000); Montserrat Guibernau, *Nationalisms: The Nation-State and Nationalism in the Twentieth Century* (Cambridge: Polity Press, 1996).

12. See Jürgen Habermas, *Between Facts and Norms: Contributions to a Discourse Theory of Law and Democracy*, trans. William Rehg (Cambridge, MA: MIT Press, 1998), 492–515; Max Pensky, *The Ends of Solidarity: Discourse Theory in Ethics and Politics* (New York: SUNY Press, 2008), 41–43.

13. Immanuel Kant, *Kant: The Metaphysics of Morals*, ed. Mary J. Gregor, 2nd ed. (Cambridge: Cambridge University Press, 1996), 89; Seyla Benhabib, *The Rights of Others: Aliens, Residents, and Citizens* (Cambridge: Cambridge University Press, 2004), 32–40.

14. Michael Walzer, *Spheres of Justice* (New York: Basic Books Inc, 1983), 42–48.

15. Shaye J. D. Cohen, *The Beginnings of Jewishness: Boundaries, Varieties, Uncertainties* (Berkeley: University of California Press, 1999), 5.

16. Roger Parker, "Verdi and Milan: A Gresham College Lecture," Gresham College, May 14, 2007, http://www.gresham.ac.uk/lectures-and-events/verdi-and-milan.

17. The famous saying, in Italian, is *Fatta l'Italia, bisogna fare gli italiani.*

18. Walker Connor, *Ethnonationalism: The Quest for Understanding* (Princeton, NJ: Princeton University Press, 1993).

19. Anthony D. Smith, *The Cultural Foundations of Nations: Hierarchy, Covenant, and Republic* (Malden, MA: Wiley-Blackwell, 2008).

20. Halvor Moxnes, *Jesus and the Rise of Nationalism: A New Quest for the Nineteenth Century Historical Jesus* (London: I. B. Tauris, 2011).

Notes

21. Martha Nussbaum and Joshua Cohen, eds., *For Love of Country?* (Boston: Beacon Press, 2002); Kwame Anthony Appiah, *Cosmopolitanism: Ethics in a World of Strangers* (New York: W. W. Norton, 2007).

22. Kurt Bayertz, ed., *Solidarity*, Philosophical Studies in Contemporary Culture, v. 5 (Boston: Kluwer Academic Publishers, 1999).

23. Peter Sheridan Dodds, Roby Muhamad, and Duncan J. Watts, "An Experimental Study of Search in Global Social Networks," *Science* 301, no. 5634 (August 8, 2003): 827–29, https://doi.org/10.1126/science.1081058.

24. Pope Francis and Grand Imam Ahmad Al-Tayyeb, "Abu Dhabi Document on 'Human Fraternity for World Peace and Living Together," https://www.vatican.va/content/francesco/en/travels/2019/outside/documents/papa-francesco_20190204_documento-fratellanza-umana.html.

25. David Hollenbach, *Humanity in Crisis: Ethical and Religious Response to Refugees* (Washington, DC: Georgetown University Press, 2019); Raimond Gaita, *A Common Humanity: Thinking about Love and Truth and Justice* (New York: Routledge, 2002).

26. Christine Pohl, *Making Room: Recovering Hospitality as a Christian Tradition* (Grand Rapids, MI: Eerdmans, 1999).

27. "Internally Displaced People, Sovereignty, and the Responsibility to Protect," in *Refugee Rights: Ethics, Advocacy, and Africa*, ed. David Hollenbach (Washington, DC: Georgetown University Press, 2008), 188.

28. David Hollenbach, ed., *Driven from Home: Protecting the Rights of Forced Migrants* (Washington, DC: Georgetown University Press, 2010), chap. 7.

29. *The Common Good and Christian Ethics* (Cambridge: Cambridge University Press, 2002), 187.

30. Hollenbach, *Driven from Home*, 184.

31. Hollenbach, *Driven from Home*, 184.

32. Hollenbach, *Driven from Home*, 188.

33. Regarding the link between *caritas* and solidarity in the Catholic tradition, see René Coste, "Solidarité," in *Dictionnaire de spiritualité—ascétique et mystique, doctrine et histoire*, ed. Ferdinand Cavallera, et al. (Paris: Beauchesne, 2004), 999–1006. Coste's article also provides an account of the historical development of the notion of solidarity in Catholic Social Teaching, from its introduction by Pius XII in 1939 (*Summi Pontificatus*) until the 1990s.

34. Elias J. Bickerman, *The Jews in the Greek Age* (Cambridge, MA: Harvard University Press, 1990), 81.

35. Michael Ungar, "Resilience across Cultures," *British Journal of Social Work* 38, no. 2 (November 8, 2006): 218–35.

36. Frans de Waal, *The Bonobo and the Atheist: In Search of Humanism among the Primates* (New York: W. W. Norton, 2014).

37. Mary Douglas, *Purity and Danger: An Analysis of Concepts of Pollution and Taboo* (London: Routledge and Kegan Paul, 1966).

38. Anne Sophie Krossa, *Analysing Society in a Global Context: Empirical Studies on Sociation Processes of Volunteers and Refugees* (Cham, Switzerland: Palgrave Macmillan, 2020).

39. Mark Juergensmeyer, *Terror in the Mind of God: The Global Rise of Religious Violence*, 3rd ed. (Berkeley: University of California Press, 2003).

40. Cohen, *Beginnings of Jewishness*, 5.

41. Roger Waldinger, "The Sociology of Immigration: Second Thoughts and Reconsiderations," in *Host Societies and the Reception of Immigrants*, ed. Jeffrey G. Reitz (La Jolla, CA: Center for Comparative Immigration, 2003), 21–22.

42. Diana Edelman, "Ethnicity in Early Israel," in *Ethnicity and the Bible*, ed. Mark G. Brett (Leiden: Brill, 2002), 25; my emphasis.

43. Peter Machinist, "The Question of Distinctiveness in Ancient Israel," in *Essential Papers on Israel and the Ancient Near East*, ed. Frederick E. Greenspahn (New York: New York University Press, 1991), 426.

44. Machinist, "Question of Distinctiveness," n22.

45. Machinist, "Question of Distinctiveness," 431.

46. Machinist, "Question of Distinctiveness," 432.

47. Moshe Weinfeld has discovered similar reversals in the tales of the foundation of cities in the Greek and Roman world: city founders are often portrayed as descendants of a hero coming from the outside: "The Pattern of Israelite Settlement in Canaan," in *Congress Volume: Jerusalem, 1986*, ed. John Adney Emerton (Leiden: Brill, 1988), 270–83; "The Promise to the Patriarchs and Its Realization: An Analysis of Foundation Stories," in *Society and Economy in the Eastern Mediterranean (c. 1500–1000 B.C.): Proceedings of the International Symposium Held at the University of Haifa from the 28th of April to the 2nd of May 1985*, ed. Michael Heltzer and Edward Lipiński (Leuven: Peeters, 1988), 353–70; "Historical Facts behind the Israelite Settlement Pattern," *Vetus Testamentum* 38, no. 3 (July 1, 1988): 324–32.

48. Rainer Albertz, *A History of Israelite Religion in the Old Testament Period*, trans. John Bowden (Louisville, KY: Westminster John Knox, 1994), 45.

49. William G. Dever, *Who Were the Early Israelites, and Where Did They Come From?* (Grand Rapids, MI: Eerdmans, 2003), 167. The scenario of a total conquest (Josh 11:23) is contradicted by the Bible itself (Josh 13:1), and the assumption that most of the indigenous peoples were eliminated through the ban and disappeared is also contradicted in the Bible (Josh 11:13 claims that only Hazor was utterly destroyed). See Michael D. Coogan, *The Old Testament: A Historical and Literary Introduction to the Hebrew Scriptures*, 3rd ed. (New York: Oxford University Press, 2013), 207–10. Regarding the other scenarios cf. Coogan, *The Old Testament*, 224, Stager "Forging an Identity: The Emergence of Ancient Israel," in *The Oxford History of the Biblical World*, ed. Michael D. Coogan (New York: Oxford University Press, 2001), 93–105, and Jo Ann Hackett, "'There Was No King in Israel': The Era of the Judges," in *The*

Notes

Oxford History of the Biblical World, ed. Michael D. Coogan (New York: Oxford University Press, 2001), 145–154.

50. Donald Senior, John Collins, and Mary Ann Getty, eds., *The Catholic Study Bible*, 3rd ed. (New York: Oxford University Press, 2016), reading guide 44–45; Benjamin W. Porter, "Assembling the Iron Age Levant: The Archaeology of Communities, Polities, and Imperial Peripheries," *Journal of Archaeological Research*, 24 no. 4 (December 2016): 388.

51. See Lawrence E. Stager, "The Archaeology of the Family in Ancient Israel," *Bulletin of the American Schools of Oriental Research*, no. 260 (October 1, 1985): 1–35; Stager, "Forging an Identity," 128–42; Israel Finkelstein and Neil Asher Silberman, *The Bible Unearthed: Archaeology's New Vision of Ancient Israel and the Origin of Its Sacred Texts* (New York: Free Press, 2002); Mario Liverani, *Oltre la Bibbia. Storia antica di Israele*, 6th ed. (Rome: Laterza, 2017), 59–116.

52. Peter Machinist, "Outsiders or Insiders: The Biblical View of Emergent Israel and Its Contexts," in *The Other in Jewish Thought and History: Constructions of Jewish Culture and Identity*, ed. Laurence J. Silberstein and Robert L. Cohn (New York: NYU Press, 1994), 35.

53. Christian Lenhardt, "Anamnestic Solidarity: The Proletariat and Its Manes," *Telos* 1975, no. 25 (October 1, 1975): 133–54; Max Pensky, "On the Use and Abuse of Memory: Habermas, 'Anamnestic Solidarity,' and the *Historikerstreit*," *Philosophy & Social Criticism* 15, no. 4 (October 1, 1989): 351–80.

54. Walter Benjamin, *Illuminations: Essays and Reflections*, ed. Hannah Arendt, trans. Harry Zohn (New York: Schocken, 1969), 253–57; Marsha Hewitt, "The Redemptive Power of Memory: Walter Benjamin and Elisabeth Schüssler Fiorenza," *Journal of Feminist Studies in Religion* 10, no. 1 (1994): 76.

55. William O'Neill, "Anamnestic Solidarity: Immigration from the Perspective of Restorative Justice," *Catholic Theological Society of America Proceedings* 64 (2009): 158–59; "'No Longer Strangers' (Ephesians 2:19): The Ethics of Migration," *Word and World* 29, no. 3 (2009): 229.

56. Nadav Na'aman, "Ḥabiru and Hebrews: The Transfer of a Social Term to the Literary Sphere," *Journal of Near Eastern Studies* 45, no. 4 (1986): 271–88.

57. The *'ayin* in the root is usually replaced by *ḫ* in Akkadian. See Jan Assmann, *The Invention of Religion: Faith and Covenant in the Book of Exodus*, trans. Robert Savage (Princeton, NJ: Princeton University Press, 2018), 44.

58. Ernest Klein, "Klein Dictionary, עָבְרִי," www.sefaria.org.

59. Edelman, "Ethnicity in Early Israel," 25; my emphasis.

60. Edelman, "Ethnicity in Early Israel," 36.

61. See Machinist, "Outsiders or Insiders," 47–48.

62. See Marit Skjeggestad, "Ethnic Groups in Early Iron Age Palestine: Some Remarks on the Use of the Term 'Israelite' in Recent Research," *Scandinavian Journal of the Old Testament* 6, no. 2 (1992): 159–86; Edelman, "Ethnicity

in Early Israel"; Keith W. Whitelam, "Israel's Traditions of Origin: Reclaiming the Land," *Journal for the Study of the Old Testament* 44 (June 1989): 19–42; Israel Finkelstein, *The Archaeology of the Israelite Settlement* (Jerusalem and Leiden: Israel Exploration Society and Brill, 1988), 28.

63. Liverani, *Oltre la Bibbia*, 104–25.

64. Dermot Nestor, *Cognitive Perspectives on Israelite Identity* (New York: T & T Clark, 2010), 208–15.

65. McGuire Gibson, "Nippur—Sacred City of Enlil, Supreme God of Sumer and Akkad," *Al-Rafidan* 14 (1993): 1–18; Andrew R. George, "Die Kosmogonie des alten Mesopotamien," in *Anfang und Ende. Vormoderne Szenarien von Weltentstehung und Weltuntergang*, ed. Marion Gindhart and Tanja Pommerening (Darmstadt: Philipp von Zabern, 2016), 7–25.

66. Machinist, "The Question of Distinctiveness in Ancient Israel," 434; Albertz, *A History of Israelite Religion in the Old Testament Period*, 24–25.

67. Paul Ricœur, *The Symbolism of Evil* (Boston: Beacon Press, 1986).

68. Innocenzo Cardellini, "Le Migrazioni Nelle Società Del Vicino Oriente Antico e l'idea Di 'Straniero' Nella Bibbia Ebraica," *Studi Emigrazione / Migration Studies* 52, no. 198 (2015): 272–94.

69. "Genesis 1—3: Permission to Exploit Nature?," *The Bible Today* 26 (1988): 132–37.

70. Daniel L. Smith-Christopher, *The Religion of the Landless: The Social Context of the Babylonian Exile* (Eugene OR: Wipf and Stock, 2015), 139–40.

71. Claus Westermann, *Genesis 1—11: A Continental Commentary* (Minneapolis: Fortress, 1984).

72. Enrique Sanz Giménez-Rico, *Ya en el principio: Fundamentos veterotestamentarios de la moral cristiana* (Madrid: San Pablo–Universidad Pontificia Comillas, 2008), 64.

73. Christoph Uehlinger, *Weltreich und "eine rede": eine neue deutung der sogenannten tumbauerzählung (Gen 11, 1–9)* (Freiburg: Universitätsverlag, 1990).

74. Sanz Giménez-Rico, *Ya en el principio*, 67–68.

75. Machinist, "The Question of Distinctiveness in Ancient Israel," 432; Machinist, "Outsiders or Insiders," 50–51.

Chapter 6

1. Mark A. Awabdy, *Immigrants and Innovative Law: Deuteronomy's Theological and Social Vision for the גר* (Tübingen: Mohr Siebeck, 2014), 127–64.

2. Peter Machinist, "Outsiders or Insiders: The Biblical View of Emergent Israel and Its Contexts," in *The Other in Jewish Thought and History: Constructions*

Notes

of *Jewish Culture and Identity*, ed. Laurence J. Silberstein and Robert L. Cohn (New York: NYU Press, 1994), 49.

3. Machinist, "Outsiders or Insiders,"49.

4. Mario Liverani, *Oltre la Bibbia. Storia antica di Israele*, 6th ed. (Rome: Laterza, 2017), 194–98.

5. See Rainer Albertz, *A History of Israelite Religion in the Old Testament Period*, trans. John Bowden, vol. 1 (Louisville, KY: Westminster John Knox, 1994), 1:110–14.

6. Rolf Rendtorff, "The *Gēr* in the Priestly Laws of the Pentateuch," in *Ethnicity and the Bible*, ed. Mark G. Brett (Leiden: Brill, 2002), 77.

7. Patrick D. Miller, "Israel as Host to Strangers," in *Today's Immigrants and Refugees: A Christian Understanding*, ed. US Catholic Bishops' Committee on Migration (Washington DC: United States Catholic Conference, 1988), 1.

8. See David Novak, "Land and People: One Jewish Perspective," in *Boundaries and Justice: Diverse Ethical Perspectives*, ed. David Leslie Miller and Sohail H. Hashmi (Princeton, NJ: Princeton University Press, 2001), 222–24.

9. Miller, "Israel as Host to Strangers," 2. Furthermore, in Trito-Isaiah (Isa 56:3, 6), *bęn-han-nekār* is used in a positive sense, as a foreigner who could be joined to Israel.

10. Shaye J. D. Cohen, *The Beginnings of Jewishness: Boundaries, Varieties, Uncertainties* (Berkeley: University of California Press, 1999), 109–39.

11. Christopher G. Frechette, "Destroying the Internalized Perpetrator: A Healing Function of the Violent Language against Enemies in the Psalms," in *Trauma and Traumatization in Individual and Collective Dimensions: Insights from Biblical Studies and Beyond*, ed. Eve-Marie Becker, Jan Dochhorn, and Else Kragelund Holt (Göttingen: Vandenhoeck & Ruprecht, 2014), 71–84.

12. Carol M. Bechtel, *Esther: Interpretation: A Bible Commentary for Teaching and Preaching* (Louisville, KY: Westminster John Knox, 2002), 1–4; Michael V. Fox, *Character and Ideology in the Book of Esther*, 2nd ed. (Eugene, OR: Wipf and Stock, 2010), 49.

13. Yochanan Muffs, *Studies in the Aramaic Legal Papyri from Elephantine* (Leiden: Brill, 2003).

14. "Sojourner," in *The New Interpreters Dictionary of the Bible*, ed. Katharine Doob Sakenfeld (Nashville: Abingdon, 2009), 314.

15. Christoph Bultmann, *Der Fremde im antiken Juda: Eine Untersuchung zum sozialen Typenbegriff ger und seinem Bedeutungswandel in der alttestamentlichen Gesetzgebung* (Göttingen: Vandenhoeck & Ruprecht, 1992), 93; Ambrogio Spreafico, "Lo straniero e la difesa delle categorie più deboli come simbolo di giustizia e di civiltà nell'opera deuteronomico-deuteronomistica," in *Lo "straniero" nella Bibbia. Aspetti storici, istituzionali e teologici. XXXIII Settimana biblica nazionale*, ed. Innocenzo Cardellini, Ricerche storico-bibliche, VIII (Bologna: EDB, 1996), 117–22.

16. Jobling, "Sojourner," 315.
17. Rendtorff, "The Gēr in the Priestly Laws of the Pentateuch," 79.
18. Novak, "Land and People: One Jewish Perspective," 223.
19. Cohen, *The Beginnings of Jewishness*, 121.
20. The Hasmonean kings were vassals of the Seleucid Empire (140–110 BCE) and subsequently rulers of an independent kingdom (110–63 BCE). Hasmonean Judea (*Yəhūda*) then became a client state of the Roman Republic (63–40 BCE) and of the Parthian Empire (40–37 BCE).
21. Cohen, *The Beginnings of Jewishness*, 210.
22. José E. Ramírez Kidd, *Alterity and Identity in Israel: The "Ger" in the Old Testament* (Berlin: De Gruyter, 1999), 130.
23. Robert W. Heimburger, *God and the Illegal Alien: United States Immigration Law and a Theology of Politics* (New York: Cambridge University Press, 2018), 25–43.
24. *The Alien in Israelite Law* (Sheffield: JSOT Press, 1991), 158–65.
25. Van Houten, *The Alien in Israelite Law*, 175.
26. "Between Ezra and Isaiah: Exclusion, Transformation and Inclusion of the 'Foreigner' in Post-exilic Biblical Theology" in *Ethnicity and the Bible*, ed. Mark G. Brett (Leiden: Brill, 1996), 117–42.
27. For instance, Van Seters argues that the Covenant Code could be postexilic in origin and ultimately based on the Deuteronomic and Holiness Codes. Such a late dating would bring us to question the historical reconstruction attempted below, but it is rejected by most scholars, and we will not take it into account. John Van Seters, "Revision in the Study of the Covenant Code and a Response to My Critics," *Scandinavian Journal of the Old Testament* 21, no. 1 (January 2007): 5–28.
28. Jobling, "Sojourner," 315.
29. Albertz, *A History of Israelite Religion in the Old Testament Period*, 182–83.
30. M. Broshi, "The Expansion of Jerusalem in the Reigns of Hezekiah and Manasseh," *Israel Exploration Journal* 24, no. 1 (January 1, 1974): 21, https://www.jstor.org/stable/27925434.
31. Ramírez Kidd, *Alterity and Identity in Israel*, 131.
32. See Miller, "Israel as Host to Strangers," 12.
33. See Albertz, *A History of Israelite Religion in the Old Testament Period*, 58.
34. Some authors cite the dismantling of a temple in the Royal Citadel of Arad on the southern border, but the stratigraphy is inconclusive. Secular buildings were placed directly over the temple site during the reforms of Hezekiah (prior to Josiah), probably to prevent it from being rebuilt, but the dismantling was probably done before Hezekiah, in an effort to preserve the temple rather than to destroy it. See Lisbeth S. Fried, "The High Places (*Bāmôt*)

Notes

and the Reforms of Hezekiah and Josiah: An Archaeological Investigation," *Journal of the American Oriental Society* 122, no. 3 (2002): 445–47.

35. Fried, "The High Places," 450; 457–58; 460–61.

36. Albertz, *A History of Israelite Religion in the Old Testament Period,* 208–9; cf. 219–22. According to Albertz, 222, the reformers attempted to integrate them into the Zadokite priesthood in Jerusalem, but the Jerusalem priesthood looked at them with suspicion as possibly unorthodox, theologically syncretistic competitors.

37. According to some authors, the "urbanization" of rural land for legal purposes in postexilic Judea and the commercialization that ensued "led to the gradual obliteration of the old distinctions between those who owned land and those who were landless. Thus the Levites, who were only assigned a number of villages that could not support sufficient agriculture for their needs and thus had to live off of the tithes that the rest of the people paid them, were eventually integrated into the rest of the population." Novak, "Land and People: One Jewish Perspective," 220.

38. Ramírez Kidd, *Alterity and Identity in Israel,* 131.

39. Ramírez Kidd, *Alterity and Identity in Israel,* 83–84.

40. Ramírez Kidd, *Alterity and Identity in Israel,* 94–98. For a different approach to the distinction between the *'ebed*-in-Egypt and the *gēr*-in-Egypt passages, see Awabdy, *Immigrants and Innovative Law,* 127–64.

41. Ruth Ebach, *Das Fremde und das Eigene: Die Fremdendarstellungen des Deuteronomiums im Kontext israelitischer Identitätskonstruktionen* (Berlin: De Gruyter, 2014), 172; 314–16.

42. Ebach, *Das Fremde und das Eigene,* 317.

43. Ebach, *Das Fremde und das Eigene,* 317.

44. Daniel L. Smith-Christopher, *The Religion of the Landless: The Social Context of the Babylonian Exile* (Eugene, OR: Wipf and Stock, 2015), 32–35.

45. Gianni Barbiero, "Lo straniero nel Codice dell'Alleanza e nel Codice di Santità: Tra separazione e accoglienza," in *Lo "straniero" nella Bibbia. Aspetti storici, istituzionali e teologici. XXXIII Settimana biblica nazionale,* ed. Innocenzo Cardellini, Ricerche storico-bibliche, VIII (Bologna: EDB, 1996), 65–68; Esias E. Meyer, *The Jubilee in Leviticus 25: A Theological Ethical Interpretation from a South African Perspective* (Munster: LIT Verlag, 2005), chap. 6.

46. Ramírez Kidd, *Alterity and Identity in Israel,* 64.

47. Ramírez Kidd, *Alterity and Identity in Israel,* 58–59.

48. Ramírez Kidd, *Alterity and Identity in Israel,* 118.

49. Jobling, "Sojourner," 315.

50. Cf. Novak, "Land and People: One Jewish Perspective," 223.

51. Albertz, *A History of Israelite Religion in the Old Testament Period,* 92–94.

52. Isa 5:20, 23; Amos 5:10; Mic 3:1–3, 9, 11; cf. Albertz, *A History of Israelite Religion in the Old Testament Period*, 165-67.

53. Jobling, "Sojourner," 315.

54. The masculine here is clearly intended. As we shall see below, the rights of women were generally less than those of wayfarers. Even claiming that female *gērîm* had legally recognized "rights" would seem grossly anachronistic.

55. Spreafico, "Lo straniero e la difesa delle categorie più deboli," 123–26.

56. Awabdy, *Immigrants and Innovative Law*, 66–83; Ebach, *Das Fremde und das Eigene*, 69–104.

57. See Donald E. Gowan, "Wealth and Poverty in the Old Testament: The Case of the Widow, the Orphan, and the Sojourner," *Interpretation* 41, no. 4 (1987): 341–53.

58. Harold V. Bennett, *Injustice Made Legal: Deuteronomic Law and the Plight of Widows, Strangers, and Orphans in Ancient Israel* (Grand Rapids, MI: Eerdmans, 2002).

59. See Albertz, *A History of Israelite Religion in the Old Testament Period*, 217–18; 435.

60. Gowan, "Wealth and Poverty in the Old Testament."

61. Jobling, "Sojourner," 316.

62. Ramírez Kidd, *Alterity and Identity in Israel*, 16–17.

63. Albertz, *A History of Israelite Religion in the Old Testament Period*, 232–36; Bennett, *Injustice Made Legal*.

64. Kathryn Sikkink, *Evidence for Hope: Making Human Rights Work in the 21st Century* (Princeton, NJ: Princeton University Press, 2017).

Chapter 7

1. David Novak, "Land and People: One Jewish Perspective," in *Boundaries and Justice: Diverse Ethical Perspectives*, ed. David Leslie Miller and Sohail H. Hashmi (Princeton, NJ: Princeton University Press, 2001), 232.

2. Donald Senior, John J. Collins, and Mary Ann Getty-Sullivan, eds., *The Catholic Study Bible: With the New American Bible*, 2nd ed. (New York: Oxford University Press, 2011); Gianfranco Ravasi and Bruno Maggioni, eds., *La Bibbia—Via verità e vita. Nuova versione ufficiale della CEI*, 2nd ed. (Cinisello Balsamo: San Paolo, 2012).

3. For instance, Letellier's elegant analysis of Gen 18 and 19, which integrates various exegetical methods, can be a second step in the process. See Robert Ignatius Letellier, *Day in Mamre, Night in Sodom: Abraham and Lot in Genesis 18 and 19*, Biblical Interpretation Series 10 (Leiden: Brill, 1995).

4. John R. Kohlenberger, ed., *The Interlinear NIV Hebrew-English Old Testament* (Grand Rapids, MI: Zondervan, 1993); Lyman Coleman,

Notes

ed., *Serendipity Bible: New International Version*, 4th ed. (Grand Rapids, MI: Zondervan, 1996).

5. For a morphological analysis of some of the terms in the text, issues regarding the unique pointing in the Hebrew manuscripts, and variants in the Samaritan Pentateuch, see Gordon J Wenham, *Genesis 16—50*, vol. 2 (Dallas: Word Books, 1994), 36–40.

6. Senior, Collins, and Getty-Sullivan, *Catholic Study Bible*, 35.

7. Ravasi and Maggioni, *La Bibbia* (author's translation of the original Italian), note at Gen 19:1.

8. Susan Niditch, "The 'Sodomite' Theme in Judges 19—20: Family, Community; and Social Disintegration," *The Catholic Biblical Quarterly* 44, no. 3 (1982): 367–69.

9. Senior, Collins, and Getty-Sullivan, *Catholic Study Bible*, 36.

10. Wenham, *Genesis 16—50*, 2:44.

11. Trent C. Butler, *Judges*, Word Biblical Commentary (Nashville: Thomas Nelson, 2009), 412–13; Philippe Guillaume, *Waiting for Josiah: The Judges* (London: T & T Clark, 2006), 226; Niditch, "The 'Sodomite' Theme in Judges 19–20."

12. Wenham, *Genesis 16—50*, 2:42–43.

13. Lot's two guests are called "messengers" or "angels" (*mal'āḵîm*) in vv. 1 and 15, and "humans" (*'anāšîm*) in vv. 8, 5, 12, and 16.

14. Wenham, *Genesis 16—50*, 2:41.

15. Wenham, *Genesis 16—50*, 2:43–44. Letellier proposes a more complex parallel structure wherein Gen 19 mirrors Gen 18: *Day in Mamre, Night in Sodom*, 64–66.

16. Luigi Di Pinto, *Ospitare lo straniero. Cultura e teologia dell'ospitalità nella Bibbia* (Trapani: Il Pozzo di Giacobbe, 2020), 25–55. Cf. Marianne Moyaert, "Biblical, Ethical and Hermeneutical Reflections on Narrative Hospitality," in *Hosting the Stranger: Between Religions*, ed. James Taylor and Richard Kearney (New York: Bloomsbury, 2011), 95–108; Jonathan Sacks, "Arguments for the Sake of Heaven: Vayera 5767," *Covenant & Conversation*, November 11, 2006, https://www.rabbisacks.org/covenant-conversation/vayera/arguments-for-the-sake-of-heaven/.

17. Michael Walzer, *In God's Shadow: Politics in the Hebrew Bible* (New Haven, CT: Yale University Press, 2012), chap. 3.

18. Susan Niditch, *War in the Hebrew Bible: A Study in the Ethics of Violence* (New York: Oxford University Press, 1993).

19. See Christopher G. Frechette, "Destroying the Internalized Perpetrator: A Healing Function of the Violent Language against Enemies in the Psalms," in *Trauma and Traumatization in Individual and Collective Dimensions: Insights from Biblical Studies and Beyond*, ed. Eve-Marie Becker, Jan Dochhorn, and Else Kragelund Holt (Göttingen: Vandenhoeck & Ruprecht,

2014), 73–75; Erich Zenger, *A God of Vengeance? Understanding the Psalms of Divine Wrath* (Louisville, KY: Westminster John Knox, 1995).

20. Butler, *Judges*, 461.

21. Debora Tonelli, "Tra mito e rivelazione: Guerra e violenza nel canto di Debora," *Annali di studi religiosi* 13 (2012): 77; 82; 86–87.

22. Giacomo Danesi and Salvatore Garofalo, *Migrazioni e accoglienza nella Sacra Scrittura* (Padua: Edizioni Messaggero, 1987), 152–55.

23. Walter Gross, *Richter* (Freiburg i.B.: Herder, 2009), 285, 334.

24. In general, "to bless" in Scripture means "to recognize relationship to someone favorably." See Christopher G. Frechette, "Blessing and Cursing," in *The Oxford Encyclopedia of the Bible and Law*, ed. B. Strawn, vol. 1 (New York: Oxford University Press, 2015), 59–63.

25. Giovanni Garbini, *Letteratura e politica nell'Israele antico* (Brescia: Paideia, 2010), 32–60.

26. Faraz Haider, "Countries with the Largest Aging Population in the World," *WorldAtlas*, April 25, 2017, https://www.worldatlas.com/articles/countries-with-the-largest-aging-population-in-the-world.html.

27. *AAS* 45 (1953), 41 (author's translation of the original Italian).

28. Randall Hansen and Desmond King, "Eugenic Ideas, Political Interests, and Policy Variance: Immigration and Sterilization Policy in Britain and the U.S.," *World Politics* 53, no. 2 (January 2001): 237–63; Randall Hansen, "Migration, Citizenship and Race in Europe: Between Incorporation and Exclusion," *European Journal of Political Research* 35, no. 4 (June 1, 1999): 415–44.

29. René M. Micallef, "Das katholische Sozialdenken zur Mobilität der Menschen im 20. und 21. Jahrhundert: Kontinuität und Aggiornamento" in *Aggiornamento—damals und heute: Perspektiven für die Zukunft*, ed. Annette Schavan and Hans Zollner (Freiburg i.B.: Herder, 2017), 86–121; Thomas Massaro, *Mercy in Action: The Social Teachings of Pope Francis* (Lanham, MD: Rowman & Littlefield, 2018), 119–48.

30. Juliet Stumpf, "The Crimmigration Crisis: Immigrants, Crime, and Sovereign Power," *American University Law Review* 56, no. 2 (December 2006): 367–419.

31. Danesi and Garofalo, *Migrazioni e Accoglienza Nella Sacra Scrittura*, 197–239.

32. James F. Keenan, "Jesuit Hospitality?" in *Promise Renewed: Jesuit Higher Education for a New Millennium*, ed. Martin R. Tripole (Chicago: Jesuit Way, 1999), 230–44.

33. Kurt Aland, *Synopsis of the Four Gospels: Greek-English Edition of the* Synopsis Quattuor Evangeliorum. (Stuttgart: German Bible Society, 2013), sec. 151.

34. Roland Meynet, *Treatise on Biblical Rhetoric* (Leiden: Brill, 2012), 5.

35. Meynet, *Treatise on Biblical Rhetoric*, 3.

Notes

36. Authors such as Scaglione note that the five classical "canons" or "functions of the orator" are among "the most constant features in the systematic treatment of the art of rhetoric, starting with the earliest and most illustrious of the extant treatises, that of Aristotle, down to Martianus Capella." See Aldo Scalgione, *The Classical Theory of Composition, from Its Origins to the Present: A Historical Survey* (Chapel Hill: University of North Carolina Press, 1972), 14. Indeed, various works of Cicero list the canons of discovery (*inventio*), disposition (*dispositio*), elocution (*elocutio*), memory (*memoria*), and delivery (*actio*), which are discussed at length in Quintillian's *Institutes of Oratory*. However, we should approach such lists critically, wary of past positivistic tendencies that overschematized classical rhetoric and glossed over the differences among authors so to present classical rhetoric as a "heritage" rather than a complex reality to be approached dialectically. See Kathleen E. Welch, *The Contemporary Reception of Classical Rhetoric: Appropriations of Ancient Discourse* (Hillsdale, NJ: Lawrence Erlbaum, 1990), 8–11; 21–22; 95–96; 130–32.

37. Roland Meynet, "L'analyse rhétorique. Une nouvelle méthode pour comprendre la Bible," *Nouvelle Revue Théologique* 116, no. 5 (1994): 642. An English translation by Leo Arnold of this brief introduction to the method is provided on the website of the International Society for the Study of Biblical and Semitic Rhetoric: https://www.retoricabiblicaesemitica.org/wp-content/uploads/2018/11/inglese_121019.pdf, together with practical resources and exercises.

38. Meynet, *Treatise on Biblical Rhetoric*, 187–299.

39. See Bibical and Semitic Rethoric [*sic*], "Resources," https://www.retoricabiblicaesemitica.org/en/resources/.

40. Roland Meynet, *L'évangile de Marc*, Rhétorique sémitique 16 (Pendé: Gabalda, 2014), 220–28.

41. See, for instance, Gal 2:5, where Titus is called a "Greek."

42. Meynet, *L'évangile de Marc*, 221.

43. Meynet, *L'évangile de Marc*, 221.

44. Meynet, *L'évangile de Marc*, 222.

45. Meynet, *L'évangile de Marc*, 222.

46. Meynet, *L'évangile de Marc*, 222.

47. In the first block (Mark 7:17–23) I use the NRSV translation, which I modify slightly based on the Greek to make the semantic fields more evident to the reader. In the second block (Mark 7:24–30), I use my translation from the previous section, with the sentence construction slightly modified to make it more readable in English.

48. Stephen Castles, Hein de Haas, and Mark J. Miller, *The Age of Migration: International Population Movements in the Modern World*, 5th ed. (New York: Guilford Press, 2013).

49. Anne Sophie Krossa, *Analysing Society in a Global Context: Empirical Studies on Sociation Processes of Volunteers and Refugees* (Cham, Switzerland: Palgrave Macmillan, 2020).

50. Michelle Alexander, *The New Jim Crow: Mass Incarceration in the Age of Colorblindness* (New York: New Press, 2010).

Chapter 8

1. Mark A. Awabdy, *Immigrants and Innovative Law: Deuteronomy's Theological and Social Vision for the* גר (Tübingen: Mohr Siebeck, 2014), 66–82.

2. Awabdy, *Immigrants and Innovative Law*, 81.

3. David Novak, "Land and People: One Jewish Perspective," in *Boundaries and Justice: Diverse Ethical Perspectives*, ed. David Leslie Miller and Sohail H. Hashmi (Princeton, NJ: Princeton University Press, 2001), 223.

4. Shaye J. D. Cohen, *The Beginnings of Jewishness: Boundaries, Varieties, Uncertainties* (Berkeley: University of California Press, 1999), 110–35.

5. Cardellini analyzes various manuscripts and Greek translations of Lev 25:35; Num 35:14–15; 15:14–15; Judg 17:7; 19:1, 12; Isa 5:17; Gen 49:14–15; Gen 38:2; Num 12:1. Innocenzo Cardellini, "Ingegnose interpretazioni di un termine scomodo: Il gēr," in *"Canterò in eterno le misericordie del Signore" (Sal 89,2): Studi in onore del Prof. Gianni Barbiero in occasione del suo settantesimo compleanno*, ed. Stefan M. Attard and Marco Pavan, Analecta Biblica Studia (Rome: Gregorian & Biblical Press, 2015), 73–86.

6. Daniel L. Smith-Christopher, "Between Ezra and Isaiah: Exclusion, Transformation and Inclusion of the 'Foreigner' in Post-exilic Biblical Theology," in *Ethnicity and the Bible*, ed. Mark G. Brett (Leiden: Brill, 1996), 127–30.

7. Smith-Christopher, "Between Ezra and Isaiah," 121–27.

8. Daniel L. Smith-Christopher, *The Religion of the Landless: The Social Context of the Babylonian Exile* (Eugene, OR: Wipf and Stock, 2015), 32–34; 190–93.

9. Katherine E. Southwood, *Ethnicity and the Mixed Marriage Crisis in Ezra 9—10: An Anthropological Approach* (New York: Oxford University Press, 2012), 193.

10. Deut 7:3 is considered by most scholars a later elaboration on 7:2; its narrative setting in premonarchic Israel does not allow it to be understood as a timeless, apodictic rule. There is no similar rule in the law codes of the Pentateuch or in the prophetic books. See Ulrich Berges, "Trito-Isaiah and the Reforms of Ezra/Nehemiah," *Biblica* 2 (2017): 183.

11. Southwood, *Ethnicity and the Mixed Marriage Crisis*, 73–122.

Notes

12. Neil Glover, "Your People, My People: An Exploration of Ethnicity in Ruth," *Journal for the Study of the Old Testament* 33, no. 3 (March 2009): 306, https://doi.org/10.1177/0309089209102498.

13. Southwood, *Ethnicity and the Mixed Marriage Crisis.*

14. Southwood, *Ethnicity and the Mixed Marriage Crisis*, 203–10; 215–18.

15. Smith-Christopher, "Between Ezra and Isaiah," n14; David Jobling, "Sojourner" in *The New Interpreters Dictionary of the Bible*, ed. Katharine Doob Sakenfeld (Nashville: Abingdon, 2009), 316.

16. Southwood, *Ethnicity and the Mixed Marriage Crisis*, 203.

17. Southwood, *Ethnicity and the Mixed Marriage Crisis*, 197.

18. Smith-Christopher, *The Religion of the Landless*, 108–15.

19. "The Mixed Marriage Crisis of Ezra 9–10 and Nehemiah 13: A Study of the Sociology of Post-exilic Judean Community," in *Second Temple Studies: Temple and Community in the Persian Period*, ed. Tamara Cohn Eskenazi and Kent Harold Richards, *Journal for the Study of the Old Testament* 175 (Sheffield, UK: JSOT Press, 1994), 243–65.

20. Smith-Christopher, *The Religion of the Landless*, 79–80.

21. Smith-Christopher, *The Religion of the Landless*, 193–96.

22. Smith-Christopher, "The Mixed Marriage Crisis," 258-261; Smith-Christopher, "Between Ezra and Isaiah," 126.

23. The name Tobiah (Tovi-YAH, "YHWH is good") indicates a YHWH worshiper. Sanballat, according to many historians, was a "Samaritan," a person living in Persian Samaria, culturally and religiously "Israelite" just as most of the "people of the land" in the neighboring Yehud (though not a "Jew," as defined by the Babylonian Golah). Albertz argues that the text in 2 Kgs 17:24–41, which polemically depicts the population of Samaria as alien syncretists, probably does not apply to the postexilic population of Samaria in general; see Albertz, *A History of Israelite Religion in the Old Testament Period*, trans. John Bowden (Louisville, KY: Westminster John Knox, 1994), 524; Smith-Christopher, *The Religion of the Landless*, 183–85.

24. Cf. Josephus's *Antiquities* (XI, ch. 8); Albertz, *A History of Israelite Religion in the Old Testament Period*, 526–33.

25. Smith-Christopher, *The Religion of the Landless*, 103–6.

26. Smith-Christopher, "Between Ezra and Isaiah," 119.

27. Ulrich Berges, "Isaiah," in *The Oxford Handbook of the Prophets*, ed. Carolyn J. Sharp (Oxford: Oxford University Press, 2016), 163.

28. Berges, "Isaiah," 162.

29. Berges, "Isaiah," 164.

30. Berges, "Trito-Isaiah and the Reforms of Ezra/Nehemiah," 175–79; 188–89.

31. Berges, "Trito-Isaiah and the Reforms of Ezra/Nehemiah," 180; 185; 189.

32. W. A. M. Beuken, "The Main Theme of Trito-Isaiah, 'the Servants of Yhwh,'" *Journal for the Study of the Old Testament* 15, no. 47 (June 1, 1990): 74–5; Claus Westermann, *Isaiah 40—66* (Louisville, KY: Westminster John Knox, 2001), 212–13.

33. Berges, "Trito-Isaiah and the Reforms of Ezra/Nehemiah," 182; Christoph Bultmann, *Der Fremde im antiken Juda: Eine Untersuchung zum sozialen Typenbegriff ger und seinem Bedeutungswandel in der alttestamentlichen Gesetzgebung* (Göttingen: Vandenhoeck & Ruprecht, 1992), 216.

34. Berges, "Trito-Isaiah and the Reforms of Ezra/Nehemiah," 186–87.

35. Berges, "Trito-Isaiah and the Reforms of Ezra/Nehemiah," 185.

36. Berges, "Isaiah," 163–64.

37. Shaye J. D. Cohen, "Crossing the Boundary and Becoming a Jew," *The Harvard Theological Review* 82, no. 1 (January 1, 1989): 26.

38. Innocenzo Cardellini, "Riflessioni sullo 'straniero' nella Bibbia alla luce del Vicino Oriente antico," *Studi Emigrazione / Migration Studies* 36, no. 133 (1999): 125–28.

39. Avi Sagi and Zvi Zohar, "Giyyur, Jewish Identity, and Modernization: An Analysis of Halakhic Sources," *Modern Judaism* 15, no. 1 (February 1, 1995): 49–68.

40. Noam J. Zohar, "Contested Boundaries: Judaic Visions of a Shared World," in *Boundaries and Justice: Diverse Ethical Perspectives*, ed. David Leslie Miller and Sohail H. Hashmi (Princeton, NJ: Princeton University Press, 2001), 242–46.

41. Jürgen Habermas, *Between Facts and Norms: Contributions to a Discourse Theory of Law and Democracy*, trans. William Rehg (Cambridge, MA: MIT Press, 1998); Seyla Benhabib, *The Rights of Others: Aliens, Residents, and Citizens* (Cambridge: Cambridge University Press, 2004).

42. Benhabib, *The Rights of Others*, 171–212.

43. Glover, "Your People, My People," 295.

44. Glover, "Your People, My People," 299.

45. Glover, "Your People, My People," 303.

46. Jean-Luc Vesco, "La date du livre de Ruth," *Revue Biblique (1946–)* 74, no. 2 (1967): 235–47; Tamara Cohn Eskenazi and Tikva Frymer-Kensky, *Ruth*, The JPS Bible Commentary (Philadelphia: Jewish Publication Society, 2011), xvi–xix.

47. Christian Frevel, *Das Buch Rut*, Neuer Stuttgarter Kommentar. Altes Testament (Stuttgart: Katholisches Bibelwerk, 1992), 31–34; 156–58.

48. Kirsten Nielsen, *Ruth: A Commentary*, The Old Testament Library (Louisville, KY: Westminster John Knox, 1997), 28–29.

49. Frederic William Bush, *Ruth, Esther*, Word Biblical Commentary (Dallas: Word Books, 1996), 16–30.

50. Bush, *Ruth, Esther*, 27–30.

Notes

51. Alice L. Laffey and Mahri Leonard-Fleckman, *Ruth* (Collegeville, MN: Liturgical Press, 2017), lix, 59; Alice L. Laffey, "Ruth," in *The Paulist Biblical Commentary*, ed. José Enrique Aguilar Chiu, et al. (Mahwah, NJ: Paulist Press, 2018), 240–247.

52. "Un alegato en favor del mestizaje: el libro de Rut," *Reseña Bíblica* 40 (2003): 25.

53. Daniel Marguerat, "Entrer dans le monde du récit," *Cahier Évangile* 127 (March 2004): 7. English translations of all Marguerat and Aletti texts in this chapter are by the present author.

54. Umberto Eco, *Lector in fabula: La cooperazione interpretativa nei testi narrativi*, Studi Bompiani (Milan: Bompiani, 1979).

55. Marguerat, "Entrer Dans Le Monde Du Récit," 9–10.

56. Jean-Noël Aletti, *Il racconto come teologia: studio narrativo del terzo vangelo e del libro degli Atti degli Apostoli*, trans. Carlo Valentino, Collana biblica (Rome: Edizioni Dehoniane, 1996), 213–18.

57. Cardellini, "Ingegnose interpretazioni di un termine scomodo: Il gēr."

58. Giulio Michelini's reading of Ruth, using a reader-response criticism approach combined with rabbinic exegesis, points in this direction. He uses the Midrash to underscore that in Scripture, famine implies a sin and argues that in order to shed light on the main plot of Ruth, we need to recall Judg 19—21 (the rape of the Levite's concubine at Gibeah) and in particular the last line of Judges ("In those days there was no king in Israel; all the people did what was right in their own eyes" [21:25]). See Giulio Michelini, "Prossimità e distanza. Lettura pragmatica del libro di rut a Partire dall'esegesi rabbinica," in *Il diverso e lo straniero nella Bibbia ebraico-cristiana: Uno studio esegetico-teologico in chiave interculturale*, ed. Massimo Grilli and Joseph Maleparampil (Bologna: Edizioni Dehoniane, 2013), 133–59.

59. In the Midrash, Rabbi Zeira (in *Ruth Rabbah* 2:14) claims that the Book of Ruth was written "to teach us the greatness of the reward for acts of lovingkindness," https://www.sefaria.org/Ruth_Rabbah.2.14.

60. Katharine D. Sakenfeld, *The Meaning of Hesed in the Hebrew Bible: A New Inquiry* (Eugene, OR: Wipf & Stock, 2002), 3. Sakenfeld accepts, in part, the results of Nelson Glueck's classical 1927 study of the obligatory nature of *hesed*, which refutes the dichotomy between "mercy" and "justice" spread in Christian popular culture during modernity as a result of certain theologies and spiritualties. Biblical mercy is intimately linked with justice, and hence is morally obligatory. Sakenfeld, however, does not accept Glueck's claim that the obligation is one imposed by law or social pressure, and hence recovers the popular notion that mercy is, in a sense, "freely-imparted." Cf. Nelson Glueck, *Das Wort Ḥesed im alttestamentlichen Sprachgebrauche als menschliche und*

göttliche gemeinschaftgemässe Verhaltungsweise (Giessen: Alfred Töpelmann, 1927).

61. Eskenazi and Frymer-Kensky, *Ruth*, l.

62. Bush, *Ruth, Esther*, 204.

63. Bush, *Ruth, Esther*, 204; Nielsen, *Ruth*, 83; Eskenazi and Frymer-Kensky, *Ruth*, 73.

64. Eskenazi and Frymer-Kensky, *Ruth*, xlv–xlvii.

65. Nielsen, *Ruth*, 14–15.

66. Eskenazi and Frymer-Kensky, *Ruth*, 44.

67. John Hall Elliott, *A Home for the Homeless: A Sociological Exegesis of 1 Peter, Its Situation and Strategy* (Philadelphia: Fortress, 1981), 7–13.

68. Elliott, *Home for the Homeless*, 13.

69. This translation reproduces that of Elliott, *Home for the Homeless*, 23.

70. Elliott, *Home for the Homeless*, 65–67.

71. Elliott, *Home for the Homeless*, 24–49.

72. Richard Carrier, "The Prospect of a Christian Interpolation in Tacitus, Annals 15.44," *Vigiliae Christianae* 68, no. 3 (July 2, 2014): 264–83.

73. Elliott, *Home for the Homeless*, 46–47; 232.

74. Elliott, *Home for the Homeless*, 78–87; 106–48.

75. Elliott, *Home for the Homeless*, 221.

Conclusion

1. Bible scholars like Peter Machinist argue that this idea of migrant origins must have had deep roots in Israel's history, given that, with very few exceptions, the many biblical texts tracing the origins of Israel agree that the "Israelites" had entered Syria-Palestine as outsiders. See his "Outsiders or Insiders: The Biblical View of Emergent Israel and Its Contexts," in *The Other in Jewish Thought and History: Constructions of Jewish Culture and Identity*, ed. Laurence J. Silberstein and Robert L. Cohn (New York: NYU Press, 1994), 35–60. Machinist actually lists and categorizes all the texts. The only three texts with a seemingly dissonant narrative can be explained as polemical provocations (Ezra 16:3, 45) or truncated versions of the "orthodox" narrative/genealogy (Deut 32:10–14; 1 Chr 1—9).

INDEX OF SCRIPTURE REFERENCES

308

SUBJECT INDEX

Subject Index

109–13, 114, 121, 127–29, 179, 209, 219, 258
criticism, textual (lower), 99, 111, 114, 127–28, 192, 210
cross-disciplinarity, xxiv
Cyrus, king, 55, 225, 232, 233

David, king, 55, 162, 247, 251, 254, 256
de Bono, Edward, 32, 279
Deborah, prophetess and judge, 190, 205–6
De Doctrina Christiana. See *On Christian Doctrine*
Deidun, Tom, 95, 285
Dei Verbum, 98, 104, 122
Demmer, Klaus, 54, 108, 286
denizen. See *paroikos*
deontology, 26, 36, 53–54, 62, 69, 127, 152, 187, 236, 277
De Pastorali Migratorum Cura / Nemo Est, xxviii
Deuteronomic Code, 167, 169, 174–76, 177–82, 184, 185–86, 187–88, 220, 294, 300
Deuteronomic reform, 170–71, 177–78, 185–86, 225, 294–95
devotional use of Scripture in decision-making, 43–48, 63, 98, 100, 280. *See also* implicit channel
diachronic approaches in exegesis. *See* criticism, higher historical; exegesis: diachronic
dialectics, 42, 69–73, 81–84, 207, 235, 259, 280, 299
DiCaprio, Leonardo, 48
dignity, human, 50, 52, 137, 149–50, 203, 208
Dilthey, Wilhelm, 79, 89
Di Pinto, Luigi, 199, 297
direction, spiritual. *See* accompaniment

discernment, 26, 41, 45, 66–69, 77, 100, 116–17, 123, 130, 235
Divino Afflante Spiritu, 104
Duhigg, Charles, 63, 281
Duhm, Bernhard, 233
Dunbar, Robin, 138, 141, 146–47
Durkheim, Émile, 146
dynamic encounter experiences (linking the world of Scripture and the world of the reader), 49, 81–84, 96, 129–30, 259

Ebach, Ruth, 180, 295–96
Eco, Umberto, 75, 93–94, 284, 303
Edelman, Diana, 162, 290–91
Egypt (including Egyptian persons) 34, 145, 158–59, 163, 166, 169–71, 183, 185, 201, 222, 226, 268, 295
eisegesis. *See* proof-texting
Elliott, John, 262–64, 304
encounter, theology of the, 6–7, 19–20, 100, 190, 200, 212–14, 244–46, 277
Erga Migrantes Caritas Christi, xxviii
Estévez López, María Elisa, 239, 303
ethnonationalism. *See* nationalism: ethnic
European Union (including EU citizens), 137, 146, 184
exegesis: diachronic, 110–13, 127–29, 175, 180–83, 188, 193–97, 241; patristic (typological), 3, 24–25, 111; synchronic, 110–13, 127–29, 180, 186, 200, 241, 258. *See also* criticism, higher historical; human sciences in biblical interpretation; liberation, theologies and philosophies of; narratological analysis; Semitic (and biblical) rhetorical analysis

313

Subject Index

Ricœur, Paul, 6, 20, 32, 62, 69, 75–76, 79, 82, 85–92, 94–96, 112, 276–78, 281, 283–85, 292
right natural reason (natural law), 22, 26, 52, 54, 101, 103, 106, 139, 206–7, 235, 280
rights: human and natural, 1, 18, 21–22, 29, 48, 51–52, 103–4, 134, 137, 149, 187–88, 191, 206–7, 264, 270, 280; legal, 30, 51, 71, 134, 141, 149–50, 156, 167, 172, 174–75, 183–88, 191, 194, 197, 235–36, 288–89, 296
ritual impurity. *See* kosherness
Roukema, Reimer, 25, 278
Ruether, Rosemary Radford, 109

Samaritans (inhabitants of Samaria), 11, 15, 58, 72, 74, 208, 262, 301. *See also* Good Samaritan; Northern Israelite Kingdom
Samaritans (rescuers), 7–8. *See also* Good Samaritan
Sanz Giménez-Rico, Enrique, 165, 292
Savonarola, Girolamo, 102, 285
Schneiders, Sandra, 82, 118–20, 283–84, 286–87
Schulz, Hermann, 178
Schüssler Fiorenza, Elisabeth, 106, 108, 291
Second World War, xx, 142, 209
secularism and secularization: in biblical interpretation, 77, 97, 110–12, 121–22; as social phenomena, 29, 41, 44, 47–49, 50, 100, 110–12, 121–22, 216, 264, 272, 280
Semitic (and biblical) rhetorical analysis, 110–11, 128, 190, 197–99, 209–16
Senghor, Léopold Sédar, 229

Sennacherib, king, 177–78
Sessions, Jeff, 115
Shallow Pond case, 7
Shamaneser V, king, 178
Sheshonq I, pharaoh, 178
Siker, Jeffrey, 108, 286
Singer, Peter, 7
Sitz im Leben (life setting of a text), 79, 128, 177, 228–306
slaves and slavery, 37, 51–52, 130, 144, 156, 160, 170, 174, 185, 212, 221, 268–69, 295
Smith, Anthony D., 145, 288
Smith-Christopher, Daniel L., 176, 224, 228, 230–31, 292, 295, 300–301
Sobrino, Jon, 106
socialism, 17, 103, 110, 161, 241. *See also* Marxian social analysis; National Socialism
sociology: in biblical interpretation, 6, 89, 111, 128, 154, 203, 219, 230, 259, 262–64, 267, 277, 301, 304; in general, 5, 14–15, 19, 63–64, 121, 136, 138–41, 147, 149, 156–57, 216–17, 281, 290
Socrates, 60
Soderbergh, Steven, 58
Sollicitudo Rei Socialis, xxviii, 149
Solomon, king, 35, 55, 162
Southern Israelite Kingdom, 157, 177–79, 182, 184, 225–28, 230, 233–34, 238, 246, 250–51, 253–55, 258–60, 269. *See also* Judea
Southwood, Katerine, 228–29, 300–301
sovereignty, national, 134, 136, 143–44, 172, 221, 269–72, 289, 298
Spinoza, Baruch, 116

319

world, hermeneutical: of the reader,
70, 75, 79–80, 81–82, 83, 86–88,
90–91, 133; of the text, 70, 81–82,
84, 86–96, 127, 133–34
worldview, 4, 48, 63, 102, 112, 114,
116, 165–66, 191, 213, 216
Wright, Christopher J. H., 55

xenophobia and racism, 9–10,
13–14, 22–23, 34, 58, 63, 102,
114, 169, 189, 197, 218, 224, 228,
237–40, 263, 268–69, 271

Yehud Medinata. *See* Judea
Yoder, John Howard, 108